MONOLINGUAL

OXFORD PICTURE DICTIONARY

SECOND EDITION

Jayme Adelson-Goldstein

Norma Shapiro

OXFORD
UNIVERSITY PRESS

198 Madison Avenue
New York, NY 10016 USA

Great Clarendon Street, Oxford OX2 6DP UK

Oxford University Press is a department of the University of Oxford.
It furthers the University's objective of excellence in research, scholarship,
and education by publishing worldwide in

Oxford New York

Auckland Cape Town Dar es Salaam Hong Kong Karachi
Kuala Lumpur Madrid Melbourne Mexico City Nairobi
New Delhi Shanghai Taipei Toronto

With offices in

Argentina Austria Brazil Chile Czech Republic France Greece
Guatemala Hungary Italy Japan Poland Portugal Singapore
South Korea Switzerland Thailand Turkey Ukraine Vietnam

OXFORD and OXFORD ENGLISH are registered trademarks of
Oxford University Press.

© Oxford University Press 2008

Library of Congress Cataloging-in-Publication Data

Adelson-Goldstein, Jayme.
The Oxford picture dictionary. Monolingual /
Jayme Adelson-Goldstein and Norma Shapiro.– 2nd ed.
p. cm.
Includes index.
ISBN: 978-0-19-436976-3

1. Picture dictionaries, English. 2. English
language–Textbooks for foreign speakers.
I. Shapiro, Norma. II. Title.
PE1629.S52 2008
423'.1–dc22

2007041017

Database right Oxford University Press (maker)

Executive Publishing Manager: Stephanie Karras
Managing Editor: Sharon Sargent
Development Editors: Glenn Mathes II, Bruce Myint, Katie La Storia
Associate Development Editors: Olga Christopoulos, Hannah Ryu
Design Manager: Maj-Britt Hagsted
Project Manager: Allison Harm
Senior Designers: Stacy Merlin, Michael Steinhofer
Designer: Jaclyn Smith
Senior Production Artist: Julie Armstrong
Production Layout Artist: Colleen Ho
Cover Design: Stacy Merlin
Senior Image Editor: Justine Eun
Image Editors: Robin Fadool, Fran Newman, Jenny Vainisi
Manufacturing Manager: Shanta Persaud
Manufacturing Controller: Eve Wong

ISBN: 978 0 19 436976 3

Printed in China

13

This book is printed on paper from certified and well-managed sources.

The OPD team thanks the following artists for their storyboarding and sketches:
Cecilia Aranovich, Chris Brandt, Giacomo Ghiazza, Gary Goldstein, Gordan Kljucec,
Vincent Lucido, and Glenn Urieta

Illustrations by: Lori Anzalone: 13, 70-71, 76-77; Joe "Fearless" Arenella/Will Sumpter:
178; Argosy Publishing: 66-67 (call-outs), 98-99, 108-109, 112-113 (call-outs), 152, 178,
193, 194-195, 196, 197, 205; Barbara Bastian: 4, 15, 17, 20-21, 162 (map), 198, 216-217
(map), 220-221; Philip Batini/AA Reps: 50; Thomas Bayley/Sparks Literary Agency:
158-159; Sally Bensusen: 211, 214; Annie Bissett: 112; Peter Bollinger/Shannon
Associates: 14-15; Higgens Bond/Anita Grien: 226; Molly Borman-Pullman: 116,
117; Jim Fanning/Ravenhill Represents: 80-81; Mike Gardner: 10, 12, 17, 22, 132,
114-115, 142-143, 174, 219, 228-229; Garth Glazier/AA Reps: 106, 118-119; Dennis
Godfrey/Mike Wepplo: 204; Steve Graham: 124-125, 224; Graphic Map & Chart Co.:
200-201, 202-203; Julia Green/Mendola Art: 225; Glenn Gustafson: 9, 27, 48, 76,
100, 101, 117, 132, 133, 136, 155, 161, 179, 196; Barbara Harmon: 212-213, 215; Ben
Hasler/NB Illustration: 94-95, 101, 148-149, 172, 182, 186-187; Betsy Hayes: 134,
138-139; Matthew Holmes: 75; Stewart Holmes/Illustration Ltd.: 192; Janos Jantner/
Beehive Illustration: 5, 13, 82-83, 122-123, 130-131, 146-147, 164-165, 184, 185; Ken
Joudrey/Munro Campagna: 52, 68-69, 177, 208-209; Bob Kaganich/Deborah Wolfe:
10, 40-41, 121; Steve Karp: 230, 231; Mike Kasun/Munro Campagna: 218; Graham
Kennedy: 27; Marcel Laverdet/AA Reps: 23; Jeffrey Lindberg: 33, 42-43, 92-93, 133,
160-161, 170-171, 176; Dennis Lyall/Artworks: 198; Chris Lyons:/Lindgren & Smith:
173, 191; Alan Male/Artworks: 210, 211; Jeff Mangiat/Mendola Art: 53, 54, 55, 56, 57,
58, 59, 66-67; Adrian Mateescu/The Studio: 188-189, 232-233; Karen Minot: 28-29;
Paul Mirocha/The Wiley Group: 194, 216-217; Peter Miserendino/P.T. Pie Illustrations:
198; Lee Montgomery/Illustration Ltd.: 4; Roger Motzkus: 229; Laurie O'Keefe: 111,
216-217; Daniel O'Leary/Illustration Ltd.: 8-9, 26, 34-35, 78, 135, 136-137, 238; Vilma
Ortiz-Dillon: 16, 20-21, 60, 98-99, 100, 211; Terry Pazcko: 46-47, 144-145, 152, 180,
227; David Preiss/Munro Campagna: 5; Pronk & Associates: 192-193; Tony Randazzo/
AA Reps: 156, 234-235; Mike Renwick/Creative Eye: 126-127; Mark Riedy/Scott Hull
Associates: 48-49, 79, 140, 153; Jon Rogers/AA Reps: 112; Jeff Sanson/Schumann &
Co.: 84-85, 240-241; David Schweitzer/Munro Campagna: 162-163; Ben Shannon/
Magnet Reps: 11, 64-65, 90, 91, 96, 97, 166-167, 168-169, 179, 239; Reed Sprunger/
Jae Wagoner Artists Rep.: 18-19, 232-233; Studio Liddell/AA Reps: 27; Angelo Tillary:
108-109; Ralph Voltz/Deborah Wolfe: 50-51, 128-129, 141, 154, 175, 236-237;
Jeff Wack/Mendola Art: 24, 25, 86-87, 102-103, 134-135, 231; Brad Walker: 104-105,
150-151, 157, 206-207; Wendy Wassink: 110-111; John White/The Neis Group: 199;
Eric Wilkerson: 32, 138; Simon Williams/Illustration Ltd.: 2-3, 6-7, 30-31, 36, 38-39,
44-45, 72-73; Lee Woodgate/Eye Candy Illustration: 222-223; Andy Zito: 62-23; Craig
Zuckerman: 14, 88-89, 112-113, 120-121, 194-195.

Chapter icons designed by Von Glitschka/Scott Hull Associates

Cover Art by CUBE/Illustration Ltd (hummingbird, branch); Paul Mirocha/The Wiley
Group (cherry); Mark Riedy/Scott Hull Associates (stamp); 9 Surf Studios (lettering).

Studio photography for Oxford University Press done by Dennis Kitchen Studio: 37,
61, 72, 73, 74, 75, 95, 96, 100, 180, 181, 183, 226.

Stock Photography: Age FotoStock: 238 (flute; clarinet; bassoon; saxophone; violin; cello;
bass; guitar; trombone; trumpet; xylophone; harmonica); Comstock, 61 (window);
Morales, 221 (bat); Franco Pizzochero, 98 (cashmere); Thinkstock, 61 (sink); Alamy:
Corbis, 61 (table); Gary Crabbe, 220 (park ranger); The Associated Press: 198 (strike;
soldiers in trench); Joe Rosenthal, 198 (Iwo Jima); Neil Armstrong, 198 (Buzz Aldrin
on Moon); CORBIS: Philip Gould, 198 (Civil War); Photo Library, 220 (Yosemite Falls);
Danita Delimont: Greg Johnston, 220 (snorkeling); Jamie & Judy Wild, 220 (El Capitan);
Getty Images: 198 (Martin Luther King, Jr.); Amana Images, 61 (soapy plates); The
Granger Collection: 198 (Jazz Age); The Image Works: Kelly Spranger, 220 (sea turtle);
Inmagine: 238 (oboe; tuba; French horn; piano; drums; tambourine; accordion);
istockphoto: 61 (oven), 98 (silk), 99 (suede; lace; velvet); Jupiter Images: 61 (tiles); 98
(wool); 99 (corduroy); Foodpix, 98 (linen); Rob Melnychuk/Brand X Pictures, 61 (glass
shower door); Jupiter Unlimited: 220 (seagulls); 238 (electric keyboard); Comstock, 99
(denim); Mary Evans Picture Library: 198 (women in factory); NPS Photo: Peter Jones, 221
(Carlsbad Cavern entrance; tour; cavern; spelunker); OceanwideImages.com: Gary Bell,
220 (coral); Photo Edit, Inc: David Young-Wolff, 220 (trail); Picture History: 198 (Hiram
Rhodes); Robertstock: 198 (Great Depression); Punchstock: 98 (t-shirt), Robert Glusic,
31 (Monument Valley); Roland Corporation: 238 (organ); SuperStock: 99 (leather); 198
(Daniel Boone); Shutterstock: Marek Szumlas, 94 (watch); United States Mint: 126;
Veer: Brand X Pictures, 220 (deer); Photodisc, 220 (black bear); Yankee Fleet, Inc.: 220
(Fort Jefferson; Yankee Freedom Ferry), Emil von Maltitz/Lime Photo, 37 (baby carrier).

This second edition of
the Oxford Picture Dictionary
is lovingly dedicated to
the memory of Norma Shapiro.

Her ideas, her pictures, and
her stories continue to teach,
inspire, and delight.

Acknowledgments

The publisher and authors would like to acknowledge the following individuals for their invaluable feedback during the development of this program:

Dr. Macarena Aguilar, Cy-Fair College, Houston, TX

Joseph F. Anselme, Atlantic Technical Center, Coconut Creek, FL

Stacy Antonopoulos, Monterey Trail High School, Elk Grove, CA

Carol Antunano, The English Center, Miami, FL

Irma Arencibia, Thomas A. Edison School, Union City, NJ

Suzi Austin, Alexandria City Public School Adult Program, Alexandria, FL

Patricia S. Bell, Lake Technical Center, Eustis, FL

Jim Brice, San Diego Community College District, San Diego, CA

Phil Cackley, Arlington Education and Employment Program (REEP), Arlington, VA

Frieda Caldwell, Metropolitan Adult Education Program, San Jose, CA

Sandra Cancel, Robert Waters School, Union City, NJ

Anne Marie Caney, Chula Vista Adult School, Chula Vista, CA

Patricia Castro, Harvest English Institute, Newark, NJ

Paohui Lola Chen, Milpitas Adult School, Milpitas, CA

Lori Cisneros, Atlantic Vo-Tech, Ft. Lauderdale, FL

Joyce Clapp, Hayward Adult School, Hayward, CA

Stacy Clark, Arlington Education and Employment Program (REEP), Arlington, VA

Nancy B. Crowell, Southside Programs for Adults in Continuing Education, Prince George, VA

Doroti da Cunha, Hialeah-Miami Lakes Adult Education Center, Miami, FL

Paula Da Silva-Michelin, La Guardia Community College, Long Island City, NY

Cynthia L. Davies, Humble I.S.D., Humble, TX

Christopher Davis, Overfelt Adult Center, San Jose, CA

Beverly De Nicola, Capistrano Unified School District, San Juan Capistrano, CA

Beatriz Diaz, Miami-Dade County Public Schools, Miami, FL

Druci J. Diaz, Hillsborough County Public Schools, Tampa, FL

Marion Donahue, San Dieguito Adult School, Encinitas, CA

Nick Doorn, International Education Services, South Lyon, MI

Mercedes Douglass, Seminole Community College, Sanford, FL

Jenny Elliott, Montgomery College, Rockville, MD

Paige Endo, Mt. Diablo Adult Education, Concord, CA

Megan Ernst, Glendale Community College, Glendale, CA

Elizabeth Escobar, Robert Waters School, Union City, NJ

Joanne Everett, Dave Thomas Education Center, Pompano Beach, FL

Jennifer Fadden, Arlington Education and Employment Program (REEP), Arlington, VA

Judy Farron, Fort Myers Language Center, Fort Myers, FL

Sharyl Ferguson, Montwood High School, El Paso, TX

Dr. Monica Fishkin, University of Central Florida, Orlando, FL

Nancy Frampton, Reedley College, Reedley, CA

Lynn A. Freeland, San Dieguito Union High School District, Encinitas, CA

Cathy Gample, San Leandro Adult School, San Leandro, CA

Hillary Gardner, Center for Immigrant Education and Training, Long Island City, NY

Martha C. Giffen, Alhambra Unified School District, Alhambra, CA

Jill Gluck, Hollywood Community Adult School, Los Angeles, CA

Carolyn Grimaldi, LaGuardia Community College, Long Island City, NY

William Gruenholz, USD Adult School, Concord, CA

Sandra G. Gutierrez, Hialeah-Miami Lakes Adult Education Center, Miami, FL

Conte Gúzman-Hoffman, Triton College, River Grove, IL

Amanda Harllee, Palmetto High School, Palmetto, FL

Mercedes Hearn, Tampa Bay Technical Center, Tampa, FL

Robert Hearst, Truman College, Chicago, IL

Patty Heiser, University of Washington, Seattle, WA

Joyce Hettiger, Metropolitan Education District, San Jose, CA

Karen Hirsimaki, Napa Valley Adult School, Napa, CA

Marvina Hooper, Lake Technical Center, Eustis, FL

Katie Hurter, North Harris College, Houston, TX

Nuchamon James, Miami Dade College, Miami, FL

Linda Jennings, Montgomery College, Rockville, MD

Bonnie Boyd Johnson, Chapman Education Center, Garden Grove, CA

Fayne B. Johnson, Broward County Public Schools, Fort Lauderdale, FL

Stavroula Katseyeanis, Robert Waters School, Union City, NJ

Dale Keith, Broadbase Consulting, Inc. at Kidworks USA, Miami, FL

Blanche Kellawon, Bronx Community College, Bronx, NY

Mary Kernel, Migrant Education Regional Office, Northwest Educational Service District, Anacortes, WA

Karen Kipke, Antioch High School Freshman Academy, Antioch, TN

Jody Kirkwood, ABC Adult School, Cerritos, CA

Matthew Kogan, Evans Community Adult School, Los Angeles, CA

Ineza Kuceba, Renton Technical College, Renton, WA

John Kuntz, California State University, San Bernadino, San Bernadino, CA

Claudia Kupiec, DePaul University, Chicago, IL

E.C. Land, Southside Programs for Adult Continuing Education, Prince George, VA

Betty Lau, Franklin High School, Seattle, WA

Patt Lemonie, Thomas A. Edison School, Union City, NJ

Lia Lerner, Burbank Adult School, Burbank, CA

Krystyna Lett, Metropolitan Education District, San Jose, CA

Renata Lima, TALK International School of Languages, Fort Lauderdale, FL

Luz M. Lopez, Sweetwater Union High School District, Chula Vista, CA

Osmara Lopez, Bronx Community College, Bronx, NY

Heather Lozano, North Lake College, Irving, TX

Betty Lynch, Arlington Education and Employment Program (REEP), Arlington, VA

Meera Madan, REID Park Elementary School, Charlotte, NC

Ivanna Mann Thrower, Charlotte Mecklenburg Schools, Charlotte, NC

Michael R. Mason, Loma Vista Adult Center, Concord, CA

Holley Mayville, Charlotte Mecklenburg Schools, Charlotte, NC

Margaret McCabe, United Methodist Cooperative Ministries, Clearwater, FL

Todd McDonald, Hillsborough Adult Education, Tampa, FL

Nancy A. McKeand, ESL Consultant, St. Benedict, LA

Rebecca L. McLain, Gaston College, Dallas, NC

John M. Mendoza, Redlands Adult School, Redlands, CA

Bet Messmer, Santa Clara Adult Education Center, Santa Clara, CA

Christina Morales, BEGIN Managed Programs, New York, NY

Lisa Munoz, Metropolitan Education District, San Jose, CA

Mary Murphy-Clagett, Sweetwater Union High School District, Chula Vista, CA

Jonetta Myles, Rockdale County High School, Conyers, GA

Marwan Nabi, Troy High School, Fullerton, CA

Dr. Christine L. Nelsen, Salvation Army Community Center, Tampa, FL

Michael W. Newman, Arlington Education and Employment Program (REEP), Arlington, VA

Rehana Nusrat, Huntington Beach Adult School, Huntington Beach, CA

Cindy Oakley-Paulik, Embry-Riddle Aeronautical University, Daytona Beach, FL

Acknowledgments

Janet Ochi-Fontanott, Sweetwater Union High School District, Chula Vista, CA

Lorraine Pedretti, Metropolitan Education District, San Jose, CA

Isabel Pena, BE/ESL Programs, Garland, TX

Margaret Perry, Everett Public Schools, Everett, WA

Dale Pesmen, PhD, Chicago, IL

Cathleen Petersen, Chapman Education Center, Garden Grove, CA

Allison Pickering, Escondido Adult School, Escondido, CA

Ellen Quish, LaGuardia Community College, Long Island City, NY

Teresa Reen, Independence Adult Center, San Jose, CA

Kathleen Reynolds, Albany Park Community Center, Chicago, IL

Melba I. Rillen, Palmetto High School, Palmetto, FL

Lorraine Romero, Houston Community College, Houston, TX

Eric Rosenbaum, BEGIN Managed Programs, New York, NY

Blair Roy, Chapman Education Center, Garden Grove, CA

Arlene R. Schwartz, Broward Community Schools, Fort Lauderdale, FL

Geraldyne Blake Scott, Truman College, Chicago, IL

Sharada Sekar, Antioch High School Freshman Academy, Antioch, TN

Dr. Cheryl J. Serrano, Lynn University, Boca Raton, FL

Janet Setzekorn, United Methodist Cooperative Ministries, Clearwater, FL

Terry Shearer, EDUCALL Learning Services, Houston, TX

Elisabeth Sklar, Township High School District 113, Highland Park, IL

Robert Stein, BEGIN Managed Programs, New York, NY

Ruth Sutton, Township High School District 113, Highland Park, IL

Alisa Takeuchi, Chapman Education Center, Garden Grove, CA

Grace Tanaka, Santa Ana College School of Continuing Education, Santa Ana, CA

Annalisa Te, Overfelt Adult Center, San Jose, CA

Don Torluemke, South Bay Adult School, Redondo Beach, CA

Maliheh Vafai, Overfelt Adult Center, San Jose, CA

Tara Vasquez, Robert Waters School, Union City, NJ

Nina Velasco, Naples Language Center, Naples, FL

Theresa Warren, East Side Adult Center, San Jose, CA

Lucie Gates Watel, Truman College, Chicago, IL

Wendy Weil, Arnold Middle School, Cypress, TX

Patricia Weist, TALK International School of Languages, Fort Lauderdale, FL

Dr. Carole Lynn Weisz, Lehman College, Bronx, NY

Desiree Wesner, Robert Waters School, Union City, NJ

David Wexler, Napa Valley Adult School, Napa, CA

Cynthia Wiseman, Borough of Manhattan Community College, New York, NY

Debbie Cullinane Wood, Lincoln Education Center, Garden Grove, CA

Banu Yaylali, Miami Dade College, Miami, FL

Hongyan Zheng, Milpitas Adult Education, Milpitas, CA

Arlene Zivitz, ESOL Teacher, Jupiter, FL

The publisher, authors, and editors would like to thank the following people for their expertise in reviewing specific content areas:

Ross Feldberg, Tufts University, Medford, MA

William J. Hall, M.D. FACP/FRSM (UK), Cumberland Foreside, ME

Jill A. Horohoe, Arizona State University, Tempe, AZ

Phoebe B. Rouse, Louisiana State University, Baton Rouge, LA

Dr. Susan Rouse, Southern Wesleyan University, Central, SC

Dr. Ira M. Sheskin, University of Miami, Coral Gables, FL

Maiko Tomizawa, D.D.S., New York, NY

The author lovingly acknowledges the extraordinary people at Oxford who worked so tirelessly to make OPD 2e an OPD for the 21st century. Special thanks to Stephanie—for her vision and verve; Glenn—for his brilliant ideas and constant support; Bruce—for his unerring eye and rapier wit; Katie—for always getting to the heart of the issue; Sharon—for her ability to make the impossible possible; Maj—for "getting OPD" so completely; Stacy, Michael and Claudia—for their absolutely wonderful sense of design; Fran, Justine, Robin and Jenni—for their artistic understanding; Myndee, Joe, Laura and Margaret—for believing in a second edition; and Shanta and Eve—for making sure that edition got into print.

There are many other people who stood beside me during this project. I humbly thank Gordan, Chris, Vincent, Glenn, Cecilia and my own Gary for sketching out each page of the book with me. I am indebted to Jane, Jenni, Marjorie and Margot for the time they spent reviewing word lists and art while working on their own books. Norma, of course, made her presence known many times. (See page 169.) I am also grateful to Karen Clark and my own Emily. Without their organizational skills, I would still be drowning in reams and reams of art and words.

And last, but certainly not least, I thank all the students and teachers I've worked with over the past 25 years. Your input is on every page.

xo j/me

Table of Contents

Introduction . . . . .ix–xi

1. Everyday Language

Meeting and Greeting 2–3
Personal Information 4
School 5
A Classroom 6–7
Studying 8–9
Succeeding in School 10
A Day at School 11
Everyday Conversation 12
Weather 13
The Telephone 14–15
Numbers 16
Measurements 17
Time 18–19
The Calendar 20–21
Calendar Events 22
Describing Things 23
Colors 24
Prepositions 25
Money 26
Shopping 27
Same and Different 28–29

2. People

Adults and Children 30–31
Describing People 32
Describing Hair 33
Families 34–35
Childcare and Parenting 36–37
Daily Routines 38–39
Life Events and Documents 40–41
Feelings 42–43
A Family Reunion 44–45

3. Housing

The Home 46–47
Finding a Home 48–49
Apartments 50–51
Different Places to Live 52
A House and Yard 53
A Kitchen 54
A Dining Area 55
A Living Room 56
A Bathroom 57
A Bedroom 58
The Kids' Bedroom 59
Housework 60
Cleaning Supplies 61
Household Problems and Repairs 62–63
The Tenant Meeting 64–65

Contents

4. Food

Back from the Market	66–67
Fruit	68
Vegetables	69
Meat and Poultry	70
Seafood and Deli	71
A Grocery Store	72–73
Containers and Packaging	74
Weights and Measurements	75
Food Preparation and Safety	76–77
Kitchen Utensils	78
Fast Food Restaurant	79
A Coffee Shop Menu	80–81
A Restaurant	82–83
The Farmers' Market	84–85

5. Clothing

Everyday Clothes	86–87
Casual, Work, and Formal Clothes	88–89
Seasonal Clothing	90
Underwear and Sleepwear	91
Workplace Clothing	92–93
Shoes and Accessories	94–95
Describing Clothes	96–97
Making Clothes	98–99
Making Alterations	100
Doing the Laundry	101
A Garage Sale	102–103

6. Health

The Body	104–105
Inside and Outside the Body	106–107
Personal Hygiene	108–109
Symptoms and Injuries	110
Illnesses and Medical Conditions	111
A Pharmacy	112–113
Taking Care of Your Health	114–115
Medical Emergencies	116
First Aid	117
Medical Care	118
Dental Care	119
Hospital	120–121
A Health Fair	122–123

7. Community

Downtown 124–125
City Streets 126–127
An Intersection 128–129
A Mall 130–131
The Bank 132
The Library 133
The Post Office 134–135
Department of Motor Vehicles (DMV) 136–137
Government and Military Service 138–139
Civic Rights and Responsibilities 140
The Legal System 141
Crime 142
Public Safety 143
Emergencies and Natural Disasters 144–145
Emergency Procedures 146–147
Community Cleanup 148–149

8. Transportation

Basic Transportation 150–151
Public Transportation 152
Prepositions of Motion 153
Traffic Signs 154
Directions and Maps 155
Cars and Trucks 156
Buying and Maintaining a Car 157
Parts of a Car 158–159
An Airport 160–161
Taking a Trip 162–163

9. Work

The Workplace 164–165
Jobs and Occupations A-C 166
Jobs and Occupations C-H 167
Jobs and Occupations H-P 168
Jobs and Occupations P-W 169
Job Skills 170
Office Skills 171
Career Planning 172
Job Search 173
Interview Skills 174
A Factory 175
Landscaping and Gardening 176
Farming and Ranching 177
Construction 178
Job Safety 179
Tools and Building Supplies 180–181
An Office 182–183
A Hotel 184
Food Service 185
A Bad Day at Work 186–187

Contents

10. Areas of Study

Schools and Subjects 188–189
English Composition 190–191
Mathematics 192–193
Science 194–195
Computers 196
The Internet 197
U.S. History 198
World History 199
North America and Central America 200–201
World Map 202–203
Geography and Habitats 204
The Universe 205
A Graduation 206–207

11. Plants and Animals

Nature Center 208–209
Trees and Plants 210
Flowers 211
Marine Life, Amphibians, and Reptiles 212–213
Birds, Insects, and Arachnids 214
Domestic Animals and Rodents 215
Mammals 216–217
Energy and Conservation 218–219
U.S. National Parks 220–221

12. Recreation

Places to Go 222–223
The Park and Playground 224
The Beach 225
Outdoor Recreation 226
Winter and Water Sports 227
Individual Sports 228
Team Sports 229
Sports Verbs 230
Sports Equipment 231
Hobbies and Games 232–233
Electronics and Photography 234–235
Entertainment 236–237
Music 238
Holidays 239
A Birthday Party 240–241

Verb Guide 242–244
How to Use the Index 245
Index 246–281
Geographical Index 282–284
Research Bibliography 285

Teaching with the *Oxford Picture Dictionary* Program

The following general guidelines will help you prepare single and multilevel lessons using the OPD program. For step-by-step, topic-specific lesson plans, see *OPD Lesson Plans*.

1. Use Students' Needs to Identify Lesson Objectives

- Create communicative objectives based on your learners' needs assessments (*see OPD 2e Assessment Program*).
- Make sure objectives state what students will be able to do at the end of the lesson. For example: *Students will be able to respond to basic classroom commands and requests for classroom objects.* (pp. 6–7, A Classroom)
- For multilevel classes, identify a low-beginning, high-beginning, and low-intermediate objective for each topic.

2. Preview the Topic

Identify what your students already know about the topic.

- Ask general questions related to the topic.
- Have students list words they know from the topic.
- Ask questions about the picture(s) on the page.

3. Present the New Vocabulary

Research shows that it is best to present no more than 5–7 new words at a time. Here are a few presentation techniques:

- Say each new word and describe it within the context of the picture. Have volunteers act out verbs and verb sequences.
- Use Total Physical Response commands to build vocabulary comprehension.
- For long or unfamiliar word lists, introduce words by categories or select the words your students need most.
- Ask a series of questions to build comprehension and give students an opportunity to say the new words. Begin with *yes/no* questions: *Is #16 chalk?* Progress to *or* questions: *Is #16 chalk or a marker?* Finally, ask *Wh-* questions: *What can I use to write on this paper?*
- Focus on the words that students want to learn. Have them write 3–5 new words from each topic, along with meaning clues such as a drawing, translation, or sentence.

More vocabulary and **Grammar Point** sections provide additional presentation opportunities (see p. 5, School). For multilevel presentation ideas, see *OPD Lesson Plans*.

4. Check Comprehension

Make sure that students understand the target vocabulary. Here are two activities you can try:

- Say vocabulary words, and have students point to the correct items in their books. Walk around the room, checking if students are pointing to the correct pictures.
- Make true/false statements about the target vocabulary. Have students hold up two fingers for true, three for false.

5. Provide Guided and Communicative Practice

The exercise bands at the bottom of the topic pages provide a variety of guided and communicative practice opportunities and engage students' higher-level thinking.

6. Provide More Practice

OPD Second Edition offers a variety of components to facilitate vocabulary acquisition. Each of the print and electronic materials listed below offers suggestions and support for single and multilevel instruction.

OPD Lesson Plans Step-by-step multilevel lesson plans feature 3 CDs with multilevel listening, context-based pronunciation practice, and leveled reading practice. Includes multilevel teaching notes for *The OPD Reading Library*.

OPD Audio CDs or Audio Cassettes Each word in *OPD*'s word list is recorded by topic.

Low-Beginning, High-Beginning, and Low-Intermediate Workbooks Guided practice for each page in *OPD* features linked visual contexts, realia, and listening practice.

Classic Classroom Activities A photocopiable resource of interactive multilevel activities, grammar practice, and communicative tasks.

The OPD Reading Library Readers include civics, academic content, and workplace themes.

Overhead Transparencies Vibrant transparencies help to focus students on the lesson.

OPD Presentation Software A multilevel interactive teaching tool using interactive whiteboard and LCD technology. Audio, animation, and video instructional support bring each dictionary topic to life.

The OPD CD-ROM An interactive learning tool featuring four-skill practice based on *OPD* topics.

Bilingual Editions *OPD* is available in numerous bilingual editions including Spanish, Chinese, Vietnamese, Arabic, Korean, and many more.

My hope is that OPD makes it easier for you to take your learners from comprehension to communication. Please share your thoughts with us as you make the book your own.

Jayme Adelson-Goldstein

Jayme Adelson-Goldstein

OPDteam.us@oup.com

Welcome to the
OPD SECOND EDITION

The second edition of the *Oxford Picture Dictionary* expands on the best aspects of the 1998 edition with:

- New artwork presenting words within meaningful, real-life contexts
- An updated word list to meet the needs of today's English language learners
- 4,000 English words and phrases, including 285 verbs
- 40 new topics with 12 intro pages and 12 story pages
- Unparalleled support for vocabulary teaching

Subtopics present the words in easy-to-learn "chunks."

Color coding and icons make it easy to navigate through *OPD*.

New art and rich contexts improve vocabulary acquisition.

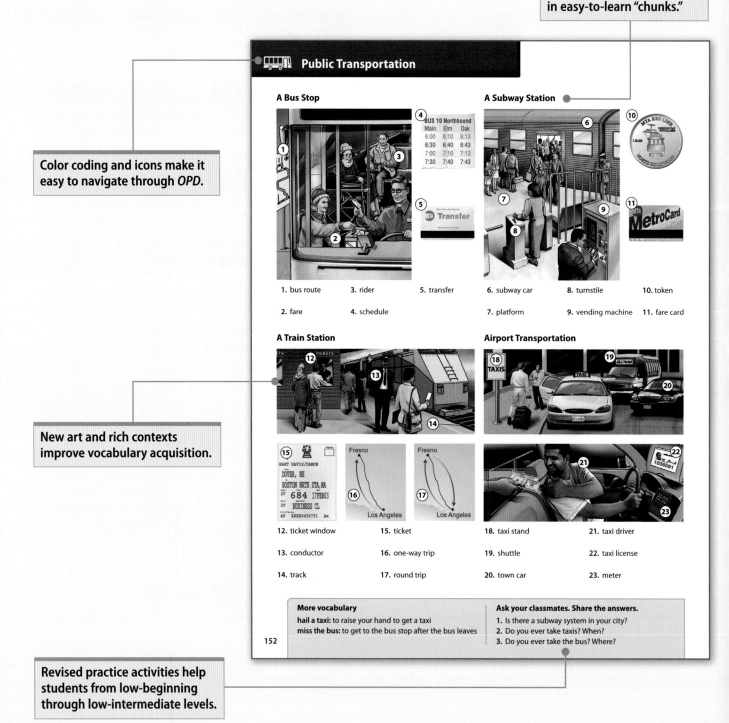

Public Transportation

A Bus Stop

A Subway Station

1. bus route
2. fare
3. rider
4. schedule
5. transfer

6. subway car
7. platform
8. turnstile
9. vending machine
10. token
11. fare card

A Train Station

Airport Transportation

12. ticket window
13. conductor
14. track

15. ticket
16. one-way trip
17. round trip

18. taxi stand
19. shuttle
20. town car

21. taxi driver
22. taxi license
23. meter

More vocabulary
hail a taxi: to raise your hand to get a taxi
miss the bus: to get to the bus stop after the bus leaves

Ask your classmates. Share the answers.
1. Is there a subway system in your city?
2. Do you ever take taxis? When?
3. Do you ever take the bus? Where?

152

Revised practice activities help students from low-beginning through low-intermediate levels.

Each intro page teaches key vocabulary items within the unit theme.

Practice activities make it easy to manage multilevel classrooms.

NEW! Story pages close each unit with a lively scene for reviewing vocabulary and teaching additional language. Meanwhile, rich visual contexts recycle words from the unit.

Pre-reading questions build students' previewing and predicting skills.

High-interest readings promote literacy skills.

Post-reading questions and role-play activities support critical thinking and encourage students to use the language they have learned.

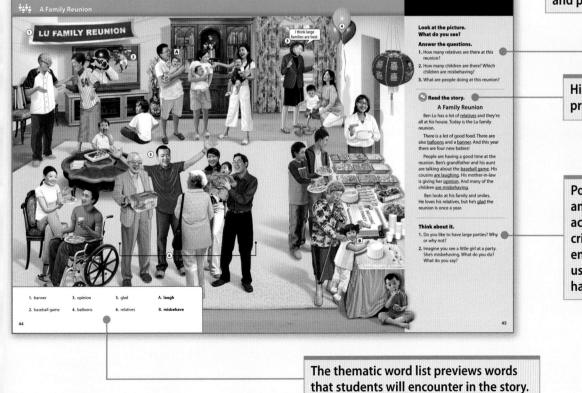

The thematic word list previews words that students will encounter in the story.

A. **Say**, "Hello."

B. **Ask**, "How are you?"

C. **Introduce** yourself.

D. **Smile**.

E. **Hug**.

F. **Wave**.

Tell your partner what to do. Take turns.

1. *Say, "Hello."*   4. *Shake hands.*
2. *Bow.*   5. *Wave.*
3. *Smile.*   6. *Say, "Goodbye."*

Dictate to your partner. Take turns.

A: *Write smile.*
B: *Is it spelled s-m-i-l-e?*
A: *Yes, that's right.*

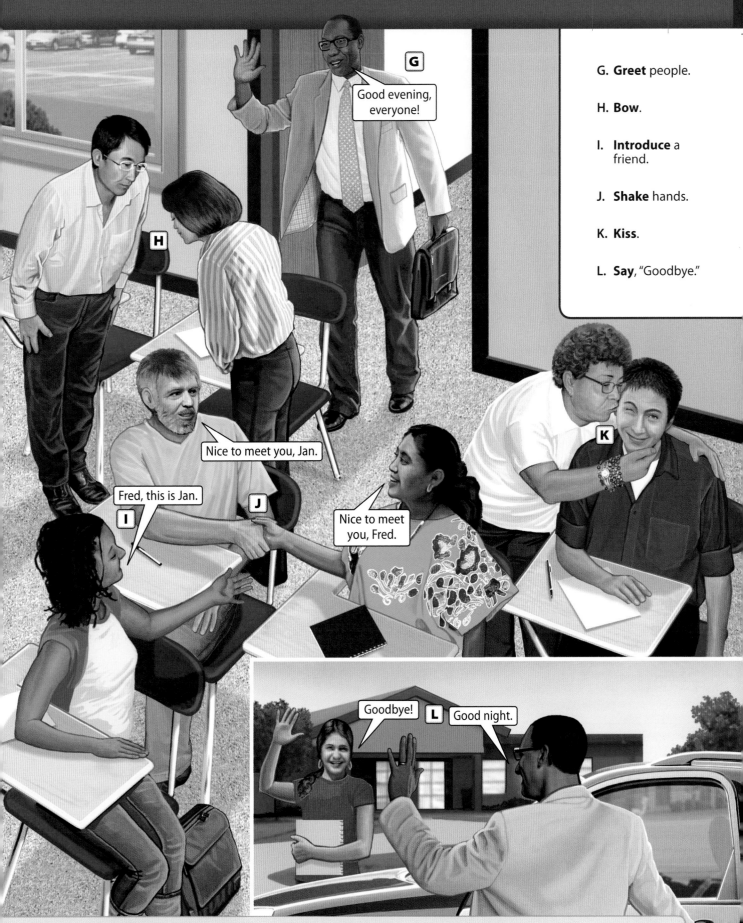

G. **Greet** people.

H. **Bow**.

I. **Introduce** a friend.

J. **Shake** hands.

K. **Kiss**.

L. **Say**, "Goodbye."

Ways to greet people

Good morning.
Good afternoon.
Good evening.

Ways to introduce yourself

I'm Tom.
My name is Tom.

Pair practice. Make new conversations.

A: *Good morning. My name is Tom.*
B: *Nice to meet you, Tom. I'm Sara.*
A: *Nice to meet you, Sara.*

A. Say your name.

B. Spell your name.

C. Print your name.

D. Sign your name.

Filling Out a Form

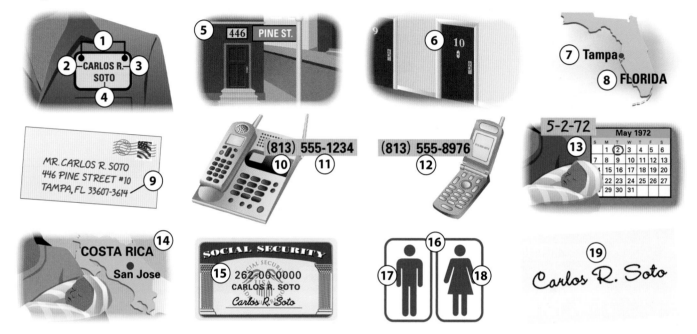

School Registration Form

1. name:

_____

2. first name **3.** middle initial **4.** last name **5.** address **6.** apartment number

_____

7. city **8.** state **9.** ZIP code **10.** area code **11.** phone number

( )

12. cell phone number **13.** date of birth (DOB) **14.** place of birth

____ - __ - ____ **16.** sex: **17.** male ☐ **19.** signature

15. Social Security number **18.** female ☐

Pair practice. Make new conversations.

A: *My first name is Carlos.*
B: *Please spell Carlos for me.*
A: *C-a-r-l-o-s*

Ask your classmates. Share the answers.

1. Do you like your first name?
2. Is your last name from your mother? father? husband?
3. What is your middle name?

Campus

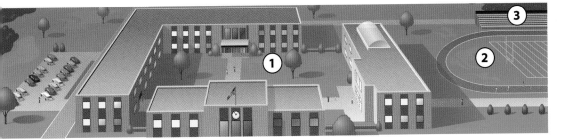

1. quad
2. field
3. bleachers
4. principal
5. assistant principal
6. counselor
7. classroom
8. teacher
9. restrooms
10. hallway
11. locker
12. main office
13. clerk
14. cafeteria
15. computer lab
16. teacher's aide
17. library
18. auditorium
19. gym
20. coach
21. track

Administrators

Around Campus

More vocabulary

Students do not pay to go to a **public school**.
Students pay to go to a **private school**.
A church, mosque, or temple school is a **parochial school**.

Grammar Point: contractions of the verb *be*

He + is = He's   *He's a teacher.*
She + is = She's   *She's a counselor.*
They + are = They're   *They're students.*

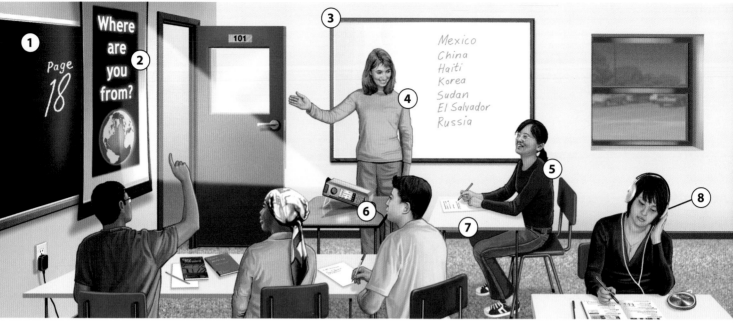

A Classroom

1. chalkboard
2. screen
3. whiteboard
4. teacher / instructor
5. student
6. LCD projector
7. desk
8. headphones

A. **Raise** your hand.

B. **Talk** to the teacher.

C. **Listen** to a CD.

D. **Stand up**.

E. **Write** on the board.

F. **Sit down**. / **Take** a seat.

G. **Open** your book.

H. **Close** your book.

I. **Pick up** the pencil.

J. **Put down** the pencil.

ABCDEFGHIJKLMNOPQRSTUVWXYZ

9. clock

10. bookcase

11. chair

12. map

13. alphabet

14. bulletin board

15. computer

16. overhead projector

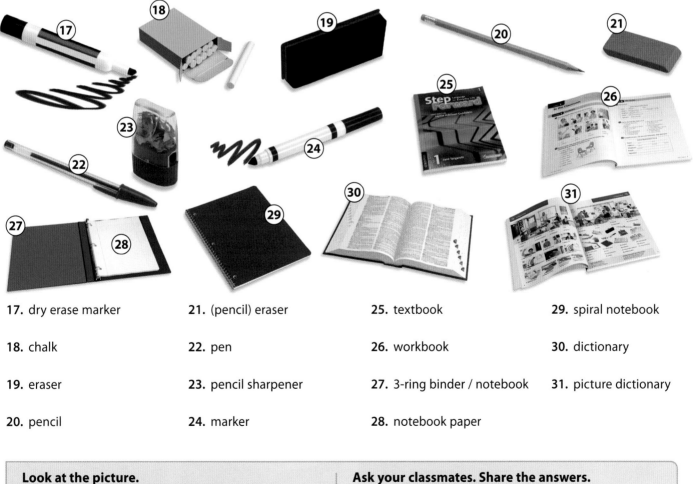

17. dry erase marker

18. chalk

19. eraser

20. pencil

21. (pencil) eraser

22. pen

23. pencil sharpener

24. marker

25. textbook

26. workbook

27. 3-ring binder / notebook

28. notebook paper

29. spiral notebook

30. dictionary

31. picture dictionary

Look at the picture.
Describe the classroom.

A: There's a chalkboard.
B: There are fifteen students.

Ask your classmates. Share the answers.

1. Do you like to raise your hand in class?
2. Do you like to listen to CDs in class?
3. Do you ever talk to the teacher?

7

Learning New Words

A. **Look up** the word.

B. **Read** the definition.

C. **Translate** the word.

D. **Check** the pronunciation.

E. **Copy** the word.

F. **Draw** a picture.

Working with Your Classmates

G. **Discuss** a problem.

H. **Brainstorm** solutions / answers.

I. **Work** in a group.

J. **Help** a classmate.

Working with a Partner

K. **Ask** a question.

L. **Answer** a question.

M. **Share** a book.

N. **Dictate** a sentence.

Following Directions

O

Read a book.

O. **Fill in** the blank.

P

5. How much is the book?
a. $99.99
b. $9.99
c. $0.99

Study Skills For You
$9.99

P. **Choose** the correct answer.

Q

Read the book. pencil.

Q. **Circle** the answer.

R

pen
pencil
book
chalk
marker

R. **Cross out** the word.

S

Underline the action.
1. Open the book.
2. Close the book.
3. Give me the book.

S. **Underline** the word.

T

1. read ___ a. pencil
2. write ___ b. chair
3. sit ___ c. book

T. **Match** the items.

U

Check the box next to each action.

☑ stand ☑ sit
☐ pen ☑ write
☐ paper ☐ book

U. **Check** the correct boxes.

V

Study Skills For You
$9.99

book

V. **Label** the picture.

W

1. enp pen
2. rappe paper
3. okob book

W. **Unscramble** the words.

X

4 Close the book.
1 Pick up the book.
2 Open the book.
3 Read the book.

X. **Put** the sentences in order.

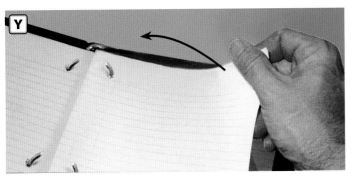

Y. **Take out** a piece of paper.

Z. **Put away** your books.

Ask your classmates. Share the answers.

1. Do you like to work in a group?
2. Do you ever share a book?
3. Do you like to answer questions?

Think about it. Discuss.

1. How can classmates help each other?
2. Why is it important to ask questions in class?
3. How can students check their pronunciation? Explain.

9

Ways to Succeed

Learn 5 words a day.

A. **Set** goals.

Goal

B. **Participate** in class.

Goal Progress Succeed

C. **Take** notes.

progress

D. **Study** at home.

VOCABULARY TEST 78% PASS

E. **Pass** a test.

Will you help me?
Sure.

F. **Ask** for help.

VOCABULARY TEST 96% GREAT!

G. **Make** progress.

GRADE REPORT Vocabulary A Writing B Reading A

H. **Get** good grades.

Taking a Test

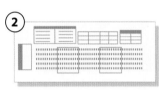
① READING Level A R ESL

②

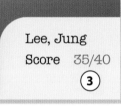
Lee, Jung
Score 35/40
③

④

A	90%-100%	Outstanding
B	80%-89%	Very good
C	70%-79%	Satisfactory
D	60%-69%	Barely passing
F	0%-59%	Fail

1. test booklet

2. answer sheet

3. score

4. grades

I. **Clear off** your desk.

J. **Work** on your own.

3. He is at _____.
a. home
b. bed
c. book

K. **Bubble in** the answer.

4. It is an _____.
a. erasers
b. book
c. eraser

L. **Check** your work.

4. Ⓐ Ⓑ Ⓒ Ⓓ Ⓔ

M. **Erase** the mistake.

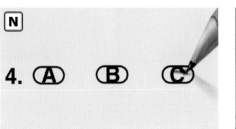
4. Ⓐ Ⓑ Ⓒ

N. **Correct** the mistake.

O. **Hand in** your test.

A. **Enter** the room.

B. **Turn on** the lights.

C. **Walk** to class.

D. **Run** to class.

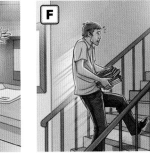

E. **Lift / Pick up** the books.

F. **Carry** the books.

G. **Deliver** the books.

H. **Take** a break.

I. **Eat**.

J. **Drink**.

K. **Buy** a snack.

L. **Have** a conversation.

M. **Go back** to class.

N. **Throw away** trash.

O. **Leave** the room.

P. **Turn off** the lights.

Grammar Point: present continuous

Use **be** + verb + **ing**
He **is** walk**ing**. They **are** enter**ing**.
Note: He is run**ning**. They are leav**ing**.

Look at the pictures.
Describe what is happening.

A: They are _entering the room_.
B: He is _walking_.

11

A. **start** a conversation

B. **make** small talk

C. **compliment** someone

D. **offer** something

E. **thank** someone

F. **apologize**

G. **accept** an apology

H. **invite** someone

I. **accept** an invitation

J. **decline** an invitation

K. **agree**

L. **disagree**

M. **explain** something

N. **check** your understanding

More vocabulary

request: to ask for something
accept a compliment: to thank someone for a compliment

Pair practice. Follow the directions.

1. Start a conversation with your partner.
2. Make small talk with your partner.
3. Compliment each other.

Temperature

1. Fahrenheit
2. Celsius
3. hot
4. warm
5. cool
6. cold
7. freezing
8. degrees

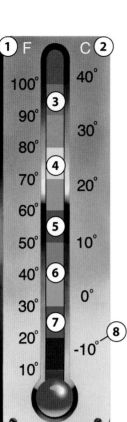

A Weather Map

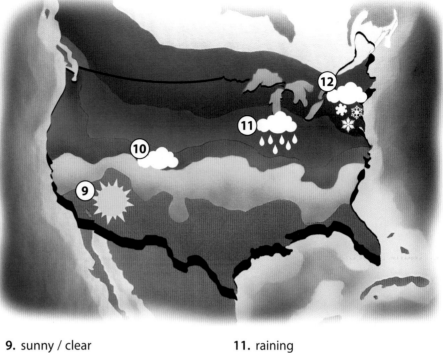

9. sunny / clear

10. cloudy

11. raining

12. snowing

Weather Conditions

13. heat wave
14. smoggy
15. humid

16. thunderstorm
17. lightning
18. windy

19. dust storm
20. foggy
21. hailstorm

22. icy
23. snowstorm / blizzard

Ways to talk about the weather

It's <u>sunny</u> in <u>Dallas</u>.
What's the temperature?
It's <u>108</u>. They're having <u>a heat wave</u>.

Pair practice. Make new conversations.

A: *What's the weather like in <u>Chicago</u>?*
B: *It's <u>raining</u> and it's <u>cold</u>. It's <u>30</u> degrees.*

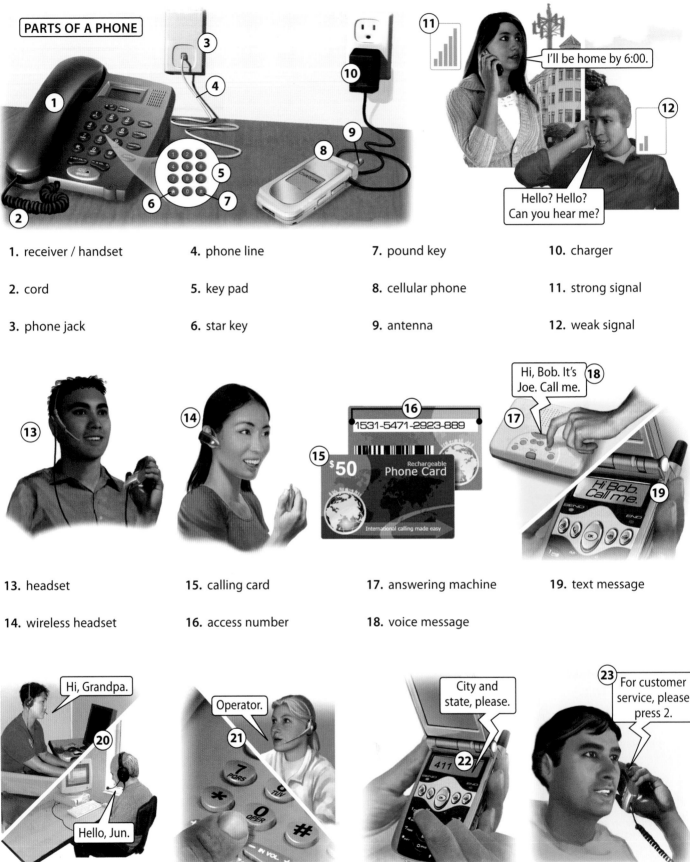

PARTS OF A PHONE

I'll be home by 6:00.

Hello? Hello? Can you hear me?

1. receiver / handset
2. cord
3. phone jack
4. phone line
5. key pad
6. star key
7. pound key
8. cellular phone
9. antenna
10. charger
11. strong signal
12. weak signal

Hi, Bob. It's Joe. Call me.

Hi Bob. Call me.

13. headset
14. wireless headset
15. calling card
16. access number
17. answering machine
18. voice message
19. text message

Hi, Grandpa.

Hello, Jun.

Operator.

City and state, please.

For customer service, please press 2.

20. Internet phone call
21. operator
22. directory assistance
23. automated phone system

24. cordless phone

25. pay phone

26. TDD*

27. smart phone

Reading a Phone Bill

28. phone bill

29. area code

30. phone number

31. local call

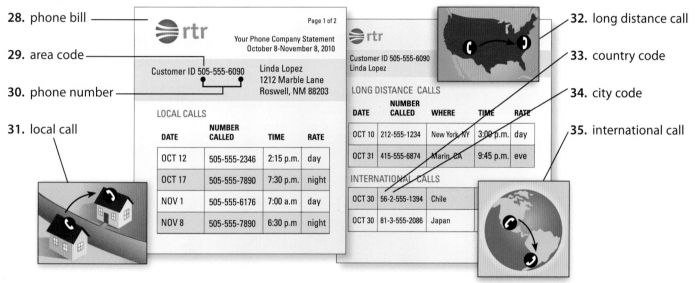

32. long distance call

33. country code

34. city code

35. international call

Page 1 of 2

rtr
Your Phone Company Statement
October 8-November 8, 2010

Customer ID 505-555-6090 | Linda Lopez
1212 Marble Lane
Roswell, NM 88203

LOCAL CALLS

DATE	NUMBER CALLED	TIME	RATE
OCT 12	505-555-2346	2:15 p.m.	day
OCT 17	505-555-7890	7:30 p.m.	night
NOV 1	505-555-6176	7:00 a.m	day
NOV 8	505-555-7890	6:30 p.m	night

rtr
Customer ID 505-555-6090
Linda Lopez

LONG DISTANCE CALLS

DATE	NUMBER CALLED	WHERE	TIME	RATE
OCT 10	212-555-1234	New York, NY	3:00 p.m.	day
OCT 31	415-555-6874	Marin, CA	9:45 p.m.	eve

INTERNATIONAL CALLS

DATE	NUMBER CALLED	WHERE		
OCT 30	56-2-555-1394	Chile		
OCT 30	81-3-555-2086	Japan		

Making a Phone Call

A. Dial the phone number.

B. Press "send".

C. Talk on the phone.

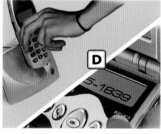
D. Hang up. / **Press** "end".

Making an Emergency Call

E. Dial 911.

This is Roy Chu.

F. Give your name.

There's a fire on 5th and Oak.

G. State the emergency.

Please stay on the line.

H. Stay on the line.

*telecommunication device for the deaf

Cardinal Numbers

0 zero	20 twenty
1 one	21 twenty-one
2 two	22 twenty-two
3 three	23 twenty-three
4 four	24 twenty-four
5 five	25 twenty-five
6 six	30 thirty
7 seven	40 forty
8 eight	50 fifty
9 nine	60 sixty
10 ten	70 seventy
11 eleven	80 eighty
12 twelve	90 ninety
13 thirteen	100 one hundred
14 fourteen	101 one hundred one
15 fifteen	1,000 one thousand
16 sixteen	10,000 ten thousand
17 seventeen	100,000 one hundred thousand
18 eighteen	1,000,000 one million
19 nineteen	1,000,000,000 one billion

Ordinal Numbers

1st first	16th sixteenth
2nd second	17th seventeenth
3rd third	18th eighteenth
4th fourth	19th nineteenth
5th fifth	20th twentieth
6th sixth	21st twenty-first
7th seventh	30th thirtieth
8th eighth	40th fortieth
9th ninth	50th fiftieth
10th tenth	60th sixtieth
11th eleventh	70th seventieth
12th twelfth	80th eightieth
13th thirteenth	90th ninetieth
14th fourteenth	100th one hundredth
15th fifteenth	1,000th one thousandth

Roman Numerals

I = 1	VII = 7	XXX = 30
II = 2	VIII = 8	XL = 40
III = 3	IX = 9	L = 50
IV = 4	X = 10	C = 100
V = 5	XV = 15	D = 500
VI = 6	XX = 20	M = 1,000

A. **divide**

B. **calculate**

C. **measure**

D. **convert**

Fractions and Decimals

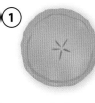

1. one whole
   1 = 1.00

2. one half
   1/2 = .5

3. one third
   1/3 = .333

4. one fourth
   1/4 = .25

5. one eighth
   1/8 = .125

Percents

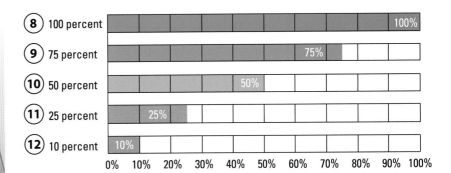

8. 100 percent
9. 75 percent
10. 50 percent
11. 25 percent
12. 10 percent

6. calculator

7. decimal point

Measurement

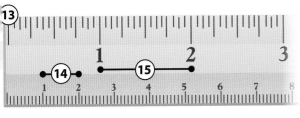

13. ruler

15. inch [in.]

14. centimeter [cm]

Dimensions

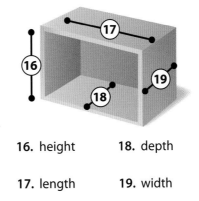

16. height

18. depth

17. length

19. width

Equivalencies

12 inches = 1 foot

3 feet = 1 yard

1,760 yards = 1 mile

1 inch = 2.54 centimeters

1 yard = .91 meters

1 mile = 1.6 kilometers

Telling Time

1. hour **2.** minutes **3.** seconds **4.** a.m. **5.** p.m.

6. 1:00
one o'clock

7. 1:05
one-oh-five
five after one

8. 1:10
one-ten
ten after one

9. 1:15
one-fifteen
a quarter after one

10. 1:20
one-twenty
twenty after one

11. 1:30
one-thirty
half past one

12. 1:40
one-forty
twenty to two

13. 1:45
one-forty-five
a quarter to two

Times of Day

14. sunrise **15.** morning **16.** noon **17.** afternoon

18. sunset **19.** evening **20.** night **21.** midnight

Ways to talk about time

I wake up at <u>6:30</u> <u>a.m.</u>
I wake up at <u>6:30</u> <u>in the morning</u>.
I <u>wake up</u> at <u>6:30</u>.

Pair practice. Make new conversations.

A: *What time do you <u>wake up</u> on <u>weekdays</u>?*
B: *At <u>6:30</u> <u>a.m.</u> How about you?*
A: *I <u>wake up</u> at <u>7:00</u>.*

22. early

23. on time

24. late

25. daylight saving time

26. standard time

Time Zones

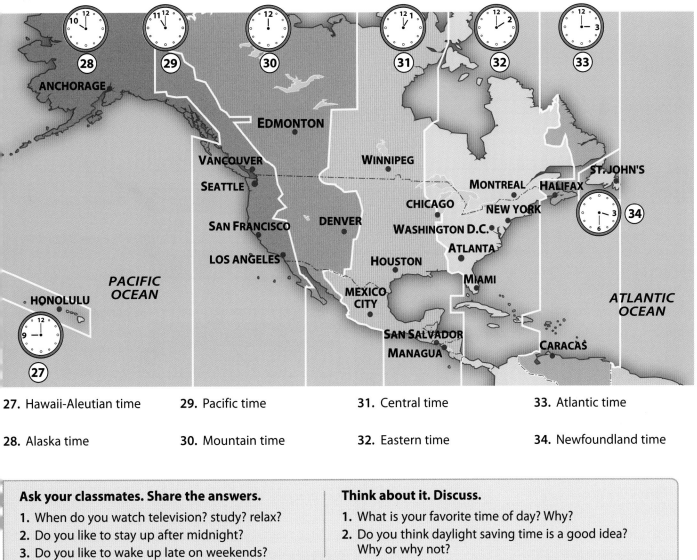

27. Hawaii-Aleutian time

28. Alaska time

29. Pacific time

30. Mountain time

31. Central time

32. Eastern time

33. Atlantic time

34. Newfoundland time

Ask your classmates. Share the answers.

1. When do you watch television? study? relax?
2. Do you like to stay up after midnight?
3. Do you like to wake up late on weekends?

Think about it. Discuss.

1. What is your favorite time of day? Why?
2. Do you think daylight saving time is a good idea? Why or why not?

1. date
2. day
3. month
4. year

5. today
6. tomorrow
7. yesterday

Days of the Week

8. Sunday
9. Monday
10. Tuesday
11. Wednesday
12. Thursday
13. Friday
14. Saturday

15. week
16. weekdays
17. weekend

MAY

SUN	MON	TUE	WED	THU	FRI	SAT
1	2	3	4	5	6	7
8	9	10	11	12	13	14
15	16	17	18	19	20	21
22	23	24	25	26	27	28
29	30	31				

Frequency

18. last week
19. this week
20. next week

21. every day / daily
22. once a week
23. twice a week
24. three times a week

MAY

SUN	MON	TUE	WED	THU	FRI	SAT
X1	X2	X3	X4	X5	X6	X7
8	9	10	11	12	13	14
15	16	17	18	19	20	21
22	23	24	25	26	27	28

Ways to say the date

Today is _May 10th_. It's the _tenth_.
Yesterday was _May 9th_.
The party is on _May 21st_.

Pair practice. Make new conversations.

A: The _test_ is on _Friday_, _June 14th_.
B: Did you say _Friday_, the _fourteenth_?
A: Yes, the _fourteenth_.

Months of the Year

25 JAN

SUN	MON	TUE	WED	THU	FRI	SAT
					1	2
3	4	5	6	7	8	9
10	11	12	13	14	15	16
17	18	19	20	21	22	23
24/31	25	26	27	28	29	30

26 FEB

SUN	MON	TUE	WED	THU	FRI	SAT
	1	2	3	4	5	6
7	8	9	10	11	12	13
14	15	16	17	18	19	20
21	22	23	24	25	26	27
28						

27 MAR

SUN	MON	TUE	WED	THU	FRI	SAT
	1	2	3	4	5	6
7	8	9	10	11	12	13
14	15	16	17	18	19	20
21	22	23	24	25	26	27
28	29	30	31			

28 APR

SUN	MON	TUE	WED	THU	FRI	SAT
				1	2	3
4	5	6	7	8	9	10
11	12	13	14	15	16	17
18	19	20	21	22	23	24
25	26	27	28	29	30	

29 MAY

SUN	MON	TUE	WED	THU	FRI	SAT
						1
2	3	4	5	6	7	8
9	10	11	12	13	14	15
16	17	18	19	20	21	22
23/30	24/31	25	26	27	28	29

30 JUN

SUN	MON	TUE	WED	THU	FRI	SAT
		1	2	3	4	5
6	7	8	9	10	11	12
13	14	15	16	17	18	19
20	21	22	23	24	25	26
27	28	29	30			

31 JUL

SUN	MON	TUE	WED	THU	FRI	SAT
				1	2	3
4	5	6	7	8	9	10
11	12	13	14	15	16	17
18	19	20	21	22	23	24
25	26	27	28	29	30	31

32 AUG

SUN	MON	TUE	WED	THU	FRI	SAT
1	2	3	4	5	6	7
8	9	10	11	12	13	14
15	16	17	18	19	20	21
22	23	24	25	26	27	28
29	30	31				

33 SEP

SUN	MON	TUE	WED	THU	FRI	SAT
			1	2	3	4
5	6	7	8	9	10	11
12	13	14	15	16	17	18
19	20	21	22	23	24	25
26	27	28	29	30		

34 OCT

SUN	MON	TUE	WED	THU	FRI	SAT
					1	2
3	4	5	6	7	8	9
10	11	12	13	14	15	16
17	18	19	20	21	22	23
24/31	25	26	27	28	29	30

35 NOV

SUN	MON	TUE	WED	THU	FRI	SAT
	1	2	3	4	5	6
7	8	9	10	11	12	13
14	15	16	17	18	19	20
21	22	23	24	25	26	27
28	29	30				

36 DEC

SUN	MON	TUE	WED	THU	FRI	SAT
			1	2	3	4
5	6	7	8	9	10	11
12	13	14	15	16	17	18
19	20	21	22	23	24	25
26	27	28	29	30	31	

Months of the Year

25. January

26. February

27. March

28. April

29. May

30. June

31. July

32. August

33. September

34. October

35. November

36. December

Seasons

37. spring

38. summer

39. fall / autumn

40. winter

Dictate to your partner. Take turns.

A: *Write Monday.*

B: *Is it spelled M-o-n-d-a-y?*

A: *Yes, that's right.*

Ask your classmates. Share the answers.

1. What is your favorite day of the week? Why?
2. What is your busiest day of the week? Why?
3. What is your favorite season of the year? Why?

1. birthday

2. wedding

3. anniversary

4. appointment

5. parent-teacher conference

6. vacation

7. religious holiday

8. legal holiday

Legal Holidays

Happy New Year!

JAN 1

I have a dream.

JAN

FEB

MAY

JUL 4

SEP

OCT

PROUD TO WORK

NOV

NOV

DEC 25

9. New Year's Day

10. Martin Luther King Jr. Day

11. Presidents' Day

12. Memorial Day

13. Fourth of July / Independence Day

14. Labor Day

15. Columbus Day

16. Veterans Day

17. Thanksgiving

18. Christmas

Pair practice. Make new conversations.

A: *When is your birthday?*
B: *It's on January 31st. How about you?*
A: *It's on December 22nd.*

Ask your classmates. Share the answers.

1. What are the legal holidays in your native country?
2. When is Labor Day in your native country?
3. When do you celebrate the New Year in your native country?

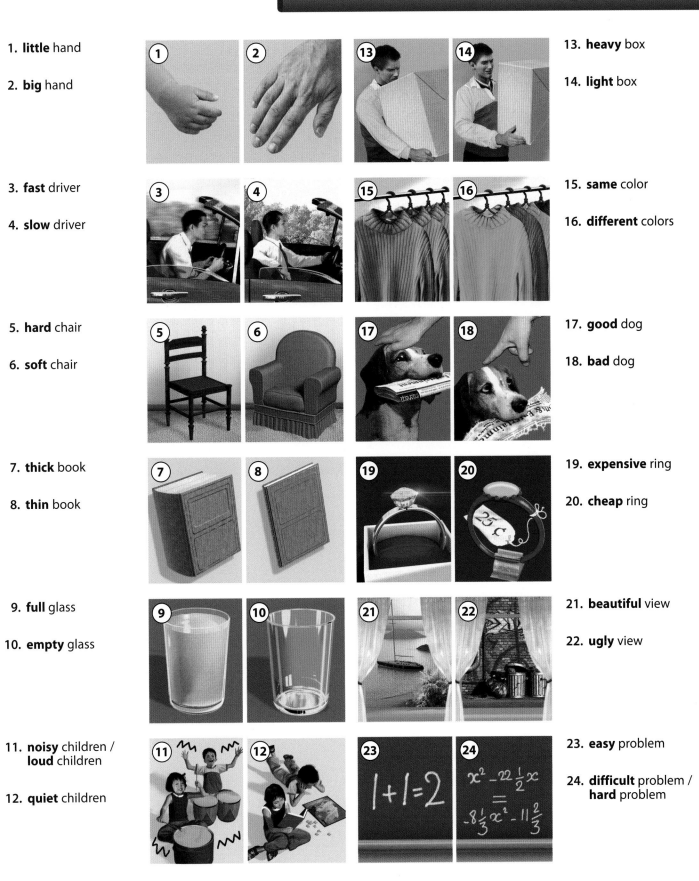

1. **little** hand
2. **big** hand

3. **fast** driver
4. **slow** driver

5. **hard** chair
6. **soft** chair

7. **thick** book
8. **thin** book

9. **full** glass
10. **empty** glass

11. **noisy** children / **loud** children
12. **quiet** children

13. **heavy** box
14. **light** box

15. **same** color
16. **different** colors

17. **good** dog
18. **bad** dog

19. **expensive** ring
20. **cheap** ring

21. **beautiful** view
22. **ugly** view

23. **easy** problem
24. **difficult** problem / **hard** problem

$$1 + 1 = 2$$

$$x^2 - 22\tfrac{1}{2}x = -8\tfrac{1}{3}x^2 - 11\tfrac{2}{3}$$

Ask your classmates. Share the answers.

1. Are you a slow driver or a fast driver?
2. Do you prefer a hard bed or a soft bed?
3. Do you like loud parties or quiet parties?

Use the new words.

Look at page 150–151. Describe the things you see.

A: _The street_ is _hard_.
B: _The truck_ is _heavy_.

Basic Colors

1. red
2. yellow
3. blue
4. orange
5. green
6. purple

7. pink
8. violet
9. turquoise
10. dark blue
11. light blue
12. bright blue

Neutral Colors

13. black
14. white
15. gray
16. cream / ivory
17. brown
18. beige / tan

Ask your classmates. Share the answers.
1. What colors are you wearing today?
2. What colors do you like?
3. Is there a color you don't like? What is it?

Use the new words. Look at pages 86–87.
Take turns naming the colors you see.

A: *His shirt is <u>blue</u>.*
B: *Her shoes are <u>white</u>.*

1. The yellow sweaters are **on the left**.

2. The purple sweaters are **in the middle**.

3. The brown sweaters are **on the right**.

4. The red sweaters are **above** the blue sweaters.

5. The blue sweaters are **below** the red sweaters.

6. The turquoise sweater is **in** the box.

7. The white sweater is **in front of** the black sweater.

8. The black sweater is **behind** the white sweater.

9. The violet sweater is **next to** the gray sweater.

10. The gray sweater is **under** the orange sweater.

11. The orange sweater is **on** the gray sweater.

12. The green sweater is **between** the pink sweaters.

More vocabulary
near: in the same area
far from: not near

Role play. Make new conversations.
A: *Excuse me. Where are the <u>red</u> sweaters?*
B: *They're <u>on the left</u>, <u>above</u> the <u>blue</u> sweaters.*
A: *Thanks very much.*

Coins

1. $.01 = 1¢
a penny / 1 cent

3. $.10 = 10¢
a dime / 10 cents

5. $.50 = 50¢
a half dollar

2. $.05 = 5¢
a nickel / 5 cents

4. $.25 = 25¢
a quarter / 25 cents

6. $1.00
a dollar coin

Bills

7. $1.00
a dollar

8. $5.00
five dollars

9. $10.00
ten dollars

10. $20.00
twenty dollars

11. $50.00
fifty dollars

12. $100.00
one hundred dollars

A. Get change.

B. Borrow money.

C. Lend money.

D. Pay back the money.

Pair practice. Make new conversations.

A: *Do you have change for a dollar?*
B: *Sure. How about two quarters and five dimes?*
A: *Perfect!*

Think about it. Discuss.

1. Is it a good idea to lend money to a friend? Why or why not?
2. Is it better to carry a dollar or four quarters? Why?
3. Do you prefer dollar coins or dollar bills? Why?

Ways to Pay

A. **pay** cash

B. **use** a credit card

C. **use** a debit card

D. **write** a (personal) check

E. **use** a gift card

F. **cash** a traveler's check

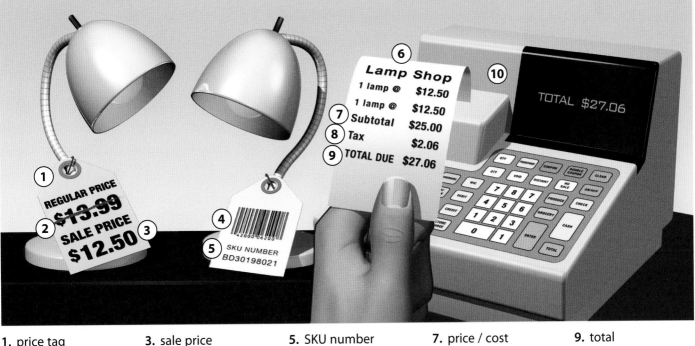

Lamp Shop
1 lamp @ $12.50
1 lamp @ $12.50
Subtotal $25.00
Tax $2.06
TOTAL DUE $27.06

TOTAL $27.06

REGULAR PRICE $13.99
SALE PRICE $12.50

SKU NUMBER
BD30198021

1. price tag

2. regular price

3. sale price

4. bar code

5. SKU number

6. receipt

7. price / cost

8. sales tax

9. total

10. cash register

G. **buy / pay for**

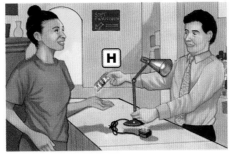

H. **return**

I. **exchange**

27

1. twins
2. sweater
3. matching
4. disappointed
5. navy blue
6. happy

A. **shop**
B. **keep**

Look at the pictures.
What do you see?

Answer the questions.

1. Who is the woman shopping for?

2. Does she buy matching sweaters or different sweaters?

3. How does Anya feel about her green sweater? What does she do?

4. What does Manda do with her sweater?

📖 **Read the story.**

Same and Different

Mrs. Kumar likes to <u>shop</u> for her <u>twins</u>. Today she's looking at <u>sweaters</u>. There are many different colors on sale. Mrs. Kumar chooses two <u>matching</u> green sweaters.

The next day, Manda and Anya open their gifts. Manda likes the green sweater, but Anya is <u>disappointed</u>. Mrs. Kumar understands the problem. Anya wants to be different.

Manda <u>keeps</u> her sweater. But Anya goes to the store. She exchanges her green sweater for a <u>navy blue</u> sweater. It's an easy answer to Anya's problem. Now the twins can be warm, <u>happy</u>, and different.

Think about it.

1. Do you like to shop for other people? Why or why not?

2. Imagine you are Anya. Would you keep the sweater or exchange it? Why?

1. man

2. woman

3. women

4. men

5. senior citizen

Listen and point. Take turns.

A: *Point to a woman.*
B: *Point to a senior citizen.*
A: *Point to an infant.*

Dictate to your partner. Take turns.

A: *Write woman.*
B: *Is that spelled w-o-m-a-n?*
A: *Yes, that's right, woman.*

6. infant

7. baby

8. toddler

9. 6-year-old boy

10. 10-year-old girl

11. teenager / teen

Ways to talk about age

1 month – 3 months old = **infant**

18 months – 3 years old = **toddler**

3 years old – 12 years old = **child**

13 – 19 years old = **teenager**

18+ years old = **adult**

62+ years old = **senior citizen**

Pair practice. Make new conversations.

A: *How old is Sandra?*

B: *She's thirteen years old.*

A: *Wow, she's a teenager now!*

31

Age

1. young
2. middle-aged
3. elderly

Height

4. tall
5. average height
6. short

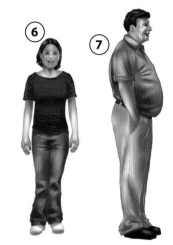
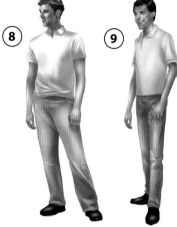

Weight

7. heavy / fat
8. average weight
9. thin / slender

Disabilities

10. physically challenged
11. sight impaired / blind
12. hearing impaired / deaf

Appearance

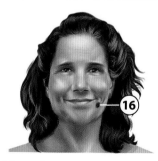

13. attractive   14. cute   15. pregnant   16. mole   17. pierced ear

18. tattoo

Ways to describe people

He's a <u>heavy</u>, <u>young</u> man.
She's a <u>pregnant</u> woman with <u>a mole</u>.
He's <u>sight impaired</u>.

Use the new words. Look at pages 2–3.
Describe the people and point. Take turns.

A: *He's a <u>tall</u>, <u>thin</u>, <u>middle-aged</u> man.*
B: *She's a <u>short</u>, <u>average-weight</u> <u>young</u> woman.*

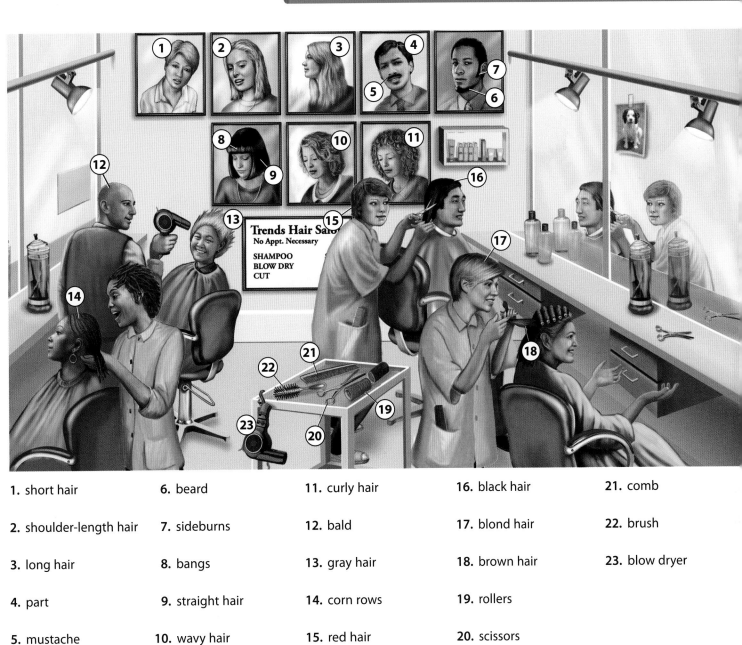

1. short hair
2. shoulder-length hair
3. long hair
4. part
5. mustache

6. beard
7. sideburns
8. bangs
9. straight hair
10. wavy hair

11. curly hair
12. bald
13. gray hair
14. corn rows
15. red hair

16. black hair
17. blond hair
18. brown hair
19. rollers
20. scissors

21. comb
22. brush
23. blow dryer

Style Hair

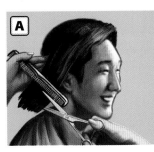

A. cut hair

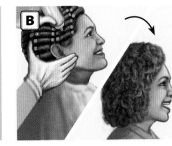

B. perm hair

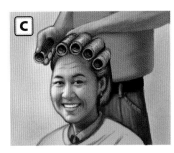

C. set hair

D. color hair / **dye** hair

Ways to talk about hair
Describe hair in this order: length, style, and then color.
She has <u>long</u>, <u>straight</u>, <u>brown</u> hair.

Role play. Talk to a stylist.
A: *I need a new hairstyle.*
B: *How about <u>short</u> and <u>straight</u>?*
A: *Great. Do you think I should <u>dye</u> it?*

33

Families

1. grandmother
2. grandfather
3. mother
4. father
5. sister
6. brother
7. aunt
8. uncle
9. cousin

10. mother-in-law
11. father-in-law
12. wife
13. husband
14. daughter
15. son
16. sister-in-law
17. brother-in-law
18. niece
19. nephew

Tim Lee's Family

GRANDPARENTS — Min (1), Lu (2)

Immediate Family

PARENTS — Rose (3), Ken (4), Lynn (7), Dan (8)

CHILDREN — Tim, Lily (5), Alex (6), Emily (9)

Ana Garcia's Family

Eva (10), Sam (11)

Extended Family

Ana (12), Tito (13), Marta (16), Carlos (17)

Sara (14), Felix (15), Alice (18), Eddie (19)

More vocabulary

Tim is Min and Lu's **grandson**.
Lily and Emily are Min and Lu's **granddaughters**.
Alex is Min's youngest **grandchild**.

Ana is Tito's **wife**.
Ana is Eva and Sam's **daughter-in-law**.
Carlos is Eva and Sam's **son-in-law**.

20. married couple

21. divorced couple

22. single mother

23. single father

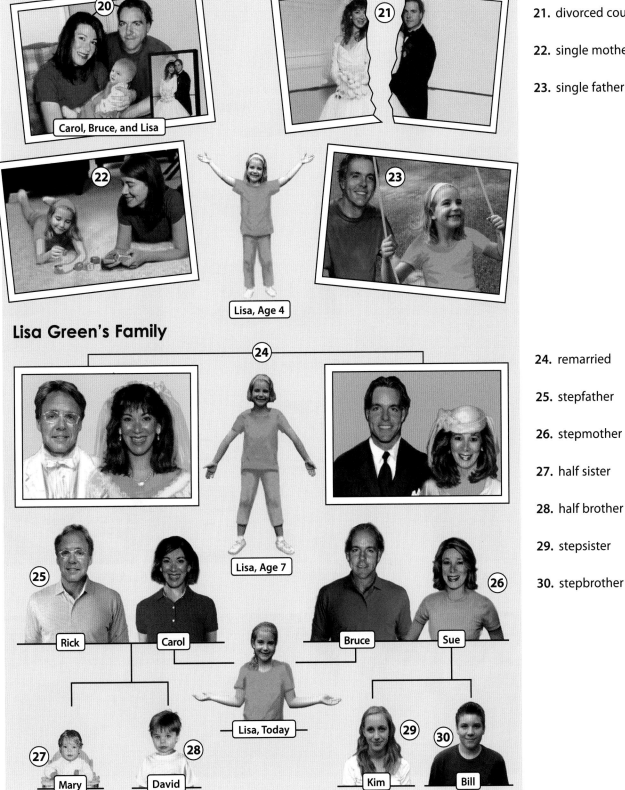

Carol, Bruce, and Lisa

Lisa, Age 4

Lisa Green's Family

24. remarried

25. stepfather

26. stepmother

27. half sister

28. half brother

29. stepsister

30. stepbrother

Lisa, Age 7

Rick   Carol   Bruce   Sue

Lisa, Today

Mary   David   Kim   Bill

More vocabulary

Bruce is Carol's **former husband** or **ex-husband**.
Carol is Bruce's **former wife** or **ex-wife**.
Lisa is the **stepdaughter** of both Rick and Sue.

Look at the pictures.
Name the people.

A: *Who is Lisa's half sister?*
B: *Mary is. Who is Lisa's stepsister?*

35

A. **hold**

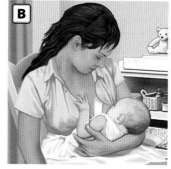

B. **nurse**

C. **feed**

D. **rock**

E. **undress**

F. **bathe**

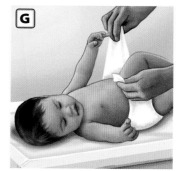

G. **change** a diaper

H. **dress**

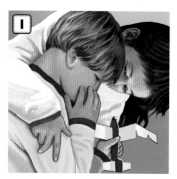

I. **comfort**

Good job!

J. **praise**

No!

K. **discipline**

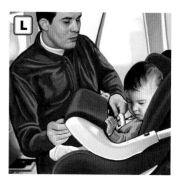

L. **buckle up**

M. **play** with

N. **read** to

O. **sing** a lullaby

P. **kiss** goodnight

Look at the pictures.
Describe what is happening.

A: *She's changing her baby's diaper.*
B: *He's kissing his son goodnight.*

Ask your classmates. Share the answers.
1. Do you like to take care of children?
2. Do you prefer to read to children or play with them?
3. Can you sing a lullaby? Which one?

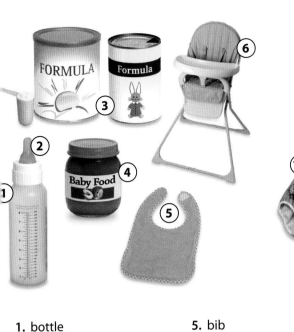

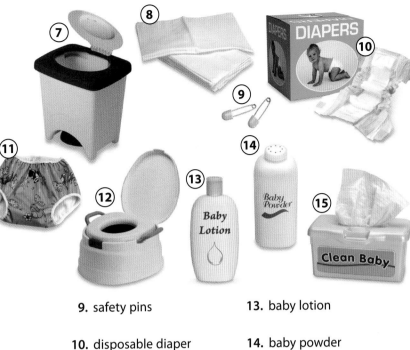

1. bottle

2. nipple

3. formula

4. baby food

5. bib

6. high chair

7. diaper pail

8. cloth diaper

9. safety pins

10. disposable diaper

11. training pants

12. potty seat

13. baby lotion

14. baby powder

15. wipes

16. baby bag

17. baby carrier

18. stroller

19. car safety seat

20. carriage

21. rocking chair

22. nursery rhymes

23. teddy bear

24. pacifier

25. teething ring

26. rattle

27. night light

Dictate to your partner. Take turns.

A: *Write pacifier.*

B: *Was that pacifier, p-a-c-i-f-i-e-r?*

A: *Yes, that's right.*

Think about it. Discuss.

1. How can parents discipline toddlers? teens?

2. What are some things you can say to praise a child?

3. Why are nursery rhymes important for young children?

A. **wake up**

B. **get up**

C. **take** a shower

D. **get dressed**

E. **eat** breakfast

F. **make** lunch

G. **take** the children to school /
drop off the kids

H. **take** the bus to school

I. **drive** to work / **go** to work

J. **go** to class

K. **work**

L. **go** to the grocery store

M. **pick up** the kids

N. **leave** work

Grammar Point: third person singular

For *he* and *she*, add **-s** or **-es** to the verb:

He wake**s** up.   He watch**es** TV.

He get**s** up.   She go**es** to the store.

These verbs are different (irregular):

Be: She **is** in school at 10:00 a.m.

Have: He **has** dinner at 6:30 p.m.

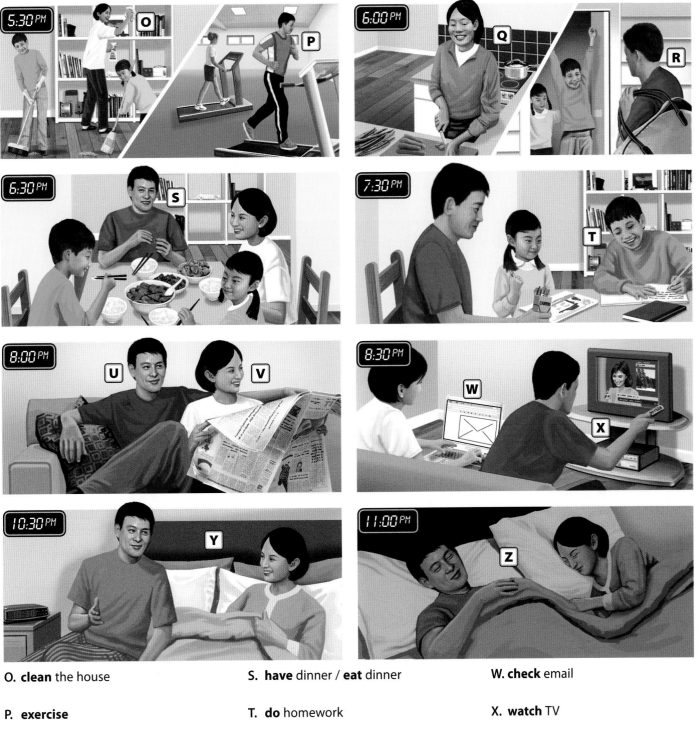

O. clean the house

P. exercise

Q. cook dinner / **make** dinner

R. come home / **get** home

S. have dinner / **eat** dinner

T. do homework

U. relax

V. read the paper

W. check email

X. watch TV

Y. go to bed

Z. go to sleep

Pair practice. Make new conversations.

A: *When does he go to work?*
B: *He goes to work at 8:00 a.m. When does she go to class?*
A: *She goes to class at 10:00 a.m.*

Ask your classmates. Share the answers.

1. Who cooks dinner in your family?
2. Who goes to the grocery store?
3. Who goes to work?

39

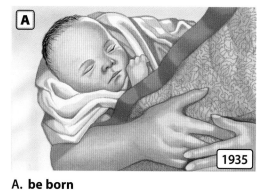

A. be born — 1935

B. start school — 1940

1. birth certificate

C. immigrate — 1950

D. graduate — 1953

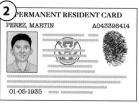

2. Resident Alien card / green card

3. diploma

E. learn to drive — 1953

F. get a job — 1954

4. driver's license

5. Social Security card

G. become a citizen — 1954

H. fall in love — 1955

6. Certificate of Naturalization

Grammar Point: past tense

start
learn   +ed
travel

immigrate   retire
graduate   die   +d

These verbs are different (irregular):

be – was   go – went   buy – bought
get – got   have – had
become – became   fall – fell

I. go to college — 1956

J. get engaged — 1958

7. college degree

K. get married — 1959

L. have a baby — 1961

8. marriage license

M. buy a home — 1965

N. become a grandparent — 1986

9. deed

O. retire — 2000

P. travel — 2005

10. passport

Q. volunteer — 2006

R. die — 2008

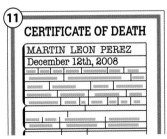

11. death certificate

More vocabulary

When a husband dies, his wife becomes a **widow**.
When a wife dies, her husband becomes a **widower**.

Ask your classmates. Share the answers.

1. When did you start school?
2. When did you get your first job?
3. Do you want to travel?

41

1. hot
2. thirsty
3. sleepy
4. cold
5. hungry
6. full / satisfied

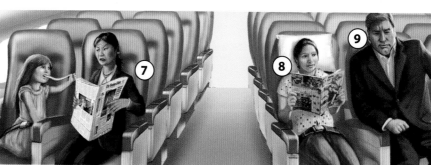

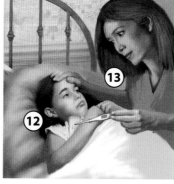

7. disgusted
8. calm
9. uncomfortable
10. nervous

11. in pain
12. sick
13. worried
14. well
15. relieved

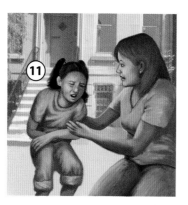

16. hurt
17. lonely
18. in love

Pair practice. Make new conversations.

A: *How are you doing?*
B: *I'm <u>hungry</u>. How about you?*
A: *I'm <u>hungry</u> and <u>thirsty</u>, too!*

Use the new words.
Look at pages 40–41. Describe what each person is feeling.

A: *Martin is <u>excited</u>.*
B: *Martin's mother is <u>proud</u>.*

19. sad

20. homesick

21. proud

22. excited

23. scared / afraid

24. embarrassed

14 (tan 63°)

$T = V_0 / g$

79.00 - .40 (79.00)

$-1/2 gt^2 + V_0 t + h$

$sin^2 t + cos^2 t + 1$

$tan (\pi - t) = -tan t$

25. bored

26. confused

27. frustrated

28. upset

29. angry

30. surprised

31. happy

32. tired

Ask your classmates. Share the answers.

1. Do you ever feel homesick?
2. What makes you feel frustrated?
3. Describe a time when you were very happy.

More vocabulary

exhausted: very tired
furious: very angry
humiliated: very embarrassed

overjoyed: very happy
starving: very hungry
terrified: very scared

LU FAMILY REUNION

1. banner 3. opinion 5. glad A. **laugh**

2. baseball game 4. balloons 6. relatives B. **misbehave**

Look at the picture.
What do you see?

Answer the questions.

1. How many relatives are there at this reunion?

2. How many children are there? Which children are misbehaving?

3. What are people doing at this reunion?

Read the story.

A Family Reunion

Ben Lu has a lot of <u>relatives</u> and they're all at his house. Today is the Lu family reunion.

There is a lot of good food. There are also <u>balloons</u> and a <u>banner</u>. And this year there are four new babies!

People are having a good time at the reunion. Ben's grandfather and his aunt are talking about the <u>baseball game</u>. His cousins <u>are laughing</u>. His mother-in-law is giving her <u>opinion</u>. And many of the children <u>are misbehaving</u>.

Ben looks at his family and smiles. He loves his relatives, but he's <u>glad</u> the reunion is once a year.

Think about it.

1. Do you like to have large parties? Why or why not?

2. Imagine you see a little girl at a party. She's misbehaving. What do you do? What do you say?

The Home

1. roof

2. bedroom

3. door

4. bathroom

5. kitchen

6. floor

7. dining area

Listen and point. Take turns.

A: *Point to the kitchen.*

B: *Point to the living room.*

A: *Point to the basement.*

Dictate to your partner. Take turns.

A: *Write kitchen.*

B: *Was that k-i-t-c-h-e-n?*

A: *Yes, that's right, kitchen.*

8. attic

9. kids' bedroom

10. baby's room

11. window

12. living room

13. basement

14. garage

Ways to give locations
I'm home.
I'm in _the kitchen_.
I'm on _the roof_.

Pair practice. Make new conversations.
A: _Where's the man?_
B: _He's in the attic. Where's the teenager?_
A: _She's in the laundry room._

1. Internet listing

2. classified ad

Abbreviations

apt = apartment
bdrm = bedroom
ba = bathroom
kit = kitchen
yd = yard
util = utilities
incl = included
mo = month
furn = furnished
unfurn = unfurnished
mgr = manager
eves = evenings

West Rentals
1 Bedroom
$900 / Month
Call for info:
818-555-4949

Apartment For Rent
2 bdrm 2ba city apt
Unfurn Sunny kit
Util incl
$850/mo
Call mgr eves
212-555-2368

3. furnished apartment

4. unfurnished apartment

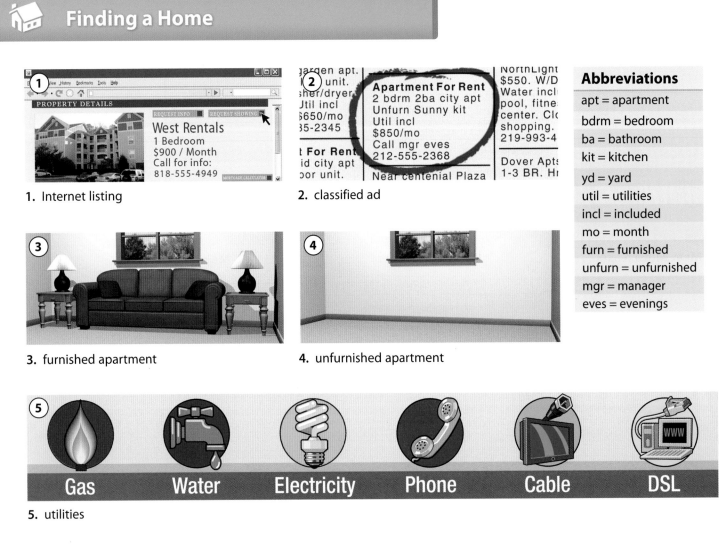

Gas   Water   Electricity   Phone   Cable   DSL

5. utilities

Renting an Apartment

A. **Call** the manager.

B. **Ask** about the features.
> Are utilities included?
> No, they aren't.

C. **Submit** an application.
Rental Application
Name: Maya Ramos
Telephone number: 818-555-8907

D. **Sign** the rental agreement.
Rental Agreement
Maya Ramos

E. **Pay** the first and last month's rent.
Maya Ramos
100 4th Street
Big City, WI 60444
Pay to the order of *Armstrong Properties* $1,700.00
Maya Ramos
For Rent $850/mo.

F. **Move in**.

More vocabulary

lease: a monthly or yearly rental agreement
redecorate: to change the paint and furniture in a home
move out: to pack and leave a home

Ask your classmates. Share the answers.

1. How did you find your home?
2. Do you like to paint or arrange furniture?
3. Does gas or electricity cost more for you?

Buying a House

G. **Meet** with a realtor.

H. **Look** at houses.

$$$$$$

I. **Make** an offer.

Congratulations!

APPROVED

J. **Get** a loan.

K. **Take** ownership.

Mr. Young Chang
4445 2nd Street
Passville, CA 00543
Pay to the order of *Towne Bank* $ 2000.00
Two Thousand and 00/100 Dollars

L. **Make** a mortgage payment.

Moving In

M. **Pack**.

N. **Unpack**.

We have a new address.

PHONE ✓
DWP ✓
GAS
CABLE ✓

GAS

O. **Put** the utilities in your name.

P. **Paint**.

Q. **Arrange** the furniture.

Welcome!

R. **Meet** the neighbors.

Ways to ask about a home's features

Are <u>utilities</u> included?
Is <u>the kitchen</u> large and sunny?
Are <u>the neighbors</u> quiet?

Role play. Talk to an apartment manager.

A: *Hi. I'm calling about <u>the apartment</u>.*
B: *OK. It's <u>unfurnished</u> and rent is $<u>800</u> a month.*
A: *<u>Are utilities included</u>?*

49

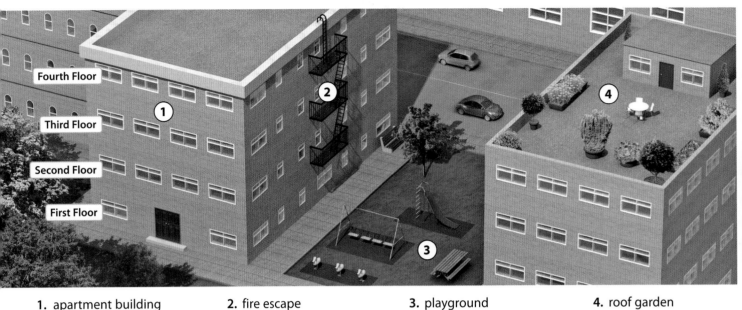

Fourth Floor 1

Third Floor

Second Floor

First Floor

2

4

3

1. apartment building   2. fire escape   3. playground   4. roof garden

Entrance

5

6

7

Apartment Available
2BD + 2BA
555-4263

8

5. intercom / speaker   7. vacancy sign

6. tenant   8. manager / superintendent

Lobby

9

10

11

9. elevator   11. mailboxes

10. stairs / stairway

Basement

12

13

LAUNDRY ROOM

14

15

RECREATION ROOM

16

17

19

18

GARAGE

12. washer   14. big-screen TV   16. security gate   18. parking space

13. dryer   15. pool table   17. storage locker   19. security camera

---

Grammar Point: *there is / there are*

singular: there is   plural: there are
***There is** a recreation room in the basement.*
***There are** mailboxes in the lobby.*

Look at the pictures.
Describe the apartment building.

A: *There's <u>a pool table</u> in the recreation room.*
B: *There are <u>parking spaces</u> in the garage.*

APARTMENT COMPLEX

20. balcony

21. courtyard

22. swimming pool

23. trash bin

24. alley

Hallway

25. emergency exit

26. trash chute

Rental Office

27. landlord

28. lease / rental agreement

An Apartment Entryway

It's Joe.

Come up.

29. smoke detector

30. key

31. buzzer

32. peephole

33. door chain

34. dead-bolt lock

More vocabulary

upstairs: the floor(s) above you
downstairs: the floor(s) below you
fire exit: another name for emergency exit

Role play. Talk to a landlord.

A: *Is there <u>a swimming pool</u> in this <u>complex</u>?*
B: *Yes, there is. It's near <u>the courtyard</u>.*
A: *Is there…?*

Different Places to Live

1. the city / an urban area   2. the suburbs   3. a small town / a village   4. the country / a rural area

5. condominium / condo

6. townhouse

7. mobile home

8. college dormitory / dorm

9. farm

10. ranch

11. senior housing

12. nursing home

13. shelter

More vocabulary

co-op: an apartment building owned by residents
duplex: a house divided into two homes
two-story house: a house with two floors

Think about it. Discuss.

1. What's good and bad about these places to live?
2. How are small towns different from cities?
3. How do shelters help people in need?

Front Yard and House

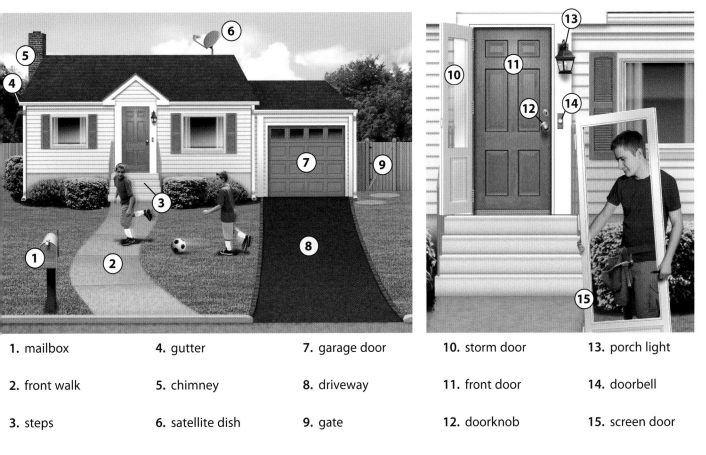

Front Porch

1. mailbox	4. gutter	7. garage door
2. front walk	5. chimney	8. driveway
3. steps	6. satellite dish	9. gate

10. storm door	13. porch light
11. front door	14. doorbell
12. doorknob	15. screen door

Backyard

16. patio	19. patio furniture	22. sprinkler	25. compost pile	A. **take** a nap
17. grill	20. flower bed	23. hammock	26. lawn	B. **garden**
18. sliding glass door	21. hose	24. garbage can	27. vegetable garden	

1. cabinet	8. dishwasher	15. toaster oven	22. counter
2. shelf	9. refrigerator	16. pot	23. drawer
3. paper towels	10. freezer	17. teakettle	24. pan
4. sink	11. coffeemaker	18. stove	25. electric mixer
5. dish rack	12. blender	19. burner	26. food processor
6. toaster	13. microwave	20. oven	27. cutting board
7. garbage disposal	14. electric can opener	21. broiler	28. mixing bowl

Ways to talk about location using *on* and *in*

Use **on** for the counter, shelf, burner, stove, and cutting board. *It's on the counter.* Use **in** for the dishwasher, oven, sink, and drawer. *Put it in the sink.*

Pair practice. Make new conversations.

A: *Please move <u>the blender</u>.*
B: *Sure. Do you want it <u>in the cabinet</u>?*
A: *No, put it <u>on the counter</u>.*

1. dish / plate

2. bowl

3. fork

4. knife

5. spoon

6. teacup

7. coffee mug

8. dining room chair

9. dining room table

10. napkin

11. placemat

12. tablecloth

13. salt and pepper shakers

14. sugar bowl

15. creamer

16. teapot

17. tray

18. light fixture

19. fan

20. platter

21. serving bowl

22. hutch

23. vase

24. buffet

Ways to make requests at the table

May I have the sugar bowl?
Would you pass the creamer, please?
Could I have a coffee mug?

Role play. Request items at the table.

A: *What do you need?*
B: *Could I have a coffee mug?*
A: *Certainly. And would you...*

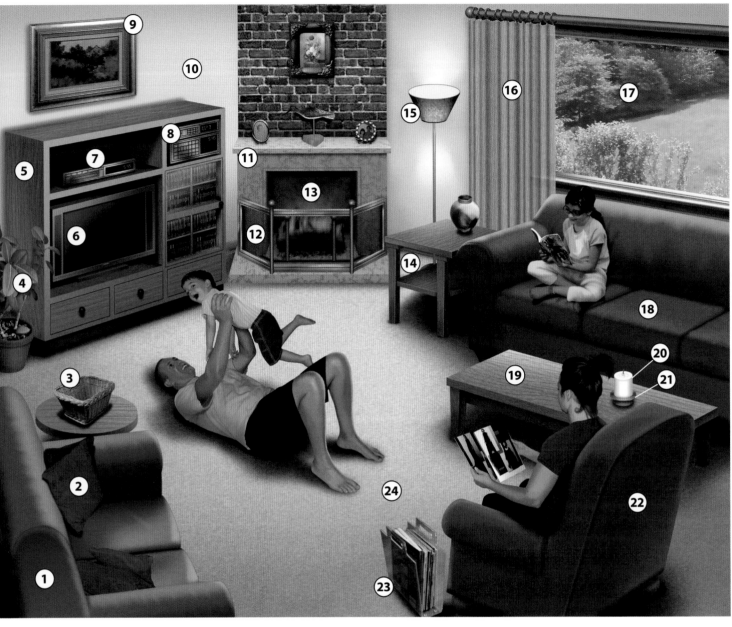

1. love seat	**7.** DVD player	**13.** fireplace	**19.** coffee table
2. throw pillow	**8.** stereo system	**14.** end table	**20.** candle
3. basket	**9.** painting	**15.** floor lamp	**21.** candle holder
4. houseplant	**10.** wall	**16.** drapes	**22.** armchair / easy chair
5. entertainment center	**11.** mantle	**17.** window	**23.** magazine holder
6. TV (television)	**12.** fire screen	**18.** sofa / couch	**24.** carpet

Use the new words.
Look at pages 44–45. Name the things in the room.

A: *There's a TV.*
B: *There's a carpet.*

More vocabulary

light bulb: the light inside a lamp
lampshade: the part of the lamp that covers the light bulb
sofa cushions: the pillows that are part of the sofa

1. hamper

2. bathtub

3. soap dish

4. soap

5. rubber mat

6. washcloth

7. drain

8. faucet

9. hot water

10. cold water

11. grab bar

12. tile

13. showerhead

14. shower curtain

15. towel rack

16. bath towel

17. hand towel

18. mirror

19. toilet paper

20. toilet brush

21. toilet

22. medicine cabinet

23. toothbrush

24. toothbrush holder

25. sink

26. wastebasket

27. scale

28. bath mat

More vocabulary

stall shower: a shower without a bathtub
half bath: a bathroom with no shower or tub
linen closet: a closet for towels and sheets

Ask your classmates. Share the answers.

1. Is your toothbrush on the sink or in the medicine cabinet?
2. Do you have a bathtub or a shower?
3. Do you have a shower curtain or a shower door?

57

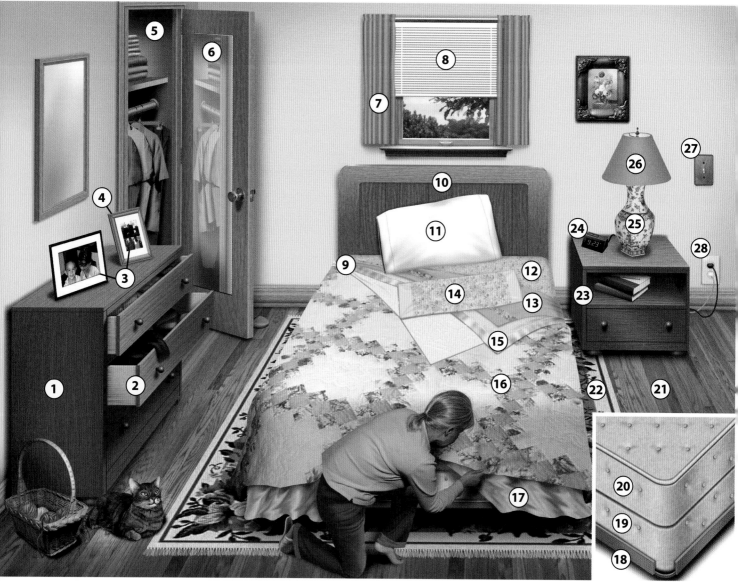

1. dresser / bureau
2. drawer
3. photos
4. picture frame
5. closet
6. full-length mirror
7. curtains

8. mini-blinds
9. bed
10. headboard
11. pillow
12. fitted sheet
13. flat sheet
14. pillowcase

15. blanket
16. quilt
17. dust ruffle
18. bed frame
19. box spring
20. mattress
21. wood floor

22. rug
23. night table / nightstand
24. alarm clock
25. lamp
26. lampshade
27. light switch
28. outlet

Look at the pictures.
Describe the bedroom.

A: There's _a lamp_ _on_ _the nightstand_.
B: There's _a mirror_ _in_ _the closet_.

Ask your classmates. Share the answers.

1. Do you prefer a hard or a soft mattress?
2. Do you prefer mini-blinds or curtains?
3. How many pillows do you like on your bed?

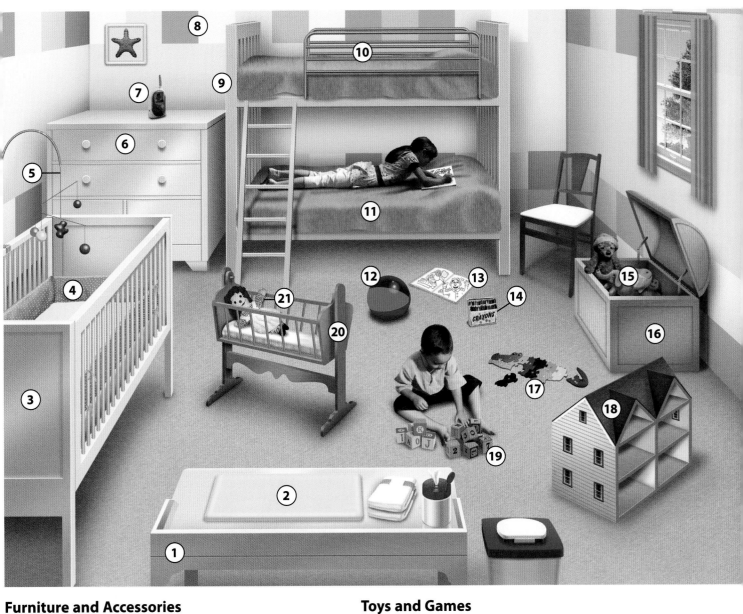

Furniture and Accessories

1. changing table
2. changing pad
3. crib
4. bumper pad
5. mobile
6. chest of drawers
7. baby monitor
8. wallpaper
9. bunk beds
10. safety rail
11. bedspread

Toys and Games

12. ball
13. coloring book
14. crayons
15. stuffed animals
16. toy chest
17. puzzle
18. dollhouse
19. blocks
20. cradle
21. doll

Pair practice. Make conversations.

A: *Where's the changing pad?*
B: *It's on the changing table.*

Think about it. Discuss.

1. Which toys help children learn? How?
2. Which toys are good for older and younger children?
3. What safety features does this room need? Why?

59

A. dust the furniture

B. recycle the newspapers

C. clean the oven

D. mop the floor

E. polish the furniture

F. make the bed

G. put away the toys

H. vacuum the carpet

I. wash the windows

J. sweep the floor

K. scrub the sink

L. empty the trash

M. wash the dishes

N. dry the dishes

O. wipe the counter

P. change the sheets

Q. take out the garbage

Pair practice. Make new conversations.

A: *Let's clean this place. First, I'll* <u>sweep the floor</u>.
B: *I'll* <u>mop the floor</u> *when you finish.*

Ask your classmates. Share the answers.

1. Who does the housework in your home?
2. How often do you wash the windows?
3. When should kids start to do housework?

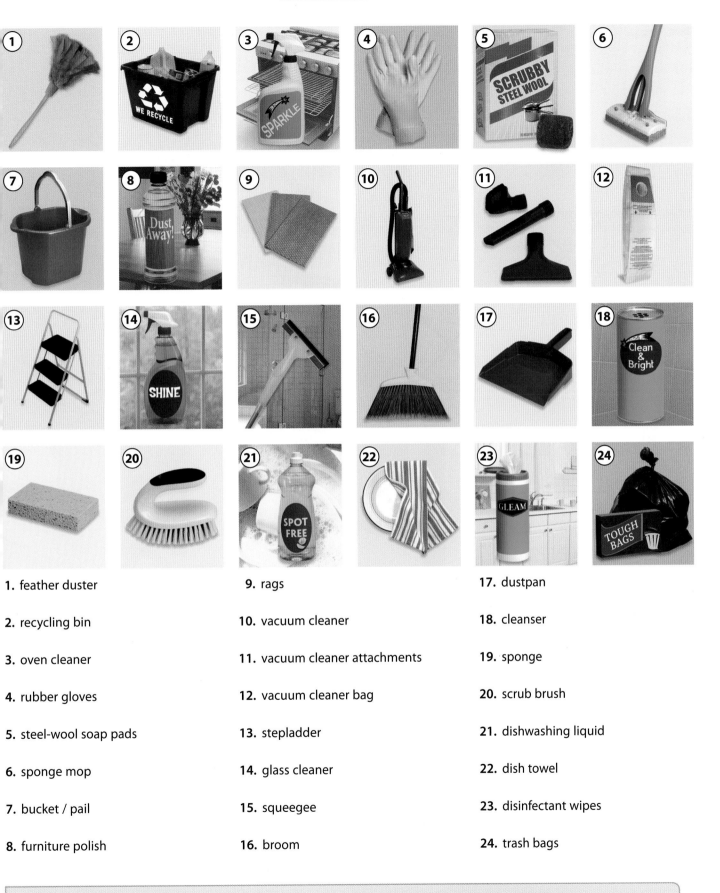

1. feather duster
2. recycling bin
3. oven cleaner
4. rubber gloves
5. steel-wool soap pads
6. sponge mop
7. bucket / pail
8. furniture polish

9. rags
10. vacuum cleaner
11. vacuum cleaner attachments
12. vacuum cleaner bag
13. stepladder
14. glass cleaner
15. squeegee
16. broom

17. dustpan
18. cleanser
19. sponge
20. scrub brush
21. dishwashing liquid
22. dish towel
23. disinfectant wipes
24. trash bags

Ways to ask for something

Please hand me the squeegee.
Can you get me the broom?
I need the sponge mop.

Pair practice. Make new conversations.

A: *Please hand me the sponge mop.*
B: *Here you go. Do you need the bucket?*
A: *Yes, please. Can you get me the rubber gloves, too?*

1. The water heater is **not working**.

2. The power is **out**.

3. The roof is **leaking**.

4. The tile is **cracked**.

5. The window is **broken**.

6. The lock is **broken**.

7. The steps are **broken**.

8. roofer

9. electrician

10. repair person

11. locksmith

12. carpenter

13. fuse box

14. gas meter

More vocabulary

fix: to repair something that is broken
pests: termites, fleas, rats, etc.
exterminate: to kill household pests

Pair practice. Make new conversations.

A: *The faucet is* <u>*leaking*</u>.
B: *Let's call* <u>*the plumber*</u>. *He can fix it.*

15. The furnace is **broken**.

16. The pipes are **frozen**.

17. The faucet is **dripping**.

18. The sink is **overflowing**.

19. The toilet is **stopped up**.

20. plumber

21. exterminator

22. termites

23. ants

24. bedbugs

25. fleas

26. cockroaches / roaches

27. rats

28. mice*

*Note: one mouse, two mice

Ways to ask about repairs

How much will this repair cost?
When can you begin?
How long will the repair take?

Role play. Talk to a repair person.

A: *Can you fix <u>the roof</u>?*
B: *Yes, but it will take <u>two weeks</u>.*
A: *How much will the repair cost?*

63

The Tenant Meeting

1. roommates
2. party
3. music
4. DJ
5. noise
6. irritated
7. rules
8. mess
9. invitation
A. **dance**

Look at the pictures.
What do you see?

Answer the questions.

1. What happened in apartment 2B? How many people were there?

2. How did the neighbor feel? Why?

3. What rules did they write at the tenant meeting?

4. What did the roommates do after the tenant meeting?

📖 **Read the story.**

The Tenant Meeting

Sally Lopez and Tina Green are <u>roommates</u>. They live in apartment 2B. One night they had a big <u>party</u> with <u>music</u> and a <u>DJ</u>. There was a <u>mess</u> in the hallway. Their neighbors were very unhappy. Mr. Clark in 2A was very <u>irritated</u>. He hates <u>noise</u>!

The next day there was a tenant meeting. Everyone wanted <u>rules</u> about parties and loud music. The girls were very embarrassed.

After the meeting, the girls cleaned the mess in the hallway. Then they gave each neighbor an <u>invitation</u> to a new party. Everyone had a good time at the rec room party. Now the tenants have two new rules and a new place to <u>dance</u>.

Think about it.

1. What are the most important rules in an apartment building? Why?

2. Imagine you are the neighbor in 2A. What do you say to Tina and Sally?

1. fish

2. meat

3. chicken

4. cheese

5. milk

6. butter

7. eggs

8. vegetables

Listen and point. Take turns.

A: *Point to the <u>vegetables</u>.*
B: *Point to the <u>bread</u>.*
A: *Point to the <u>fruit</u>.*

Pair Dictation

A: *Write <u>vegetables</u>.*
B: *Please spell <u>vegetables</u> for me.*
A: *V-e-g-e-t-a-b-l-e-s.*

9. fruit

10. rice

11. bread

12. pasta

13. grocery bag

14. shopping list

15. coupons

✓ milk
✓ bread
✓ lettuce
✓ grapes

Ways to talk about food.

Do we need eggs?
Do we have any pasta?
We have some vegetables, but we need fruit.

Role play. Talk about your shopping list.

A: *Do we need eggs?*
B: *No, we have some.*
A: *Do we have any...*

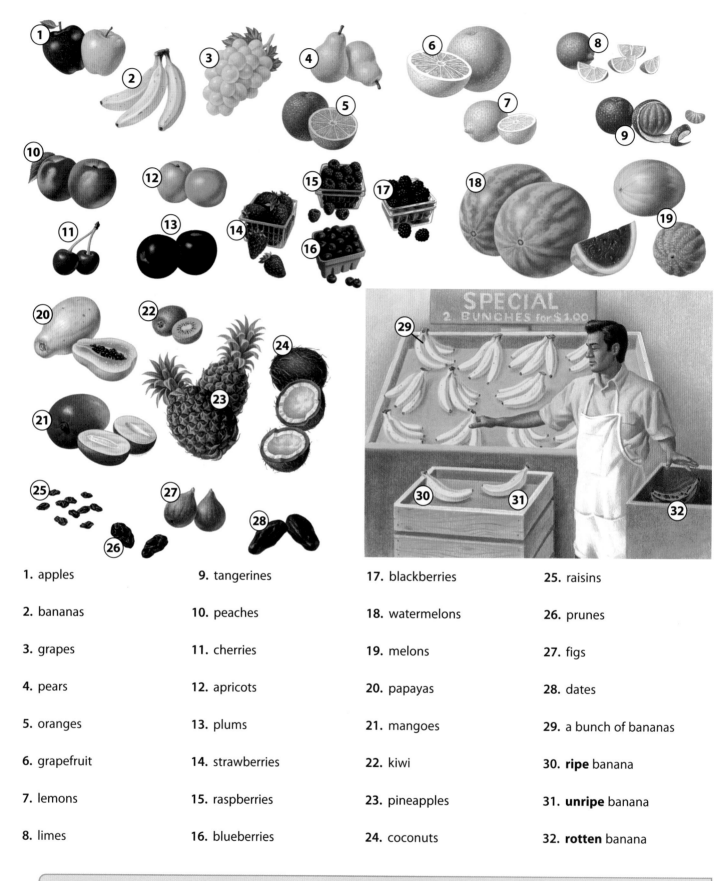

1. apples
2. bananas
3. grapes
4. pears
5. oranges
6. grapefruit
7. lemons
8. limes

9. tangerines
10. peaches
11. cherries
12. apricots
13. plums
14. strawberries
15. raspberries
16. blueberries

17. blackberries
18. watermelons
19. melons
20. papayas
21. mangoes
22. kiwi
23. pineapples
24. coconuts

25. raisins
26. prunes
27. figs
28. dates
29. a bunch of bananas
30. **ripe** banana
31. **unripe** banana
32. **rotten** banana

Pair practice. Make new conversations.

A: *What's your favorite fruit?*
B: *I like* <u>apples</u>. *Do you?*
A: *I prefer* <u>bananas</u>.

Ask your classmates. Share the answers.

1. Which fruit do you put in a fruit salad?
2. What kinds of fruit are common in your native country?
3. What kinds of fruit are in your kitchen right now?

1. lettuce
2. cabbage
3. carrots
4. radishes
5. beets
6. tomatoes
7. bell peppers
8. string beans

9. celery
10. cucumbers
11. spinach
12. corn
13. broccoli
14. cauliflower
15. bok choy
16. turnips

17. potatoes
18. sweet potatoes
19. onions
20. green onions / scallions
21. peas
22. artichokes
23. eggplants
24. squash

25. zucchini
26. asparagus
27. mushrooms
28. parsley
29. chili peppers
30. garlic
31. a **bag of** lettuce
32. a **head of** lettuce

Pair practice. Make new conversations.

A: *Do you eat* <u>broccoli</u>?
B: *Yes. I like most vegetables, but not* <u>peppers</u>.
A: *Really? Well, I don't like* <u>cauliflower</u>.

Ask your classmates. Share the answers.

1. Which vegetables do you eat raw? cooked?
2. Which vegetables do you put in a green salad?
3. Which vegetables are in your refrigerator right now?

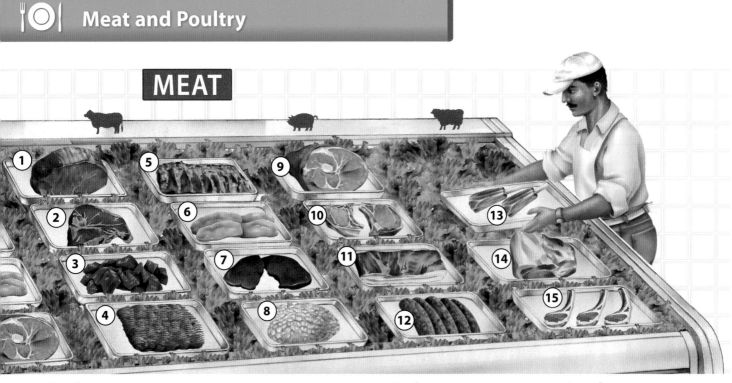

MEAT

Beef

1. roast
2. steak
3. stewing beef
4. ground beef
5. beef ribs
6. veal cutlets
7. liver
8. tripe

Pork

9. ham
10. pork chops
11. bacon
12. sausage

Lamb

13. lamb shanks
14. leg of lamb
15. lamb chops

POULTRY

Poultry

16. chicken
17. turkey
18. duck
19. breasts
20. wings
21. legs
22. thighs
23. drumsticks
24. **raw** chicken
25. **cooked** chicken

More vocabulary

vegetarian: a person who doesn't eat meat
boneless: meat and poultry without bones
skinless: poultry without skin

Ask your classmates. Share the answers.

1. What kind of meat do you eat most often?
2. What kind of meat do you use in soups?
3. What part of the chicken do you like the most?

SEAFOOD

Fish

1. trout
2. catfish
3. whole salmon
4. salmon steak
5. swordfish

6. halibut steak
7. tuna
8. cod

Shellfish

9. crab
10. lobster
11. shrimp
12. scallops
13. mussels

14. oysters
15. clams
16. **fresh** fish
17. **frozen** fish

DELI

18. white bread
19. wheat bread
20. rye bread

21. roast beef
22. corned beef
23. pastrami

24. salami
25. smoked turkey
26. American cheese

27. Swiss cheese
28. cheddar cheese
29. mozzarella cheese

Ways to order at the counter

I'd like some <u>roast beef</u>.
I'll have <u>a halibut steak</u> and some <u>shrimp</u>.
Could I get some <u>Swiss cheese</u>?

Pair practice. Make new conversations.

A: What can I get for you?
B: <u>I'd like some roast beef</u>. How about a pound?
A: A pound of <u>roast beef</u> coming up!

71

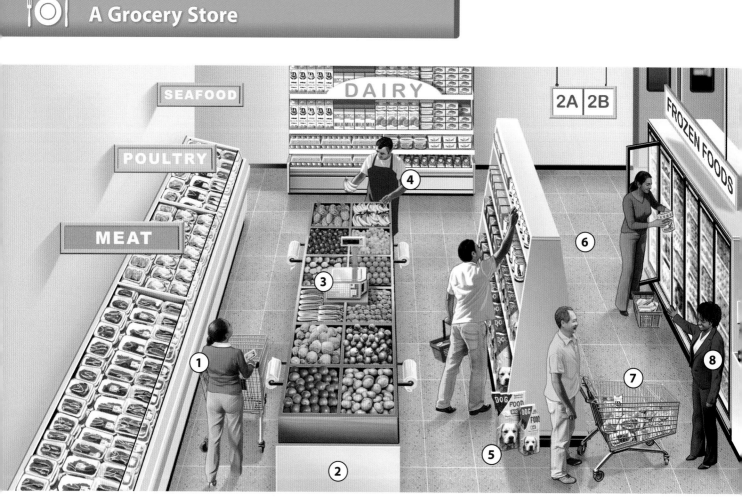

SEAFOOD

POULTRY

MEAT

DAIRY

2A 2B

FROZEN FOODS

1. customer
2. produce section
3. scale
4. grocery clerk
5. pet food
6. aisle
7. cart
8. manager

Canned Foods

17. beans
18. soup
19. tuna

Dairy

20. margarine
21. sour cream
22. yogurt

Grocery Products

23. aluminum foil
24. plastic wrap
25. plastic storage bags

Frozen Foods

26. ice cream
27. frozen vegetables
28. frozen dinner

Ways to ask for information in a grocery store

Excuse me, where are <u>the carrots</u>?
Can you please tell me where to find <u>the dog food</u>?
Do you have any <u>lamb chops</u> today?

Pair practice. Make conversations.

A: *<u>Can you please tell me where to find the dog food</u>?*
B: *Sure. It's in <u>aisle 1B</u>. Do you need anything else?*
A: *Yes, where are <u>the carrots</u>?*

BAKERY

15 items or less

3A 3B

SNACKS

Best Baked Goods

Cash for Bottles | Cash for Bottle

IN | OUT

9. shopping basket

10. self-checkout

11. line

12. checkstand

13. cashier

14. bagger

15. cash register

16. bottle return

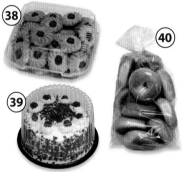

Baking Products

29. flour

30. sugar

31. oil

Beverages

32. apple juice

33. coffee

34. soda / pop

Snack Foods

35. potato chips

36. nuts

37. candy bar

Baked Goods

38. cookies

39. cake

40. bagels

Ask your classmates. Share the answers.

1. What is your favorite grocery store?
2. Do you prefer to shop alone or with friends?
3. Which foods from your country are hard to find?

Think about it. Discuss.

1. Is it better to shop every day or once a week? Why?
2. Why do grocery stores put snacks near the checkstands?
3. What's good and what's bad about small grocery stores?

①
1. bottles

②
2. jars

③
3. cans

④
4. cartons

⑤
5. containers

⑥
6. boxes

⑦
7. bags

⑧
8. packages

⑨
9. six-packs

⑩
10. loaves

⑪
11. rolls

⑫
12. tubes

⑬

⑭

⑮

⑯

⑰

⑱ Friendly O's

⑲ ENRICHED FLOUR

⑳

㉑ FIZZ FIZZ FIZZ

㉒ Whole Grain

㉓

㉔

13. a bottle of water

14. a jar of jam

15. a can of beans

16. a carton of eggs

17. a container of cottage cheese

18. a box of cereal

19. a bag of flour

20. a package of cookies

21. a six-pack of soda (pop)

22. a loaf of bread

23. a roll of paper towels

24. a tube of toothpaste

Grammar Point: count and non-count

Some foods can be counted: *an apple, two apples*.
Some foods can't be counted: *some rice, some water*.
For non-count foods, count containers: *two bags of rice*.

Pair practice. Make conversations.

A: *How many boxes of cereal do we need?*
B: *We need two boxes.*

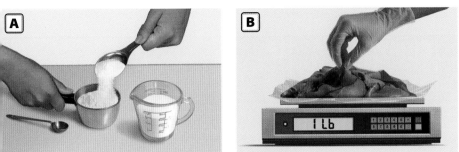

A. **Measure** the ingredients.

B. **Weigh** the food.

C. **Convert** the measurements.

1 cup = 237 milliliters

Liquid Measures

(1) 1 fl. oz.

(2) 1 c.

(3) 1 pt.

(4) 1 qt.

(5) 1 gal.

Dry Measures

(6) 1 tsp.

(7) 1 TBS.

(8) 1/4 c.

(9) 1/2 c.

(10) 1 c.

Weight

(11) 0 Lb 1 oz

(12) 1 Lb

1. a fluid ounce of milk	**5.** a gallon of water	**9.** a half cup of raisins
2. a cup of oil	**6.** a teaspoon of salt	**10.** a cup of flour
3. a pint of frozen yogurt	**7.** a tablespoon of sugar	**11.** an ounce of cheese
4. a quart of milk	**8.** a quarter cup of brown sugar	**12.** a pound of roast beef

Equivalencies

3 tsp. = 1 TBS.	2 c. = 1 pt.
2 TBS. = 1 fl. oz.	2 pt. = 1 qt.
8 fl. oz. = 1 c.	4 qt. = 1 gal.

Volume

1 fl. oz. = 30 ml
1 c. = 237 ml
1 pt. = .47 L
1 qt. = .95 L
1 gal. = 3.79 L

Weight

1 oz. = 28.35 grams (g)
1 lb. = 453.6 g
2.205 lbs. = 1 kilogram (kg)
1 lb. = 16 oz.

Food Safety

A. **clean**

B. **separate**

C. **cook**

D. **chill**

A Clean counters! **20 SECONDS** Wash your hands!

B Use separate cutting boards for vegetables and meat!

C Cook to the right temperature!

D Refrigerate leftovers quickly!

Ways to Serve Meat and Poultry

1. fried chicken

2. barbecued / grilled ribs

3. broiled steak

4. roasted turkey

5. boiled ham

6. stir-fried beef

Ways to Serve Eggs

7. scrambled eggs

8. hardboiled eggs

9. poached eggs

10. eggs sunny-side up

11. eggs over easy

12. omelet

Role play. Make new conversations.

A: *How do you like your eggs?*
B: *I like them <u>scrambled</u>. And you?*
A: *I like them <u>hardboiled</u>.*

Ask your classmates. Share the answers.

1. Do you use separate cutting boards?
2. What is your favorite way to serve meat? poultry?
3. What are healthy ways of preparing meat? poultry?

Cheesy Tofu Vegetable Casserole

A. **Preheat** the oven.

B. **Grease** a baking pan.

C. **Slice** the tofu.

D. **Steam** the broccoli.

E. **Saute** the mushrooms.

F. **Spoon** sauce on top.

G. **Grate** the cheese.

H. **Bake**.

Easy Chicken Soup

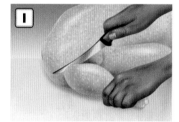

I. **Cut up** the chicken.

J. **Dice** the celery.

K. **Peel** the carrots.

L. **Chop** the onions.

M. **Boil** the chicken.

N. **Add** the vegetables.

O. **Stir**.

P. **Simmer**.

Quick and Easy Cake

Q. **Break** 2 eggs into a microwave-safe bowl.

R. **Mix** the ingredients.

S. **Beat** the mixture.

T. **Microwave** for 5 minutes.

1. can opener
2. grater
3. steamer
4. plastic storage container
5. frying pan
6. pot
7. ladle
8. double boiler

9. wooden spoon
10. casserole dish
11. garlic press
12. carving knife
13. roasting pan
14. roasting rack
15. vegetable peeler
16. paring knife

17. colander
18. kitchen timer
19. spatula
20. eggbeater
21. whisk
22. strainer
23. tongs
24. lid

25. saucepan
26. cake pan
27. cookie sheet
28. pie pan
29. pot holders
30. rolling pin
31. mixing bowl

Pair practice. Make new conversations.

A: *Please hand me the whisk.*
B: *Here's the whisk. Do you need anything else?*
A: *Yes, pass me the casserole dish.*

Use the new words.
Look at page 77. Name the kitchen utensils you see.

A: *Here's a grater.*
B: *This is a mixing bowl.*

1. hamburger

2. french fries

3. cheeseburger

4. onion rings

5. chicken sandwich

6. hot dog

7. nachos

8. taco

9. burrito

10. pizza

11. soda

12. iced tea

13. ice-cream cone

14. milkshake

15. donut

16. muffin

17. counterperson

18. straw

19. plastic utensils

20. sugar substitute

21. ketchup

22. mustard

23. mayonnaise

24. salad bar

Grammar Point: yes/no questions (do)

Do you like hamburgers? *Yes, I do.*
Do you like nachos? *No, I don't.*

Think about it. Discuss.

1. Do you think that fast food is bad for people? Why or why not?
2. What fast foods do you have in your country?
3. Do you have a favorite fast food restaurant? Which one?

1. bacon

2. sausage

3. hash browns

4. toast

5. English muffin

6. biscuits

7. pancakes

8. waffles

9. hot cereal

10. grilled cheese sandwich

11. pickle

12. club sandwich

13. spinach salad

14. chef's salad

15. dinner salad

16. soup

17. rolls

18. coleslaw

19. potato salad

20. pasta salad

21. fruit salad

BREAKFAST SPECIAL

Served 6 a.m. to 11 a.m.

Two egg omelet with one side

HONEY

JELLY

SYRUP

LUNCH

Served 11 a.m. to 2 p.m.

All sandwiches come with soup or salad

SIDE SALADS

SALAD DRESSINGS

Thousand Island

Ranch

Italian

Blue Cheese

Ways to order from a menu

I'd like <u>a grilled cheese sandwich</u>.
I'll have <u>a bowl of tomato soup</u>.
Could I get <u>the chef's salad</u> with <u>ranch dressing</u>?

Pair practice. Make conversations.

A: *I'd like <u>a grilled cheese sandwich</u>, please.*
B: *Anything else for you?*
A: *Yes, I'll have <u>a bowl of tomato soup</u> with that.*

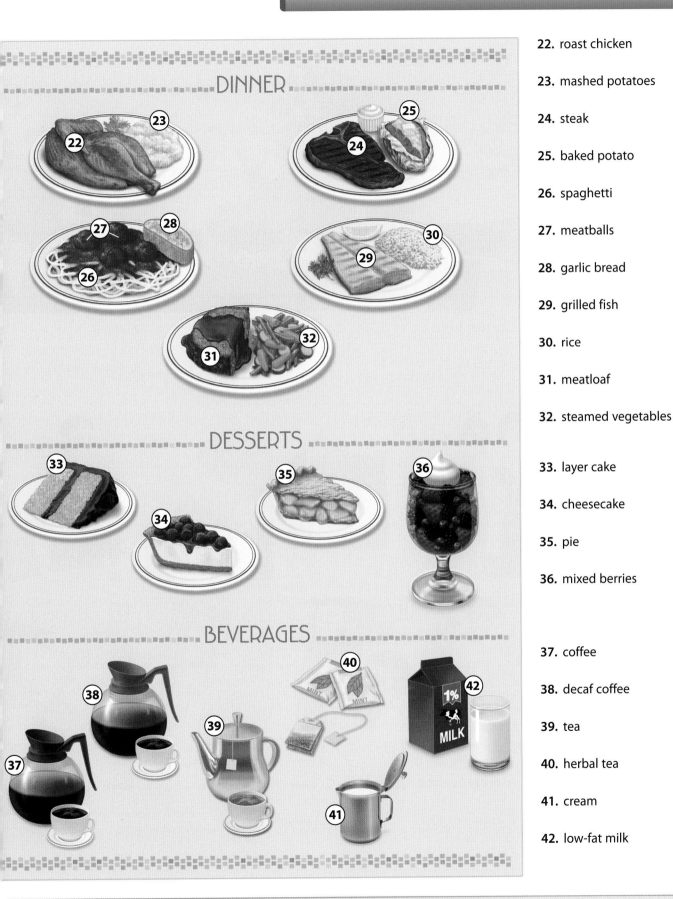

DINNER

DESSERTS

BEVERAGES

22. roast chicken
23. mashed potatoes
24. steak
25. baked potato
26. spaghetti
27. meatballs
28. garlic bread
29. grilled fish
30. rice
31. meatloaf
32. steamed vegetables

33. layer cake
34. cheesecake
35. pie
36. mixed berries

37. coffee
38. decaf coffee
39. tea
40. herbal tea
41. cream
42. low-fat milk

Ask your classmates. Share the answers.

1. Do you prefer vegetable soup or chicken soup?
2. Do you prefer tea or coffee?
3. Which desserts on the menu do you like?

Role play. Order a dinner from the menu.

A: *Are you ready to order?*
B: *I think so. I'll have* <u>the roast chicken</u>.
A: *Would you also like…?*

1. dining room
2. hostess
3. high chair
4. booth
5. to-go box
6. patron / diner
7. menu
8. server / waiter

A. **set** the table

B. **seat** the customer

C. **pour** the water

D. **order** from the menu

E. **take** the order

F. **serve** the meal

G. **clear** / **bus** the dishes

H. **carry** the tray

I. **pay** the check

J. **leave** a tip

More Vocabulary

eat out: to go to a restaurant to eat
take out: to buy food at a restaurant and take it home to eat

Look at the pictures.
Describe what is happening.

A: *She's seating the customer.*
B: *He's taking the order.*

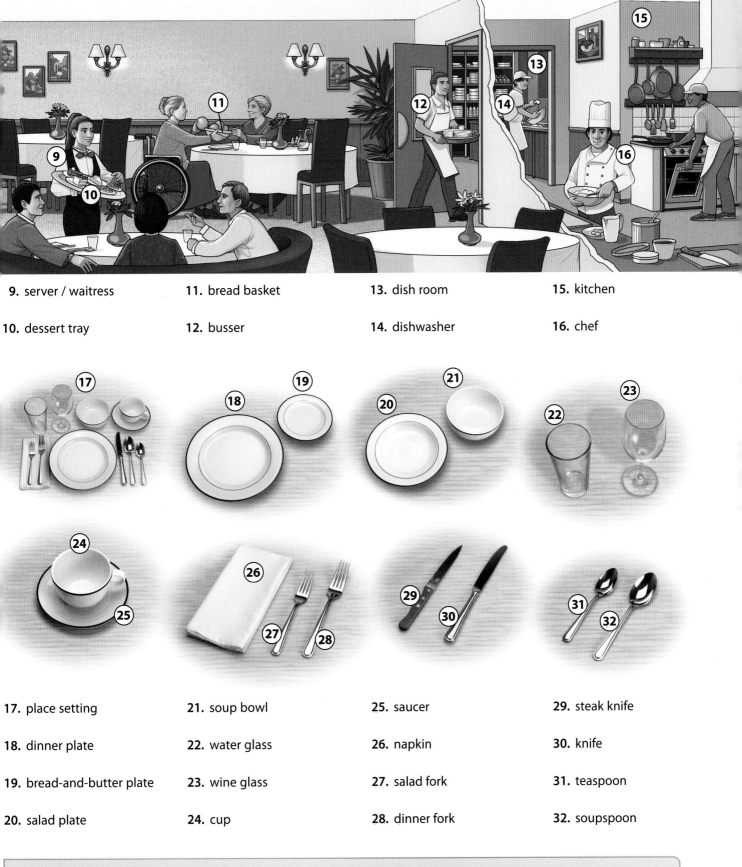

9. server / waitress

10. dessert tray

11. bread basket

12. busser

13. dish room

14. dishwasher

15. kitchen

16. chef

17. place setting

18. dinner plate

19. bread-and-butter plate

20. salad plate

21. soup bowl

22. water glass

23. wine glass

24. cup

25. saucer

26. napkin

27. salad fork

28. dinner fork

29. steak knife

30. knife

31. teaspoon

32. soupspoon

Pair practice. Make new conversations.

A: *Excuse me, this <u>spoon</u> is dirty.*
B: *I'm so sorry. I'll get you a clean <u>spoon</u> right away.*
A: *Thanks.*

Role play. Talk to a new busser.

A: *Do the <u>salad forks</u> go on <u>the left</u>?*
B: *Yes. They go <u>next to the dinner forks</u>.*
A: *What about the…?*

83

1. live music
2. organic
3. lemonade
4. sour
5. samples
6. avocados
7. vendors
8. sweets
9. herbs
A. **count**

HOT FOOD

Cara's Bakery

CHIVES

DILL

PARSLEY

**Look at the pictures.
What do you see?**

Answer the questions.

1. How many vendors are at the market today?

2. Which vegetables are organic?

3. What are the children eating?

4. What is the woman counting? Why?

📖 **Read the story.**

The Farmers' Market

On Saturdays, the Novaks go to the farmers' market. They like to visit the <u>vendors</u>. Alex Novak always goes to the hot food stand for lunch. His children love to eat the fruit <u>samples</u>. Alex's father usually buys some <u>sweets</u> and <u>lemonade</u>. The lemonade is very <u>sour</u>.

Nina Novak likes to buy <u>organic</u> <u>herbs</u> and vegetables. Today, she is buying <u>avocados</u>. The market worker <u>counts</u> eight avocados. She gives Nina one more for free.

There are other things to do at the market. The Novaks like to listen to the <u>live music</u>. Sometimes they meet friends there. The farmers' market is a great place for families on a Saturday afternoon.

Think about it.

1. What's good or bad about shopping at a farmers' market?

2. Imagine you are at the farmers' market. What will you buy?

Everyday Clothes

1. shirt

2. jeans

3. dress

4. T-shirt

5. baseball cap

6. socks

7. athletic shoes

A. **tie**

BEST OF JAZZ CONCERT

TICKETS

BEST OF JAZZ

Listen and point. Take turns.

A: *Point to the dress.*
B: *Point to the T-shirt.*
A: *Point to the baseball cap.*

Dictate to your partner. Take turns.

A: *Write dress.*
B: *Is that spelled d-r-e-s-s?*
A: *Yes. That's right.*

ONE NIGHT
ONLY

DOORS OPEN AT 8:00

8. blouse

9. handbag

10. skirt

11. suit

12. slacks / pants

13. shoes

14. sweater

B. **put on**

Ways to compliment clothes

That's a pretty <u>dress</u>!
Those are great <u>shoes</u>!
I really like your <u>baseball cap</u>!

Role play. Compliment a friend.

A: <u>*That's a pretty dress!*</u> <u>*Green*</u> *is a great color on you.*
B: *Thanks! I really like your…*

Casual Clothes

1. cap
2. cardigan sweater
3. pullover sweater
4. sports shirt
5. maternity dress

6. overalls
7. knit top
8. capris
9. sandals

Work Clothes

10. uniform
11. business suit
12. tie
13. briefcase

More vocabulary

three piece suit: matching jacket, vest, and slacks
outfit: clothes that look nice together
in fashion / in style: clothes that are popular now

Describe the people. Take turns.

A: *She's wearing a maternity dress.*
B: *He's wearing a uniform.*

Formal Clothes

14. sports jacket / sports coat

15. vest

16. bow tie

17. tuxedo

18. evening gown

19. clutch bag

20. cocktail dress

21. high heels

Exercise Wear

22. sweatshirt / hoodie

23. sweatpants

24. tank top

25. shorts

Ask your classmates. Share the answers.

1. What's your favorite outfit?
2. Do you like to wear formal clothes? Why or why not?
3. Do you prefer to exercise in shorts or sweatpants?

Think about it. Discuss.

1. What jobs require formal clothes? Uniforms?
2. What's good and bad about wearing school uniforms?
3. What is your opinion of today's popular clothing?

89

1. hat	**5.** winter scarf
2. (over)coat	**6.** gloves
3. headband	**7.** headwrap
4. leather jacket	**8.** jacket

9. parka	**13.** earmuffs
10. mittens	**14.** down vest
11. ski hat	**15.** ski mask
12. leggings	**16.** down jacket

17. umbrella	**20.** rain boots
18. raincoat	**21.** trench coat
19. poncho	

22. swimming trunks	**25.** cover-up
23. straw hat	**26.** swimsuit / bathing suit
24. windbreaker	**27.** sunglasses

Grammar Point: *should*

*It's raining. You **should** take an umbrella.*
*It's snowing. You **should** wear a scarf.*
*It's sunny. You **should** wear a straw hat.*

Pair practice. Make new conversations.

A: *It's <u>snowing</u>. You should wear <u>a scarf</u>.*
B: *Don't worry. I'm wearing my <u>parka</u>.*
A: *Good, and don't forget your <u>mittens</u>.*

Unisex Underwear

1. undershirt
2. thermal undershirt
3. long underwear

Men's Underwear

4. boxer shorts
5. briefs
6. athletic supporter / jockstrap

Unisex Socks

7. ankle socks
8. crew socks
9. dress socks

Women's Socks

10. low-cut socks
11. anklets
12. knee highs

Women's Underwear

13. (bikini) panties
14. briefs / underpants
15. body shaper / girdle
16. garter belt
17. stockings
18. panty hose
19. tights
20. bra
21. camisole
22. full slip
23. half slip

Sleepwear

24. pajamas
25. nightgown
26. slippers
27. blanket sleeper
28. nightshirt
29. robe

More vocabulary

lingerie: underwear or sleepwear for women
loungewear: very casual clothing for relaxing around the home

Ask your classmates. Share the answers.

1. What kind of socks are you wearing today?
2. What kind of sleepwear do you prefer?
3. Do you wear slippers at home?

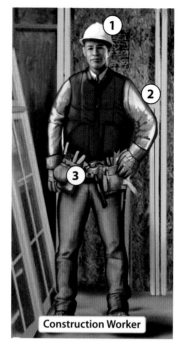

Construction Worker

Road Worker

Automotive Painter

Food Processor

1. hard hat

2. work shirt

3. tool belt

4. Hi-Visibility safety vest

5. work pants

6. steel toe boots

7. ventilation mask

8. coveralls

9. bump cap

10. safety glasses

11. apron

Manager

Salesperson

Farmworker

Ranch Hand

12. blazer

13. tie

14. polo shirt

15. name tag

16. bandana

17. work gloves

18. cowboy hat

19. jeans

Pair practice. Make new conversations.

A: *What do construction workers wear to work?*
B: *They wear hard hats and tool belts.*
A: *What do road workers wear to work?*

Use the new words.

Look at pages 166–169. Name the workplace clothing you see.

A: *He's wearing a hard hat.*
B: *She's wearing scrubs.*

Security Guard

Emergency Worker

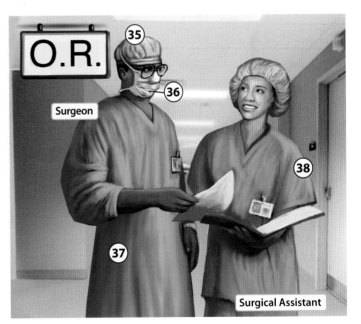

Counterperson

Chef

Line Cook

20. security shirt

21. badge

22. security pants

23. helmet

24. jumpsuit

25. hairnet

26. smock

27. disposable gloves

28. chef's hat

29. chef's jacket

30. waist apron

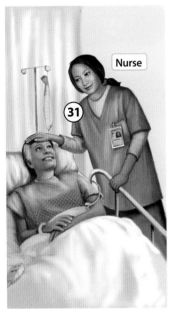

Nurse

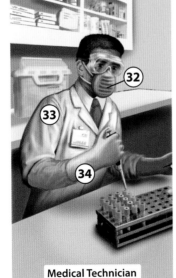

Medical Technician

O.R.

Surgeon

Surgical Assistant

31. scrubs

32. face mask

33. lab coat

34. latex gloves

35. surgical scrub cap

36. surgical mask

37. surgical gown

38. surgical scrubs

Ask your classmates. Share the answers.

1. Which of these outfits would you like to wear?
2. Which of these items are in your closet?
3. Do you wear safety clothing at work? What kinds?

Think about it. Discuss.

1. What other jobs require helmets? disposable gloves?
2. Is it better to have a uniform or wear your own clothes at work? Why?

A. purchase

B. wait in line

1. suspenders

2. purses / handbags

3. salesclerk

4. customer

5. display case

6. belts

13. wallet

14. change purse / coin purse

15. cell phone holder

16. (wrist)watch

17. shoulder bag

18. backpack

19. tote bag

20. belt buckle

21. sole

22. heel

23. toe

24. shoelaces

More vocabulary

gift: something you give or receive from friends or family for a special occasion

present: a gift

Grammar Point: object pronouns

*My **sister** loves jewelry. I'll buy **her** a necklace.*
*My **dad** likes belts. I'll buy **him** a belt buckle.*
*My **friends** love scarves. I'll buy **them** scarves.*

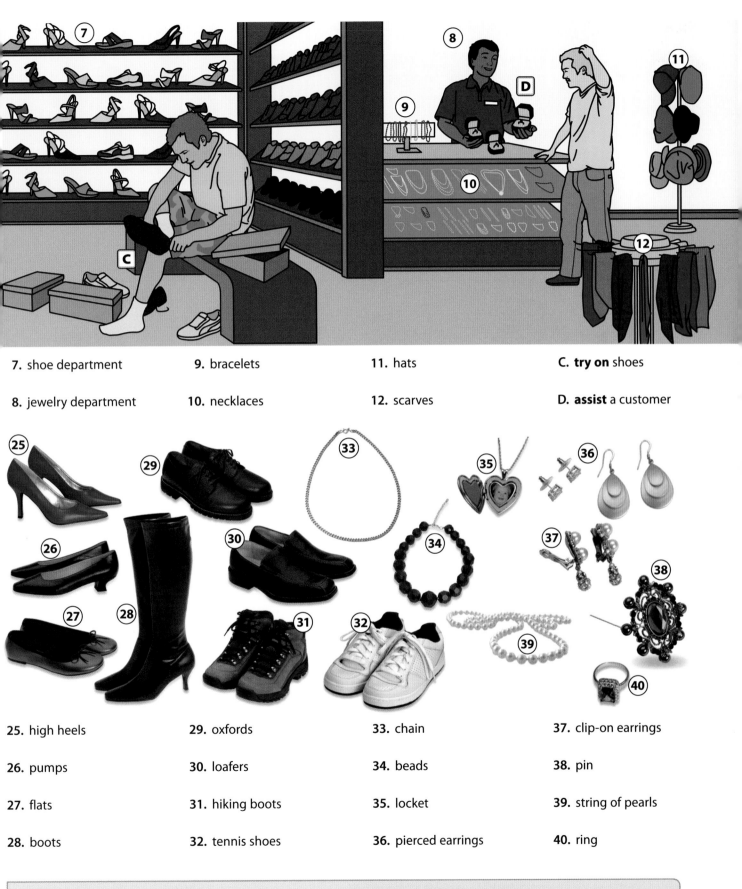

7. shoe department	9. bracelets	11. hats	C. **try on** shoes
8. jewelry department	10. necklaces	12. scarves	D. **assist** a customer

25. high heels	29. oxfords	33. chain	37. clip-on earrings
26. pumps	30. loafers	34. beads	38. pin
27. flats	31. hiking boots	35. locket	39. string of pearls
28. boots	32. tennis shoes	36. pierced earrings	40. ring

Ways to talk about accessories

I need *a hat* to wear with *this scarf*.
I'd like *earrings* to go with *the necklace*.
Do you have *a belt* that would go with my *shoes*?

Role play. Talk to a salesperson.

A: *Do you have boots that would go with this skirt?*
B: *Let me see. How about these brown ones?*
A: *Perfect. I also need…*

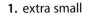

Describing Clothes

Sizes

1. extra small   **2.** small   **3.** medium   **4.** large   **5.** extra large   **6.** one-size-fits-all

Styles

7. **crewneck** sweater

8. **V-neck** sweater

9. **turtleneck** sweater

10. **scoop neck** sweater

11. **sleeveless** shirt

12. **short-sleeved** shirt

13. **3/4-sleeved** shirt

14. **long-sleeved** shirt

15. **mini**-skirt

16. **short** skirt

17. **mid-length / calf-length** skirt

18. **long** skirt

Patterns

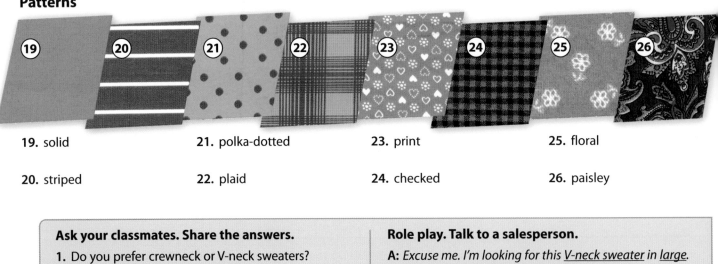

19. solid

20. striped

21. polka-dotted

22. plaid

23. print

24. checked

25. floral

26. paisley

Ask your classmates. Share the answers.

1. Do you prefer crewneck or V-neck sweaters?

2. Do you prefer checked or striped shirts?

3. Do you prefer short-sleeved or sleeveless shirts?

Role play. Talk to a salesperson.

A: *Excuse me. I'm looking for this V-neck sweater in large.*

B: *Here's a large. It's on sale for $19.99.*

A: *Wonderful! I'll take it. I'm also looking for…*

Comparing Clothing

27. **heavy** jacket	29. **tight** pants	31. **low** heels	33. **plain** blouse	35. **narrow** tie
28. **light** jacket	30. **loose** / **baggy** pants	32. **high** heels	34. **fancy** blouse	36. **wide** tie

Clothing Problems

   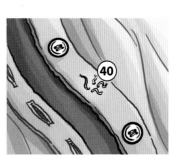

37. It's **too small**.	38. It's **too big**.	39. The zipper is **broken**.	40. A button is **missing**.

  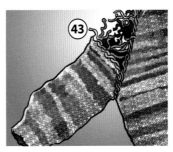 

41. It's **ripped** / **torn**.	42. It's **stained**.	43. It's **unraveling**.	44. It's **too expensive**.

More vocabulary

refund: money you get back when you return an item to the store
complaint: a statement that something is not right
customer service: the place customers go with their complaints

Role play. Return an item to a salesperson.

A: *Welcome to Shopmart. How may I help you?*
B: *This sweater is new, but it's unraveling.*
A: *I'm sorry. Would you like a refund?*

97

Types of Material

1. cotton

2. linen

3. wool

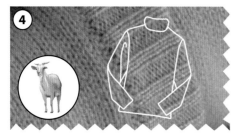

4. cashmere

5. silk

6. leather

A Garment Factory

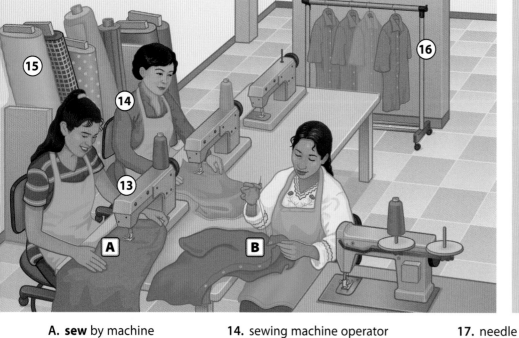

Parts of a Sewing Machine

A. **sew** by machine	14. sewing machine operator
B. **sew** by hand	15. bolt of fabric
13. sewing machine	16. rack

17. needle	20. feed dog / feed bar
18. needle plate	21. bobbin
19. presser foot	

More vocabulary

fashion designer: a person who makes original clothes
natural materials: cloth made from things that grow in nature
synthetic materials: cloth made by people, such as nylon

Use the new words.
Look at pages 86–87. Name the materials you see.

A: *That's denim.*
B: *That's leather.*

Types of Material

7. denim

8. suede

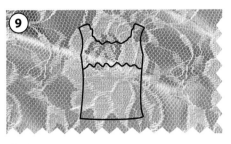

9. lace

10. velvet

11. corduroy

12. nylon

A Fabric Store

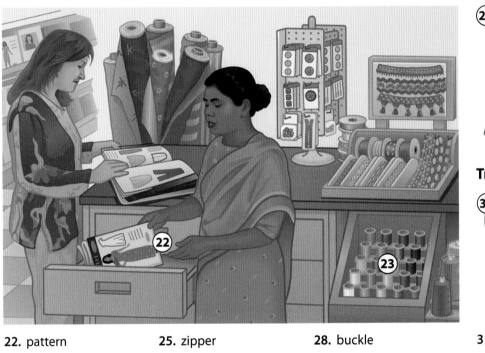

Closures

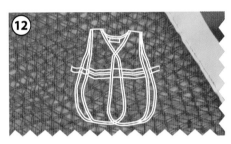

Trim

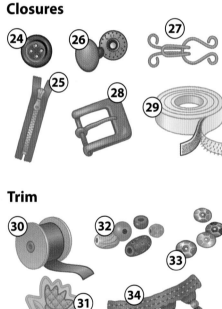

22. pattern

23. thread

24. button

25. zipper

26. snap

27. hook and eye

28. buckle

29. hook and loop fastener

30. ribbon

31. appliqué

32. beads

33. sequins

34. fringe

Ask your classmates. Share the answers.

1. Can you sew?
2. What's your favorite type of material?
3. How many types of material are you wearing today?

Think about it. Discuss.

1. Do most people make or buy clothes in your country?
2. Is it better to make or buy clothes? Why?
3. Which materials are best for formal clothes?

An Alterations Shop

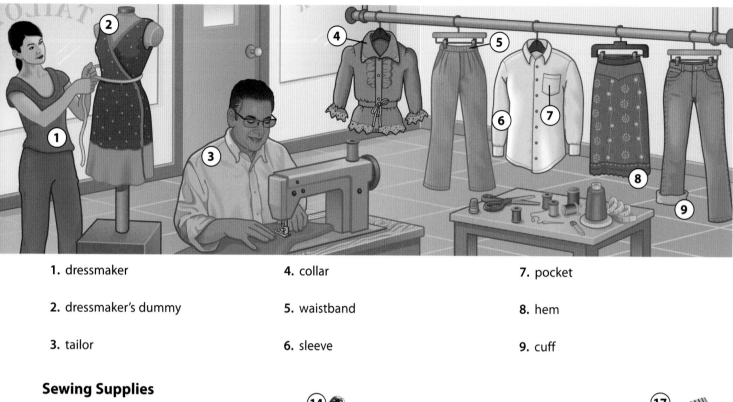

1. dressmaker
2. dressmaker's dummy
3. tailor
4. collar
5. waistband
6. sleeve
7. pocket
8. hem
9. cuff

Sewing Supplies

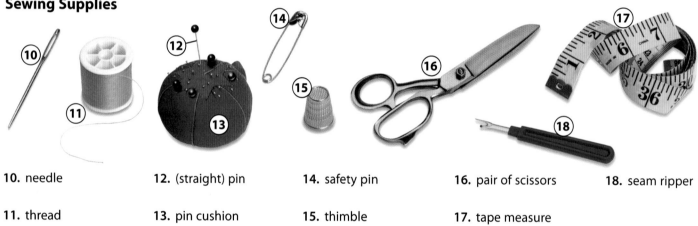

10. needle
11. thread
12. (straight) pin
13. pin cushion
14. safety pin
15. thimble
16. pair of scissors
17. tape measure
18. seam ripper

Alterations

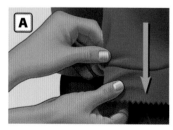

A. **Lengthen** the pants.
B. **Shorten** the pants.
C. **Let out** the pants.
D. **Take in** the pants.

Pair practice. Make new conversations.

A: *Would you hand me the thread?*
B: *OK. What are you going to do?*
A: *I'm going to take in these pants.*

Ask your classmates. Share the answers.

1. Is there an alterations shop near your home?
2. Do you ever go to a tailor or a dressmaker?
3. What sewing supplies do you have at home?

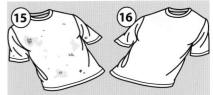

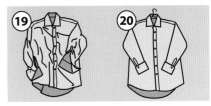

1. laundry

2. laundry basket

3. washer

4. dryer

5. dryer sheets

6. fabric softener

7. bleach

8. laundry detergent

9. clothesline

10. clothespin

11. hanger

12. spray starch

13. iron

14. ironing board

15. dirty T-shirt

16. clean T-shirt

17. wet shirt

18. dry shirt

19. wrinkled shirt

20. ironed shirt

A. **Sort** the laundry.

B. **Add** the detergent.

C. **Load** the washer.

D. **Clean** the lint trap.

E. **Unload** the dryer.

F. **Fold** the laundry.

G. **Iron** the clothes.

H. **Hang up** the clothes.

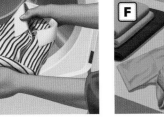

wash in cold water

no bleach

line dry

dry clean only, do not wash

Pair practice. Make new conversations.

A: *I have to <u>sort the laundry</u>. Can you help?*
B: *Sure. Here's <u>the laundry basket</u>.*
A: *Thanks a lot!*

1. flyer
2. used clothing
3. sticker
4. folding card table
5. folding chair
6. clock radio
7. VCR

A. **bargain**
B. **browse**

Look at the pictures. What do you see?

Answer the questions.

1. What kind of used clothing do you see?
2. What information is on the flyer?
3. Why are the stickers different colors?
4. How much is the clock radio? the VCR?

📖 Read the story.

A Garage Sale

Last Sunday, I had a garage sale. At 5:00 a.m., I put up <u>flyers</u> in my neighborhood. Next, I put price <u>stickers</u> on my <u>used clothing</u>, my <u>VCR</u>, and some other old things. At 7:00 a.m., I opened my <u>folding card table</u> and <u>folding chair</u>. Then I waited.

At 7:05 a.m., my first customer arrived. She asked, "How much is the sweatshirt?"

"Two dollars," I said.

She said, "It's stained. I can give you seventy-five cents." We <u>bargained</u> for a minute and she paid $1.00.

All day people came to <u>browse</u>, bargain, and buy. At 7:00 p.m., I had $85.00.

Now I know two things: Garage sales are hard work and nobody wants to buy an old <u>clock radio</u>!

Think about it.

1. Do you like to buy things at garage sales? Why or why not?
2. Imagine you want the VCR. How will you bargain for it?

103

The Body

1. head
2. hair
3. neck
4. chest
5. back
6. nose
7. mouth
8. foot

Listen and point. Take turns.

A: *Point to the chest.*
B: *Point to the neck.*
A: *Point to the mouth.*

Dictate to your partner. Take turns.

A: *Write hair.*
B: *Did you say hair?*
A: *That's right, h-a-i-r.*

9. leg
10. toe
11. eye
12. ear
13. shoulder
14. arm
15. hand
16. finger

Grammar Point: imperatives

Please touch your right foot.
Put your hands on your feet.
Don't put your hands on your shoulders.

Pair practice. Take turns giving commands.

A: <u>Raise</u> your <u>arms</u>.
B: <u>Touch</u> your <u>feet</u>.
A: <u>Put</u> your <u>hand</u> on your <u>shoulder</u>.

105

The Face

1. chin
2. forehead
3. cheek
4. jaw

The Mouth

5. lip
6. gums
7. teeth
8. tongue

The Eye

9. eyebrow
10. eyelid
11. eyelashes

The Senses

A. **see**
B. **hear**
C. **smell**
D. **taste**
E. **touch**

The Arm, Hand, and Fingers

12. elbow
13. forearm
14. wrist
15. palm
16. thumb
17. knuckle
18. fingernail

The Leg and Foot

19. thigh
20. knee
21. shin
22. calf
23. ankle
24. heel

More vocabulary

torso: the part of the body from the shoulders to the pelvis
limbs: arms and legs
toenail: the nail on your toe

Pair practice. Make new conversations.

A: *Is your <u>arm</u> OK?*
B: *Yes, but now my <u>elbow</u> hurts.*
A: *I'm sorry to hear that.*

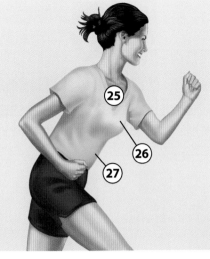

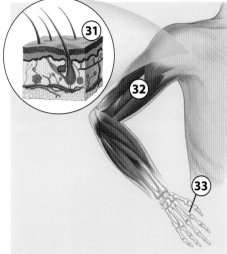

25. chest

26. breast

27. abdomen

28. shoulder blade

29. lower back

30. buttocks

31. skin

32. muscle

33. bone

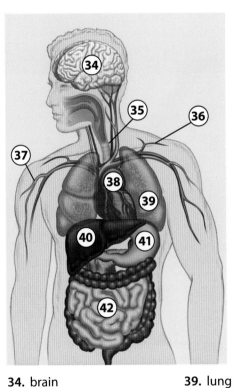

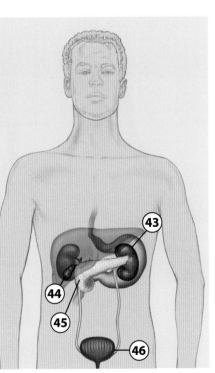

THE SKELETON

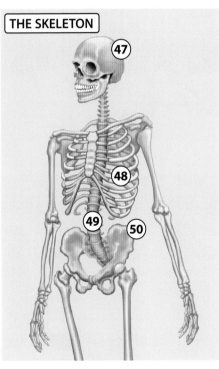

34. brain

35. throat

36. artery

37. vein

38. heart

39. lung

40. liver

41. stomach

42. intestines

43. kidney

44. gallbladder

45. pancreas

46. bladder

47. skull

48. rib cage

49. spinal column

50. pelvis

Personal Hygiene

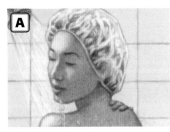

A. take a shower

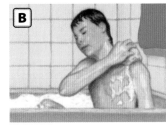

B. take a bath / **bathe**

C. use deodorant

D. put on sunscreen

1. shower cap
2. shower gel
3. soap

4. bath powder
5. deodorant / antiperspirant
6. perfume / cologne

7. sunscreen
8. sunblock
9. body lotion / moisturizer

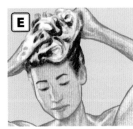

E. wash…hair

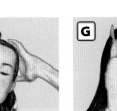

F. rinse…hair

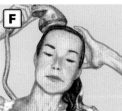

G. comb…hair

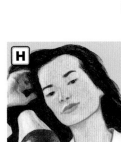

H. dry…hair

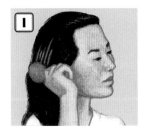

I. brush…hair

10. shampoo
11. conditioner
12. hair spray

13. comb
14. brush
15. pick

16. hair gel
17. curling iron
18. blow dryer

19. hair clip
20. barrette
21. bobby pins

More vocabulary

unscented: a product without perfume or scent
hypoallergenic: a product that is better for people with allergies

Think about it. Discuss.

1. Which personal hygiene products should someone use before a job interview?
2. What is the right age to start wearing makeup? Why?

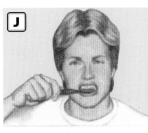 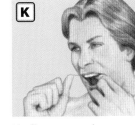  

J. brush…teeth   **K. floss**…teeth   **L. gargle**   **M. shave**

  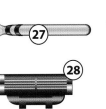

22. toothbrush

23. toothpaste

24. dental floss

25. mouthwash

26. electric shaver

27. razor

28. razorblade

29. shaving cream

30. aftershave

N. cut…nails   **O. polish**…nails   **P. put on / apply**   **Q. take off / remove**

 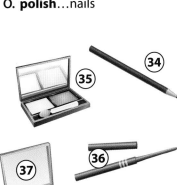 

Makeup

31. nail clipper

32. emery board

33. nail polish

34. eyebrow pencil

35. eye shadow

36. eyeliner

37. blush

38. lipstick

39. mascara

40. foundation

41. face powder

42. makeup remover

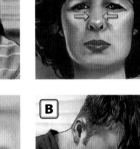
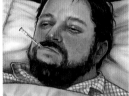

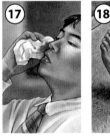

1. headache	**6.** sore throat	**A. cough**
2. toothache	**7.** nasal congestion	**B. sneeze**
3. earache	**8.** fever / temperature	**C. feel** dizzy
4. stomachache	**9.** chills	**D. feel** nauseous
5. backache	**10.** rash	**E. throw up / vomit**

11. insect bite	**13.** cut	**15.** blister	**17.** bloody nose
12. bruise	**14.** sunburn	**16.** swollen finger	**18.** sprained ankle

Look at the pictures.
Describe the symptoms and injuries.

A: *He has a backache.*
B: *She has a toothache.*

Think about it. Discuss.
1. What are some common cold symptoms?
2. What do you recommend for a stomachache?
3. What is the best way to stop a bloody nose?

Common Illnesses and Childhood Diseases

1. cold

2. flu

3. ear infection

4. strep throat

5. measles

6. chicken pox

7. mumps

8. allergies

Serious Medical Conditions and Diseases

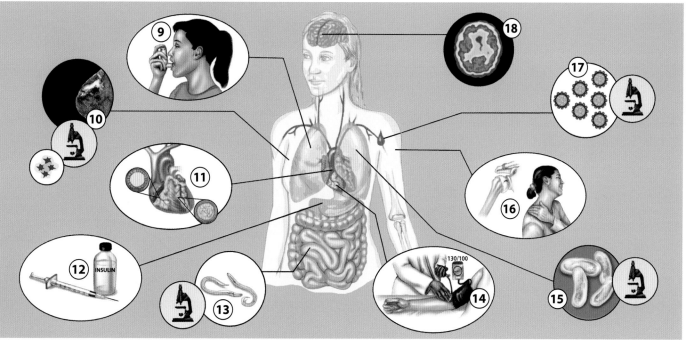

9. asthma

10. cancer

11. heart disease

12. diabetes

13. intestinal parasites

14. high blood pressure / hypertension

15. TB (tuberculosis)

16. arthritis

17. HIV (human immunodeficiency virus)

18. dementia

More vocabulary

AIDS (acquired immune deficiency syndrome): a medical condition that results from contracting the HIV virus

Alzheimer's disease: a disease that causes dementia

coronary disease: heart disease

infectious disease: a disease that is spread through air or water

influenza: flu

A Pharmacy

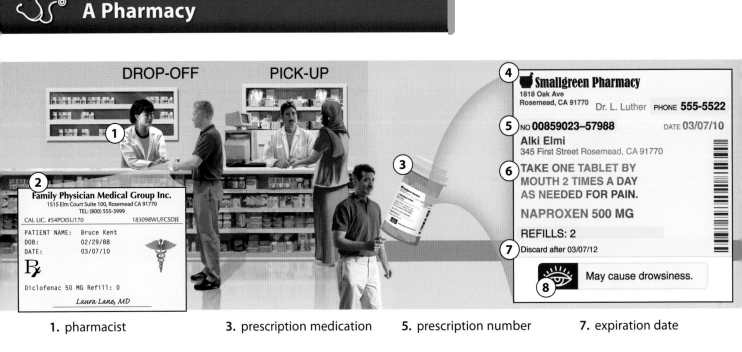

DROP-OFF PICK-UP

Smallgreen Pharmacy
1818 Oak Ave
Rosemead, CA 91770 Dr. L. Luther PHONE **555-5522**

NO **00859023–57988** DATE **03/07/10**

Alki Elmi
345 First Street Rosemead, CA 91770

TAKE ONE TABLET BY MOUTH 2 TIMES A DAY AS NEEDED FOR PAIN.

NAPROXEN 500 MG

REFILLS: 2

Discard after 03/07/12

May cause drowsiness.

Family Physician Medical Group Inc.
1515 Elm Court Suite 100, Rosemead CA 91770
TEL: (800) 555-3999
CAL LIC. #54POI5U170   183098WUFCSDJE

PATIENT NAME: Bruce Kent
DOB: 02/29/88
DATE: 03/07/10

℞
Diclofenac 50 MG Refill: 0
Laura Lane, MD

1. pharmacist
2. prescription
3. prescription medication
4. prescription label
5. prescription number
6. dosage
7. expiration date
8. warning label

Medical Warnings

A. Take with food or milk.

B. Take one hour before eating.

C. Finish all medication.

D. Do not take with dairy products.

E. Do not drive or operate heavy machinery.

F. Do not drink alcohol.

More vocabulary

prescribe medication: to write a prescription
fill prescriptions: to prepare medication for patients
pick up a prescription: to get prescription medication

Role play. Talk to the pharmacist.

A: *Hi. I need to pick up a prescription for Jones.*
B: *Here's your medication, Mr. Jones. Take these once a day with milk or food.*

112

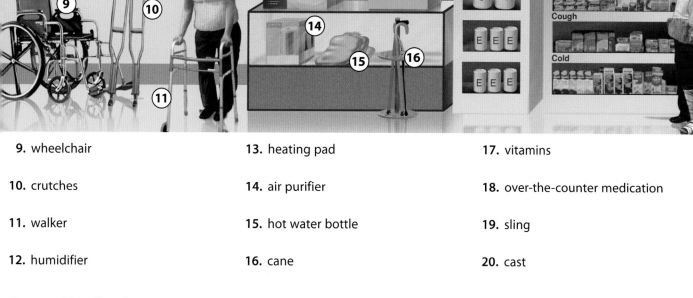

9. wheelchair

10. crutches

11. walker

12. humidifier

13. heating pad

14. air purifier

15. hot water bottle

16. cane

17. vitamins

18. over-the-counter medication

19. sling

20. cast

Types of Medication

21. pill

22. tablet

23. capsule

24. ointment

25. cream

Over-the-Counter Medication

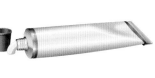

26. pain reliever

27. cold tablets

28. antacid

29. cough syrup

30. throat lozenges

31. eye drops

32. nasal spray

33. inhaler

Ways to talk about medication

Use *take* for pills, tablets, capsules, and cough syrup.
Use *apply* for ointments and creams.
Use *use* for drops, nasal sprays, and inhalers.

Ask your classmates. Share the answers.

1. What pharmacy do you go to?
2. Do you ever ask the pharmacist for advice?
3. Do you take any vitamins? Which ones?

Ways to Get Well

A. **Seek** medical attention.

B. **Get** bed rest.

C. **Drink** fluids.

D. **Take** medicine.

Ways to Stay Well

E. **Stay** fit.

F. **Eat** a healthy diet.

G. **Don't smoke**.

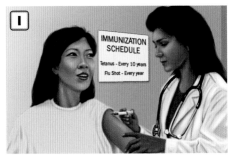

H. **Have** regular checkups.

I. **Get** immunized.

J. **Follow** medical advice.

More vocabulary

injection: medicine in a syringe that is put into the body

immunization / vaccination: an injection that stops serious diseases

Ask your classmates. Share the answers.

1. How do you stay fit?
2. What do you do when you're sick?
3. Which two foods are a part of your healthy diet?

Types of Health Problems

1. vision problems   2. hearing loss   3. pain   4. stress   5. depression

Help with Health Problems

6. optometrist   8. contact lenses   9. audiologist   10. hearing aid

7. glasses

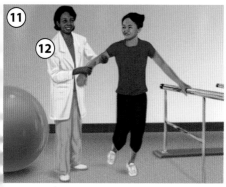

11. physical therapy   13. talk therapy   15. support group

12. physical therapist   14. therapist

Ways to ask about health problems	Pair practice. Make new conversations.
Are you in pain?	**A:** *Do you know a good optometrist?*
Are you having vision problems?	**B:** *Why? Are you having vision problems?*
Are you experiencing depression?	**A:** *Yes, I might need glasses.*

115

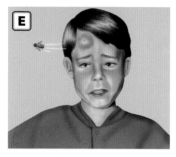

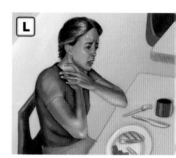

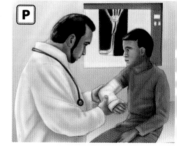

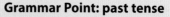

1. ambulance

2. paramedic

A. **be** unconscious

B. **be** in shock

C. **be** injured / **be** hurt

D. **have** a heart attack

E. **have** an allergic reaction

F. **get** an electric shock

G. **get** frostbite

H. **burn** (your)self

I. **drown**

J. **swallow** poison

K. **overdose** on drugs

L. **choke**

M. **bleed**

N. **can't breathe**

O. **fall**

P. **break** a bone

Grammar Point: past tense

For past tense add –ed:
burned, drowned, swallowed,
overdosed, choked

These verbs are different (irregular):

be – was, were	bleed – bled	fall – fell
have – had	can't – couldn't	
get – got	break – broke	

First Aid

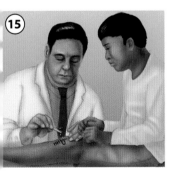

1. first aid kit

2. first aid manual

3. medical emergency bracelet

Inside the Kit

4. tweezers

5. adhesive bandage

6. sterile pad

7. sterile tape

8. gauze

9. hydrogen peroxide

10. antihistamine cream

11. antibacterial ointment

12. elastic bandage

13. ice pack

14. splint

First Aid Procedures

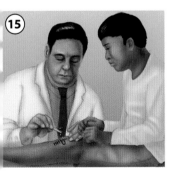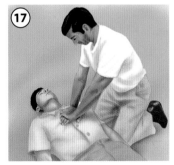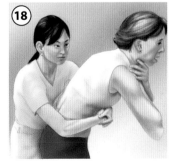

15. stitches

16. rescue breathing

17. CPR (cardiopulmonary resuscitation)

18. Heimlich maneuver

Pair practice. Make new conversations.

A: *What do we need in the first aid kit?*
B: *We need <u>tweezers</u> and <u>gauze</u>.*
A: *I think we need <u>sterile tape</u>, too.*

Think about it. Discuss.

1. What are the three most important first aid items? Why?
2. Which first aid procedures should everyone know? Why?
3. What are some good places to keep a first aid kit?

In the Waiting Room

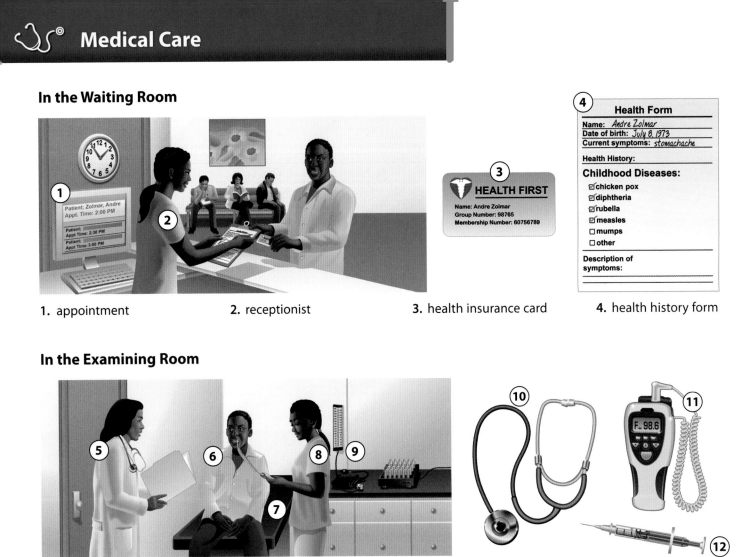

Health Form

Name: *Andre Zolmar*
Date of birth: *July 8, 1973*
Current symptoms: *stomachache*

Health History:

Childhood Diseases:
☑ chicken pox
☑ diphtheria
☑ rubella
☑ measles
☐ mumps
☐ other

Description of symptoms:

HEALTH FIRST
Name: Andre Zolmar
Group Number: 98765
Membership Number: 60756789

Patient: Zolmar, Andre
Appt. Time: 2:00 PM

Patient:
Appt Time: 2:30 PM
Patient:
Appt Time: 3:00 PM

1. appointment
2. receptionist
3. health insurance card
4. health history form

In the Examining Room

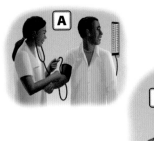

5. doctor
6. patient
7. examination table
8. nurse
9. blood pressure gauge
10. stethoscope
11. thermometer
12. syringe

F. 98.6

Medical Procedures

A. **check**…blood pressure
B. **take**…temperature
C. **listen** to…heart
D. **examine**…eyes
E. **examine**…throat
F. **draw**…blood

Grammar Point: future tense with *will* + verb

To show a future action, use *will* + verb.
The subject pronoun contraction of *will* is *-'ll*.
She **will draw** your blood. = She**'ll draw** your blood.

Role play. Talk to a medical receptionist.

A: *Will the nurse <u>examine my eyes</u>?*
B: *No, but she'll <u>draw your blood</u>.*
A: *What will the doctor do?*

Dentistry

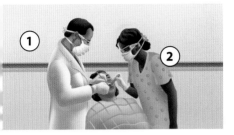

1. dentist
2. dental assistant

3. dental hygienist
4. dental instruments

Orthodontics

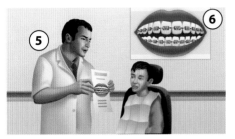

5. orthodontist
6. braces

Dental Problems

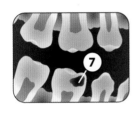

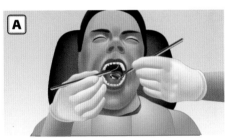

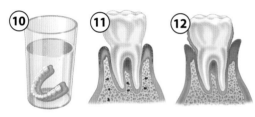

7. cavity / decay
8. filling

9. crown
10. dentures

11. gum disease
12. plaque

An Office Visit

A. **clean**…teeth

B. **take** x-rays

C. **numb** the mouth

D. **drill** a tooth

E. **fill** a cavity

F. **pull** a tooth

Ask your classmates. Share the answers.

1. Do you know someone with braces? Who?
2. Do dentists make you nervous? Why or why not?
3. How often do you go to the dentist?

Role play. Talk to a dentist.

A: *I think I have <u>a cavity</u>.*
B: *Let me take a look.*
A: *Will I need <u>a filling</u>?*

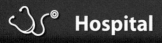
Medical Specialists

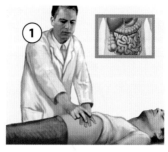

1. internist

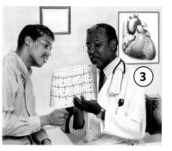

2. obstetrician

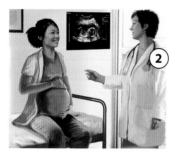

3. cardiologist

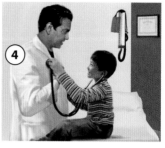

4. pediatrician

5. oncologist

6. radiologist

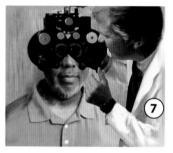

7. ophthalmologist

8. psychiatrist

Nursing Staff

9. surgical nurse

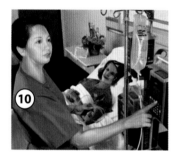

10. registered nurse (RN)

11. licensed practical nurse (LPN)

12. certified nursing assistant (CNA)

Hospital Staff

13. administrator

14. admissions clerk

15. dietician

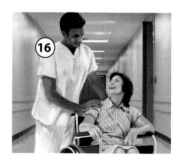

16. orderly

More vocabulary

Gynecologists examine and treat women.
Nurse practitioners can give medical exams.
Nurse midwives deliver babies.

Chiropractors move the spine to improve health.
Orthopedists treat bone and joint problems.

A Hospital Room

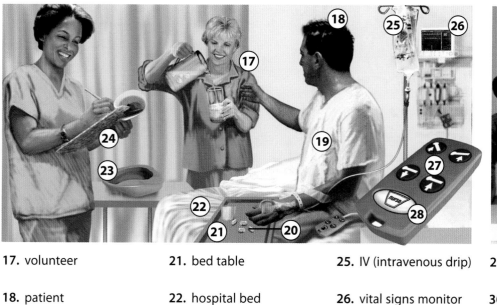

Lab

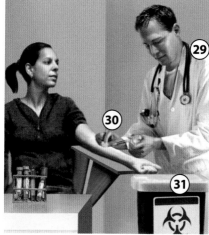

17. volunteer
18. patient
19. hospital gown
20. medication

21. bed table
22. hospital bed
23. bed pan
24. medical chart

25. IV (intravenous drip)
26. vital signs monitor
27. bed control
28. call button

29. phlebotomist
30. blood work / blood test
31. medical waste disposal

Emergency Room Entrance

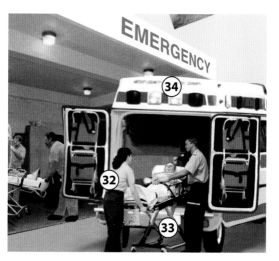

Operating Room

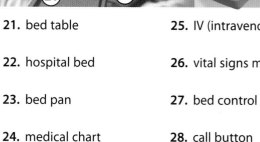

32. emergency medical technician (EMT)

33. stretcher / gurney

34. ambulance

35. anesthesiologist

36. surgeon

37. surgical cap

38. surgical gown

39. surgical gloves

40. operating table

Dictate to your partner. Take turns.

A: *Write this sentence. She's a volunteer.*

B: *She's a what?*

A: *Volunteer. That's v-o-l-u-n-t-e-e-r.*

Role play. Ask about a doctor.

A: *I need to find a good surgeon.*

B: *Dr. Jones is a great surgeon. You should call him.*

A: *I will! Please give me his number.*

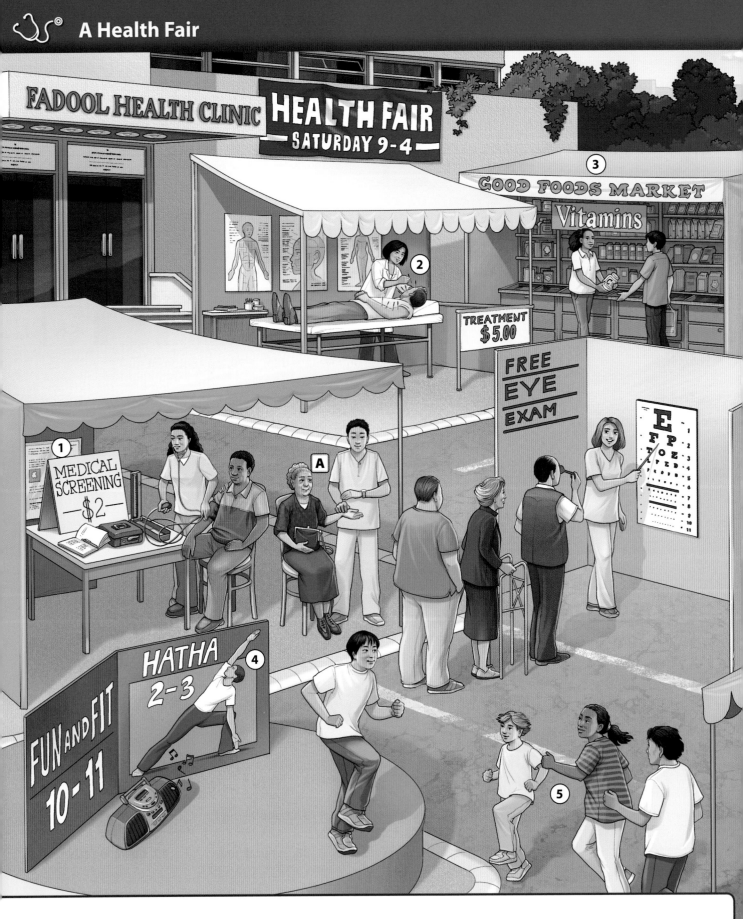

1. low-cost exam
2. acupuncture
3. booth
4. yoga
5. aerobic exercise
6. demonstration
7. sugar-free
8. nutrition label
A. **check** ... pulse
B. **give** a lecture

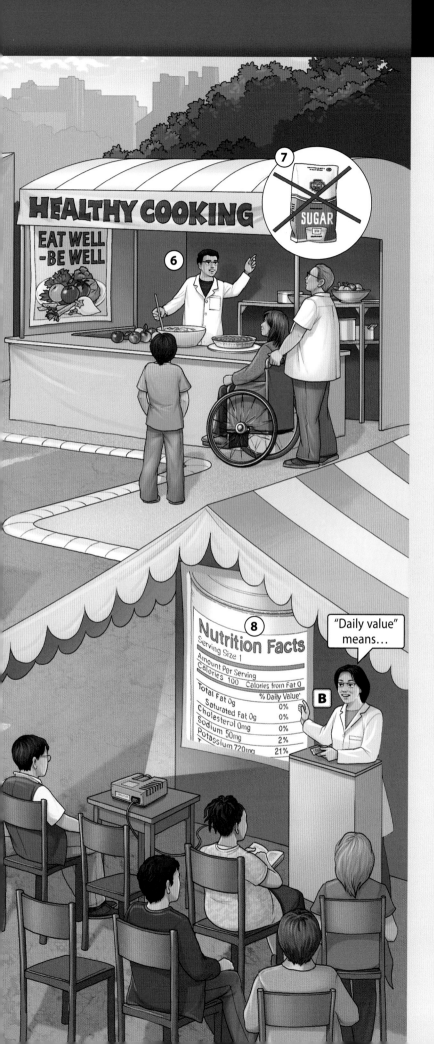

Look at the picture. What do you see?

Answer the questions.

1. How many different booths are there at the health fair?

2. What kinds of exams and treatments can you get at the fair?

3. What kinds of lectures and demonstrations are there?

4. How much is an acupuncture treatment? a medical screening?

📖 Read the story.

A Health Fair

Once a month the Fadool Health Clinic has a health fair. You can get a <u>low-cost</u> medical <u>exam</u> at one <u>booth</u>. The nurses check your blood pressure and <u>check your pulse</u>. At another booth you can get a free eye exam. And an <u>acupuncture</u> treatment is only $5.00.

You can learn a lot at the fair. This month a doctor <u>is giving a lecture</u> on <u>nutrition labels</u>. There is also a <u>demonstration</u> on <u>sugar-free</u> cooking. You can learn to do <u>aerobic exercise</u> and <u>yoga</u>, too.

Do you want to get healthy and stay healthy? Then come to the Fadool Clinic Health Fair!

Think about it.

1. Which booths at this fair look interesting to you? Why?

2. Do you read nutrition labels? Why or why not?

1. parking garage

2. office building

3. hotel

4. Department of Motor Vehicles

5. bank

6. police station

7. bus station

8. city hall

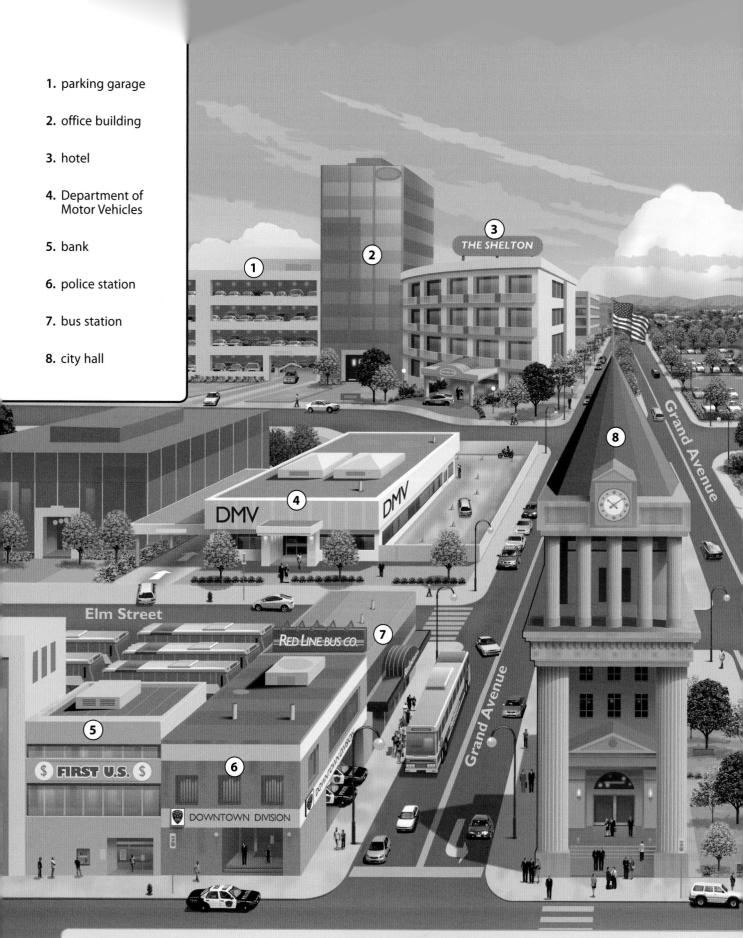

Listen and point. Take turns.

A: *Point to the bank.*
B: *Point to the hotel.*
A: *Point to the restaurant.*

Dictate to your partner. Take turns.

A: *Write bank.*
B: *Is that spelled b-a-n-k?*
A: *Yes, that's right.*

9. hospital

10. gas station

11. post office

12. fire station

13. courthouse

14. restaurant

15. library

Grammar Point: *in* and *at* with locations

Use **in** when you are inside the building. *I am in (inside) the bank.* Use **at** to describe your general location. *I am at the bank.*

Pair practice. Make new conversations.

A: *I'm in the <u>bank</u>. Where are you?*
B: *I'm at the <u>bank</u>, too, but I'm outside.*
A: *OK. I'll meet you there.*

1. stadium
2. construction site
3. factory
4. car dealership

5. mosque
6. movie theater
7. shopping mall
8. furniture store

9. school
10. gym
11. coffee shop
12. motel

Ways to state your destination using *to* and *to the*

Use *to* for schools, churches, and synagogues.
I'm going to <u>school</u>.
Use *to the* for all other locations. *I have to go to the <u>bakery</u>.*

Pair practice. Make new conversations.

A: *Where are you going today?*
B: *I'm going to <u>school</u>. How about you?*
A: *I have to go to the <u>bakery</u>.*

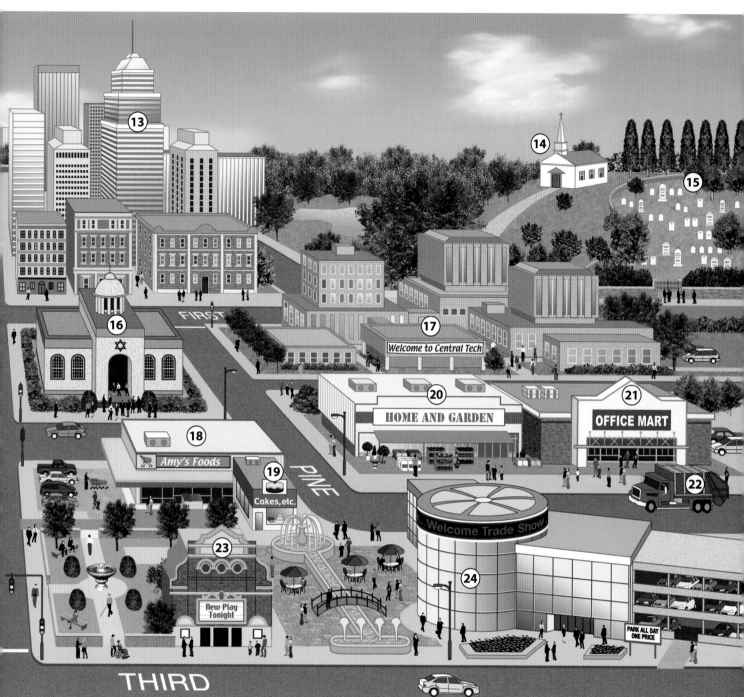

13. skyscraper / high-rise

14. church

15. cemetery

16. synagogue

17. community college

18. supermarket

19. bakery

20. home improvement store

21. office supply store

22. garbage truck

23. theater

24. convention center

Ways to give locations

The mall is on 2nd Street.
The mall is on the corner of 2nd and Elm.
The mall is next to the movie theater.

Ask your classmates. Share the answers.

1. Where's your favorite coffee shop?
2. Where's your favorite supermarket?
3. Where's your favorite movie theater?

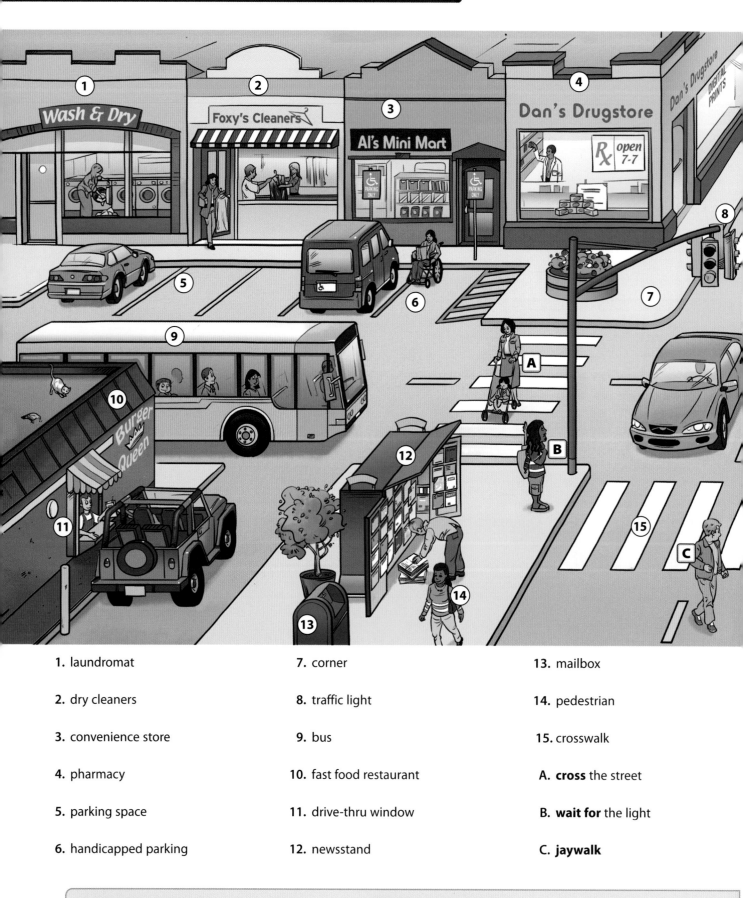

1. laundromat	**7.** corner	**13.** mailbox
2. dry cleaners	**8.** traffic light	**14.** pedestrian
3. convenience store	**9.** bus	**15.** crosswalk
4. pharmacy	**10.** fast food restaurant	**A. cross** the street
5. parking space	**11.** drive-thru window	**B. wait for** the light
6. handicapped parking	**12.** newsstand	**C. jaywalk**

Pair practice. Make new conversations.

A: *I have a lot of errands to do today.*
B: *Me, too. First, I'm going to the laundromat.*
A: *I'll see you there after I stop at the copy center.*

Think about it. Discuss.

1. Which businesses are good to have in a neighborhood? Why?
2. Would you like to own a small business? If yes, what kind? If no, why not?

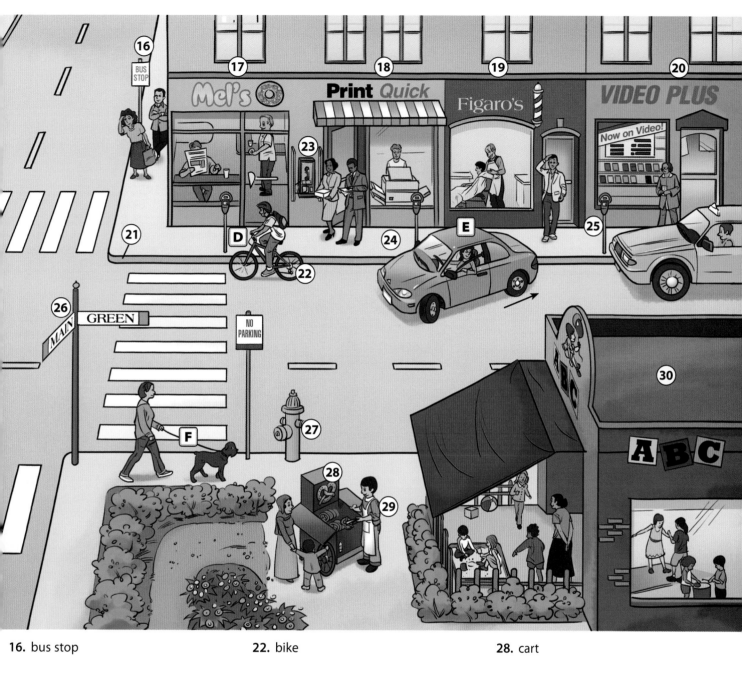

16. bus stop	**22.** bike	**28.** cart
17. donut shop	**23.** pay phone	**29.** street vendor
18. copy center	**24.** sidewalk	**30.** childcare center
19. barbershop	**25.** parking meter	**D. ride** a bike
20. video store	**26.** street sign	**E. park** the car
21. curb	**27.** fire hydrant	**F. walk** a dog

More vocabulary

neighborhood: the area close to your home
do errands: to make a short trip from your home to buy or pick up things

Ask your classmates. Share the answers.

1. What errands do you do every week?
2. What stores do you go to in your neighborhood?
3. What things can you buy from a street vendor?

129

1. music store

2. jewelry store

3. nail salon

4. bookstore

5. toy store

6. pet store

7. card store

8. florist

9. optician

10. shoe store

11. play area

12. guest services

More vocabulary

beauty shop: hair salon
men's store: men's clothing store
gift shop: a store that sells t-shirts, mugs, and other small gifts

Pair practice. Make new conversations.

A: *Where is the florist?*
B: *It's on the first floor, next to the optician.*

13. department store	**17.** candy store	**21.** elevator
14. travel agency	**18.** hair salon	**22.** cell phone kiosk
15. food court	**19.** maternity store	**23.** escalator
16. ice cream shop	**20.** electronics store	**24.** directory

Ways to talk about plans

Let's go to the <u>card store</u>.
I have to go to the <u>card store</u>.
I want to go to the <u>card store</u>.

Role play. Talk to a friend at the mall.

A: *Let's go to the <u>card store</u>. I need to buy <u>a card</u> for Maggie's birthday.*
B: *OK, but can we go to the <u>shoe store</u> next?*

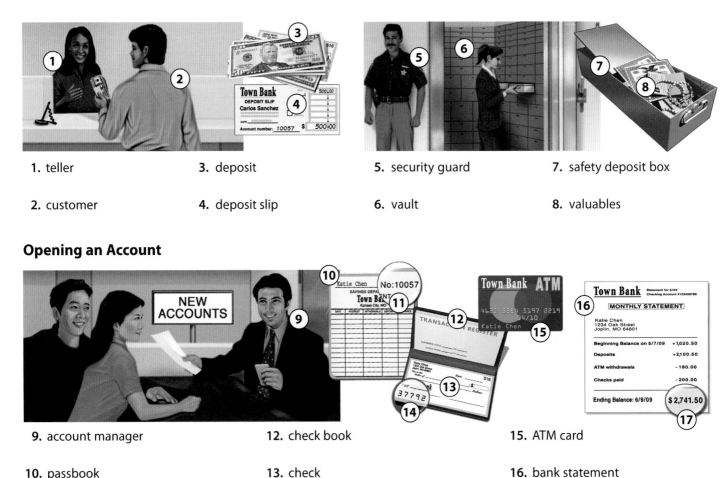

1. teller
3. deposit
5. security guard
7. safety deposit box

2. customer
4. deposit slip
6. vault
8. valuables

Opening an Account

9. account manager
12. check book
15. ATM card

10. passbook
13. check
16. bank statement

11. savings account number
14. checking account number
17. balance

A. **Cash** a check.

B. **Make** a deposit.

C. **Bank** online.

The ATM (Automated Teller Machine)

D. **Insert** your ATM card.

E. **Enter** your PIN.*

F. **Withdraw** cash.

G. **Remove** your card.

*PIN = personal identification number

132

A. get a library card

B. look for a book

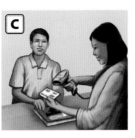

C. check out a book

D. return a book

E. pay a late fine

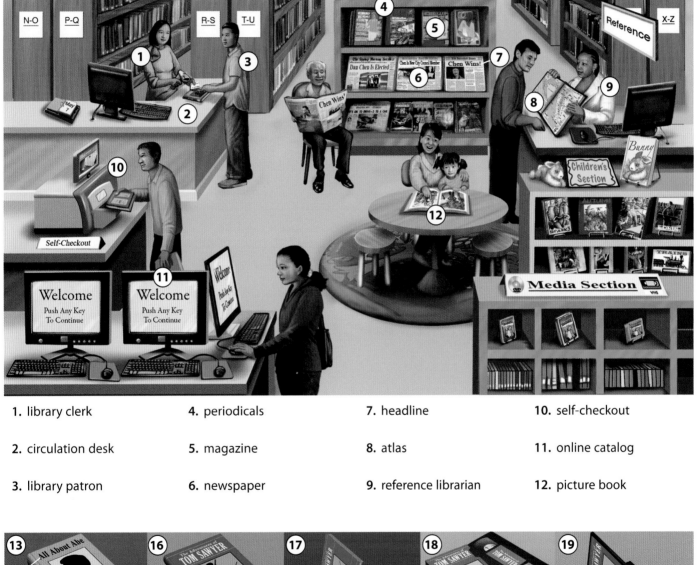

1. library clerk
2. circulation desk
3. library patron

4. periodicals
5. magazine
6. newspaper

7. headline
8. atlas
9. reference librarian

10. self-checkout
11. online catalog
12. picture book

13. biography
14. title

15. author
16. novel

17. audiobook

18. videocassette

19. DVD

1. Priority Mail®
2. Express Mail®
3. media mail
4. Certified Mail™
5. airmail
6. ground post / parcel post

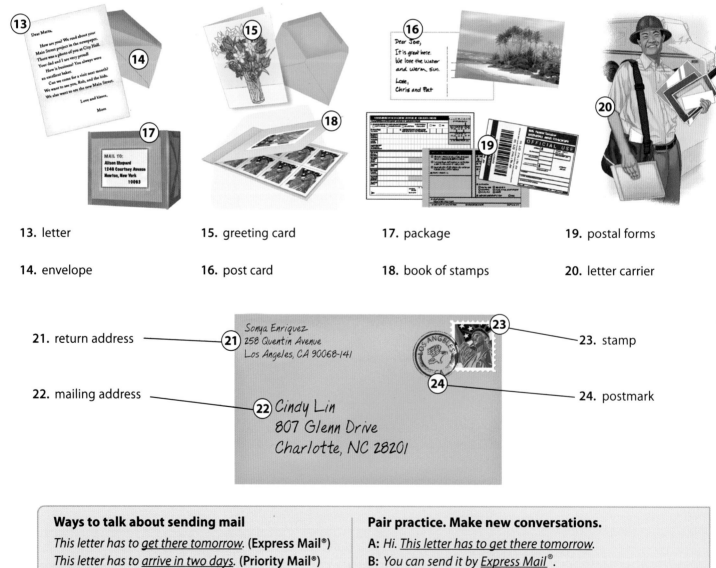

13. letter
14. envelope
15. greeting card
16. post card
17. package
18. book of stamps
19. postal forms
20. letter carrier

21. return address
22. mailing address
23. stamp
24. postmark

Sonya Enriquez
258 Quentin Avenue
Los Angeles, CA 90068-141

LOS ANGELES

Cindy Lin
807 Glenn Drive
Charlotte, NC 28201

Ways to talk about sending mail

This letter has to get there tomorrow. (**Express Mail®**)
This letter has to arrive in two days. (**Priority Mail®**)
This letter can go in regular mail. (**First Class**)

Pair practice. Make new conversations.

A: *Hi. This letter has to get there tomorrow.*
B: *You can send it by Express Mail®.*
A: *OK. I need a book of stamps, too.*

7. postal clerk

8. scale

9. post office box (PO box)

10. automated postal center (APC)

11. stamp machine

12. mailbox

Sending a Card

A. Write a note in a card.

B. Address the envelope.

C. Put on a stamp.

D. Mail the card.

E. Deliver the card.

F. Receive the card.

G. Read the card.

H. Write back.

More vocabulary

overnight / next day mail: Express Mail®
postage: the cost to send mail
junk mail: mail you don't want

Think about it. Discuss.

1. What kind of mail do you send overnight?
2. Do you want to be a letter carrier? Why or why not?
3. Do you get junk mail? What do you do with it?

135

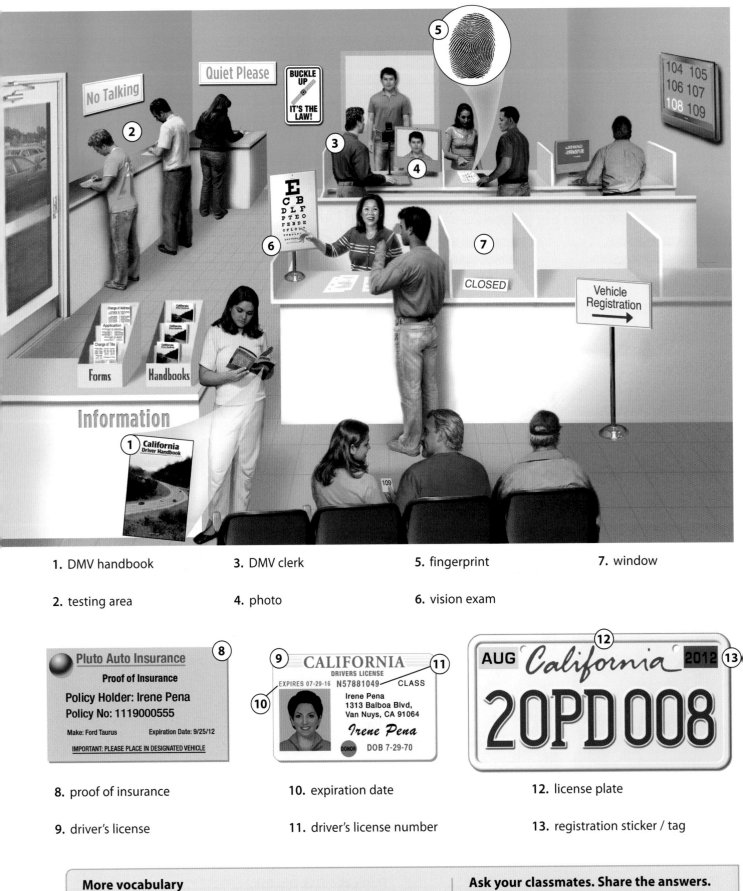

Department of Motor Vehicles (DMV)

1. DMV handbook
2. testing area
3. DMV clerk
4. photo
5. fingerprint
6. vision exam
7. window

8. proof of insurance
9. driver's license
10. expiration date
11. driver's license number
12. license plate
13. registration sticker / tag

Pluto Auto Insurance
Proof of Insurance
Policy Holder: Irene Pena
Policy No: 1119000555
Make: Ford Taurus   Expiration Date: 9/25/12
IMPORTANT: PLEASE PLACE IN DESIGNATED VEHICLE

CALIFORNIA
DRIVERS LICENSE
EXPIRES 07-29-16   N57881049   CLASS
Irene Pena
1313 Balboa Blvd,
Van Nuys, CA 91064
Irene Pena
DONOR   DOB 7-29-70

AUG *California* 2012
2OPD008

More vocabulary

expire: a license is no good, or **expires**, after the expiration date
renew a license: to apply to keep a license before it expires
vanity plate: a more expensive, personal license plate

Ask your classmates. Share the answers.

1. How far is the DMV from your home?
2. Do you have a driver's license? If yes, when does it expire? If not, do you want one?

Getting Your First License

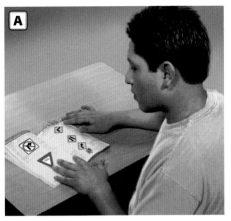

A. **Study** the handbook.

B. **Take** a driver education course.*

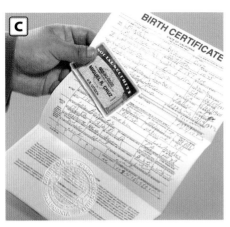

C. **Show** your identification.

D. **Pay** the application fee.

E. **Take** a written test.

F. **Get** a learner's permit.

G. **Take** a driver's training course.*

H. **Pass** a driving test.

I. **Get** your license.

*Note: This is not required for drivers 18 and older.

Ways to request more information

What do I do next?
What's the next step?
Where do I go from here?

Role play. Talk to a DMV clerk.

A: *I want to apply for a driver's license.*
B: *Did you study the handbook?*
A: *Yes, I did. What do I do next?*

Government and Military Service

Federal Government

Legislative Branch

1. U.S. Capitol
2. Congress
3. House of Representatives
4. congressperson
5. Senate
6. senator

Executive Branch

7. White House
8. president
9. vice president
10. Cabinet

Judicial Branch

11. Supreme Court
12. justices
13. chief justice

The Military

14. Army
15. Navy
16. Air Force
17. Marines
18. Coast Guard
19. National Guard

State Government

20. governor

21. lieutenant governor

22. state capital

23. Legislature

24. assemblyperson

25. state senator

City Government

26. mayor

27. city council

28. councilperson

An Election

A. **run for** office

29. political campaign

B. **debate**

30. opponent

C. **get elected**

31. election results

D. **serve**

32. elected official

More vocabulary

term: the period of time an elected official serves
political party: a group of people with the same political goals

Think about it. Discuss.

1. Should everyone have to serve in the military? Why or why not?
2. Would you prefer to run for city council or mayor? Why?

Responsibilities

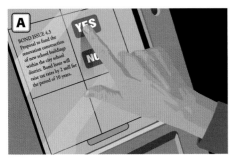

A. **vote**

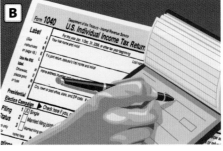

B. **pay** taxes

C. **obey** the law

D. **register** with Selective Service*

E. **serve** on a jury

F. **be** informed

Citizenship Requirements

G. **be** 18 or older

H. **live** in the U.S. for 5 years

I. **take** a citizenship test

Rights

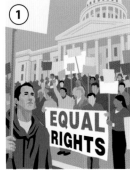

1. peaceful assembly

2. free speech

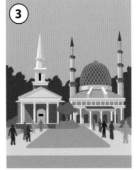

3. freedom of religion

4. freedom of the press

5. fair trial

*Note: All males 18 to 26 who live in the U.S. are required to register with Selective Service.

A. **arrest** a suspect

1. police officer
2. handcuffs

B. **hire** a lawyer / **hire** an attorney

3. guard
4. defense attorney

C. **appear** in court

5. defendant
6. judge

D. **stand** trial

7. courtroom
8. jury
9. evidence
10. prosecuting attorney
11. witness
12. court reporter
13. bailiff

E. **convict** the defendant

14. verdict*

F. **sentence** the defendant

G. **go** to jail / **go** to prison

15. convict / prisoner

H. **be** released

*Note: There are two possible verdicts, "guilty" and "not guilty."

Look at the pictures.
Describe what happened.

A: The _police officer_ _arrested a suspect_.
B: He put _handcuffs_ on him.

Think about it. Discuss.

1. Would you want to serve on a jury? Why or why not?
2. Look at the crimes on page 142. What sentence would you give for each crime? Why?

1. vandalism

2. burglary

3. assault

4. gang violence

5. drunk driving

6. illegal drugs

7. arson

8. shoplifting

9. identity theft

10. victim

11. mugging

12. murder

13. gun

More vocabulary

steal: to take money or things from someone illegally
commit a crime: to do something illegal
criminal: someone who does something illegal

Think about it. Discuss.

1. Is there too much crime on TV or in the movies? Explain.
2. How can communities help stop crime?

A

B

A. Walk with a friend.

B. Stay on well-lit streets.

C

D

C. Conceal your PIN number.

D. Protect your purse or wallet.

E

F

E. Lock your doors.

F. Don't **open** your door to strangers.

G

H

G. Don't **drink** and **drive**.

H. Shop on secure websites.

I

J

I. Be aware of your surroundings.

J. Report suspicious packages.

K

L

K. Report crimes to the police.

L. Join a Neighborhood Watch.

More vocabulary

sober: not drunk
designated drivers: sober drivers who drive drunk people home safely

Ask your classmates. Share the answers.

1. Do you feel safe in your neighborhood?
2. Look at the pictures. Which of these things do you do?
3. What other things do you do to stay safe?

1. lost child
2. car accident
3. airplane crash
4. explosion
5. earthquake
6. mudslide
7. forest fire
8. fire
9. firefighter
10. fire truck

Ways to report an emergency

First, give your name. *My name is <u>Tim Johnson</u>.*
Then, state the emergency and give the address.
There was <u>a car accident</u> at <u>219 Elm Street</u>.

Role play. Call 911.

A: *911 Emergency Operator.*
B: *My name is <u>Lisa Diaz</u>. There is <u>a fire</u> at <u>323 Oak Street</u>.
Please hurry!*

11. drought

12. famine

13. blizzard

14. hurricane

15. tornado

16. volcanic eruption

17. tidal wave / tsunami

18. avalanche

19. flood

20. search and rescue team

Ask your classmates. Share the answers.

1. Which natural disaster worries you the most?
2. Which natural disaster worries you the least?
3. Which disasters are common in your local area?

Think about it. Discuss.

1. What organizations can help you in an emergency?
2. What are some ways to prepare for natural disasters?
3. Where would you go in an emergency?

Before an Emergency

A. **Plan** for an emergency.

1. meeting place

2. out-of-state contact

3. escape route

4. gas shut-off valve

5. evacuation route

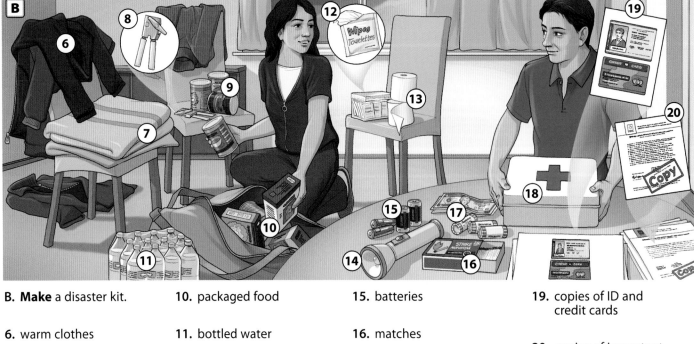

B. **Make** a disaster kit.

6. warm clothes

7. blankets

8. can opener

9. canned food

10. packaged food

11. bottled water

12. moist towelettes

13. toilet paper

14. flashlight

15. batteries

16. matches

17. cash and coins

18. first aid kit

19. copies of ID and credit cards

20. copies of important papers

Pair practice. Make new conversations.

A: *What do we need for our disaster kit?*
B: *We need blankets and matches.*
A: *I think we also need batteries.*

Ask your classmates. Share the answers.

1. Who would you call first after an emergency?
2. Do you have escape and evacuation routes planned?
3. Are you a calm person in case of an emergency?

During an Emergency

C. **Watch** the weather.

D. **Pay attention** to warnings.

E. **Remain** calm.

F. **Follow** directions.

G. **Help** people with disabilities.

H. **Seek** shelter.

I. **Stay away** from windows.

J. **Take** cover.

K. **Evacuate** the area.

After an Emergency

L. **Call** out-of-state contacts.

M. **Clean up** debris.

N. **Inspect** utilities.

Ways to say you're OK

I'm fine.
We're OK here.
Everything's under control.

Ways to say you need help

We need help.
Someone is hurt.
I'm injured. Please get help.

Role play. Prepare for an emergency.

A: *They just issued <u>a hurricane</u> warning.*
B: *OK. We need to stay calm and follow directions.*
A: *What do we need to do first?*

Community Cleanup

1. graffiti
2. litter
3. streetlight
4. hardware store
5. **petition**
A. **give** a speech
B. **applaud**
C. **change**

Look at the pictures. What do you see?

Answer the questions.

1. What were the problems on Main Street?
2. What was the petition for?
3. Why did the city council applaud?
4. How did the people change the street?

📖 Read the story.

Community Cleanup

Marta Lopez has a donut shop on Main Street. One day she looked at her street and was very upset. She saw <u>graffiti</u> on her donut shop and the other stores. <u>Litter</u> was everywhere. All the <u>streetlights</u> were broken. Marta wanted to fix the lights and clean up the street.

Marta started a <u>petition</u> about the streetlights. Five hundred people signed it. Then she <u>gave a speech</u> to the city council. The council members voted to repair the streetlights. Everyone <u>applauded</u>. Marta was happy, but her work wasn't finished.

Next, Marta asked for volunteers to clean up Main Street. The <u>hardware store</u> manager gave the volunteers free paint. Marta gave them free donuts and coffee. The volunteers painted and cleaned. They <u>changed</u> Main Street. Now Main Street is beautiful and Marta is proud.

Think about it.

1. What are some problems in your community? How can people help?
2. Imagine you are Marta. What do you say in your speech to the city council?

1. car

2. passenger

3. taxi

4. motorcycle

5. street

6. truck

7. train

8. (air)plane

Listen and point. Take turns.

A: *Point to the motorcycle.*
B: *Point to the truck.*
A: *Point to the train.*

Dictate to your partner. Take turns.

A: *Write motorcycle.*
B: *Could you repeat that for me?*
A: *Motorcycle. M-o-t-o-r-c-y-c-l-e.*

9. helicopter

10. airport

11. subway station

12. subway

13. bus stop

14. bus

15. bicycle

Ways to talk about using transportation

Use **take** for buses, trains, subways, taxis, planes, and helicopters. Use **drive** for cars and trucks. Use **ride** for bicycles and motorcycles.

Pair practice. Make new conversations.

A: *How do you get to school?*
B: *I take the bus. How about you?*
A: *I ride a bicycle to school.*

A Bus Stop

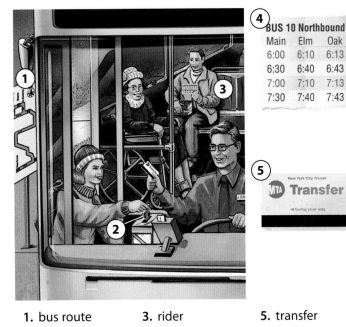

BUS 10 Northbound		
Main	Elm	Oak
6:00	6:10	6:13
6:30	6:40	6:43
7:00	7:10	7:13
7:30	7:40	7:43

New York City Transit
MTA Transfer
◀ Going your way

1. bus route
2. fare
3. rider
4. schedule
5. transfer

A Subway Station

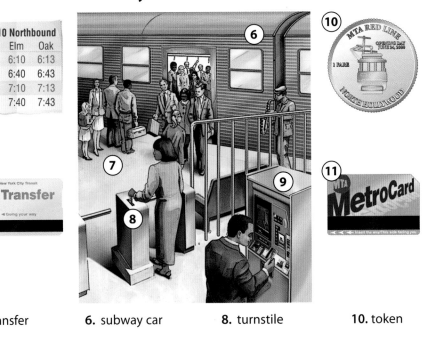

MTA RED LINE
OPENING DAY
JUNE 24, 2000
1 FARE
NORTH HOLLYWOOD

MTA
MetroCard
◀◀ Insert this way/This side facing you

6. subway car
7. platform
8. turnstile
9. vending machine
10. token
11. fare card

A Train Station

TICKETS   TICKETS

15 🚂 Baggage
HART DAVIS/DAMON
From
DOVER, NH
To
BOSTON NRTH STA,MA
Carrier Train   Date
2V   684 17FEB03
Accom   Space/Car
2V   BUSINESS CL
Form of Payment
AP   XXXX0456791   Ax

Fresno

Los Angeles

Fresno

Los Angeles

12. ticket window
13. conductor
14. track
15. ticket
16. one-way trip
17. round trip

Airport Transportation

TAXIS

TAXI

J&J Hotel

metro
1036081

22.00

18. taxi stand
19. shuttle
20. town car
21. taxi driver
22. taxi license
23. meter

More vocabulary

hail a taxi: to raise your hand to get a taxi
miss the bus: to get to the bus stop after the bus leaves

Ask your classmates. Share the answers.

1. Is there a subway system in your city?
2. Do you ever take taxis? When?
3. Do you ever take the bus? Where?

A. **go under** the bridge

B. **go over** the bridge

C. **walk up** the steps

D. **walk down** the steps

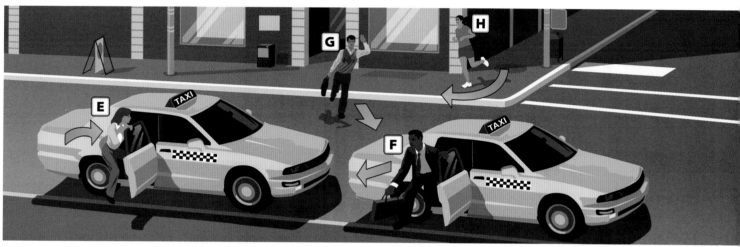

E. **get into** the taxi

F. **get out of** the taxi

G. **run across** the street

H. **run around** the corner

I. **get on** the highway

J. **get off** the highway

K. **drive through** the tunnel

Grammar Point: *into, out of, on, off*

Use ***get into*** for taxis and cars.
Use ***get on*** for buses, trains, planes, and highways.

Use ***get out of*** for taxis and cars.
Use ***get off*** for buses, trains, planes, and highways.

1. stop

2. do not enter / wrong way

3. one way

4. speed limit

5. U-turn OK

6. no outlet / dead end

7. right turn only

8. no left turn

9. yield

10. merge

11. no parking

12. handicapped parking

13. pedestrian crossing

15. school crossing

17. U.S. route / highway marker

14. railroad crossing

16. road work

18. hospital

Pair practice. Make new conversations.

A: *Watch out! The sign says <u>no left turn</u>.*
B: *Sorry, I was looking at the <u>stop</u> sign.*
A: *That's OK. Just be careful!*

Ask your classmates. Share the answers.

1. How many traffic signs are on your street?
2. What's the speed limit on your street?
3. What traffic signs are the same in your native country?

Directions

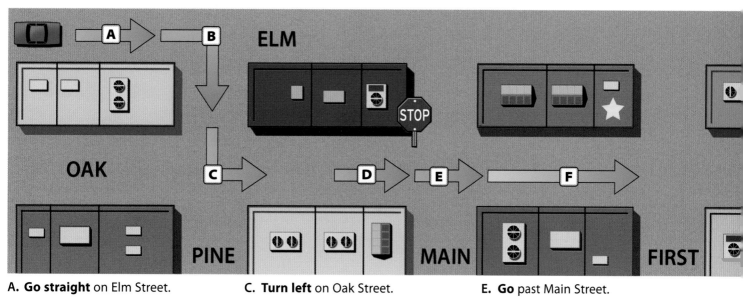

A. Go straight on Elm Street.

B. Turn right on Pine Street.

C. Turn left on Oak Street.

D. Stop at the corner.

E. Go past Main Street.

F. Go one block to First Street.

Maps

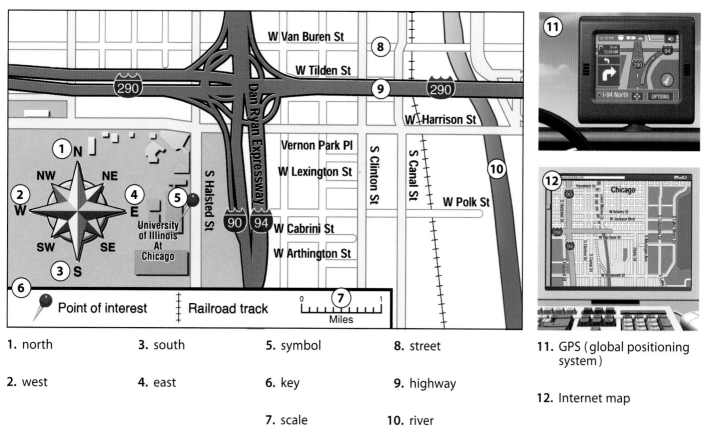

1. north
2. west
3. south
4. east
5. symbol
6. key
7. scale
8. street
9. highway
10. river
11. GPS (global positioning system)
12. Internet map

Role play. Ask for directions.

A: *I'm lost. I need to get to Elm and Pine.*
B: *Go straight on Oak and make a right on Pine.*
A: *Thanks so much.*

Ask your classmates. Share the answers.

1. How often do you use Internet maps? GPS? paper maps?
2. What was the last map you used? Why?

155

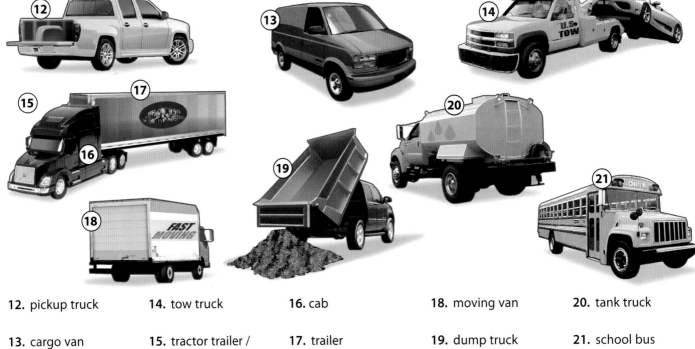

1. 4-door car / sedan

2. 2-door car / coupe

3. hybrid

4. sports car

5. convertible

6. station wagon

7. SUV (sport–utility vehicle)

8. minivan

9. camper

10. RV (recreational vehicle)

11. limousine / limo

12. pickup truck

13. cargo van

14. tow truck

15. tractor trailer / semi

16. cab

17. trailer

18. moving van

19. dump truck

20. tank truck

21. school bus

Pair practice. Make new conversations.

A: *I have a new car!*
B: *Did you get a hybrid?*
A: *Yes, but I really wanted a sports car.*

More vocabulary

make: the name of the company that makes the car
model: the style of the car

Buying a Used Car

A. **Look at** car ads.

B. **Ask** the seller about the car.

C. **Take** the car to a mechanic.

D. **Negotiate** a price.

E. **Get** the title from the seller.

F. **Register** the car.

Taking Care of Your Car

G. **Fill** the tank with gas.

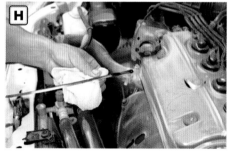

H. **Check** the oil.

I. **Put in** coolant.

J. **Go** for a smog check.*

K. **Replace** the windshield wipers.

L. **Fill** the tires with air.

*smog check = emissions test

Ways to request service

Please check the oil.
Could you fill the tank?
Put in coolant, please.

Think about it. Discuss.

1. What's good and bad about a used car?
2. Do you like to negotiate car prices? Why?
3. Do you know any good mechanics? Why are they good?

157

At the Dealer

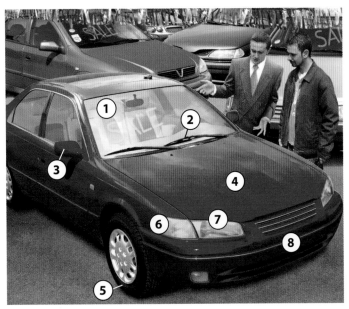

1. windshield	**5.** tire
2. windshield wipers	**6.** turn signal
3. sideview mirror	**7.** headlight
4. hood	**8.** bumper

At the Mechanic

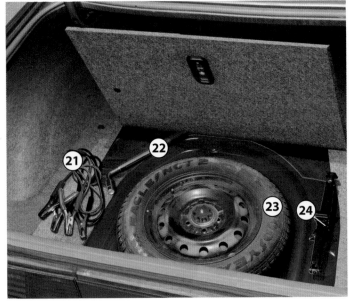

9. hubcap / wheel cover	**13.** tail light
10. gas tank	**14.** brake light
11. trunk	**15.** tail pipe
12. license plate	**16.** muffler

Under the Hood

17. fuel injection system	**19.** radiator
18. engine	**20.** battery

Inside the Trunk

21. jumper cables	**23.** spare tire
22. lug wrench	**24.** jack

The Dashboard and Instrument Panel

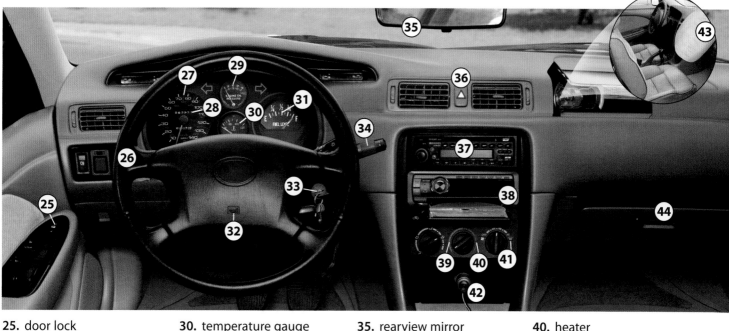

25. door lock

26. steering wheel

27. speedometer

28. odometer

29. oil gauge

30. temperature gauge

31. gas gauge

32. horn

33. ignition

34. turn signal

35. rearview mirror

36. hazard lights

37. radio

38. CD player

39. air conditioner

40. heater

41. defroster

42. power outlet

43. air bag

44. glove compartment

An Automatic Transmission

A Manual Transmission

Inside the Car

45. brake pedal

46. gas pedal / accelerator

47. gear shift

48. hand brake

49. clutch

50. stick shift

51. front seat

52. seat belt

53. child safety seat

54. backseat

In the Airline Terminal

At the Security Checkpoint

1. skycap

2. check-in kiosk

3. ticket agent

4. screening area

5. TSA* agent / security screener

6. bin

Taking a Flight

A. Check in electronically.

B. Check your bags.

C. Show your boarding pass and ID.

D. Go through security.

E. Board the plane.

F. Find your seat.

G. Stow your carry-on bag.

H. Fasten your seat belt.

I. Turn off your cell phone.

J. Take off. / Leave.

K. Land. / Arrive.

L. Claim your baggage.

* Transportation Security Administration

160

At the Gate

7. arrival and departure monitors

8. gate

9. boarding area

On the Airplane

10. cockpit

11. pilot

12. flight attendant

13. overhead compartment

14. emergency exit

15. passenger

At Customs

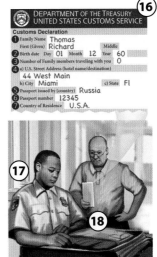

16. declaration form

17. customs officer

18. luggage / bag

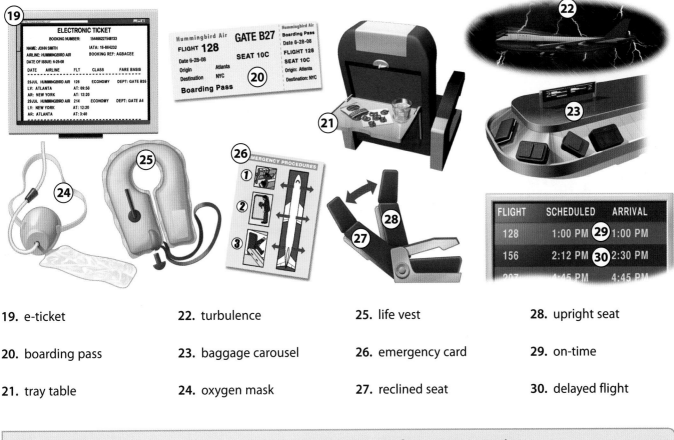

19. e-ticket

20. boarding pass

21. tray table

22. turbulence

23. baggage carousel

24. oxygen mask

25. life vest

26. emergency card

27. reclined seat

28. upright seat

29. on-time

30. delayed flight

More vocabulary

departure time: the time the plane takes off
arrival time: the time the plane lands
direct flight: a trip with no stops

Pair practice. Make new conversations.

A: *Excuse me. Where do I <u>check in</u>?*
B: *At the <u>check-in kiosk</u>.*
A: *Thanks.*

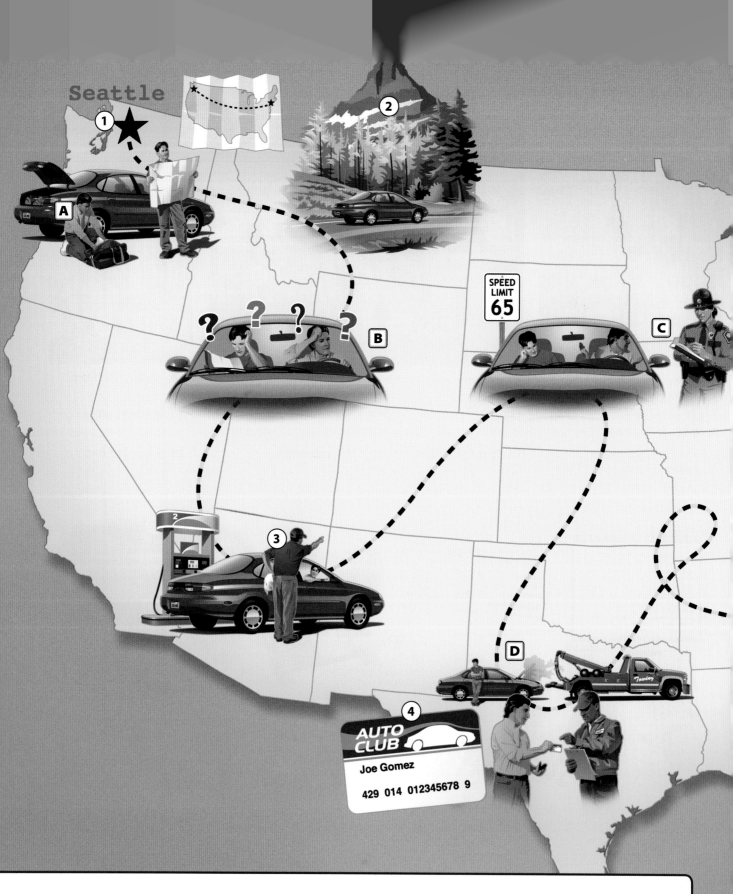

Seattle

1. starting point
2. scenery
3. gas station attendant
4. auto club card
5. destination
A. **pack**
B. **get** lost
C. **get** a speeding ticket
D. **break down**
E. **run out** of gas
F. **have** a flat tire

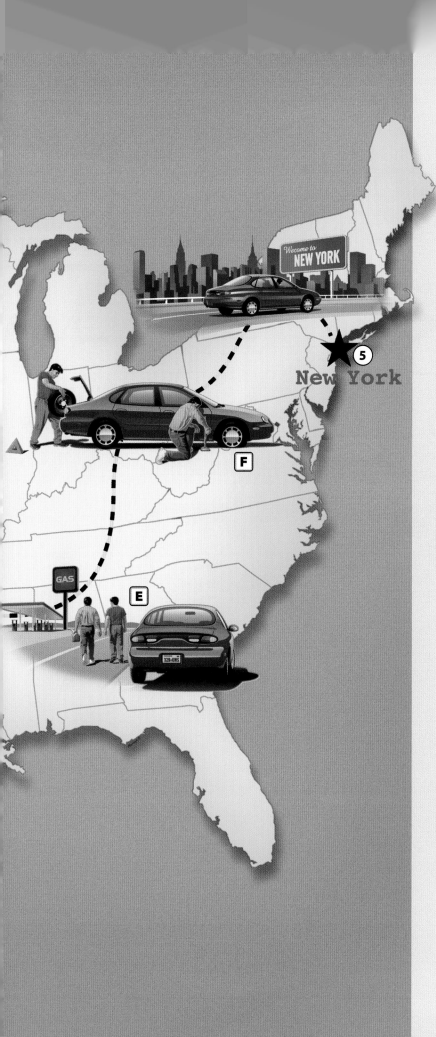

**Look at the pictures.
What do you see?**

Answer the questions.

1. What are the young men's starting point and destination?

2. What do they see on their trip?

3. What kinds of problems do they have?

📖 **Read the story.**

A Road Trip

On July 7th Joe and Rob <u>packed</u> their bags for a road trip. Their <u>starting point</u> was Seattle. Their <u>destination</u> was New York City.

The young men saw beautiful <u>scenery</u> on their trip. But there were also problems. They <u>got lost</u>. Then, a <u>gas station attendant</u> gave them bad directions. Next, they <u>got a speeding ticket</u>. Joe was very upset. After that, their car <u>broke down</u>. Joe called a tow truck and used his <u>auto club card</u>.

The end of their trip was difficult, too. They <u>ran out of gas</u> and then they had a <u>flat tire</u>.

After 7,000 miles of problems, Joe and Rob arrived in New York City. They were happy, but tired. Next time, they're going to take the train.

Think about it.

1. What is the best way to travel across the U.S.? by car? by plane? by train? Why?

2. Imagine your car breaks down on the road. Who can you call?
What can you do?

1. entrance

2. customer

3. office

4. employer / boss

5. receptionist

6. safety regulations

IRINA'S COMPUTER SERVICE

6 OSHA
HAZARDS
SPILLS
CALL 911
SAFETY FIRST

COMPUTER NEWS

Irina Sarkov Owner

Listen and point. Take turns.

A: Point to <u>the front entrance</u>.
B: Point to <u>the receptionist</u>.
A: Point to <u>the time clock</u>.

Dictate to your partner. Take turns.

A: *Can you spell <u>employer</u>?*
B: *I'm not sure. Is it <u>e-m-p-l-o-y-e-r</u>?*
A: *Yes, that's right.*

7. time clock

8. supervisor

9. employee

10. payroll clerk

11. pay stub

12. wages

13. deductions

14. paycheck

Ways to talk about wages

I **earn** $250 a week.
He **makes** $7 an hour.
I'm **paid** $1,000 a month.

Role play. Talk to an employer.

A: *Is everything correct on your paycheck?*
B: *No, it isn't. I make $250 a week, not $200.*
A: *Let's talk to the payroll clerk. Where is she?*

1. accountant

2. actor

3. administrative assistant

4. appliance repair person

5. architect

6. artist

7. assembler

8. auto mechanic

9. babysitter

10. baker

11. business owner

12. businessperson

13. butcher

14. carpenter

15. cashier

16. childcare worker

Ways to ask about someone's job

What's her job?
What does he do?
What kind of work do they do?

Pair practice. Make new conversations.

A: *What kind of work <u>does she</u> do?*
B: *<u>She's an accountant</u>. What <u>do they</u> do?*
A: *<u>They're actors</u>.*

17. commercial fisher

18. computer software engineer

19. computer technician

We have that shirt in red.

20. customer service representative

21. delivery person

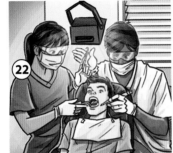

22. dental assistant

23. dockworker

24. electronics repair person

25. engineer

26. firefighter

27. florist

28. gardener

29. garment worker

30. graphic designer

31. hairdresser / hair stylist

32. home health care aide

Ways to talk about jobs and occupations

*Sue's a <u>garment worker</u>. She works **in** a factory.*
*Tom's <u>an engineer</u>. He works **for** <u>a large company</u>.*
*Ann's a <u>dental assistant</u>. She works **with** <u>a dentist</u>.*

Role play. Talk about a friend's new job.

A: *Does your friend like <u>his</u> new job?*
B: *Yes, <u>he</u> does. <u>He's a graphic designer</u>.*
A: *Does <u>he</u> work <u>in an office</u>?*

167

33. homemaker

34. housekeeper

你好 He says, "Hi."

35. interpreter / translator

36. lawyer

37. machine operator

38. manicurist

39. medical records technician

40. messenger / courier

41. model

42. mover

43. musician

44. nurse

45. occupational therapist

46. (house) painter

47. physician assistant

48. police officer

Grammar Point: past tense of _be_

I **was** a machine operator for 5 years.
She **was** a nurse for a year.
They **were** movers from 2003–2007.

Pair practice. Make new conversations.

A: _What was your first job?_
B: _I was <u>a musician</u>. How about you?_
A: _I was <u>a messenger for a small company</u>._

49. postal worker

50. printer

51. receptionist

52. reporter

53. retail clerk

54. sanitation worker

55. security guard

56. server

57. social worker

Here are some programs that will help you.

HELPING HEART AGENCY

58. soldier

59. stock clerk

Hello. I'm calling with a very special offer.

60. telemarketer

61. truck driver

62. veterinarian

63. welder

Norma's Story

64. writer / author

Ask your classmates. Share the answers.

1. Which of these jobs could you do now?
2. What is one job you don't want to have?
3. Which jobs do you want to have?

Think about it. Discuss.

1. Which jobs need special training?
2. What kind of person makes a good interpreter? A good nurse? A good reporter? Why?

169

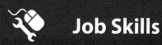
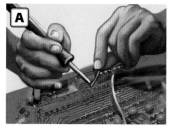

A. **assemble** components

B. **assist** medical patients

C. **cook**

D. **do** manual labor

E. **drive** a truck

F. **fly** a plane

G. **make** furniture

H. **operate** heavy machinery

I. **program** computers

J. **repair** appliances

K. **sell** cars

L. **sew** clothes

4% interest of 5K = x

M. **solve** math problems

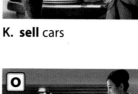

ПРИВЕТ

N. **speak** another language

O. **supervise** people

P. **take** care of children

Q. **teach**

R. **type**

S. **use** a cash register

T. **wait on** customers

Grammar Point: *can, can't*

I am a chef. I **can** *cook.*
I'm not a pilot. I **can't** *fly a plane.*
I **can't** *speak French, but I* **can** *speak Spanish.*

Role play. Talk to a job counselor.

A: *Tell me about your skills. Can you* <u>type</u>?
B: <u>No, I can't</u>, *but I* <u>can use a cash register</u>.
A: *OK. What other skills do you have?*

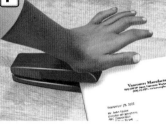

Customers need better service…

Scan Complete

Let's meet at 2:00.

Sure.

Dear Mr. Smith…

Hello. ABC Company. How may I help you?

Please hold.

Mr. Perez, I'm transferring you.

Hello. This is Sue Jones. Please call me.

Message Pad
Call From: Ana Puerta
Tel: 555-1234
Message:
Please Call

This is Lee Tran. Please call me back.

Office Skills

A. **type** a letter

B. **enter** data

C. **transcribe** notes

D. **make** copies

E. **collate** papers

F. **staple**

G. **fax** a document

H. **scan** a document

I. **print** a document

J. **schedule** a meeting

K. **take** dictation

L. **organize** materials

Telephone Skills

M. **greet** the caller

N. **put** the caller on hold

O. **transfer** the call

P. **leave** a message

Q. **take** a message

R. **check** messages

171

Career Path

1. entry-level job

2. training

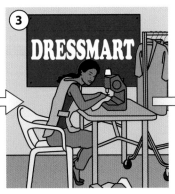

3. new job

4. promotion

Types of Job Training

5. vocational training

6. internship

7. on-the-job training

8. online course

Planning a Career

9. resource center

10. career counselor

11. interest inventory

12. skill inventory

13. job fair

14. recruiter

Ways to talk about job training

I'm looking into <u>an online course</u>.
I'm interested in <u>on-the-job training</u>.
I want to sign up for <u>an internship</u>.

Ask your classmates. Share the answers.

1. What kind of job training are you interested in?
2. Would your rather learn English in an online course or in a classroom?

A. **talk** to friends / **network**

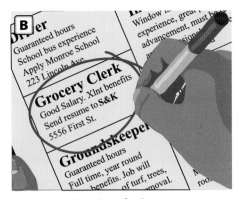

B. **look in** the classifieds

C. **look for** help wanted signs

D. **check** Internet job sites

E. **go** to an employment agency

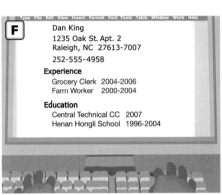

F. **write** a resume

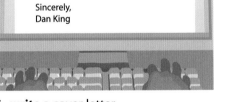

G. **write** a cover letter

H. **send in** your resume and cover letter

I. **set up** an interview

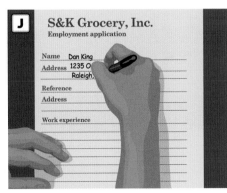

J. **fill out** an application

K. **go on** an interview

L. **get** hired

A. **Prepare** for the interview.

B. **Dress** appropriately.

C. **Be** neat.

D. **Bring** your resume and ID.

E. **Don't be** late.

F. **Be** on time.

G. **Turn off** your cell phone.

H. **Greet** the interviewer.

I. **Shake** hands.

J. **Make** eye contact.

K. **Listen** carefully.

L. **Talk** about your experience.

M. **Ask** questions.

N. **Thank** the interviewer.

O. **Write** a thank-you note.

More vocabulary

benefits: health insurance, vacation pay, or other things the employer can offer an employee
inquire about benefits: ask about benefits

Think about it. Discuss.

1. How can you prepare for an interview?
2. Why is it important to make eye contact?
3. What kinds of questions should you ask?

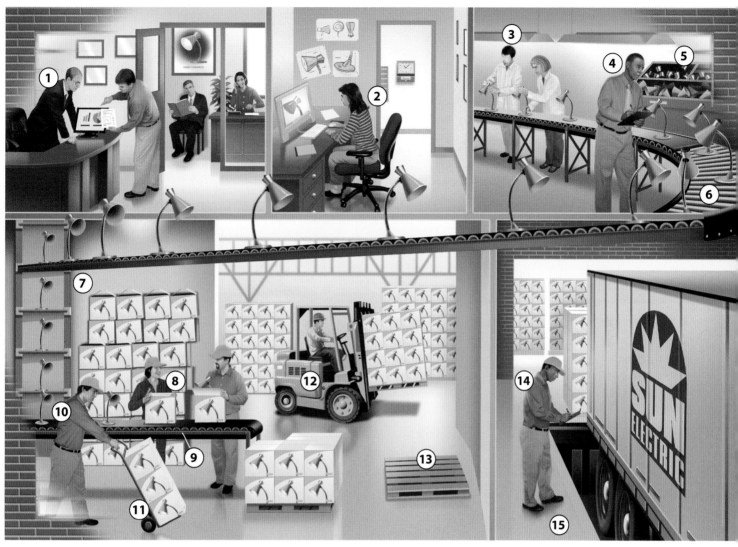

1. factory owner
2. designer
3. factory worker
4. line supervisor
5. parts
6. assembly line
7. warehouse
8. packer
9. conveyer belt
10. order puller
11. hand truck
12. forklift
13. pallet
14. shipping clerk
15. loading dock

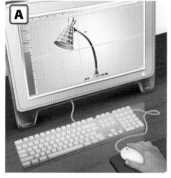

A. design

B. manufacture

C. assemble

D. ship

1. gardening crew
2. leaf blower
3. wheelbarrow
4. gardening crew leader

5. landscape designer
6. lawn mower
7. shovel
8. rake

9. pruning shears
10. trowel
11. hedge clippers
12. weed whacker / weed eater

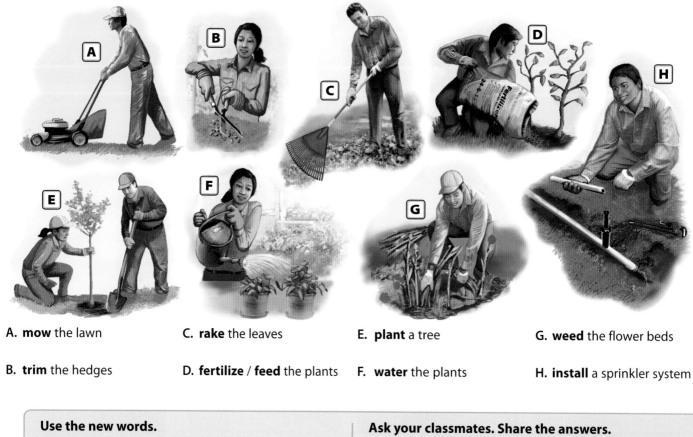

A. **mow** the lawn

B. **trim** the hedges

C. **rake** the leaves

D. **fertilize** / **feed** the plants

E. **plant** a tree

F. **water** the plants

G. **weed** the flower beds

H. **install** a sprinkler system

Use the new words.
Look at page 53. Name what you can do in the yard.
A: I can _mow the lawn_.
B: I can _weed the flower bed_.

Ask your classmates. Share the answers.
1. Do you know someone who does landscaping? Who?
2. Do you enjoy gardening? Why or why not?
3. Which gardening activity is the hardest to do? Why?

Crops

1. rice
2. wheat
3. soybeans
4. corn
5. alfalfa
6. cotton

7. field	12. farm equipment	17. corral	22. rancher
8. farmworker	13. farmer / grower	18. hay	A. **plant**
9. tractor	14. vegetable garden	19. fence	B. **harvest**
10. orchard	15. livestock	20. hired hand	C. **milk**
11. barn	16. vineyard	21. cattle	D. **feed**

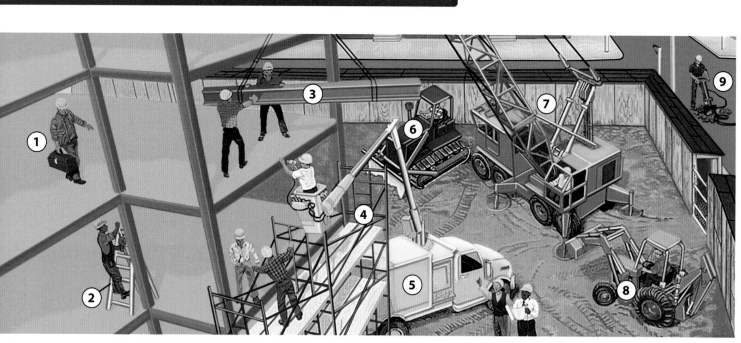

1. construction worker
2. ladder
3. I beam/girder
4. scaffolding
5. cherry picker
6. bulldozer
7. crane
8. backhoe
9. jackhammer / pneumatic drill

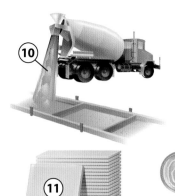
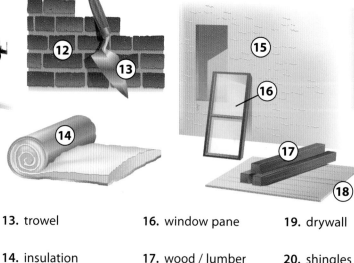
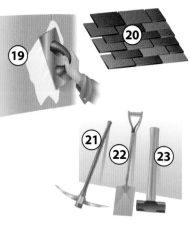

10. concrete
11. tile
12. bricks
13. trowel
14. insulation
15. stucco
16. window pane
17. wood / lumber
18. plywood
19. drywall
20. shingles
21. pickax
22. shovel
23. sledgehammer

A. **paint**

B. **lay** bricks

C. **install** tile

D. **hammer**

Safety Hazards and Hazardous Materials

1. careless worker
2. careful worker
3. poisonous fumes
4. broken equipment
5. frayed cord
6. slippery floor
7. radioactive materials
8. flammable liquids

Safety Equipment

9. hard hat
10. safety glasses
11. safety goggles
12. safety visor
13. respirator
14. particle mask
15. ear plugs
16. earmuffs
17. work gloves
18. back support belt
19. knee pads
20. safety boots
21. fire extinguisher
22. two-way radio

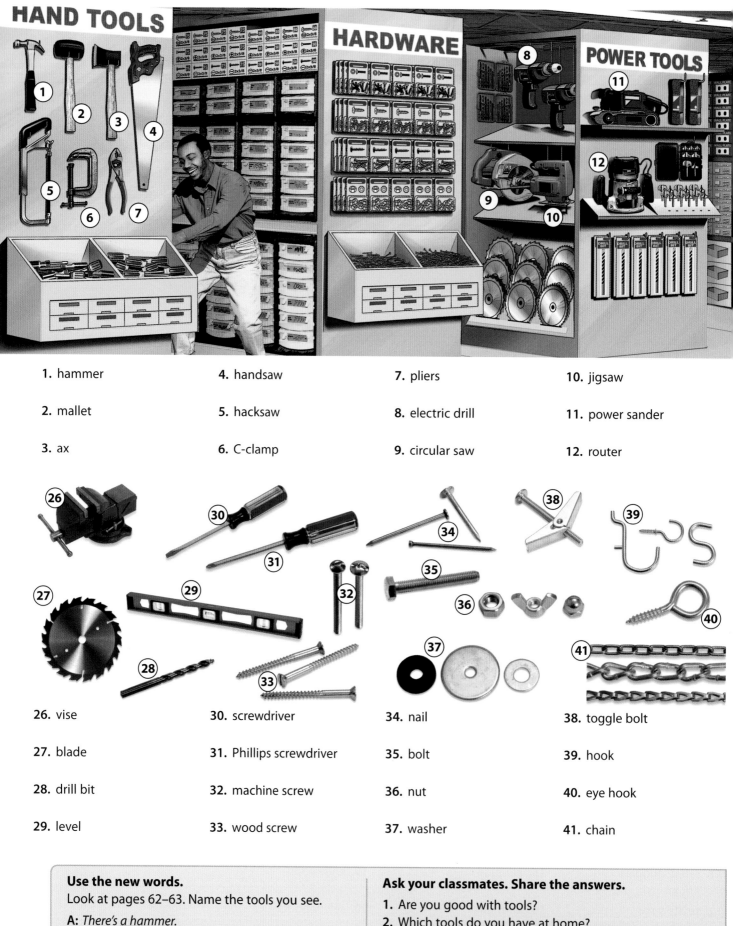

HAND TOOLS

HARDWARE

POWER TOOLS

1. hammer
2. mallet
3. ax
4. handsaw
5. hacksaw
6. C-clamp
7. pliers
8. electric drill
9. circular saw
10. jigsaw
11. power sander
12. router

26. vise
27. blade
28. drill bit
29. level
30. screwdriver
31. Phillips screwdriver
32. machine screw
33. wood screw
34. nail
35. bolt
36. nut
37. washer
38. toggle bolt
39. hook
40. eye hook
41. chain

Use the new words.
Look at pages 62–63. Name the tools you see.

A: *There's a hammer*.
B: *There's a pipe wrench*.

Ask your classmates. Share the answers.
1. Are you good with tools?
2. Which tools do you have at home?
3. Where can you shop for building supplies?

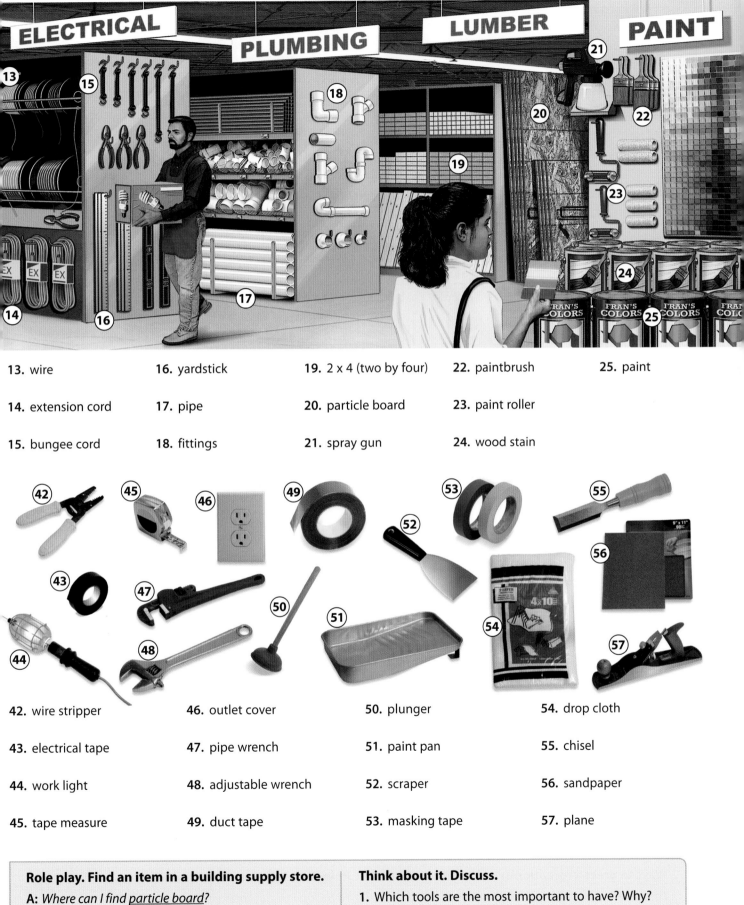

ELECTRICAL

PLUMBING

LUMBER

PAINT

13. wire

14. extension cord

15. bungee cord

16. yardstick

17. pipe

18. fittings

19. 2 x 4 (two by four)

20. particle board

21. spray gun

22. paintbrush

23. paint roller

24. wood stain

25. paint

42. wire stripper

43. electrical tape

44. work light

45. tape measure

46. outlet cover

47. pipe wrench

48. adjustable wrench

49. duct tape

50. plunger

51. paint pan

52. scraper

53. masking tape

54. drop cloth

55. chisel

56. sandpaper

57. plane

Role play. Find an item in a building supply store.

A: *Where can I find <u>particle board</u>?*
B: *It's <u>on the back wall</u>, in the <u>lumber</u> section.*
A: *Great. And where <u>are the nails</u>?*

Think about it. Discuss.

1. Which tools are the most important to have? Why?
2. Which tools can be dangerous? Why?
3. Do you borrow tools from friends? Why or why not?

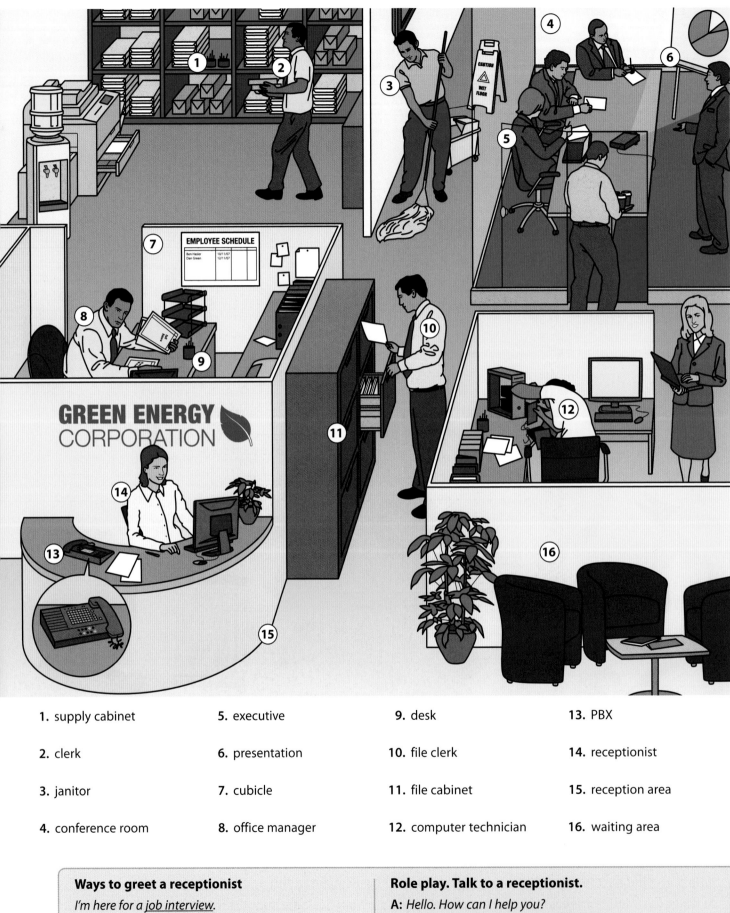

1. supply cabinet
2. clerk
3. janitor
4. conference room

5. executive
6. presentation
7. cubicle
8. office manager

9. desk
10. file clerk
11. file cabinet
12. computer technician

13. PBX
14. receptionist
15. reception area
16. waiting area

Ways to greet a receptionist

I'm here for a <u>job interview</u>.
I have a <u>9:00 a.m.</u> appointment with <u>Mr. Lee</u>.
I'd like to leave a message <u>for Mr. Lee</u>.

Role play. Talk to a receptionist.

A: *Hello. How can I help you?*
B: *<u>I'm here for a job interview with Mr. Lee.</u>*
A: *OK. What is your name?*

Office Equipment

17. computer

18. inkjet printer

19. laser printer

20. scanner

21. fax machine

22. paper cutter

23. photocopier

24. paper shredder

25. calculator

26. electric pencil sharpener

27. postal scale

Office Supplies

28. stapler

29. staples

30. clear tape

31. paper clip

32. packing tape

33. glue

34. rubber band

35. pushpin

36. correction fluid

37. correction tape

38. legal pad

39. sticky notes

40. mailer

41. mailing label

42. letterhead / stationery

43. envelope

44. rotary card file

45. ink cartridge

46. ink pad

47. stamp

48. appointment book

49. organizer

50. file folder

1. doorman

2. revolving door

3. parking attendant

4. concierge

5. gift shop

6. bell captain

7. bellhop

8. luggage cart

9. elevator

10. guest

11. desk clerk

12. front desk

13. guest room

14. double bed

15. king-size bed

16. suite

17. room service

18. hallway

19. housekeeping cart

20. housekeeper

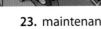

21. pool service

22. pool

23. maintenance

24. gym

25. meeting room

26. ballroom

A Restaurant Kitchen

1. short-order cook	**3.** walk-in freezer	**5.** storeroom	**7.** head chef / executive chef
2. dishwasher	**4.** food preparation worker	**6.** sous chef	

Restaurant Dining

8. server	**11.** maitre d'	**14.** banquet room
9. diner	**12.** headwaiter	**15.** runner
10. buffet	**13.** bus person	**16.** caterer

More vocabulary

line cook: short-order cook
wait staff: servers, headwaiters, and runners

Ask your classmates. Share the answers.

1. Have you ever worked in a hotel? What did you do?
2. What is the hardest job in a hotel?
3. Would you prefer to stay at a hotel in the city or in the country?

185

1. dangerous

2. clinic

3. budget

4. floor plan

5. contractor

6. electrical hazard

7. wiring

8. bricklayer

A. **call in** sick

**Look at the picture.
What do you see?**

Answer the questions.

1. How many workers are there? How many are working?

2. Why did two workers call in sick?

3. What is dangerous at the construction site?

📖 **Read the story.**

A Bad Day at Work

Sam Lopez is the <u>contractor</u> for a new building. He makes the schedule and supervises the <u>budget</u>. He also solves problems. Today there are a lot of problems.

Two <u>bricklayers</u> <u>called in sick</u> this morning. Now Sam has only one bricklayer at work. One hour later, a construction worker fell. Now he has to go to the <u>clinic</u>. Sam always tells his workers to be careful. Construction work is <u>dangerous</u>. Sam's also worried because the new <u>wiring</u> is an <u>electrical hazard</u>.

Right now, the building owner is in Sam's office. Her new <u>floor plan</u> has 25 more offices. Sam has a headache. Maybe he needs to call in sick tomorrow.

Think about it.

1. What do you say when you can't come in to work? to school?

2. Imagine you are Sam. What do you tell the building owner? Why?

187

1. preschool /
   nursery school

2. elementary school

3. middle school /
   junior high school

4. high school

5. vocational school /
   technical school

6. community college

7. college / university

8. adult school

Listen and point. Take turns.

A: *Point to the preschool.*
B: *Point to the high school.*
A: *Point to the adult school.*

Dictate to your partner. Take turns.

A: *Write preschool.*
B: *Is that p-r-e-s-c-h-o-o-l?*
A: *Yes. That's right.*

9. language arts

10. math

11. science

12. history

13. world languages

14. ESL / ESOL

15. arts

16. music

17. physical education

More vocabulary

core course: a subject students have to take. Math is a core course.

elective: a subject students choose to take. Art is an elective.

Pair practice. Make new conversations.

A: I go to <u>community college</u>.

B: What subjects are you taking?

A: I'm taking <u>history</u> and <u>science</u>.

English Composition

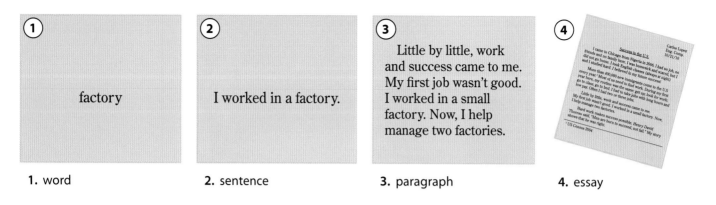

1. word

2. sentence

3. paragraph

4. essay

Parts of an Essay

5. title

6. introduction

7. body

8. conclusion

9. quotation

10. footnote

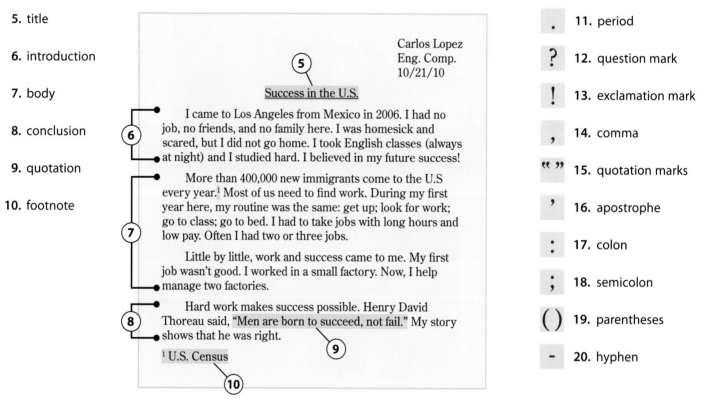

Punctuation

. **11.** period

? **12.** question mark

! **13.** exclamation mark

, **14.** comma

" " **15.** quotation marks

' **16.** apostrophe

: **17.** colon

; **18.** semicolon

( ) **19.** parentheses

- **20.** hyphen

Writing Rules

A

Carlos

Mexico

Los Angeles

A. Capitalize names.

B

Hard work makes success possible.

B. Capitalize the first letter in a sentence.

C

I was homesick and scared, but I did not go home.

C. Use punctuation.

D

I came to Los Angeles from Mexico in 2006. I had no job, no friends, and no family here. I was homesick and scared, but I did not go home. I took English classes (always at night) and I studied hard. I believed in my future success!

D. Indent the first sentence in a paragraph.

Ways to ask for suggestions on your compositions

What do you think of this <u>title</u>?

Is this <u>paragraph</u> OK? Is the <u>punctuation</u> correct?

Do you have any suggestions for the <u>conclusion</u>?

Pair practice. Make new conversations.

A: What do you think of this <u>title</u>?

B: *I think you need to <u>revise</u> it.*

A: *Thanks. Do you have any more suggestions?*

The Writing Process

PREWRITING

E. **Think about** the assignment.

F. **Brainstorm** ideas.

G. **Organize** your ideas.

WRITING AND REVISING

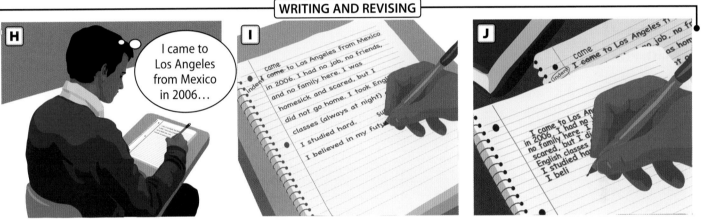

H. **Write** a first draft.

I. **Edit**. / **Proofread**.

J. **Revise**. / **Rewrite**.

SHARING AND RESPONDING

K. **Get** feedback.

L. **Write** a final draft.

M. **Turn in** your paper.

Ask your classmates. Share the answers.

1. Do you like to write essays?
2. Which part of the writing process do you like best? least?

Think about it. Discuss.

1. In which jobs are writing skills important?
2. What tools can help you edit your writing?
3. What are some good subjects for essays?

Mathematics

Integers

$$\ldots -4\ -3\ -2\ -1\ 0\ 1\ 2\ 3\ 4\ldots$$

① ②

1. negative integers

2. positive integers

Fractions

③ 1, 3, 5, 7, 9, 11...

④ 2, 4, 6, 8, 10...

$$\dfrac{3}{8} \qquad \dfrac{3}{8}$$

⑤ ⑥

3. odd numbers

4. even numbers

5. numerator

6. denominator

Math Operations

A. **add**   B. **subtract**   C. **multiply**   D. **divide**

$$\boxed{A}\ 8 + 4 = 12 \qquad \boxed{B}\ 8 - 4 = 4 \qquad \boxed{C}\ 8 \times 4 = 32 \qquad \boxed{D}\ 8 \div 4 = 2$$

⑦ ⑧ ⑨ ⑩

7. sum

8. difference

9. product

10. quotient

A Math Problem

⑪ Tom is 10 years older than Kim. Next year he will be twice as old as Kim. How old is Tom this year?

⑫ x = Kim's age now
$x + 10$ = Tom's age now
$x + 1$ = Kim's age next year
$2(x + 1)$ = Tom's age next year

$x + 10 + 1 = 2(x + 1)$
$x + 11 = 2x + 2$ ⑬
$11 - 2 = 2x - x$

$x = 9$, Kim is 9, Tom is 19 ⑭

⑮

horizontal axis

vertical axis

11. word problem

12. variable

13. equation

14. solution

15. graph

Types of Math

How much are they?

16

x = the sale price
x = 79.00 - .40 (79.00)
x = $47.40

16. algebra

How many do I need?

17

area of path = 24 square ft.
area of brick = 2 square ft.
24 / 2 = 12 bricks

17. geometry

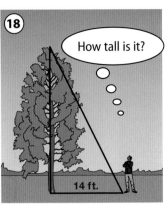

How tall is it?

18

14 ft.

$\tan 63° = $ height / 14 feet
height = 14 feet $(\tan 63°)$
height $\simeq$ 27.48 feet

18. trigonometry

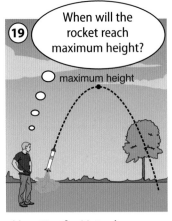

When will the rocket reach maximum height?

19

maximum height

$s(t) = -\frac{1}{2} g t^2 + V_0 t + h$
$s^{\mathrm{I}}(t) = -gt + V_0 = 0$
$t = V_0 / g$

19. calculus

Lines

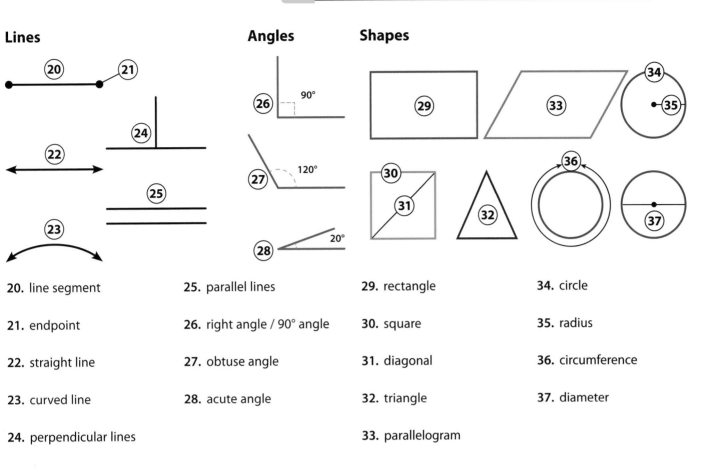

20. line segment

21. endpoint

22. straight line

23. curved line

24. perpendicular lines

25. parallel lines

Angles

26. right angle / 90° angle

27. obtuse angle

28. acute angle

Shapes

29. rectangle

30. square

31. diagonal

32. triangle

33. parallelogram

34. circle

35. radius

36. circumference

37. diameter

Geometric Solids

38. cube   **39.** pyramid   **40.** cone

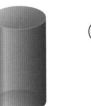 

41. cylinder   **42.** sphere

Measuring Area and Volume

$\ell \times w = \text{area}$

$6 \times f = \text{surface area}$

43. perimeter   **44.** face

$\pi \times r^2 \times h = \text{volume}$

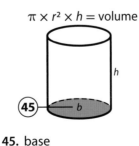

$\frac{4}{3} \times \pi \times r^3 = \text{volume}$

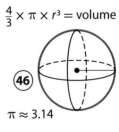

$\pi \approx 3.14$

45. base   **46.** pi

Ask your classmates. Share the answers.

1. Are you good at math?
2. Which types of math are easy for you?
3. Which types of math are difficult for you?

Think about it. Discuss.

1. What's the best way to learn mathematics?
2. How can you find the area of your classroom?
3. Which jobs use math? Which don't?

Biology

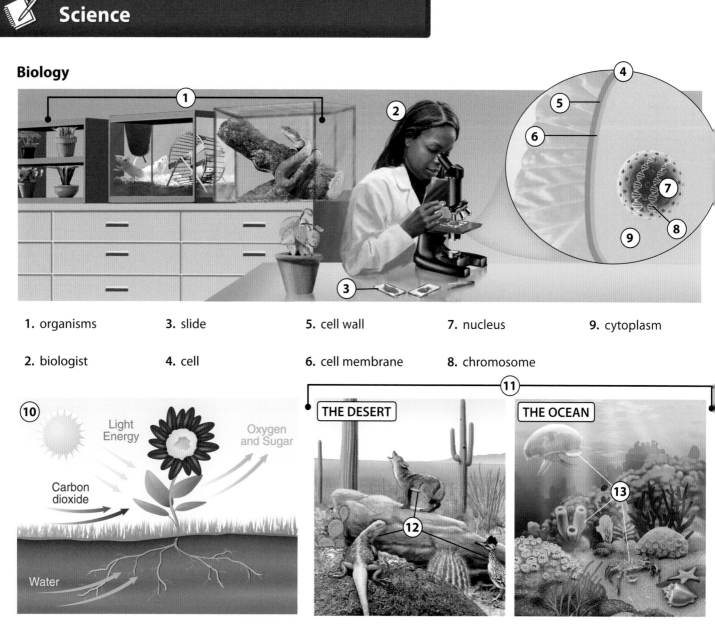

1. organisms	**3.** slide	**5.** cell wall	**7.** nucleus	**9.** cytoplasm
2. biologist	**4.** cell	**6.** cell membrane	**8.** chromosome	

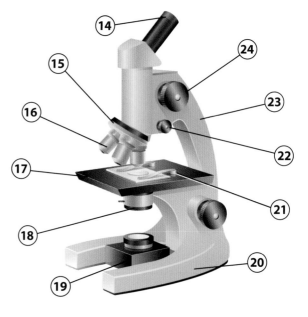

10. photosynthesis

11. habitat   **12.** vertebrates   **13.** invertebrates

A Microscope

14. eyepiece	**20.** base
15. revolving nosepiece	**21.** stage clips
16. objective	**22.** fine adjustment knob
17. stage	**23.** arm
18. diaphragm	**24.** coarse adjustment knob
19. light source	

Chemistry

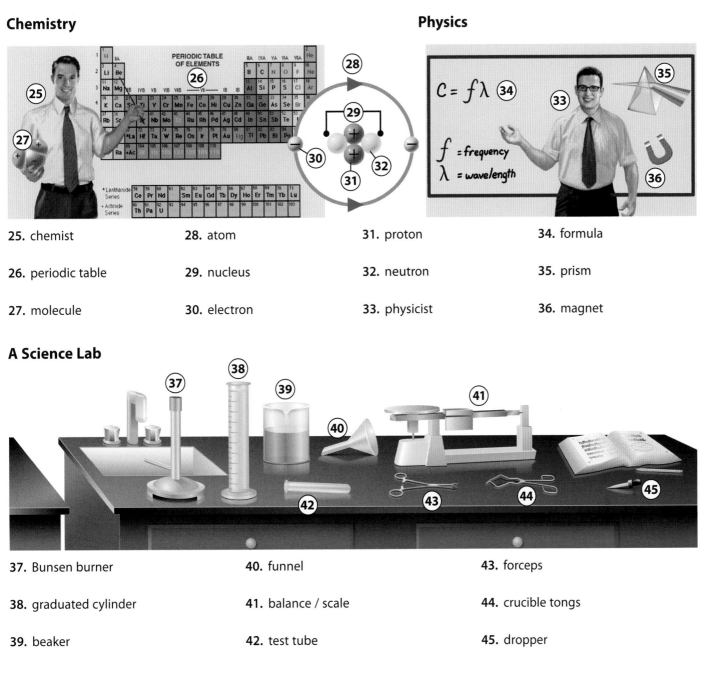

25. chemist

26. periodic table

27. molecule

28. atom

29. nucleus

30. electron

Physics

31. proton

32. neutron

33. physicist

34. formula

35. prism

36. magnet

A Science Lab

37. Bunsen burner

38. graduated cylinder

39. beaker

40. funnel

41. balance / scale

42. test tube

43. forceps

44. crucible tongs

45. dropper

An Experiment

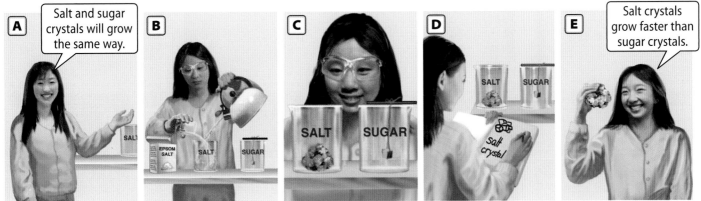

A Salt and sugar crystals will grow the same way.

E Salt crystals grow faster than sugar crystals.

A. **State** a hypothesis.   B. **Do** an experiment.   C. **Observe.**   D. **Record** the results.   E. **Draw** a conclusion.

Desktop Computer

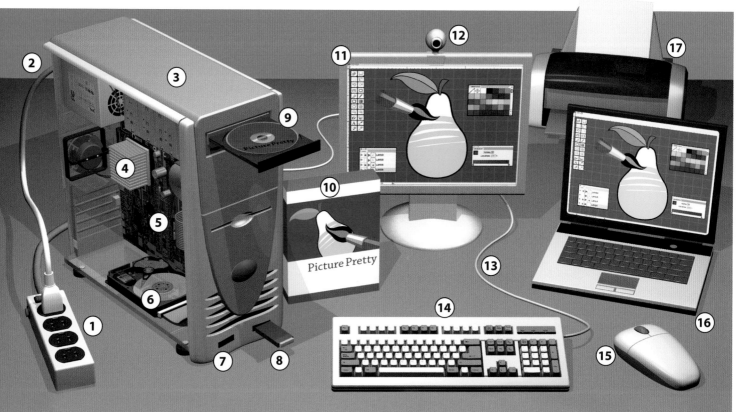

1. surge protector
2. power cord
3. tower
4. microprocessor / CPU
5. motherboard

6. hard drive
7. USB port
8. flash drive
9. DVD and CD-ROM drive
10. software

11. monitor /screen
12. webcam
13. cable
14. keyboard
15. mouse

16. laptop
17. printer

Keyboarding

A. **type**

B. **select**

C. **delete**

D. **go to** the next line

Navigating a Webpage

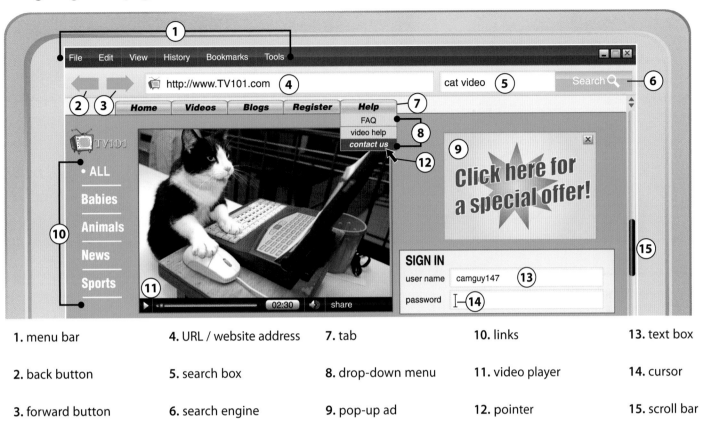

1. menu bar	4. URL / website address	7. tab	10. links	13. text box
2. back button	5. search box	8. drop-down menu	11. video player	14. cursor
3. forward button	6. search engine	9. pop-up ad	12. pointer	15. scroll bar

Logging on and Sending Email

A. **type** your password

B. **click** "sign in"

C. **address** the email

D. **type** the subject

E. **type** the message

F. **check** your spelling

G. **attach** a picture

H. **attach** a file

I. **send** the email

U.S. History

Colonial Period

1. thirteen colonies
2. colonists
3. Native Americans
4. slave
5. Declaration of Independence
6. First Continental Congress
7. founders
8. Revolutionary War
9. redcoat
10. minuteman
11. first president
12. Constitution
13. Bill of Rights

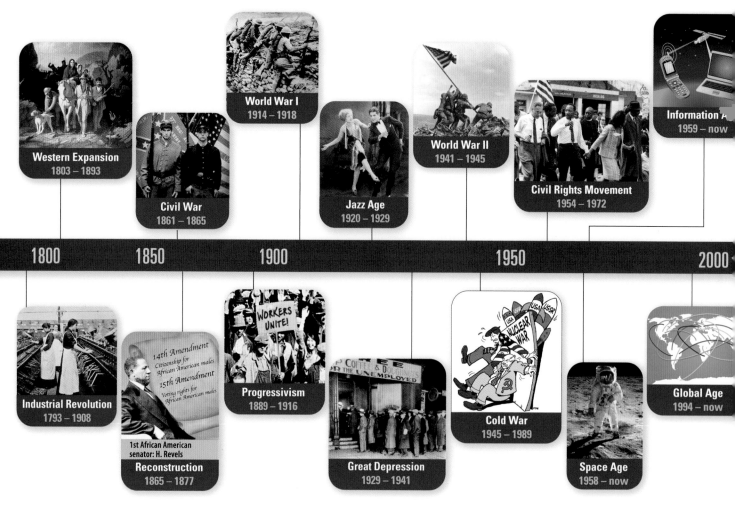

Western Expansion
1803 – 1893

Civil War
1861 – 1865

World War I
1914 – 1918

Jazz Age
1920 – 1929

World War II
1941 – 1945

Civil Rights Movement
1954 – 1972

Information Age
1959 – now

Industrial Revolution
1793 – 1908

14th Amendment
Citizenship for African American males
15th Amendment
Voting rights for African American males
1st African American senator: H. Revels
Reconstruction
1865 – 1877

WORKERS UNITE!
Progressivism
1889 – 1916

Great Depression
1929 – 1941

NUCLEAR WAR
Cold War
1945 – 1989

Space Age
1958 – now

Global Age
1994 – now

1800   1850   1900   1950   2000

Civilizations

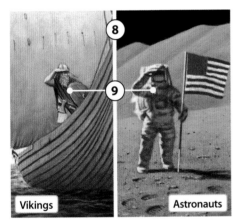
Pyramids / Parthenon — 1

Times Square — 2

Caesar — 3 / Qin Shi Huang

King Henry VIII — 4 / Queen Elizabeth I

Juarez — 5

Mussolini — 6

Churchill — 7

1. ancient

2. modern

3. emperor

4. monarch

5. president

6. dictator

7. prime minister

Historical Terms

Vikings — 8, 9 — Astronauts

war — 10, army — 11

immigration — 12, immigrant — 13

8. exploration

9. explorer

10. war

11. army

12. immigration

13. immigrant

Mozart — 14, 15 — Duke Ellington

Susan B. Anthony — 16, 17 — César Chávez

Edison — 18, 19 — Camarena

14. composer

15. composition

16. political movement

17. activist

18. inventor

19. invention

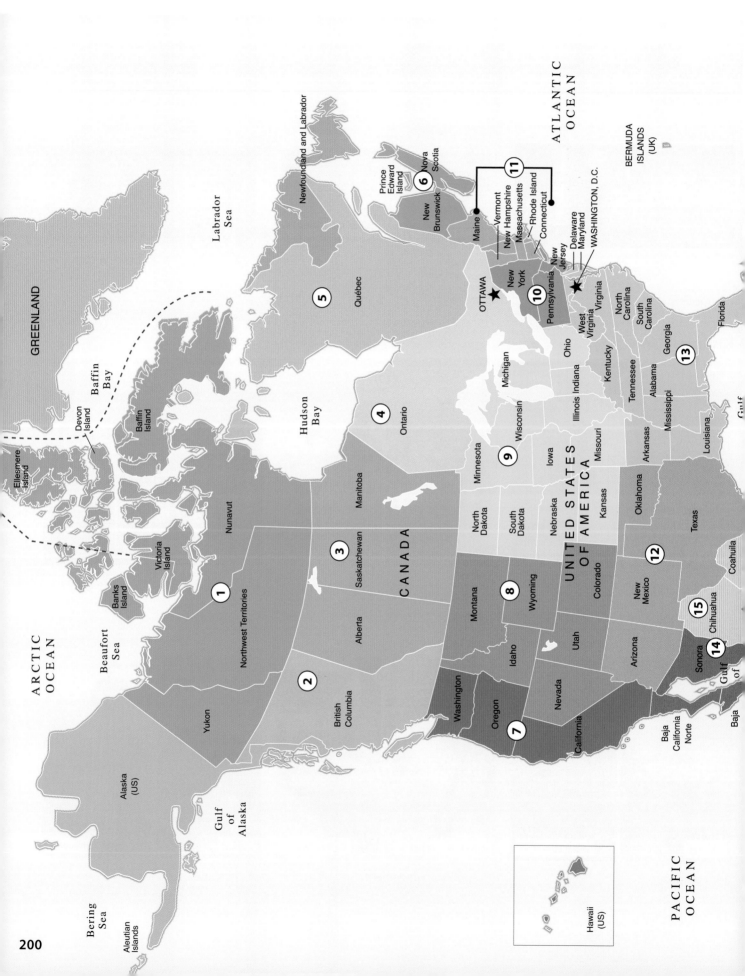

ATLANTIC OCEAN

BERMUDA ISLANDS (UK)

GREENLAND

Labrador Sea

Baffin Bay

Newfoundland and Labrador

Prince Edward Island

Nova Scotia

New Brunswick

Maine

Vermont

New Hampshire

Massachusetts

Rhode Island

Connecticut

New Jersey

Delaware

Maryland

WASHINGTON, D.C.

New York

Pennsylvania

Virginia

West Virginia

North Carolina

South Carolina

Georgia

Florida

Gulf

OTTAWA

Québec

Devon Island

Ellesmere Island

Baffin Island

Hudson Bay

Ontario

Michigan

Ohio

Kentucky

Tennessee

Alabama

Mississippi

Louisiana

Illinois Indiana

Wisconsin

Minnesota

Iowa

Missouri

Arkansas

Nunavut

Victoria Island

Banks Island

Manitoba

Saskatchewan

CANADA

North Dakota

South Dakota

Nebraska

Kansas

Oklahoma

Texas

Coahuila

Alberta

Montana

Wyoming

UNITED STATES OF AMERICA

Colorado

New Mexico

British Columbia

Northwest Territories

Idaho

Utah

Arizona

Nevada

Chihuahua

Sonora

Gulf of

Baja California Norte

Baja

Yukon

Washington

Oregon

California

Alaska (US)

Gulf of Alaska

ARCTIC OCEAN

Beaufort Sea

Bering Sea

Aleutian Islands

Hawaii (US)

PACIFIC OCEAN

1 2 3 4 5 6 7 8 9 10 11 12 13 14 15

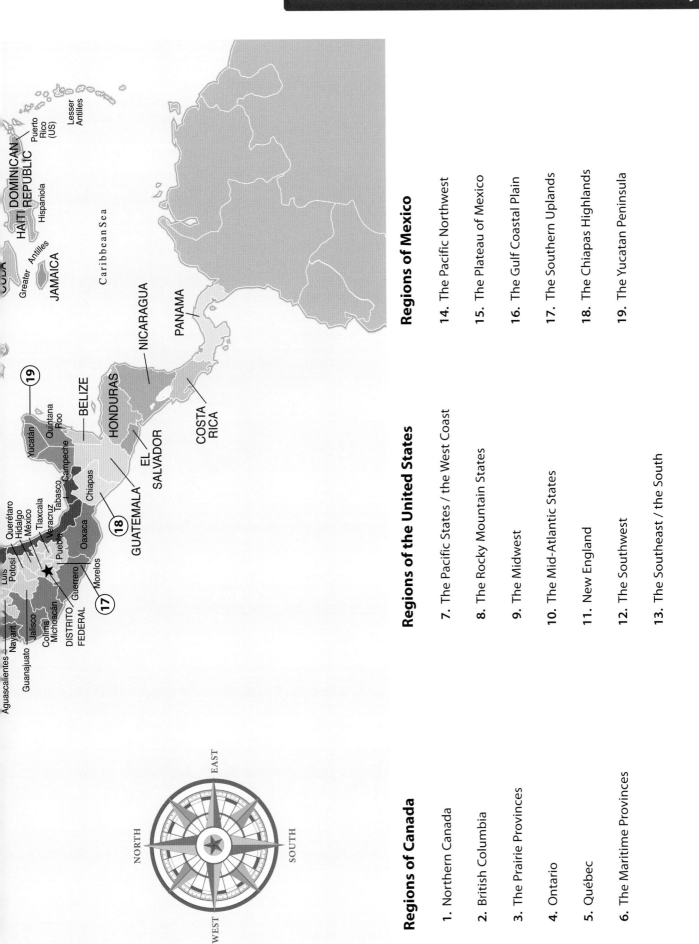

Regions of Canada

1. Northern Canada

2. British Columbia

3. The Prairie Provinces

4. Ontario

5. Québec

6. The Maritime Provinces

Regions of the United States

7. The Pacific States / the West Coast

8. The Rocky Mountain States

9. The Midwest

10. The Mid-Atlantic States

11. New England

12. The Southwest

13. The Southeast / the South

Regions of Mexico

14. The Pacific Northwest

15. The Plateau of Mexico

16. The Gulf Coastal Plain

17. The Southern Uplands

18. The Chiapas Highlands

19. The Yucatan Peninsula

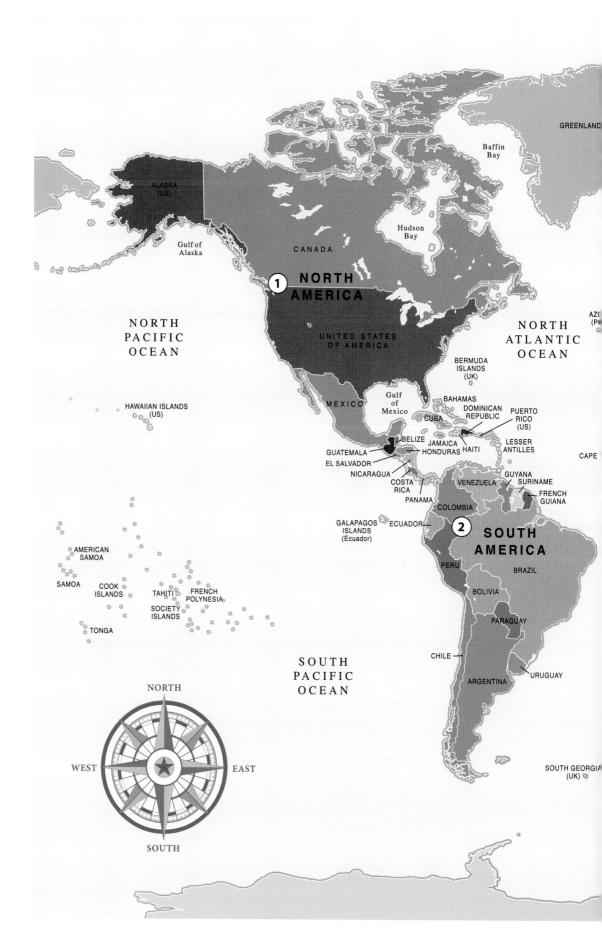

World Map

Continents

1. North America

2. South America

3. Europe

4. Asia

5. Africa

6. Australia

7. Antarctica

ARCTIC OCEAN

SVALBARD
(NORWAY)

FRANZ JOSEF LAND
(RUSSIA)

ICELAND

RUSSIA

④

ASIA

NORTH
PACIFIC
OCEAN

ALEUTIAN ISLANDS
(US)

EUROPE

③

KAZAKHSTAN

MONGOLIA

Caspian
Sea

Black Sea GEORGIA
AZERBAIJAN UZBEKISTAN KYRGYZSTAN
ARMENIA
TURKEY TURKMENISTAN TAJIKISTAN

NORTH
KOREA
SOUTH
KOREA

JAPAN

CYPRUS SYRIA
TUNISIA LEBANON IRAQ
MOROCCO Mediterranean Sea ISRAEL
JORDAN KUWAIT
ALGERIA LIBYA EGYPT BAHRAIN
Red QATAR
SAUDI UNITED
Sea ARABIA ARAB
EMIRATES
MALI NIGER CHAD OMAN
ERITREA YEMEN
BURKINA DJIBOUTI
FASO SUDAN SOMALIA

IRAN AFGHANISTAN

CHINA

PAKISTAN NEPAL BHUTAN

INDIA BANGLADESH
MYANMAR
LAOS

Taiwan

Hong
Kong

⑤

AFRICA

GUINEA
BENIN
IVORY NIGERIA
COAST GHANA TOGO CAMEROON
LIBERIA EQUATORIAL GABON
GUINEA CONGO
DEMOCRATIC
REPUBLIC
OF THE
CONGO

CENTRAL
AFRICAN
REPUBLIC
ETHIOPIA

UGANDA KENYA

RWANDA
BURUNDI
TANZANIA ZANZIBAR
SEYCHELLES

ANDAMAN THAILAND
ISLANDS VIETNAM
(INDIA) CAMBODIA

MALDIVES SRI
LANKA

Philippine
Sea

PHILIPPINES

NORTHERN
MARIANA
ISLANDS
(US)

WAKE ISLAND
(US)

GUAM
(US)

MARSHALL
ISLANDS

FEDERATED STATES
OF MICRONESIA

BRUNEI

MALAYSIA
SINGAPORE

PALAU

KIRIBATI

ANGOLA
ZAMBIA MALAWI
COMOROS

NAMIBIA ZIMBABWE
MOZAMBIQUE

BOTSWANA
MADAGASCAR MAURITIUS

SOUTH
ATLANTIC
OCEAN

SWAZILAND
LESOTHO
SOUTH
AFRICA

INDIAN
OCEAN

INDONESIA

PAPUA
NEW
GUINEA

SOLOMON
ISLANDS

Coral
Sea

VANUATU

⑥

AUSTRALIA

FIJI

NEW
CALEDONIA

SOUTH
PACIFIC
OCEAN

TASMANIA
(AUSTRALIA)

NEW
ZEALAND

ICELAND

NORWAY

SWEDEN

FINLAND

North
Sea

Baltic
Sea

ESTONIA

RUSSIA

IRELAND

UNITED
KINGDOM

DENMARK
NETHER-
LANDS

GERMANY

BELGIUM
LUXEMBOURG

POLAND

LATVIA
LITHUANIA

BELARUS

UKRAINE

CZECH
REPUBLIC
SWITZER-
LAND
FRANCE

SLOVAKIA
AUSTRIA
HUNGARY
SLOVENIA
CROATIA

MOLDOVA

ROMANIA

SOUTHERN
OCEAN

CORSICA
(FR)

MONACO

PORTUGAL

SPAIN

BOSNIA SERBIA
MONTENEGRO
ITALY MACEDONIA BULGARIA
ALBANIA

Black Sea

GREECE

MALTA

Mediterranean Sea

CYPRUS

ANTARCTICA

⑦

Geography and Habitats

1. rain forest	**6.** ocean	**10.** beach
2. waterfall	**7.** peninsula	**11.** forest
3. river	**8.** island	**12.** shore
4. desert	**9.** bay	**13.** lake
5. sand dune		

14. mountain peak	**18.** valley
15. mountain range	**19.** plains
16. hills	**20.** meadow
17. canyon	**21.** pond

More vocabulary

a body of water: a river, lake, or ocean
stream / creek: a very small river

Ask your classmates. Share the answers.

1. Would you rather live near a river or a lake?
2. Would you rather travel through a forest or a desert?
3. How often do you go to the beach or the shore?

The Solar System and the Planets

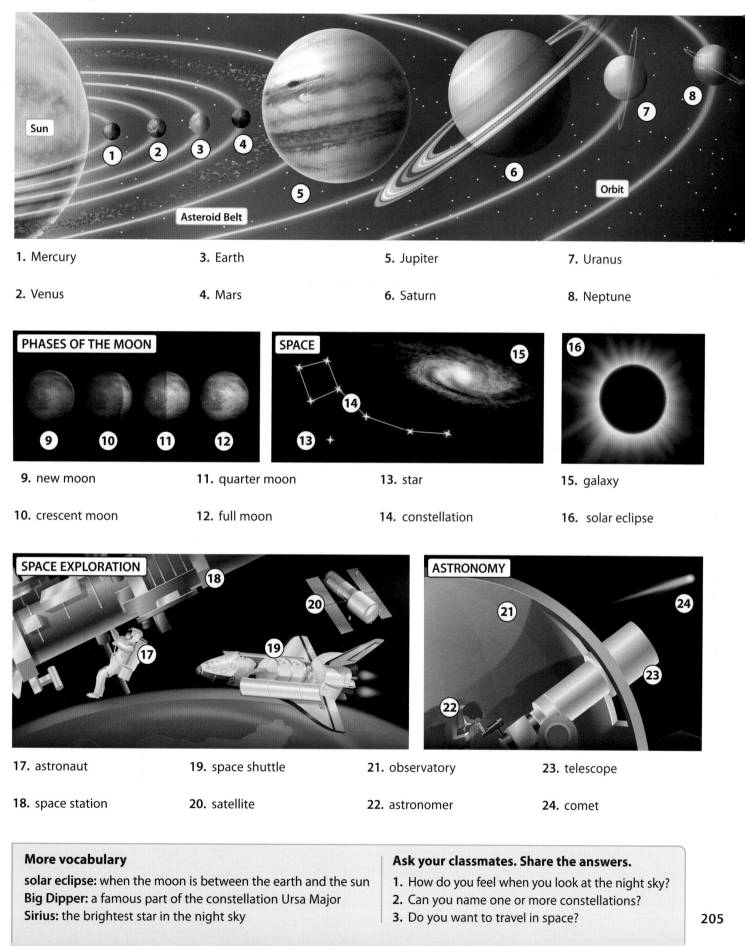

Sun

Asteroid Belt

Orbit

1. Mercury
2. Venus
3. Earth
4. Mars
5. Jupiter
6. Saturn
7. Uranus
8. Neptune

PHASES OF THE MOON

9. new moon
10. crescent moon
11. quarter moon
12. full moon

SPACE

13. star
14. constellation
15. galaxy
16. solar eclipse

SPACE EXPLORATION

17. astronaut
18. space station
19. space shuttle
20. satellite

ASTRONOMY

21. observatory
22. astronomer
23. telescope
24. comet

More vocabulary

solar eclipse: when the moon is between the earth and the sun
Big Dipper: a famous part of the constellation Ursa Major
Sirius: the brightest star in the night sky

Ask your classmates. Share the answers.

1. How do you feel when you look at the night sky?
2. Can you name one or more constellations?
3. Do you want to travel in space?

A Graduation

Home | Search | Invite | Mail |

All Adelia's photos

I loved Art History.

My last economics lesson

Marching Band is great!

The photographer was upset.

We look good!

I get my diploma.

Dad and his digital camera

1. photographer

2. funny photo

3. serious photo

4. guest speaker

5. podium

6. ceremony

7. cap

8. gown

A. **take** a picture

B. **cry**

C. **celebrate**

206

Videos | Music | Classifieds |

People	Comments	
Sara	**June 29th 8:19 p.m.**	
	Great pictures! What a day!	Delete
Zannie baby	**June 30th 10 a.m.**	
	Love the funny photo.	Delete

I'm behind the mayor.

We're all very happy.

Look at the pictures. What do you see?

Answer the questions.

1. How many people are wearing caps and gowns?

2. How many people are being funny? How many are being serious?

3. Who is standing at the podium?

4. Why are the graduates throwing their caps in the air?

📖 Read the story.

A Graduation

Look at these great photos on my web page! The first three are from my favorite classes, but the other pictures are from graduation day.

There are two pictures of my classmates in <u>caps</u> and <u>gowns</u>. In the first picture, we're laughing and the <u>photographer</u> is upset. In the second photo, we're serious. I like the <u>serious photo</u>, but I love the <u>funny photo</u>!

There's also a picture of our <u>guest speaker</u>, the mayor. She is standing at the <u>podium</u>. Next, you can see me at the graduation <u>ceremony</u>. My dad wanted to <u>take a picture</u> of me with my diploma. That's my mom next to him. She <u>cries</u> when she's happy.

After the ceremony, everyone was happy, but no one cried. We wanted to <u>celebrate</u> and we did!

Think about it.

1. What kinds of ceremonies are important for children? for teens? for adults?

2. Imagine you are the guest speaker at a graduation. What will you say to the graduates?

Nature Center

1. trees

2. soil

3. path

4. bird

5. plants

6. rock

7. flowers

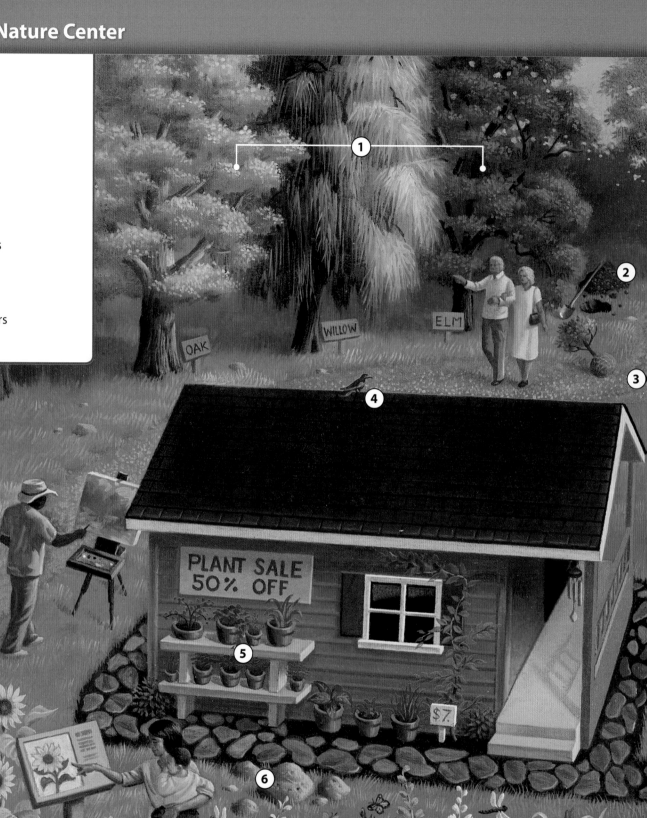

Listen and point. Take turns.

A: *Point to the trees.*
B: *Point to a bird.*
A: *Point to the flowers.*

Dictate to your partner. Take turns.

A: *Write it's a tree.*
B: *Let me check that. I-t-'s -a- t-r-e-e?*
A: *Yes, that's right.*

8. sun

9. sky

10. mammals

11. insects

12. nest

13. water

14. fish

Ways to talk about nature

Look at the sky! Isn't it beautiful?
Did you see the fish / insects?
It's / They're so interesting.

Pair practice. Make new conversations.

A: *Do you know the name of that yellow flower?*
B: *I think it's a sunflower.*
A: *Oh, and what about that blue bird?*

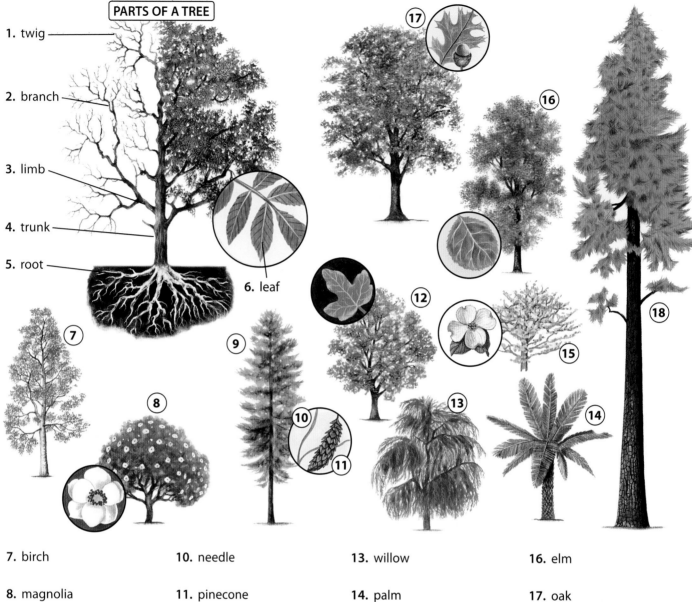

PARTS OF A TREE

1. twig
2. branch
3. limb
4. trunk
5. root
6. leaf

7. birch

8. magnolia

9. pine

10. needle

11. pinecone

12. maple

13. willow

14. palm

15. dogwood

16. elm

17. oak

18. redwood

Plants

19. holly

20. berries

21. cactus

22. vine

23. poison sumac

24. poison oak

25. poison ivy

Parts of a Flower

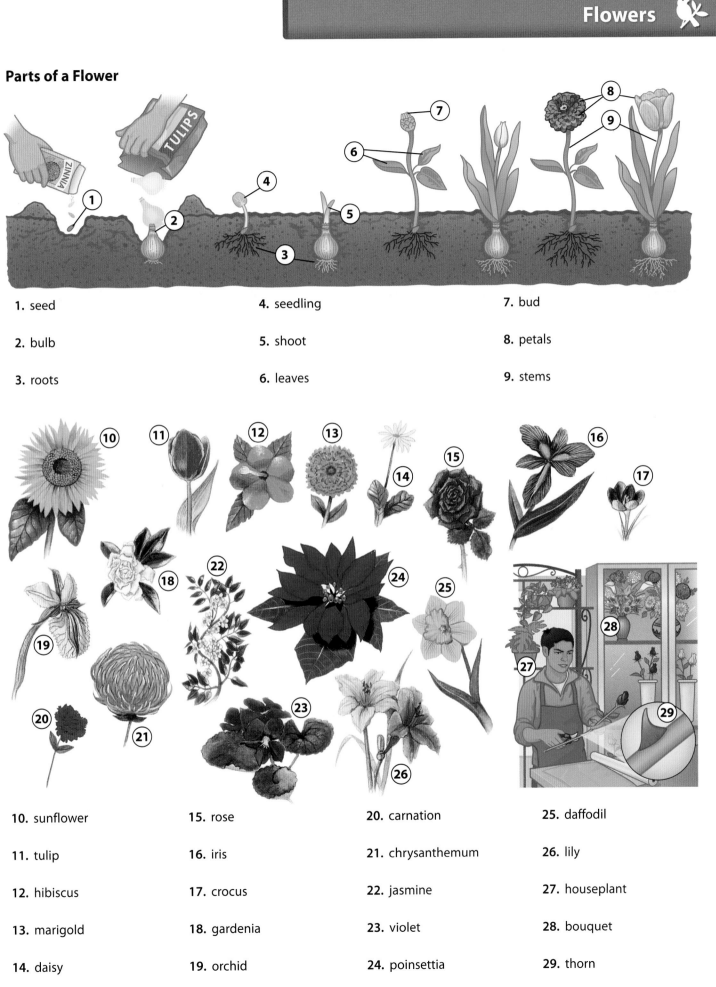

1. seed

2. bulb

3. roots

4. seedling

5. shoot

6. leaves

7. bud

8. petals

9. stems

10. sunflower

11. tulip

12. hibiscus

13. marigold

14. daisy

15. rose

16. iris

17. crocus

18. gardenia

19. orchid

20. carnation

21. chrysanthemum

22. jasmine

23. violet

24. poinsettia

25. daffodil

26. lily

27. houseplant

28. bouquet

29. thorn

Sea Animals

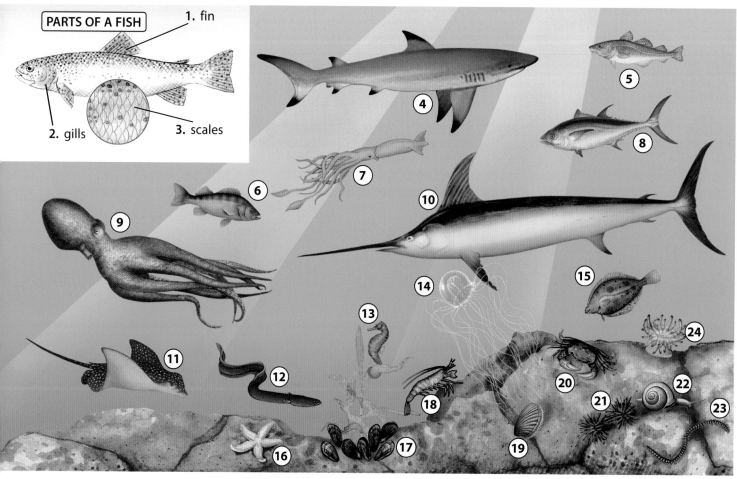

PARTS OF A FISH

1. fin
2. gills
3. scales

4. shark	9. octopus	14. jellyfish	19. scallop	24. sea anemone
5. cod	10. swordfish	15. flounder	20. crab	
6. bass	11. ray	16. starfish	21. sea urchin	
7. squid	12. eel	17. mussel	22. snail	
8. tuna	13. seahorse	18. shrimp	23. worm	

Amphibians

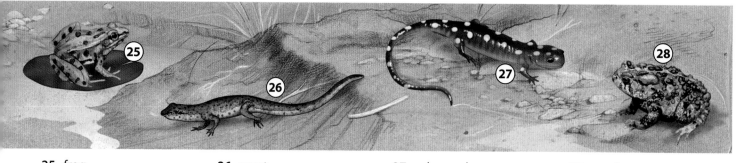

25. frog   26. newt   27. salamander   28. toad

Sea Mammals

29. whale	**31.** dolphin	**33.** sea lion	**35.** sea otter
30. porpoise	**32.** walrus	**34.** seal	

Reptiles

36. alligator	**38.** rattlesnake	**40.** lizard	**42.** tortoise
37. crocodile	**39.** garter snake	**41.** cobra	**43.** turtle

Birds, Insects, and Arachnids

PARTS OF A BIRD

1. wing
2. claw
3. beak / bill
4. feather

5. owl	8. woodpecker	11. penguin	14. peacock
6. blue jay	9. eagle	12. duck	15. pigeon
7. sparrow	10. hummingbird	13. goose	16. robin

Insects and Arachnids

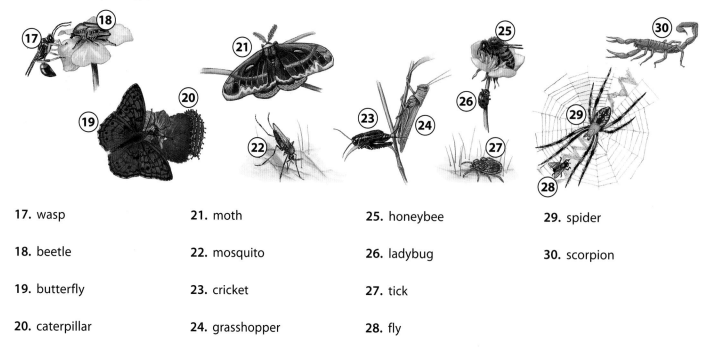

17. wasp	21. moth	25. honeybee	29. spider
18. beetle	22. mosquito	26. ladybug	30. scorpion
19. butterfly	23. cricket	27. tick	
20. caterpillar	24. grasshopper	28. fly	

Domestic Animals and Rodents

Farm Animals

1. cow
2. pig
3. donkey
4. horse
5. goat
6. sheep
7. rooster
8. hen

Pets

9. cat
10. kitten
11. dog
12. puppy
13. rabbit
14. guinea pig
15. parakeet
16. goldfish

Rodents

17. rat
18. mouse
19. gopher
20. chipmunk
21. squirrel
22. prairie dog

More vocabulary

domesticated: animals that work for and / or live with people

wild: animals that live away from people

Ask your classmates. Share the answers.

1. Have you worked with farm animals? Which ones?
2. Are you afraid of rodents? Which ones?
3. Do you have a pet? What kind?

215

1. moose	**5.** wolf	**9.** beaver	**13.** raccoon
2. mountain lion	**6.** buffalo / bison	**10.** porcupine	**14.** deer
3. coyote	**7.** bat	**11.** bear	**15.** fox
4. opossum	**8.** armadillo	**12.** skunk	

16. antlers	**18.** whiskers	**20.** paw	**22.** tail
17. hooves	**19.** coat / fur	**21.** horn	**23.** quill

24. anteater	**29.** gorilla	**34.** leopard	**39.** orangutan	**44.** kangaroo
25. llama	**30.** hyena	**35.** antelope	**40.** panther	**45.** koala
26. monkey	**31.** baboon	**36.** lion	**41.** panda	**46.** platypus
27. chimpanzee	**32.** giraffe	**37.** tiger	**42.** elephant	
28. rhinoceros	**33.** zebra	**38.** camel	**43.** hippopotamus	

47. trunk   **48.** tusk   **49.** mane   **50.** pouch   **51.** hump

Energy and Conservation

Energy Sources

1. solar energy

2. wind power

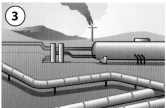

3. natural gas

4. coal

5. hydroelectric power

6. oil / petroleum

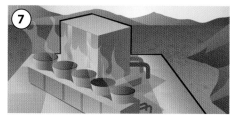

7. geothermal energy

8. nuclear energy

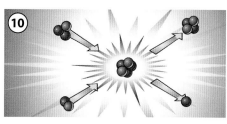

9. biomass / bioenergy

10. fusion

Pollution

11. air pollution / smog

12. hazardous waste

13. acid rain

14. water pollution

15. radiation

16. pesticide poisoning

17. oil spill

Ask your classmates. Share the answers.

1. What types of things do you recycle?
2. What types of energy sources are in your area?
3. What types of pollution do you worry about?

Think about it. Discuss.

1. How can you save energy in the summer? winter?
2. What are some other ways that people can conserve energy or prevent pollution?

Ways to Conserve Energy and Resources

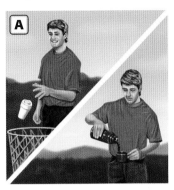

A. **reduce** trash

B. **reuse** shopping bags

C. **recycle**

D. **buy** recycled products

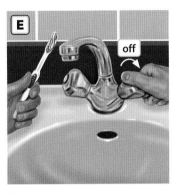

E. **save** water

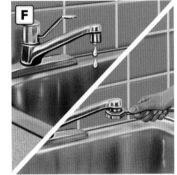

F. **fix** leaky faucets

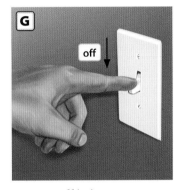

G. **turn off** lights

H. **use** energy-efficient bulbs

I. **carpool**

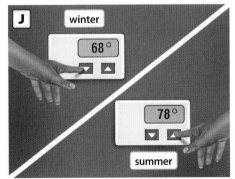

J. **adjust** the thermostat

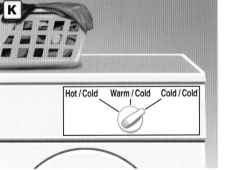

K. **wash** clothes in cold water

L. **don't litter**

M. **compost** food scraps

N. **plant** a tree

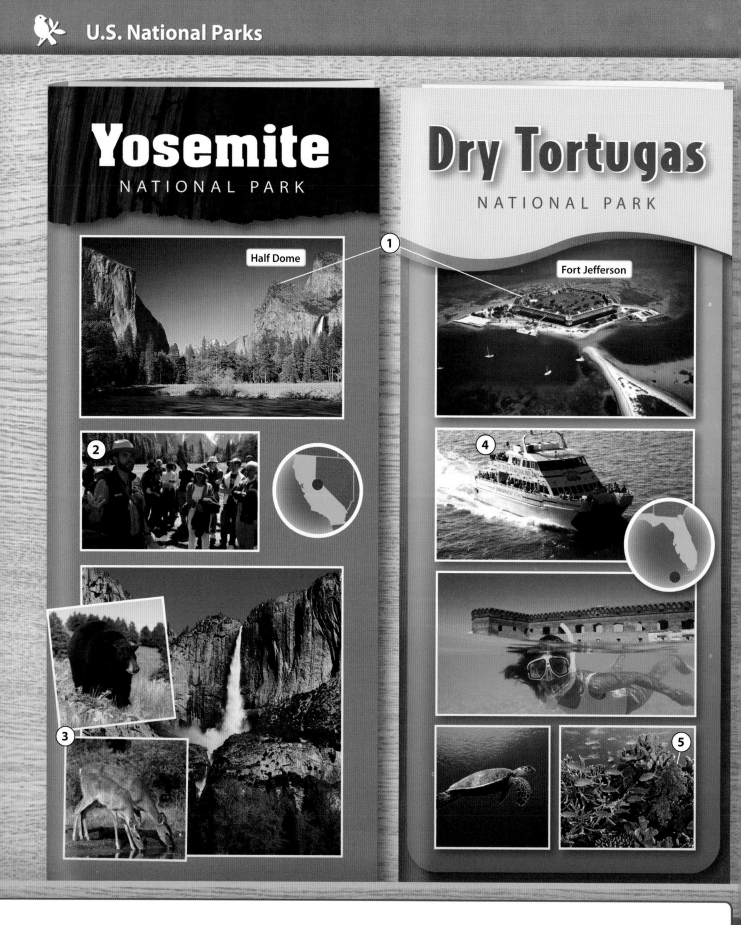

Yosemite
NATIONAL PARK

Half Dome

1

2

3

Dry Tortugas
NATIONAL PARK

Fort Jefferson

4

5

1. landmarks	**3.** wildlife	**5.** coral	**7.** caverns
2. park ranger	**4.** ferry	**6.** cave	**A. take** a tour

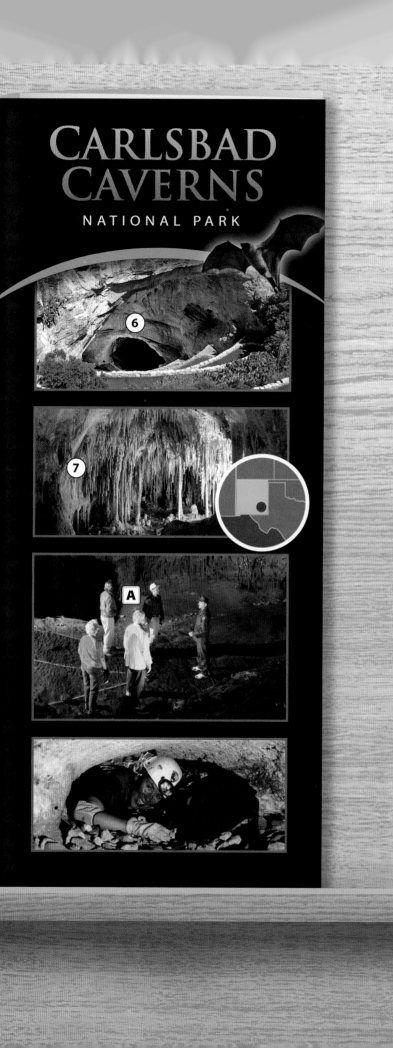

Look at the pictures. What do you see?

Answer the questions.

1. How many U.S. landmarks are in the pictures?
2. What kinds of wildlife do you see?
3. What can you do at Carlsbad Caverns?

📖 **Read the story.**

U.S. National Parks

More than 200 million people visit U.S. National Parks every year. These parks protect the <u>wildlife</u> and <u>landmarks</u> of the United States. Each park is different, and each one is beautiful.

At Yosemite, in California, you can take a nature walk with a <u>park ranger</u>. You'll see waterfalls, redwoods, and deer there.

In south Florida, you can take a <u>ferry</u> to Dry Tortugas. It's great to snorkel around the park's <u>coral</u> islands.

There are 113 <u>caves</u> at Carlsbad <u>Caverns</u> in New Mexico. The deepest cave is 830 feet below the desert! You can <u>take a tour</u> of these beautiful caverns.

There are 391 national parks to see. Go online for information about a park near you.

Think about it.

1. Why are national parks important?
2. Imagine you are a park ranger at a national park. Give your classmates a tour of the landmarks and wildlife.

221

1. zoo

2. movies

3. botanical garden

4. bowling alley

5. rock concert

6. swap meet / flea market

7. aquarium

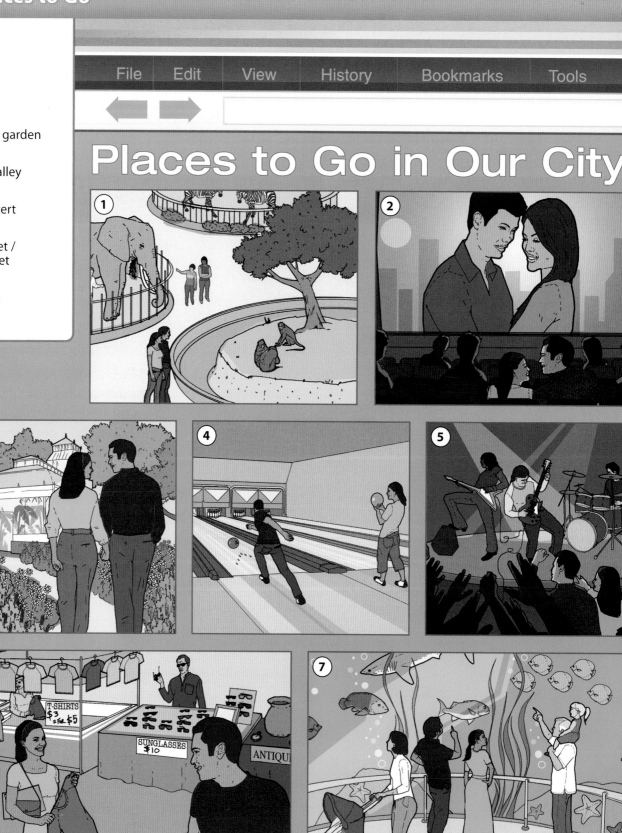

File   Edit   View   History   Bookmarks   Tools

Places to Go in Our City

Listen and point. Take turns.

A: *Point to the zoo.*
B: *Point to the flea market.*
A: *Point to the rock concert.*

Dictate to your partner. Take turns.

A: *Write these words: zoo, movies, aquarium.*
B: *Zoo, movies, and what?*
A: *Aquarium.*

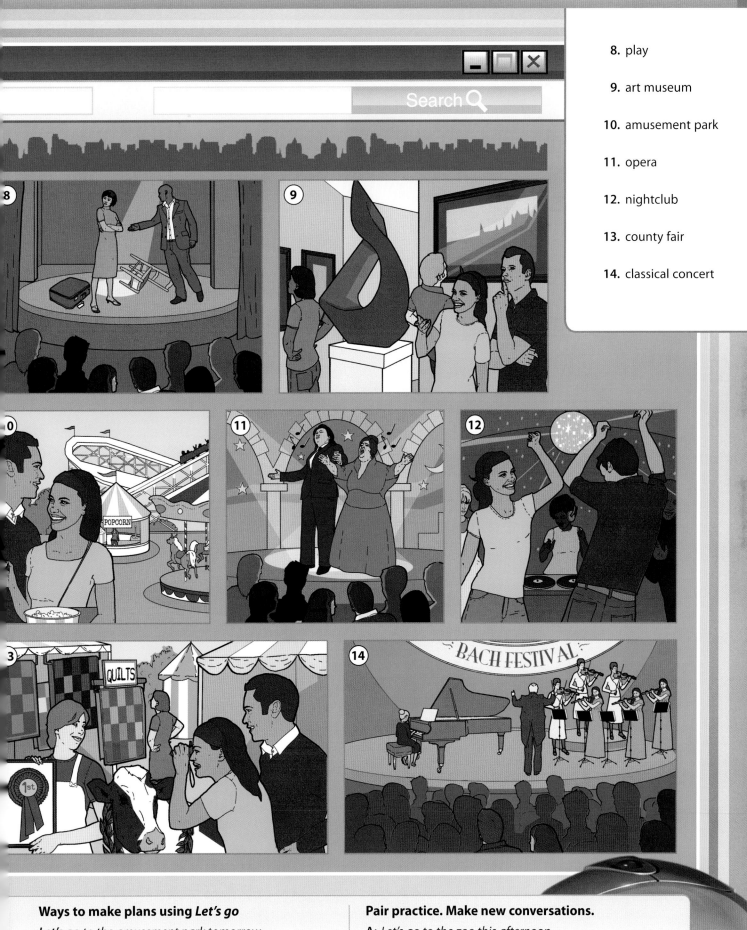

8. play

9. art museum

10. amusement park

11. opera

12. nightclub

13. county fair

14. classical concert

Ways to make plans using *Let's go*

Let's go to <u>the amusement park</u> tomorrow.
Let's go to <u>the opera</u> on Saturday.
Let's go to <u>the movies</u> tonight.

Pair practice. Make new conversations.

A: <u>Let's go to the zoo this afternoon</u>.
B: *OK. And let's go to <u>the movies tonight</u>.*
A: *That sounds like a good plan.*

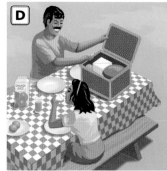

The Park and Playground

1. ball field

2. cyclist

3. bike path

4. jump rope

5. fountain

6. tennis court

7. skateboard

8. picnic table

9. water fountain

10. bench

11. swings

12. tricycle

13. slide

14. climbing apparatus

15. sandbox

16. seesaw

A. **pull** the wagon

B. **push** the swing

C. **climb** the bars

D. **picnic / have** a picnic

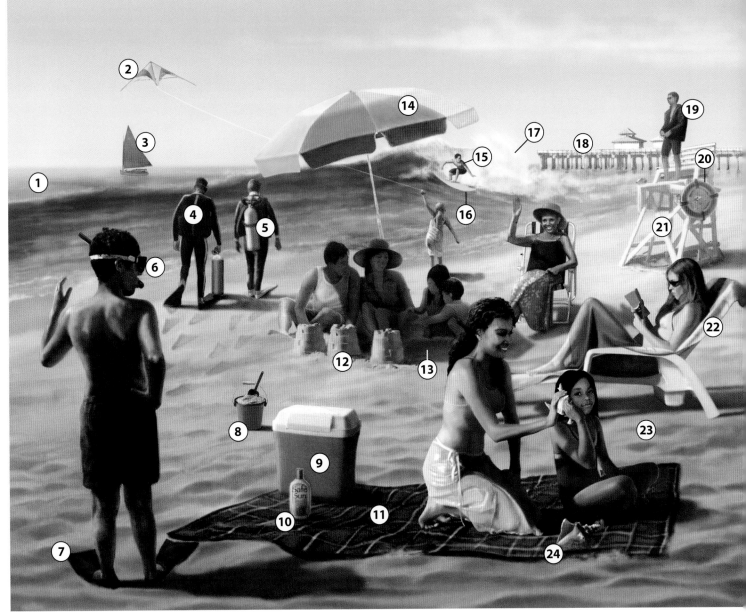

1. ocean / water
2. kite
3. sailboat
4. wet suit
5. scuba tank
6. diving mask

7. fins
8. pail / bucket
9. cooler
10. sunscreen / sunblock
11. blanket
12. sand castle

13. shade
14. beach umbrella
15. surfer
16. surfboard
17. wave
18. pier

19. lifeguard
20. lifesaving device
21. lifeguard station
22. beach chair
23. sand
24. seashell

More vocabulary

seaweed: a plant that grows in the ocean
tide: the level of the ocean. The tide goes in and out every 12 hours.

Ask your classmates. Share the answers.

1. Do you like to go to the beach?
2. Are there famous beaches in your native country?
3. Do you prefer to be on the sand or in the water?

225

1. boating
2. rafting
3. canoeing

4. fishing
5. camping
6. backpacking

7. hiking
8. mountain biking
9. horseback riding

10. tent
11. campfire
12. sleeping bag
13. foam pad
14. life vest

15. backpack
16. camping stove
17. fishing net
18. fishing pole
19. rope

20. multi-use knife
21. matches
22. lantern
23. insect repellent
24. canteen

1. downhill skiing

2. snowboarding

3. cross-country skiing

4. ice skating

5. figure skating

6. sledding

7. waterskiing

8. sailing

9. surfing

10. windsurfing

11. snorkeling

12. scuba diving

More vocabulary

speed skating: racing while ice skating
windsurfing: sailboarding

Ask your classmates. Share the answers.

1. Which of these sports do you like?
2. Which of these sports would you like to learn?
3. Which of these sports is the most fun to watch?

1. archery

2. billiards / pool

3. bowling

4. boxing

5. cycling / biking

6. badminton

7. fencing

8. golf

9. gymnastics

10. inline skating

11. martial arts

12. racquetball

13. skateboarding

14. table tennis

15. tennis

16. weightlifting

17. wrestling

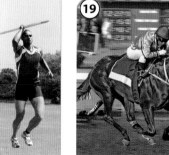
18. track and field

19. horse racing

Pair practice. Make new conversations.

A: *What sports do you like?*
B: *I like <u>bowling</u>. What do you like?*
A: *I like <u>gymnastics</u>.*

Think about it. Discuss.

1. Why do people like to watch sports?
2. Which sports can be dangerous?
3. Why do people do dangerous sports?

1. score
2. coach
3. team
4. fan
5. player
6. official / referee
7. basketball court

8. basketball

9. baseball

10. softball

11. football

12. soccer

13. ice hockey

14. volleyball

15. water polo

More Vocabulary

win: to have the best score
lose: the opposite of win
tie: to have the same score

captain: the team leader
umpire: the name of the referee in baseball
Little League: a baseball and softball program for children

229

A. pitch

B. hit

C. throw

D. catch

E. kick

F. tackle

G. pass

H. shoot

I. jump

J. dribble

K. dive

L. swim

M. stretch

N. exercise / work out

O. bend

P. serve

Q. swing

R. start

S. race

T. finish

U. skate

V. ski

Use the new words.
Look on page 229. Name the actions you see.

A: He's <u>throwing</u>.

B: She's <u>jumping</u>.

Ways to talk about your sports skills

I can <u>throw</u>, but I can't <u>catch</u>.

I <u>swim</u> well, but I don't <u>dive</u> well.

I'm good at <u>skating</u>, but I'm terrible at <u>skiing</u>.

1. golf club	**8.** arrow	**15.** catcher's mask	**22.** weights
2. tennis racket	**9.** ice skates	**16.** uniform	**23.** snowboard
3. volleyball	**10.** inline skates	**17.** glove	**24.** skis
4. basketball	**11.** hockey stick	**18.** baseball	**25.** ski poles
5. bowling ball	**12.** soccer ball	**19.** football helmet	**26.** ski boots
6. bow	**13.** shin guards	**20.** shoulder pads	**27.** flying disc*
7. target	**14.** baseball bat	**21.** football	*** Note:** one brand is Frisbee®, of Wham-O, Inc.

Use the new words.
Look at pages 228–229. Name the sports equipment you see.

A: *Those are ice skates*.
B: *That's a football*.

Ask your classmates. Share the answers.

1. Do you own any sports equipment? What kind?
2. What do you want to buy at this store?
3. Where is the best place to buy sports equipment?

A. **collect** things   B. **play** games   C. **quilt**   D. **do** crafts

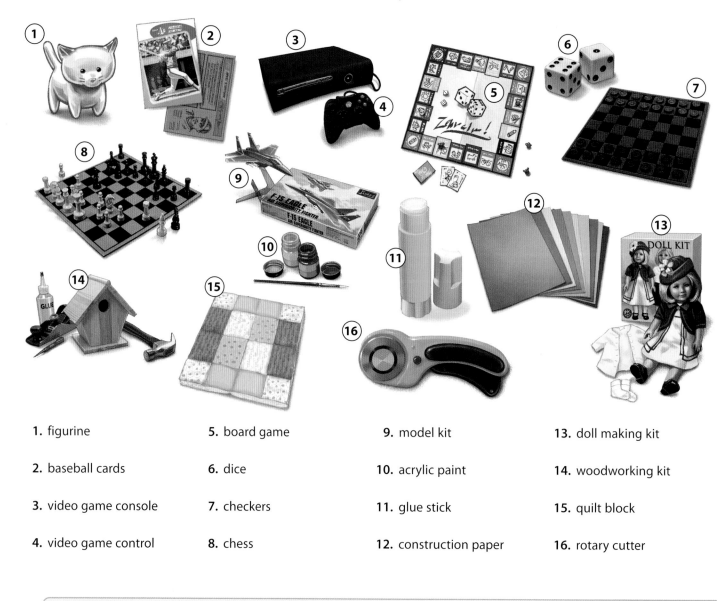

1. figurine

2. baseball cards

3. video game console

4. video game control

5. board game

6. dice

7. checkers

8. chess

9. model kit

10. acrylic paint

11. glue stick

12. construction paper

13. doll making kit

14. woodworking kit

15. quilt block

16. rotary cutter

Grammar Point: *How often do you play cards?*

*I play **all the time**. (every day)*

*I play **sometimes**. (once a month)*

*I **never** play. (0 times)*

Pair practice. Make new conversations.

A: *How often do you do your hobbies?*

B: *I play games all the time. I love chess.*

A: *Really? I never play chess.*

E. paint   **F. knit**   **G. pretend**   **H. play** cards

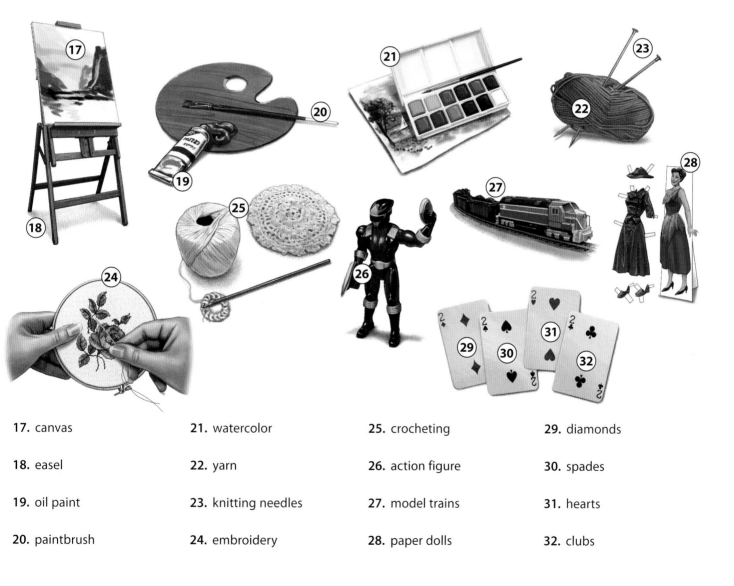

17. canvas

18. easel

19. oil paint

20. paintbrush

21. watercolor

22. yarn

23. knitting needles

24. embroidery

25. crocheting

26. action figure

27. model trains

28. paper dolls

29. diamonds

30. spades

31. hearts

32. clubs

Ways to talk about hobbies and games

*This <u>board game</u> is **interesting**. It makes me think.*
*That <u>video game</u> is **boring**. Nothing happens.*
*I love to <u>play cards</u>. It's **fun** to play with my friends.*

Ask your classmates. Share the answers.

1. Do you collect anything? What?
2. Which games do you like to play?
3. What hobbies did you have as a child?

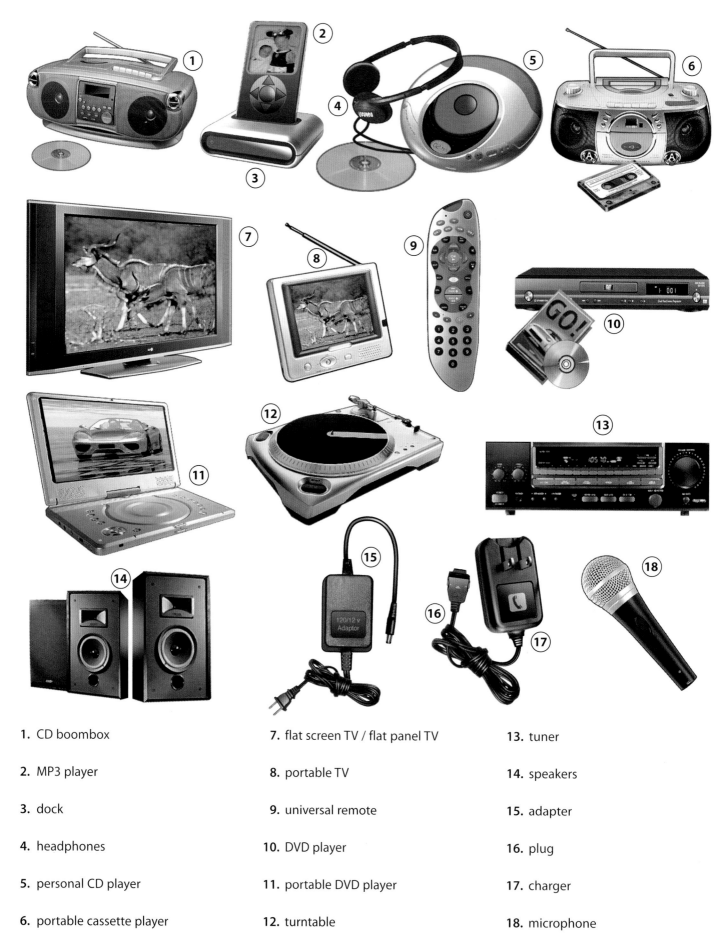

1. CD boombox
2. MP3 player
3. dock
4. headphones
5. personal CD player
6. portable cassette player

7. flat screen TV / flat panel TV
8. portable TV
9. universal remote
10. DVD player
11. portable DVD player
12. turntable

13. tuner
14. speakers
15. adapter
16. plug
17. charger
18. microphone

19. digital camera

20. memory card

21. film camera / 35 mm camera

22. film

23. zoom lens

24. camcorder

25. tripod

26. battery pack

27. battery charger

28. camera case

29. LCD projector

30. screen

31. photo album

32. digital photo album

33. out of focus

34. overexposed

35. underexposed

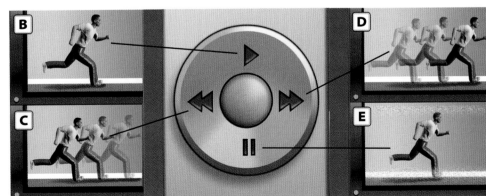

A. record

B. play

C. rewind

D. fast forward

E. pause

Types of TV Programs

1. news program

2. sitcom (situation comedy)

3. cartoon

4. talk show

5. soap opera

6. reality show

7. nature program

8. game show

9. children's program

10. shopping program

11. sports program

12. drama

Types of Movies

13. comedy

14. tragedy

15. western

16. romance

17. horror story

18. science fiction story

19. action story / adventure story

20. mystery / suspense

Types of Music

21. classical

22. blues

23. rock

24. jazz

25. pop

26. hip hop

27. country

28. R&B / soul

29. folk

30. gospel

31. reggae

32. world music

Music

A	B	C	D

A. play an instrument   **B. sing** a song   **C. conduct** an orchestra   **D. be** in a rock band

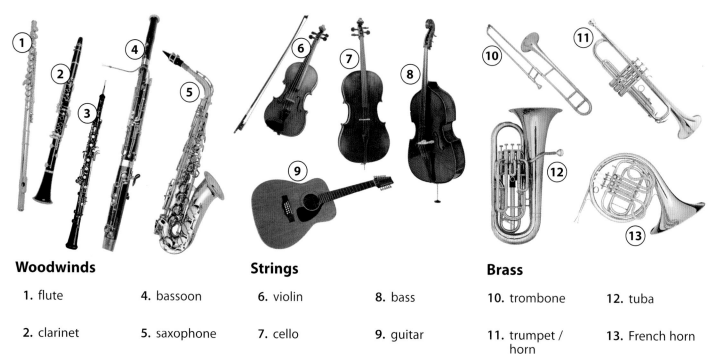

Woodwinds

1. flute
2. clarinet
3. oboe
4. bassoon
5. saxophone

Strings

6. violin
7. cello
8. bass
9. guitar

Brass

10. trombone
11. trumpet / horn
12. tuba
13. French horn

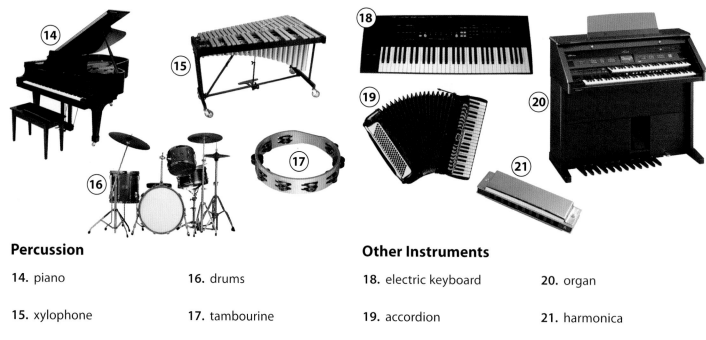

Percussion

14. piano
15. xylophone
16. drums
17. tambourine

Other Instruments

18. electric keyboard
19. accordion
20. organ
21. harmonica

1. parade
2. float
3. confetti
4. couple
5. card
6. heart
7. fireworks
8. flag
9. mask
10. jack-o'-lantern
11. costume
12. candy
13. feast
14. turkey
15. ornament
16. Christmas tree
17. candy cane
18. string lights

*Thanksgiving is on the fourth Thursday in November.

1. decorations 3. present / gift B. **make** a wish D. **hide** F. **wrap**

2. deck A. **videotape** C. **blow out** E. **bring**

**Look at the picture.
What do you see?**

Answer the questions.

1. What kinds of decorations do you see?

2. What are people doing at this birthday party?

3. What wish did the teenager make?

4. How many presents did people bring?

📖 **Read the story.**

A Birthday Party

Today is Lou and Gani Bombata's birthday barbecue. There are <u>decorations</u> around the backyard, and food and drinks on the <u>deck</u>. There are also <u>presents</u>. Everyone in the Bombata family likes to <u>bring</u> presents.

Right now, it's time for cake. Gani <u>is blowing out</u> the candles, and Lou <u>is making a wish</u>. Lou's mom wants to <u>videotape</u> everyone, but she can't find Lou's brother, Todd. Todd hates to sing, so he always <u>hides</u> for the birthday song.

Lou's sister, Amaka, has to <u>wrap</u> some <u>gifts</u>. She doesn't want Lou to see. Amaka isn't worried. She knows her family loves to sing. She can put her gifts on the present table before they finish the first song.

Think about it.

1. What wish do you think Gani made?

2. What kinds of presents do you give to relatives? What kinds of presents can you give to friends or co-workers?

241

Verb Guide

Verbs in English are either regular or irregular in the past tense and past participle forms.

Regular Verbs

The regular verbs below are marked 1, 2, 3, or 4 according to four different spelling patterns.
(See page 244 for the irregular verbs which do not follow any of these patterns.)

Spelling Patterns for the Past and the Past Participle	Example	
1. Add -ed to the end of the verb.	**ASK**	**ASKED**
2. Add -d to the end of the verb.	**LIVE**	**LIVED**
3. Double the final consonant and add -ed to the end of the verb.	**DROP**	**DROPPED**
4. Drop the final y and add -ied to the end of the verb.	**CRY**	**CRIED**

The Oxford Picture Dictionary List of Regular Verbs

accept (1)
add (1)
address (1)
adjust (1)
agree (2)
answer (1)
apologize (2)
appear (1)
applaud (1)
apply (4)
arrange (2)
arrest (1)
arrive (2)
ask (1)
assemble (2)
assist (1)
attach (1)
bake (2)
bank (1)
bargain (1)
bathe (2)
board (1)
boil (1)
borrow (1)
bow (1)
brainstorm (1)
breathe (2)
browse (2)
brush (1)
bubble (2)
buckle (2)
burn (1)
bus (1)
calculate (2)
call (1)
capitalize (2)
carpool (1)

carry (4)
cash (1)
celebrate (2)
change (2)
check (1)
chill (1)
choke (2)
chop (3)
circle (2)
claim (1)
clean (1)
clear (1)
click (1)
climb (1)
close (2)
collate (2)
collect (1)
color (1)
comb (1)
comfort (1)
commit (3)
compliment (1)
compost (1)
conceal (1)
conduct (1)
convert (1)
convict (1)
cook (1)
copy (4)
correct (1)
cough (1)
count (1)
cross (1)
cry (4)
dance (2)
debate (2)
decline (2)

delete (2)
deliver (1)
design (1)
dial (1)
dice (2)
dictate (2)
die (2)
disagree (2)
discipline (2)
discuss (1)
dive (2)
divide (2)
dress (1)
dribble (2)
drill (1)
drop (3)
drown (1)
dry (4)
dust (1)
dye (2)
edit (1)
empty (4)
enter (1)
erase (2)
evacuate (2)
examine (2)
exchange (2)
exercise (2)
expire (2)
explain (1)
exterminate (2)
fasten (1)
fast forward (1)
fax (1)
fertilize (2)
fill (1)
finish (1)

fix (1)
floss (1)
fold (1)
follow (1)
garden (1)
gargle (2)
graduate (2)
grate (2)
grease (2)
greet (1)
hail (1)
hammer (1)
hand (1)
harvest (1)
help (1)
hire (2)
hug (3)
immigrate (2)
indent (1)
inquire (2)
insert (1)
inspect (1)
install (1)
introduce (2)
invite (2)
iron (1)
jaywalk (1)
join (1)
jump (1)
kick (1)
kiss (1)
knit (3)
label (1)
land (1)
laugh (1)
learn (1)
lengthen (1)

lift (1)
listen (1)
litter (1)
live (2)
load (1)
lock (1)
look (1)
mail (1)
manufacture (2)
match (1)
measure (2)
microwave (2)
milk (1)
misbehave (2)
miss (1)
mix (1)
mop (3)
move (2)
mow (1)
multiply (4)
negotiate (2)
network (1)
numb (1)
nurse (2)
obey (1)
observe (2)
offer (1)
open (1)
operate (2)
order (1)
organize (2)
overdose (2)
pack (1)
paint (1)
park (1)
participate (2)
pass (1)
pause (2)
peel (1)
perm (1)
pick (1)

pitch (1)
plan (3)
plant (1)
play (1)
polish (1)
pour (1)
praise (2)
preheat (1)
prepare (2)
prescribe (2)
press (1)
pretend (1)
print (1)
program (3)
protect (1)
pull (1)
purchase (2)
push (1)
quilt (1)
race (2)
raise (2)
rake (2)
receive (2)
record (1)
recycle (2)
redecorate (2)
reduce (2)
register (1)
relax (1)
remain (1)
remove (2)
renew (1)
repair (1)
replace (2)
report (1)
request (1)
retire (2)
return (1)
reuse (2)
revise (2)
rinse (2)

rock (1)
sauté (1)
save (2)
scan (3)
schedule (2)
scrub (3)
seat (1)
select (1)
sentence (2)
separate (2)
serve (2)
share (2)
shave (2)
ship (3)
shop (3)
shorten (1)
sign (1)
simmer (1)
skate (2)
ski (1)
slice (2)
smell (1)
smile (2)
smoke (2)
sneeze (2)
solve (2)
sort (1)
spell (1)
spoon (1)
staple (2)
start (1)
state (2)
stay (1)
steam (1)
stir (3)
stop (3)
stow (1)
stretch (1)
study (4)
submit (3)
subtract (1)

supervise (2)
swallow (1)
tackle (2)
talk (1)
taste (2)
thank (1)
tie (2)
touch (1)
transcribe (2)
transfer (3)
translate (2)
travel (1)
trim (3)
try (4)
turn (1)
type (2)
underline (2)
undress (1)
unload (1)
unpack (1)
unscramble (2)
use (2)
vacuum (1)
videotape (2)
volunteer (1)
vomit (1)
vote (2)
wait (1)
walk (1)
wash (1)
watch (1)
water (1)
wave (2)
weed (1)
weigh (1)
wipe (2)
work (1)
wrap (3)

243

Verb Guide

Irregular Verbs

These verbs have irregular endings in the past and/or the past participle.

The Oxford Picture Dictionary List of Irregular Verbs

simple	past	past participle	simple	past	past participle
be	was	been	make	made	made
beat	beat	beaten	meet	met	met
become	became	become	pay	paid	paid
bend	bent	bent	picnic	picnicked	picnicked
bleed	bled	bled	proofread	proofread	proofread
blow	blew	blown	put	put	put
break	broke	broken	read	read	read
bring	brought	brought	rewind	rewound	rewound
buy	bought	bought	rewrite	rewrote	rewritten
catch	caught	caught	ride	rode	ridden
choose	chose	chosen	run	ran	run
come	came	come	say	said	said
cut	cut	cut	see	saw	seen
do	did	done	seek	sought	sought
draw	drew	drawn	sell	sold	sold
drink	drank	drunk	send	sent	sent
drive	drove	driven	set	set	set
eat	ate	eaten	sew	sewed	sewn
fall	fell	fallen	shake	shook	shaken
feed	fed	fed	shoot	shot	shot
feel	felt	felt	show	showed	shown
find	found	found	sing	sang	sung
fly	flew	flown	sit	sat	sat
get	got	gotten	speak	spoke	spoken
give	gave	given	stand	stood	stood
go	went	gone	steal	stole	stolen
hang	hung	hung	sweep	swept	swept
have	had	had	swim	swam	swum
hear	heard	heard	swing	swung	swung
hide	hid	hidden	take	took	taken
hit	hit	hit	teach	taught	taught
hold	held	held	think	thought	thought
keep	kept	kept	throw	threw	thrown
lay	laid	laid	wake	woke	woken
leave	left	left	withdraw	withdrew	withdrawn
lend	lent	lent	write	wrote	written
let	let	let			

Index

Index Key

Font
bold type = verbs or verb phrases (example: **catch**)
ordinary type = all other parts of speech (example: baseball)
ALL CAPS = unit titles (example: MATHEMATICS)
Initial caps = subunit titles (example: Equivalencies)

Symbols
✦ = word found in exercise band at bottom of page

Numbers/Letters
first number in **bold** type = page on which word appears
second number, or letter, following number in **bold** type = item number on page
(examples: cool [ko͞ol] **13**-5 means that the word *cool* is item number 5 on page 13;
across [ə krös/] **153**–G means that the word *across* is item G on page 153).

Pronunciation Guide

The index includes a pronunciation guide for all the words and phrases illustrated in the book. This guide uses symbols commonly found in dictionaries for native speakers. These symbols, unlike those used in pronunciation systems such as the International Phonetic Alphabet, tend to use English spelling patterns and so should help you to become more aware of the connections between written English and spoken English.

Consonants

[b] as in back [băk]	[k] as in key [kē]	[sh] as in shoe [sho͞o]
[ch] as in cheek [chēk]	[l] as in leaf [lēf]	[t] as in tape [tāp]
[d] as in date [dāt]	[m] as in match [măch]	[th] as in three [thrē]
[dh] as in this [dhĭs]	[n] as in neck [nĕk]	[v] as in vine [vīn]
[f] as in face [fās]	[ng] as in ring [rĭng]	[w] as in wait [wāt]
[g] as in gas [găs]	[p] as in park [pärk]	[y] as in yams [yămz]
[h] as in half [hăf]	[r] as in rice [rīs]	[z] as in zoo [zo͞o]
[j] as in jam [jăm]	[s] as in sand [sănd]	[zh] as in measure [mĕzhər]

Vowels

[ā] as in bake [bāk]	[ī] as in line [līn]	[o͝o] as in cook [ko͝ok]
[ă] as in back [băk]	[ĭ] as in lip [lĭp]	[ow] as in cow [kow]
[ä] as in car [kär] or box [bäks]	[ï] as in near [nïr]	[oy] as in boy [boy]
[ē] as in beat [bēt]	[ō] as in cold [kōld]	[ŭ] as in cut [kŭt]
[ĕ] as in bed [bĕd]	[ö] as in short [shört] or claw [klö]	[ü] as in curb [kürb]
[ë] as in bear [bër]	[o͞o] as in cool [ko͞ol]	[ə] as in above [ə bŭv/]

All the pronunciation symbols used are alphabetical except for the schwa [ə]. The schwa is the most frequent vowel sound in English. If you use the schwa appropriately in unstressed syllables, your pronunciation will sound more natural.

Vowels before [r] are shown with the symbol [¨] to call attention to the special quality that vowels have before [r]. (Note that the symbols [ä] and [ö] are also used for vowels not followed by [r], as in *box* or *claw*.) You should listen carefully to native speakers to discover how these vowels actually sound.

Stress

This index follows the system for marking stress used in many dictionaries for native speakers.
1. Stress is not marked if a word consisting of a single syllable occurs by itself.
2. Where stress is marked, two levels are distinguished:
a bold accent [/] is placed after each syllable with primary (or strong) stress, a light accent [/] is placed after each syllable with secondary (or weaker) stress. In phrases and other combinations of words, stress is indicated for each word as it would be pronounced within the whole phrase.

Syllable Boundaries

Syllable boundaries are indicated by a single space or by a stress mark.

Note: The pronunciations shown in this index are based on patterns of American English. There has been no attempt to represent all of the varieties of American English. Students should listen to native speakers to hear how the language actually sounds in a particular region.

Index

Abbreviations [ə brē/vē ā/shənz] **48**
abdomen [ăb/də mən] **107**–27
about [ə bowt/] **48**–B, **174**–L, **191**–E
above [ə bŭv/] **25**–4
accelerator [ĭk sĕl/ə rā/tər] **159**–46
accept [ĭk sĕpt/] **12**–G, **12**–I, **12** ✦
access number [ăk/sĕs/ nŭm/bər] **14**–16
Accessories [ĭk sĕs/ə rēz] **59, 94**–**95**
accident [ăk/sə dənt] **144**–2
accordion [ə kör/dē ən] **238**–19
account [ə kownt/] **132**–11, **132**–14
    account manager [ə kownt/ măn/ə jər] **132**–9
Account [ə kownt/] **132**
accountant [ə kown/tənt] **166**–1
ache [āk]
    backache [băk/āk/] **110**–5
    earache [ïr/āk/] **110**–3
    headache [hĕd/āk/] **110**–1
    stomachache [stŭm/ək/ āk/] **110**–4
    toothache [tooth/āk/] **110**–2
acid rain [ăs/əd rān/] **218**–13
across [ə krös/] **153**–G
acrylic paint [ə krĭl/ĭk pānt] **232**–10
action [ăk/shən]
    action figure [ăk/shən fĭg/yər] **233**–26
    action story [ăk/shən stör/ē] **237**–19
activist [ăk/tə vĭst] **199**–17
actor [ăk/tər] **166**–2
acupuncture [ăk/yə pŭngk/chər] **122**–2
acute angle [ə kyoot/ ăng/gəl] **193**–28
ad [ăd] **48**–2, **197**–9
adapter [ə dăp/tər] **234**–15
add [ăd] **77**–N, **101**–B, **192**–A
address [ə drĕs/, ă/drĕs] **4**–5
    mailing address [mā/lĭng ə drĕs/, –ă/drĕs] **134**–22
    return address [rĭ türn/ ə drĕs/, –ă/drĕs] **134**–21
    website address [wĕb/sīt ə drĕs/, –ă/drĕs] **197**–4
address [ə drĕs/] **135**–B, **197**–C
adhesive bandage [əd hē/sĭv băn/dĭj] **117**–5
adjust [ə jŭst/] **219**–J
    adjustable wrench [ə jŭs/tə bəl rĕnch/] **181**–48
    adjustment [ə jŭst/mənt] **194**–23, **194**–24
administrative assistant
    [əd mĭn/ə strā/tĭv ə sĭs/tənt] **166**–3
administrator [əd mĭn/ə strā/tər] **120**–13
Administrators [əd mĭn/ə strā/tərz] **5**
admissions clerk [əd mĭ/shənz klürk/] **120**–14
ADULTS AND CHILDREN [ə dŭlts/ en chĭl/ drən] **30**–**31**
adult school [ə dŭlt/ skool/, ăd/ŭlt–] **188**–8
adventure story [əd vĕn/chər stör/ē] **237**–19
aerobic exercise [ə rō/bĭk ĕk/sər sīz/] **122**–5
afraid [ə frād/] **43**–23
after [ăf/tər]
    afternoon [ăf/tər noon/] **18**–17
    aftershave [ăf/tər shāv/] **109**–30
    five after one [fīv/ ăf/tər wŭn/] **18**–7
    quarter after one [kwör/tər ăf/tər wŭn/] **18**–9
    ten after one [tĕn/ ăf/tər wŭn/] **18**–8
    twenty after one [twĕn/tē ăf/tər wŭn/] **18**–10
After an Emergency [ăf/tər ən ĭ mür/jən sē] **147**
Age [āj] **32**
agency [ā/jən sē] **131**–14

agent [ā/jənt] **160**–3, **160**–5
agree [ə grē/] **12**–K
agreement [ə grē/mənt] **51**–28
aid [ād]
    first aid kit [fürst/ ād/ kĭt/] **117**–1, **146**–18
    first aid manual [fürst/ ād/ măn/yoo əl] **117**–2
    hearing aid [hïr/ĭng ād/] **115**–10
aide [ād] **167**–32
AIDS (acquired immune deficiency syndrome) [ādz] /
    [ə kwī/rd ĭ myoon/ də fĭ/shən sē sĭn/dröm] **111** ✦
air [ër]
    air bag [ër/ băg/] **159**–43
    air conditioner [ër/ kən dĭsh/ə nər] **159**–39
    Air Force [ër/ förs/] **138**–16
    airmail [ër/māl/] **134**–5
    airplane [ër/plān/] **150**–8
    airplane crash [ër/plān/ krăsh/] **144**–3
    air pollution [ër/ pə loo/shən] **218**–11
    airport [ër/pört/] **151**–10
    air purifier [ër/ pyoor/ə fī ər] **113**–14
Airline Terminal [ër/līn/ tür/mə nəl] **160**
Airplane [ër/plān/] **161**
AIRPORT [ër/pört/] **160**–**161**
Airport Transportation
    [ër/pört/ trăns/pər tā/shən] **152**
aisle [īl] **72**–6
alarm clock [ə lärm/ kläk/] **58**–24
Alaska time [ə lăs/kə tīm/] **19**–28
album [ăl/bəm] **235**–31, **235**–32
alfalfa [ăl făl/fə] **177**–5
algebra [ăl/jə brə] **192**–16
allergic reaction [ə lür/jĭk rē ăk/shən] **116**–E
allergies [ăl/ər jēz] **111**–8
alley [ăl/ē] **51**–24, **222**–4
alligator [ăl/ə gā/tər] **213**–36
alphabet [ăl/fə bĕt/] **7**–13
Alterations [öl/tə rā/shənz] **100**
ALTERATIONS [öl/tə rā/shənz] **100**
Alteration Shop [öl/tə rā/shən shäp/] **100**
aluminum foil [ə loo/mə nəm foyl/] **72**–23
Alzheimer's disease [älts/hī mərz dĭ zēz/, älts–] **111** ✦
a.m. [ā/ĕm/] **18**–4
ambulance [ăm/byə ləns] **116**–1, **121**–34
AMERICA [ə mĕr/ə kə] **200**–**201**
American cheese [ə mĕr/ə kən chēz/] **71**–26
Americans [ə mĕr/ə kənz] **198**–3
Amphibians [ăm fĭb/ē ənz] **212**
AMPHIBIANS [ăm fĭb/ē ənz] **212**–**213**
amusement park [ə myooz/mənt pärk/] **223**–10
ancient [ān/shənt] **199**–1
anemone [ə nĕ/mə nē] **212**–24
anesthesiologist [ă/nəs thē/zē ä/lə jĭst] **121**–35
angle [ăng/gəl] **193**–26, **193**–27, **193**–28
Angles [ăng/gəlz] **193**
angry [ăng/grē] **43**–29
animals [ăn/ə məlz] **59**–15
Animals [ăn/ə məlz] **212, 215**
ANIMALS [ăn/ə məlz] **215**
ankle [ăng/kəl] **106**–23, **110**–18
    ankle socks [ăng/kəl säks/] **91**–7
anklets [ăngk/ləts] **91**–11
anniversary [ăn/ə vür/sə rē] **22**–3

answer [ăn/sər] **8**–L
answering machine [ăn/sə rĭng mə shēn/] **14**–17
answer sheet [ăn/sər shēt/] **10**–2
antacid [ănt ăs/əd] **113**–28
anteater [ănt/ē/tər] **217**–24
antelope [ăn/tə lōp/] **217**–35
antenna [ăn tĕ/nə] **14**–9
antibacterial ointment
    [ăn/tē băk tïr/ē əl oynt/mənt] **117**–10
antihistamine cream [ăn/tī hĭs/tə mēn krēm/] **117**–11
antiperspirant [ăn/tē pürs/pə rənt] **108**–5
antlers [ănt/lərz] **216**–16
ants [ănts] **63**–23
apartment [ə pärt/mənt] **48**–3, **48**–4
    apartment building [ə pärt/mənt bĭl/dĭng] **50**–1
    apartment number [ə pärt/mənt nŭm/bər] **4**–6
Apartment [ə pärt/mənt] **48**
Apartment Complex [ə pärt/mənt käm/plĕx] **51**
Apartment Entryway [ə pärt/mənt ĕn/trē wā/] **51**
APARTMENTS [ə pärt/mənts] **50**–**51**
APC (automated postal center) [ā/pē/sē/] /
    [ö/tə māt ĭd pōs/təl–sĕn/tər] **135**–10
apologize [ə päl/ə jīz/] **12**–F
apostrophe [ə päs/trə fē] **190**–16
apparatus [ăp/ə rā/təs] **224**–14
appear [ə pïr/] **141**–C
Appearance [ə pïr/əns] **32**
applaud [ə plöd/] **148**–B
apples [ăp/əlz] **68**–1
    apple juice [ăp/əl joos/] **73**–32
appliance repair person
    [ə plī/əns rĭ për/ pür/sən] **166**–4
appliqué [ăp/lə kā/] **99**–31
apply [ə plī/] **109**–P
appointment [ə poynt/mənt] **22**–4, **118**–1
    appointment book [ə poynt/mənt book/] **183**–48
apricots [ăp/rə käts/] **68**–12
April [ā/prəl] **21**–28
apron [ā/prən] **92**–11, **93**–30
aquarium [ə kwër/ē əm] **222**–7
Arachnids [ə răk/nĭdz/] **214**
ARACHNIDS [ə răk/nĭdz/] **214**
archery [är/chə rē] **228**–1
architect [är/kə tĕkt/] **166**–5
area [ër/ē ə]
    area code [ër/ē ə kōd/] **4**–10, **15**–29
    boarding area [bör/dĭng ër/ē ə] **161**–9
    dining area [dī/nĭng ër/ē ə] **46**–7
    play area [plā/ ër/ē ə] **130**–11
    reception area [rĭ sĕp/shən ër/ē ə] **182**–5
    rural area [roor/əl ër/ē ə] **52**–4
    screening area [skrē/nĭng ër/ē ə] **160**–4
    testing area [tĕs/tĭng ër/ē ə] **136**–2
    urban area [ür/bən ër/ē ə] **52**–1
AREA [ër/ē ə] **55**
Area and Volume [ër/ē ə ən văl/yəm, –yoom] **193**
arm [ärm] **105**–14, **194**–15
    armchair [ärm/chër/] **56**–22
armadillo [är/mə dĭl/ō] **216**–8
Arm, Hand, and Fingers [ärm/ hănd/ ən fĭng/gərz] **106**
Army [är/mē] **138**–14, **199**–11
around [ə rownd/] **153**–H

Around Campus [ə rownd/ kăm/pəs] **5**

arrange [ə rānj/] **49**–Q

arrest [ə rĕst/] **141**–A

arrival [ə rī/vəl] **161**–7, **161** ✦

arrive [ə rīv/] **160**–K

arrow [ăr/ō] **231**–8

arson [är/sən] **142**–7

artery [är/tə rē] **107**–36

arthritis [är thrī/təs] **111**–16

artichokes [är/tə chōks/] **69**–22

artist [är/tĭst] **166**–6

arts [ärts] **189**–9, **189**–15, **228**–11

    art museum [ärt/ myōō zē/əm] **223**–9

ask [ăsk] **2**–B

    ask about [ăsk/ ə bowt/] **48**–B, **157**–B

    ask for [ăsk/ för/] **10**–F

    ask questions [ăsk/ kwĕs/chənz] **8**–K, **174**–M

asparagus [ə spĕr/ə gəs] **69**–26

assault [ə sölt/] **142**–3

assemble [ə sĕm/bəl] **170**–A, **175**–C

assembler [ə sĕm/blər] **166**–7

assembly [ə sĕm/blē] **140**–1

    assembly line [ə sĕm/blē līn/] **175**–6

    assemblyperson [ə sĕm/blē pür/sən] **139**–24

assist [ə sĭst/] **95**–D, **170**–B

assistance [ə sĭs/təns] **14**–22

assistant [ə sĭs/tənt]

    administrative assistant

        [əd mĭn/ ə strā/ tĭv ə sĭs/tənt] **166**–3

    assistant principal [ə sĭs/tənt prĭn/sə pəl] **5**–5

    certified nursing assistant (CNA) [sür/tə fīd/

        nür/sĭng ə sĭs/tənt] / [sē/ĕn/ā/] **120**–12

    dental assistant [dĕn/təl ə sĭs/tənt] **119**–2, **167**–22

    physician assistant [fə zĭ/shən ə sĭs/tənt] **168**–47

Assistant [ə sĭs/tənt] **93**

asthma [ăz/mə] **111**–9

astronaut [ăs/trə nöt/] **205**–17

astronomer [ə strä/nə mər] **205**–22

Astronomy [ə strä/nə mē] **205**

At Customs [ăt/ kŭs/təmz] **161**

athletic [ăth lĕt/ĭk]

    athletic shoes [ăth lĕt/ĭk shōōz/] **86**–7

    athletic supporter [ăth lĕt/ĭk sə pör/tər] **91**–6

Atlantic time [ət lăn/tĭk tīm/] **19**–33

atlas [ăt/ləs] **133**–8

ATM (Automated Teller Machine) [ā/tē/ĕm/] /

    [ö/tə măt ĭd tē/lər mə shēn/] **132**

ATM card [ā/tē/ĕm/ kärd/] **132**–15

atom [ăt/əm] **195**–28

attach [ə tăch/] **197**–G, **197**–H

attachments [ə tăch/mənts] **61**–11

attack [ə tăk/] **116**–D

attendant [ə tĕn/dənt] **161**–12, **162**–3, **184**–3

At the Dealer [ăt/ dhə dē/lər] **158**

At the Gate [ăt/ dhə gāt/] **161**

At the Mechanic [ăt/ dhə mə kăn/ĭk] **158**

At the Security Checkpoint

    [ăt/ dhə sə kyōō/ rə tē/ chĕk/ poynt/] **160**

attic [ăt/ĭk] **47**–7

attorney [ə tür/nē] **141**–4, **141**–10

attractive [ə trăk/tĭv] **32**–13

audiobook [ö/dē ō bŏŏk/] **133**–17

audiologist [ö dē ä/lə jĭst] **115**–9

auditorium [ö/də tör/ē əm] **5**–18

August [ö/gəst] **21**–32

aunt [ănt] **34**–7

author [ö/thər] **133**–15, **169**–64

auto [ö/tō]

    auto club card [ö/tō klŭb/ kärd/] **162**–4

    auto mechanic [ö/tō mə kăn/ĭk] **166**–8

automated [ö/tə măt ĭd]

    automated phone system

        [ö/tə măt ĭd fōn/ sĭs/təm] **14**–23

    automated postal center (APC)

        [ö/tə măt ĭd pōs/təl sĕn/tər] / [ā/pē/sē/] **135**–10

Automated Teller Machine

    [ö/tə măt ĭd tĕl/ər mə shēn/] **132**

Automatic Transmission

    [ö tə măt/ĭk trănz mĭ/shən] **159**

Automotive Painter [ö tə mōt/ĭv pān/tər] **92**

autumn [ö/təm] **21**–39

avalanche [ăv/ə lănch/] **145**–18

average [ăv/rĭj]

    average height [ăv/rĭj hīt/] **32**–5

    average weight [ăv/rĭj wāt/] **32**–8

avocados [ä/və kä/dōz, ăv/ə–] **84**–6

ax [ăks] **180**–3

baboon [bă bōōn/] **217**–31

baby [bā/bē] **31**–7

    baby bag [bā/bē băg/] **37**–16

    baby carrier [bā/bē kă/rē/ər] **37**–17

    baby food [bā/bē fōōd/] **37**–4

    baby lotion [bā/bē lō/shən] **37**–13

    baby monitor [bā/bē män/ə tər] **59**–7

    baby powder [bā/bē pow/dər] **37**–14

    babysitter [bā/bē sĭt/ər] **166**–9

    baby's room [bā/bēz/ rōōm/] **47**–10

back [băk] **104**–5

    backache [băk/āk/] **110**–5

    back button [băk/ bŭt/n] **197**–2

    backhoe [băk/hō/] **178**–8

    backpack [băk/păk/] **94**–18, **226**–15

    backpacking [băk/păk/ĭng] **226**–6

    backseat [băk/sēt/] **159**–54

    back support belt [băk/ sə pört/ bĕlt/] **179**–18

    go back [gō/ băk/] **11**–M

    horseback riding [hörs/băk/ rī/dĭng] **226**–9

    lower back [lō/ər băk/] **107**–29

    pay back [pā/ băk/] **26**–D

Backyard [băk/yärd/] **53**

BACK FROM THE MARKET

    [băk/ frəm dhə mär/kət] **66**–67

bacon [bā/kən] **70**–11, **80**–1

bad [băd] **23**–18

BAD DAY AT WORK [băd/ dā/ ăt würk/] **186**–187

badge [băj] **93**–21

badminton [băd/mĭn tən] **228**–6

bag [băg] **69**–31, **74**–7, **74**–19, **161**–18

    air bag [ĕr/ băg/] **159**–43

    baby bag [bā/bē băg/] **37**–16

    clutch bag [klŭch/ băg/] **89**–19

    grocery bag [grōs/rē băg/] **67**–13

    handbag [hănd/ băg/] **87**–9, **94**–2

    plastic storage bags [plăs/tĭk stör/ĭj băgz/] **72**–25

    shoulder bag [shōl/dər băg/] **94**–17

    sleeping bag [slē/pĭng băg/] **226**–12

    totebag [tōt/ băg/] **94**–19

    trash bags [trăsh/ băgz/] **61**–24

    vacuum cleaner bag

        [văk/yōōm klē/nər băg/] **61**–12

bagels [bā/gəlz] **73**–40

baggage [băg/ĭj]

    baggage carousel [băg/ĭj kăr/ə sĕl/] **161**–23

bagger [băg/ər] **73**–14

baggy [băg/ē] **97**–30

bailiff [bā/lĭf] **141**–13

bake [bāk] **77**–H

Baked Goods [bākt/ gŏŏdz/] **73**

baked potato [bākt/ pə tā/tō] **81**–25

baker [bā/kər] **166**–10

bakery [bā/kə rē] **127**–19

Baking Products [bā/kĭng prăd/ŭkts] **73**

balance [băl/əns] **132**–17, **195**–41

balcony [băl/kə nē] **51**–20

bald [böld] **33**–12

ball [böl] **59**–12, **231**–5, **231**–12

    ball field [böl/ fēld/] **224**–1

    ballroom [böl/rōōm/] **184**–26

    baseball [bās/böl/] **231**–18, **231**–14

    basketball [băs/kət böl/] **229**–8, **231**–4

    basketball court [băs/kət böl/ kört/] **229**–7

    football [fŏŏt/böl/] **229**–11, **231**–21

    meatballs [mĕt/bölz/] **81**–27

    racquetball [răk/ət böl/] **228**–12

    softball [söft/böl/] **229**–10

    volleyball [väl/ē böl/] **229**–14, **231**–3

balloons [bə lōōnz/] **44**–4

bananas [bə năn/əz] **68**–2

band [bănd] **183**–34

    headband [hĕd/bănd/] **90**–3

    waistband [wāst/bănd/] **100**–5

bandage [băn/dĭj] **117**–5, **117**–12

bandana [băn dă/nə] **92**–16

bangs [băngz] **33**–8

bank [băngk] **124**–5

    bank statement [băngk/ stāt/mənt] **132**–16

bank online [băngk/ än līn/] **132**–C

BANK [băngk] **132**

banner [băn/ər] **44**–1

banquet room [băng/kwət rōōm/] **185**–14

bar [bär]

    bar code [bär/ kōd/] **27**–4

    candy bar [kăn/dē bär/] **73**–37

    grab bar [grăb/ bär/] **57**–9

    menu bar [mĕn/yōō bär/] **197**–1

    salad bar [săl/əd bär/] **79**–24

    scroll bar [skrōl/ bär/] **197**–15

barbecued ribs [bär/bǐ kyōō/d rĭbz/] **76**–2

barbershop [bär/bər shäp/] **129**–19

bargain [bär/gən] **102**–A

barn [bärn] **177**–11

barrette [bə rĕt/] **108**–20

base [bās] **193**–45, **194**–20

baseball [bās/böl/] **229**–9, **231**–18

    baseball bat [bās/böl/ băt/] **231**–14

    baseball cap [bās/böl/ kăp/] **86**–5

baseball cards [bās/böl/ kärds/] **232**–2
baseball game [bās/böl/ gām/] **44**–2
basement [bās/mənt] **47**–13
Basement [bās/mənt] **50**
Basic Colors [bā/sĭk kŭ/lərz] **24**
BASIC TRANSPORTATION
    [bā/sĭk trănz/pər tā/shən] **150**–151
basket [băs/kət] **56**–3
    basketball [băs/kət böl] **229**–8, **231**–4
    basketball court [băs/kət böl kört/] **229**–7
    bread basket [brĕd/ băs/kət] **83**–11
    laundry basket [lön/drē băs/kət] **101**–2
    shopping basket [shäp/ĭng băs/kət] **73**–9
    wastebasket [wāst/băs/kət] **57**–26
bass [băs] **212**–6, [băs] **238**–8
bassoon [bə sōōn/] **238**–4
bat [băt] **216**–7, **231**–14
bath [băth]
    bath mat [băth/ măt/] **57**–28
    bath powder [băth/ pow/dər] **108**–4
    bathroom [băth/rōōm/] **46**–4
    bath towel [băth/ tow/əl] **57**–13
    bathtub [băth/tŭb/] **57**–2
    half bath [hăf/ băth/] **57** ✦
bathe [bādh] **36**–F, **108**–B
bathing suit [bā/dhĭng sōōt/] **90**–26
BATHROOM [băth/rōōm/] **57**
battery / batteries [băt/ə rē] / [băt/ə rēz]
    146–15, **158**–20
    battery charger [băt/ə rē chär/jər] **235**–27
    battery pack [băt/ə rē păk/] **235**–26
bay [bā] **204**–9
be [bē]
    be aware [bē ə wër/] **143**–I
    be born [bē börn/] **40**–A
    be 18 or older [bē ā/tēn/ ör öld/ər] **140**–G
    be hurt [bē hürt/] **116**–C
    be informed [bē ĭn förmd/] **140**–F
    be injured [bē ĭn/jərd] **116**–C
    be in shock [bē ĭn shäk/] **116**–B
    be neat [bē nēt/] **174**–C
    be on time [bē ön tïm/] **174**–F
    be released [bē rĭ lēst/] **141**–H
    be unconscious [bē ŭn kän/shəs] **116**–A
    don't be late [dönt/ bē lāt/] **174**–D
beach [bēch] **204**–10
    beach chair [bēch/ chër/] **225**–22
    beach umbrella [bēch/ ŭm brĕl/ə] **225**–14
BEACH [bēch] **225**
beads [bēdz] **95**–34, **99**–32
beak [bēk] **214**–3
beaker [bē/kər] **195**–39
beam [bēm] **178**–3
beans [bēnz] **69**–8, **72**–17
    soybeans [soy/bēnz/] **177**–3
bear [bër] **37**–23, **216**–11
beard [bērd] **33**–6
beat [bēt] **77**–S
beater [bē/tər]
    eggbeater [ĕg/bē/tər] **78**–20
beautiful [byōō/tə fəl] **23**–21

beauty shop [byōō/tē shäp/] **130** ✦
beaver [bē/vər] **216**–9
become [bē kŭm/] **40**–G, **41**–N
bed [bĕd] **58**–9
    bedbugs [bĕd/bŭgz/] **63**–24
    bed control [bĕd/ kən tröl/] **121**–27
    bed frame [bĕd/ frām/] **58**–18
    bed pan [bĕd/ păn/] **121**–23
    bedroom [bĕd/rōōm/] **46**–2
    bedspread [bĕd/sprĕd/] **59**–11
    bed table [bĕd/ tā/bəl] **121**–21
    bunk beds [bŭnk/ bĕdz/] **59**–9
    double bed [dŭb/əl bĕd/] **184**–14
    flower bed [flow/ər bĕd/] **53**–20
    hospital bed [häs/pĭ tl bĕd/] **121**–22
    kids' bedroom [kïdz/ bĕd/rōōm/] **47**–9
    king-size bed [kĭng/sïz/ bĕd/] **184**–15
BEDROOM [bĕd/rōōm/] **58, 59**
bee [bē]
    honeybee [hŭn/ē bē/] **214**–25
beef [bēf]
    beef ribs [bēf/ rĭbz/] **70**–5
    corned beef [körnd/ bēf/] **71**–22
    ground beef [grownd/ bēf/] **70**–4
    roast beef [röst/ bēf/] **71**–21
    stewing beef [stōō/ĭng bēf/] **70**–3
    stir-fried beef [stür/frïd/ bēf/] **76**–6
Beef [bēf] **70**
beetle [bēt/l] **214**–18
beets [bēts] **69**–5
Before an Emergency [bĭ för/ ən ĭ mür/ jən sē] **146**
behind [bĭ hïnd/] **25**–8
beige [bāzh] **24**–18
bell [bĕl]
    bell captain [bĕl/ kăp/tən] **184**–6
    bellhop [bĕl/häp/] **184**–7
    bell peppers [bĕl/ pĕp/ərz] **69**–7
    doorbell [dör/bĕl/] **53**–14
below [bĭ lō/] **25**–5
belts [bĕlts] **94**–6
    back support belt [băk/ sə pört/ bĕlt/] **179**–18
    belt buckle [bĕlt/ bŭk/əl] **94**–20
    conveyor belt [kən vā/ər bĕlt/] **175**–9
    garter belt [gär/tər bĕlt/] **91**–16
    seat belt [sēt/ bĕlt/] **159**–52
    tool belt [tōōl/ bĕlt/] **92**–3
bench [bĕnch] **224**–10
bend [bĕnd] **230**–O
benefits [bĕn/ə fĭts] **174** ✦
berries [bĕr/ēz] **210**–20
    blackberries [blăk/bĕr/ēz] **68**–17
    blueberries [blōō/bĕr/ēz] **68**–16
    mixed berries [mïkst/ bĕr/ēz] **81**–36
    raspberries [răz/bĕr/ēz] **68**–15
    strawberries [strö/bĕr/ēz] **68**–14
between [bĭ twēn/] **25**–12
Beverages [bĕv/rə jəz] **73, 81**
bib [bĭb] **37**–5
bicycle / bike [bï/sĭ kəl] / [bïk] **129**–22, **151**–15
big [bĭg] **23**–2, **97**–38
    Big Dipper [bĭg/ dĭ/pər] **205** ✦
    big-screen TV [bĭg/skrēn/ tē/vē/] **50**–15

bike / bicycle [bïk] / [bï/sĭ kəl] **129**–22, **151**–15
    bike path [bïk/ păth/] **224**–3
biking [bï/kïng] **226**–8, **228**–5
bikini panties [bə kē/nē păn/tēz] **91**–13
bill [bĭl] **214**–3
Bill [bĭl] **15**
billiards [bĭl/yərdz] **228**–2
Bill of Rights [bĭl/ əv rïts/] **198**–10
Bills [bĭlz] **26**
bin [bĭn] **51**–23, **61**–2, **160**–6
bioenergy [bī/ō ĕn/ər jē] **218**–9
biography [bī ä/grə fē] **133**–15
biologist [bī ä/lə jïst] **194**–2
Biology [bī ä/lə jē] **194**
biomass [bī/ō măs/] **218**–9
birch [bürch] **210**–7
bird [bürd] **208**–4
Bird [bürd] **214**
BIRDS, INSECTS, AND ARACHNIDS
    [bürdz/ ĭn/sĕkts ən ə răk/nïdz] **214**
birth [bürth]
    birth certificate [bürth/ sər tĭf/ə kət] **40**–1
    birthday [bürth/dā/] **22**–1
BIRTHDAY PARTY [bürth/dā/ pär/tē] **240**–241
biscuits [bĭs/kəts] **80**–6
bison [bī/sən] **216**–6
bit [bĭt] **180**–28
bite [bït] **110**–11
black [blăk] **24**–13
    blackberries [blăk/bĕr/ēz] **68**–17
    black hair [blăk/ hër/] **33**–16
bladder [blăd/ər] **107**–46
blade [blād] **107**–28, **109**–28, **180**–27
blankets [blăng/kəts] **58**–15, **146**–7, **225**–11
    blanket sleeper [blăng/kət slē/pər] **91**–27
blazer [blā/zər] **92**–12
bleach [blēch] **101**–7
bleachers [blē/chərz] **5**–3
bleed [blēd] **116**–M
blender [blĕn/dər] **54**–12
blind [blïnd] **32**–11
blister [blĭs/tər] **110**–15
blizzard [blïz/ərd] **13**–23, **145**–13
blocks [bläks] **59**–19
    quilt block [kwĭlt/ bläk/] **232**–15
    sunblock [sŭn/bläk/] **108**–8, **225**–10
blond hair [bländ/ hër/] **33**–17
blood [blŭd] **111**–14
    blood pressure gauge [blŭd/ prĕsh/ər gāj/] **118**–9
    blood test [blŭd/ tĕst/] **121**–30
    blood work [blŭd/ würk/] **121**–30
    bloody nose [blŭd/ē nōz/] **110**–17
blouse [blows] **87**–8
blow dryer [blō/ drï/ər] **33**–23, **108**–18
blower [blō/ər] **176**–2
blow out [blō/ owt/] **240**–C
blue [blōō] **24**–3
    blueberries [blōō/bĕr/ēz] **68**–16
    blue jay [blōō/ jā/] **214**–6
    bright blue [brït/ blōō/] **24**–12
    dark blue [därk/ blōō/] **24**–10
    light blue [lït/ blōō/] **24**–11
    navy blue [nā/vē blōō/] **28**–5

blues [blo͞oz] **237**–22
blush [blŭsh] **109**–37
board [bôrd]
    board game [bôrd/ gām/] **232**–5
    bulletin board [bŏŏl/ə tn bôrd/] **7**–14
    chalkboard [chôk/bôrd/] **6**–1
    cutting board [kŭt/ĭng bôrd/] **54**–27
    emery board [ĕm/ə rē bôrd/, ĕm/rē–] **109**–32
    headboard [hĕd/bôrd/] **58**–10
    ironing board [ī/ər nĭng bôrd/] **101**–14
    motherboard [mŭdh/ər bôrd/] **196**–5
    particle board [pär/tə kəl bôrd/] **181**–20
    skateboard [skāt/bôrd/] **224**–7
    snowboard [snō/bôrd/] **231**–23
    surfboard [sürf/bôrd/] **225**–16
    whiteboard [wīt/bôrd/] **6**–3
board [bôrd] **160**–E
boarding [bôr/dĭng]
    boarding area [bôr/dĭng ër/ē ə] **161**–9
    boarding pass [bôr/dĭng păs/] **161**–20
    sailboarding [sāl/bôr/dĭng] **227** ✦
    skateboarding [skāt/bôr/dĭng] **228**–13
    snowboarding [snō/bôr/dĭng] **227**–2
boat [bōt]
    sailboat [sāl/bōt/] **225**–3
boating [bō/tĭng] **226**–1
bobbin [bä/bĭn] **98**–21
bobby pins [bäb/ē pĭnz/]**108**–21
body [bäd/ē] **190**–7
    body lotion [bäd/ē lō/shən] **108**–9
    body of water [bäd/ē əv wö/tər] **204** ✦
    body shaper [bäd/ē/ shā/pər] **91**–15
BODY [bäd/ē] **104**–**105**, **106**–**107**
boil [boyl] **77**–M
boiled ham [boyld/ hăm/] **76**–5
boiler [boy/lər] **78**–8
bok choy [bäk/ choy/] **69**–15
bolt [bōlt] **51**–34, **180**–35, **180**–38
    bolt of fabric [bōlt/ əv fäb/rĭk] **98**–15
bone [bōn] **107**–33, **116**–P
    boneless [bōn/ləs] **70** ✦
book [bŏŏk]
    appointment book [ə poynt/mənt bŏŏk/] **183**–48
    audiobook [ö/dē ō bŏŏk/] **133**–17
    bookkeeper [bŏŏk/ kē/pər] **175**–2
    book of stamps [bŏŏk/ əv stämps/] **134**–18
    bookcase [bŏŏk/ kās/] **7**–10
    bookstore [bŏŏk/ stôr/] **130**–4
    check book [chĕk/ bŏŏk/] **132**–12
    coloring book [kŭl/ə rĭng bŏŏk/] **59**–13
    DMV handbook [dē/ĕm/vē/ hănd/bŏŏk/] **136**–1
    notebook [nōt/bŏŏk/] **7**–27
    passbook [păs/bŏŏk/] **132**–10
    picture book [pĭk/chər bŏŏk/] **133**–12
    spiral notebook [spī/rəl nōt/bŏŏk/] **7**–29
    test booklet [tĕst/ bŏŏk/lət] **10**–1
    textbook [tĕkst/bŏŏk/, tĕks/–] **7**–25
    workbook [würk/bŏŏk/] **7**–26
boombox [bōōm/bäks/] **234**–1
booth [bōōth] **82**–4, **122**–3

boots [bōōts] **95**–28
    hiking boots [hī/kĭng bōōts/] **95**–31
    rain boots [rān/ bōōts/] **90**–20
    safety boots [sāf/tē bōōts/] **179**–20
    ski boots [skē/ bōōts/] **231**–26
    steel toe boots [stēl/ tō/ bōōts/] **92**–6
bored [bôrd] **43**–25
borrow [bär/ō, bör/ō] **26**–B
boss [bäs] **164**–4
botanical garden [bə tăn/ĭ kəl gär/dn] **222**–3
bottle [bät/l] **37**–1, **74**–1, **74**–13
    bottle return [bät/l rĭ türn/] **73**–16
    hot water bottle [hät/ wö/tər bät/l] **113**–15
bottled water [bät/ld wö/tər] **146**–11
bouquet [bō kā/, bōō–] **211**–28
bow [bō] **231**–6
    bow tie [bō/ tī/] **89**–16
bow [bow] **3**–H
bowl [bōl] **55**–2
    mixing bowl [mĭks/ĭng bōl/] **54**–28, **78**–31
    serving bowl [sürv/ĭng bōl/] **55**–21
    soup bowl [sōōp/ bōl/] **83**–21
    sugar bowl [shŏŏg/ər bōl/] **55**–14
bowling [bō/lĭng] **228**–3
    bowling alley [bō/lĭng ăl/ē] **222**–4
    bowling ball [bō/lĭng bōl/] **231**–5
box / boxes [bäks/, bäks/ĭz] **74**–6, **74**–18
    box spring [bäks/ sprĭng/] **58**–19
    CD boombox [sē/dē/ bōōm/bäks/] **234**–1
    fuse box [fyōōz/ bäks/] **62**–13
    mailboxes [māl/bäk/səz] **50**–11, **128**–13
    post office box (PO box)
       [pōst/ ö/fəs bäks/] / [pē/ō bäks/] **135**–9
    safety deposit box [sāf/tē dĭ päz/ət bäks/] **132**–7
    sandbox [sănd/bäks/] **224**–15
    search box [sürch/ bäks/] **197**–5
    text box [tĕkst/ bäks/] **197**–13
    to-go box [tə gō/ bäks/] **82**–5
boxer shorts [bäk/sər shôrts/] **91**–4
boxing [bäks/ĭng] **228**–4
boy [boy] **31**–9
bra [brä] **91**–20
bracelets [brās/ləts] **95**–9, **117**–3
braces [brā/səz] **119**–6
brain [brān] **107**–34
brainstorm [brān/stôrm/] **8**–H, **191**–F
brake [brāk] **159**–48
    brake light [brāk/ līt/] **158**–14
    brake pedal [brāk/ pĕd/l] **159**–45
branch [brănch] **210**–2
Branch [brănch] **138**
Brass [brăs] **238**
bread [brĕd] **67**–11
    bread-and-butter plate [brĕd/ n bŭt/ər plāt/] **83**–19
    bread basket [brĕd/ bäs/kət] **83**–11
    garlic bread [gär/lĭk brĕd/] **81**–28
    rye bread [rī/ brĕd/] **71**–20
    wheat bread [wēt/ brĕd/] **71**–19
    white bread [wīt/ brĕd/] **71**–18
break [brāk] **77**–Q, **116**–P
    break down [brāk/ down/] **162**–D

Breakfast Special [brĕk/fəst spĕ/shəl] **80**
breasts [brĕsts] **70**–19, **107**–26
breathe [brēdh] **116**–N
breathing [brē/dhĭng] **117**–16
bricklayer [brĭk/lā/ər] **186**–8
bricks [brĭks] **178**–12, **178**–B
briefcase [brēf/kās/] **88**–13
briefs [brēfs] **91**–5, **91**–14
bright blue [brīt/ blōō/] **24**–12
bring [brĭng] **174**–D, **240**–E
broccoli [bräk/ə lē] **69**–13
broiled steak [broyld/ stāk/] **76**–3
broiler [broy/lər] **54**–21
broken [brō/kən] **62**–5, **62**–6, **62**–7, **63**–15, **97**–39
    broken equipment [brō/kən ĭ kwĭp/mənt] **179**–4
broom [brōōm] **61**–16
brother [brŭdh/ər] **34**–6, **35**–28
    brother-in-law [brŭdh/ər ĭn lö/] **34**–17
    stepbrother [stĕp/brŭdh/ər] **35**–30
brown [brown] **24**–17
    brown hair [brown/ hër/] **33**–18
    hash browns [hăsh/ brownz/] **80**–3
browse [browz] **102**–B
bruise [brōōz] **110**–12
brush [brŭsh] **33**–22, **108**–14
    paintbrush [pānt/brŭsh/] **181**–22, **233**–20
    scrub brush [skrŭb/ brŭsh/] **61**–20
    toilet brush [toy/lət brŭsh/] **57**–18
    toothbrush [tōōth/brŭsh/] **109**–22
brush [brŭsh] **108**–I, **109**–J
bubble in [bŭ/bəl ĭn/] **10**–K
bucket [bŭk/ət] **61**–7, **225**–8
buckle [bŭk/əl] **94**–20, **99**–28
buckle up [bŭk/əl ŭp/] **36**–L
bud [bŭd] **211**–7
budget [bŭ jĭt/] **186**–3
buffalo [bŭf/ə lō] **216**–6
buffet [bə fā/] **55**–24, **185**–10
bugs [bŭgz]
    bedbugs [bĕd/bŭgz/] **63**–24
building [bĭl/dĭng] **50**–1, **124**–2
BUILDING SUPPLIES [bĭl/dĭng sə plīz/] **180**–**181**
bulb [bŭlb] **56** ✦, **211**–2
bulldozer [bŏŏl/dō/zər] **178**–6
bulletin board [bŏŏl/ə tn bôrd/] **7**–14
bump cap [bŭmp/ kăp/] **92**–9
bumper [bŭm/pər] **158**–8
    bumper pad [bŭm/pər păd/] **59**–4
bunch [bŭnch] **68**–29
bunk beds [bŭngk/ bĕdz/] **59**–9
Bunsen burner [bŭn/sən bür/nər] **195**–37
bureau [byŏŏr/ō] **58**–1
burger [bür/gər]
    cheeseburger [chēz/bür/gər] **79**–3
    hamburger [hăm/bür/gər] **79**–1
burglary [bür/glə rē] **142**–2
burn [bürn]
    sunburn [sŭn/bürn/] **110**–14
burn [bürn] **116**–H
burner [bür/nər] **54**–19, **195**–37
burrito [bə rē/tō] **79**–9

Index

bus [bŭs] **128**–9, **151**–14
  bus person [bŭs/ pür/sən] **185**–13
  bus route [bŭs/ rōōt/, –rowt/] **152**–1
  bus station [bŭs/ stā/shən] **124**–7
  bus stop [bŭs/ stäp/] **129**–16, **151**–13
  miss the bus [mĭs/ dhə bŭs/] **152** ✦
bus [bŭs] **82**–G
business [bĭz/nəs]
  business owner [bĭz/nəs ō/nər] **166**–11
  businessperson [bĭz/nəs pür/sən] **166**–12
  business suit [bĭz/nəs sōōt/] **88**–11
busser [bŭ/sər] **83**–12
Bus Stop [bŭs/ stäp/] **152**
butcher [bŏŏch/ər] **166**–13
butter [bŭt/ər] **66**–6, **83**–19
butterfly [bŭt/ər flī/] **214**–19
buttocks [bŭt/əks] **107**–30
button [bŭt/n] **99**–24
  back button [băk/ bŭt/n] **197**–2
  call button [köl/ bŭt/n] **121**–28
  forward button [för/wərd bŭt/n] **197**–3
buy [bī] **27**–G
  buy a home [bī/ ə hōm/] **41**–M
  buy a snack [bī/ ə snăk/] **11**–K
  buy recycled products
    [bī/ rē sī/kəld präd/ŭkts] **219**–D
Buying a House [bī/ĭng ə hows/] **49**
BUYING AND MAINTAINING A CAR
  [bī/ĭng ən mān tā/nĭng ə kär/] **157**
Buying a Used Car [bī/ĭng ə yōōzd/ kär/] **157**
buzzer [bŭz/ər] **51**–31
cab [kăb] **156**–16
cabbage [kăb/ĭj] **69**–2
Cabinet [kăb/ə nət] **138**–10
cabinet [kăb/ə nət] **54**–1
  file cabinet [fīl/ kăb/ə nət] **182**–11
  medicine cabinet [mĕd/ə sən kăb/ə nət] **57**–20
  supply cabinet [sə plī/ kăb/ə nət] **182**–1
cables [kā/bəlz] **158**–21, **196**–13
cactus [kăk/təs] **210**–21
cafeteria [kăf/ə tĭr/ē ə] **5**–14
cage [kāj] **107**–48
cake [kāk] **73**–39, **81**–33
  cake pan [kāk/ păn/] **78**–26
  cheesecake [chēz/kāk/] **81**–34
  pancakes [păn/kāks/] **80**–7
Cake [kāk] **77**
calculate [kăl/kyə lāt/] **17**–B
calculator [kăl/kyə lā/tər] **17**–6, **183**–25
calculus [kăl/kyə ləs] **192**–19
CALENDAR [kăl/ən dər] **20**–21
CALENDAR EVENTS [kăl/ən dər ĭ vĕnts/] **22**
calf [kăf] **106**–22
  calf-length [kăf/ lĕnth/] **96**–17
call [köl]
  call button [köl/ bŭt/n] **121**–28
  international call [ĭn/tər năsh/ə nəl köl/] **15**–35
  Internet phone call [ĭn/tər nĕt/ fōn/ köl/] **14**–20
  local call [lō/kəl köl/] **15**–31
  long distance call [löng/ dĭs/təns köl/] **15**–32
call [köl] **48**–A, **147**–L
  call in [köl/ ĭn/] **186**–A

calling card [kö/lĭng kärd/] **14**–15
calm [köm] **42**–8
camcorder [kăm/kör dər] **235**–24
camel [kăm/əl] **217**–38
camera [kăm/rə]
  camera case [kăm/rə kās/] **235**–28
  digital camera [dĭ/jə təl kăm/rə] **235**–19
  film camera [fĭlm/ kăm/rə] **235**–21
  security camera [sĭ kyŏŏr/ə tē kăm/rə] **50**–19
  35 mm camera
    [thür/tē fīv/ mĭl/ə mē/tər kăm/rə] **235**–21
camisole [kăm/ə sōl/] **91**–21
campaign [kăm pān/] **139**–29
camper [kăm/pər] **156**–9
campfire [kămp/fīr/] **226**–11
camping [kăm/pĭng] **226**–5
  camping stove [kăm/pĭng stōv/] **226**–16
Campus [kăm/pəs] **5**
can [kăn] **74**–3, **74**–15
  can opener [kăn/ ō/pə nər] **78**–1, **146**–8
  electric can opener [ĭ lĕk/trĭk/ kăn/ ō/pə nər] **54**–14
  garbage can [gär/bĭj kăn/] **53**–24
cancer [kăn/sər] **111**–10
candle [kăn/dl] **56**–20
  candle holder [kăn/dl hōl/dər] **56**–21
candy [kăn/dē] **239**–12
  candy bar [kăn/dē bär/] **73**–37
  candy cane [kăn/dē kān/] **239**–17
  candy store [kăn/dē stör/] **131**–17
cane [kān] **113**–16, **239**–17
canned food [kănd/ fōōd/] **146**–9
Canned Foods [kănd/ fōōdz/] **72**
canoeing [kə nōō/ĭng] **226**–3
can't breathe [kănt/ brēdh/] **116**–N
canteen [kăn tēn/] **226**–24
canvas [kăn/vəs] **233**–17
canyon [kăn/yən] **204**–17
cap [kăp] **88**–1, **206**–7
  baseball cap [bās/böl/ kăp/] **86**–5
  bump cap [bŭmp/ kăp/] **92**–9
  shower cap [show/ər kăp/] **108**–1
  surgical cap [sür/jĭ kəl kăp/] **121**–37
  surgical scrub cap [sür/jĭ kəl skrŭb/ kăp/] **93**–35
capital [kă/pət əl] **139**–22
capitalize [kă/pət əl īz/] **190**–A, **190**–B
Capitol [kă/pət əl] **138**–1
capris [kə prēz/] **88**–8
capsule [kăp/səl] **113**–23
car [kär] **150**–1
  car accident [kär/ ăk/sə dənt] **144**–2
  car dealership [kär/ dē/lər shĭp/] **126**–4
  car safety seat [kär/ sāf/tē sēt/] **37**–19
  4-door car [för/dör/ kär/] **156**–1
  sports car [spörts/kär/] **156**–4
  subway car [sŭb/wā/ kär/] **152**–6
  town car [town/ kär/] **152**–20
  2-door car [tōō/dör/ kär/] **156**–2
Car [kär] **157**, **159**
CAR [kär] **156**, **157**, **158**–**159**
card [kärd] **239**–5
  ATM card [ā/tē/ĕm/ kärd/] **132**–15
  auto club card [ö tō/ klŭb/ kärd/] **162**–4

baseball cards [bās/böl/ kärdz/] **232**–2
card store [kärd/ stör/] **130**–7
copies of ID and credit cards
  [käp/ēz əv ī/dē/ ən krĕd/ət/ kärdz/] **146**–19
emergency card [ĭ mür/jən sē/ kärd/] **161**–23
fare card [fër/ kärd/] **152**–11
folding card table [fōl/dĭng/ kärd/ tā/bəl] **102**–4
green card [grēn/ kärd/] **40**–2
greeting card [grē/tĭng kärd/] **134**–15
health insurance card
  [hĕlth/ ĭn shŏŏr/əns kärd/] **118**–3
memory card [mĕm/ə rē kärd/] **235**–20
post card [pōst/ kärd/] **134**–16
Resident Alien card [rĕz/ə dənt ā/lē ən kärd/] **40**–2
rotary card file [rō/tə rē kärd/ fīl/] **183**–44
Social Security card
  [sō/shəl sĭ kyŏŏr/ə tē kärd/] **40**–5
Card [kärd] **135**
cardigan sweater [kär/də gən swĕt/ər] **88**–2
Cardinal Numbers [kärd/nəl nŭm/bərz] **16**
cardiologist [kär/dē äl/ə jĭst] **120**–3
cardiopulmonary resuscitation (CPR)
  [kär/dē ō pŏŏl mə nër/ē rĭ sŭs/ə tā/shən] /
  [sē/pē/är/] **117**–17
care [kër] **167**–32
careful worker [kër/fəl wür/kər] **179**–2
careless worker [kër/ləs wür/kər] **179**–1
childcare worker [chīld/kër wür/kər] **166**–16
CARE [kër] **114**–**115**, **118**, **119**
Care of Your Car [kër/ əv yər kär/] **157**
career counselor [kə rër/ kown/slər] **172**–10
Career Path [kə rër/ păth/] **172**
CAREER PLANNING [kə rër/ plăn/ĭng] **172**
cargo van [kär/gō văn/] **156**–13
carnation [kär nā/shən] **211**–20
carousel [kär/ə sĕl/] **161**–23
carpenter [kär/pən tər] **62**–12, **166**–14
carpet [kär/pət] **56**–24
carpool [kär/pōōl/] **219**–I
carriage [kär/ĭj] **37**–20
carrier [kär/ē ər] **37**–17, **134**–20
carrots [kär/əts] **69**–3
carry [kär/ē] **11**–F, **82**–H
CARS AND TRUCKS [kärz/ ən trŭks/] **156**
cart [kärt] **72**–7, **129**–28
  housekeeping cart [hows/kē/pĭng kärt/] **184**–19
  luggage cart [lŭg/ĭj/ kärt/] **184**–8
carton [kär/tn] **74**–4, **74**–16
cartoon [kär/tōōn] **236**–3
cartridge [kär/trĭj] **183**–45
carving knife [kär/vĭng nīf/] **78**–12
case [kās] **94**–5, **235**–28
cash [kăsh]
  cash and coins [kăsh/ ən koynz/] **146**–17
  cash register [kăsh/ rĕj/ə stər] **27**–10, **73**–15
cash [kăsh] **27**–F, **132**–A
cashier [kă shĭr/] **73**–13, **166**–15
cashmere [kăzh/mĭr/] **98**–4
Casserole [kăs/ə rōl] **77**
casserole dish [kăs/ə rōl dĭsh/] **78**–10
cassette [kə sĕt/] **234**–6
  videocassette [vĭ/dē ō kə sĕt/] **133**–18

cast [kăst] **113**–20
castle [kă/səl] **225**–12
Casual Clothes [kăzh/ōō əl klōz/] **88**
CASUAL, WORK, AND FORMAL CLOTHES
[kăzh/ōō əl würk/ ən för/məl klōz/] **88**–89
cat [kăt] **215**–9
catfish [kăt/fĭsh/] **71**–2
catalog [kăt ə /lög] **133**–11
catch [kăch] **230**–D
catcher's mask [kăch/ərz măsk/] **231**–15
caterer [kā/tər ər] **185**–16
caterpillar [kăt/ə pĭl/ər, kăt/ər–] **214**–20
cattle [kăt/l] **177**–21
cauliflower [kö/lĭ flow/ər, kä/–] **69**–14
cave [kāv] **220**–6
caverns [kă/vərnz] **220**–7
cavity [kăv/ə tē] **119**–7
C-clamp [sē/klămp/] **180**–6
CD [sē/dē/] **196**–9, **234**–5
CD boombox [sē/dē/ bōōm/bäks/] **234**–1
CD player [sē/dē/ plā/ər] **159**–38
celebrate [sĕl/ə brāt] **206**–C
celery [sĕl/ə rē] **69**–9
cell [sĕl] **194**–4
cell membrane [sĕl/ mĕm/brān] **194**–6
cell phone holder [sĕl/ fōn/ hōl/dər] **94**–15
cell phone kiosk [sĕl/ fōn/ kē/äsk] **131**–22
cell phone number [sĕl/ fōn/ nŭm/bər] **4**–12
cell wall [sĕl/ wäl/] **194**–5
cello [chĕl/ō] **238**–7
cellular phone [sĕl/yə lər fōn/] **14**–8
Celsius [sĕl/sē əs] **13**–2
cemetery [sĕ/mə tĕr/ē] **127**–15
cent [sĕnt] **26**–1, **26**–2, **26**–3, **26**–4
center [sĕn/tər]
automated postal center (APC)
[ö/tə māt ĭd pōs/təl sĕn/tər] / [ā/pē/sē/] **135**–10
childcare center [chĭld/kër/ sĕn/tər] **129**–30
convention center [kən vĕn/shən sĕn/tər] **127**–24
copy center [käp/ē sĕn/tər] **129**–18
entertainment center
[ĕn/tər tān/mənt sĕn/tər] **56**–5
resource center [rē/sörs sĕn/tər] **172**–9
CENTER [sĕn/tər] **208**–209
centimeter [cm] [sĕn/tə mē/tər] **17**–14
CENTRAL AMERICA [sĕn/trəl ə mĕr/ə kə] **200**–201
Central time [sĕn/trəl tīm/] **19**–31
cereal [sïr/ē əl] **80**–9
ceremony [sĕr/ə mō/nē] **206**–6
certificate [sər tĭf/ə kət] **40**–1, **41**–11
Certificate of Naturalization
[sər tĭf/ə kət əv năch/rə lə zā/shən] **40**–6
certified [sür/tə fīd/]
Certified Mail® [sür/tə fīd/ māl/] **134**–4
certified nursing assistant (CNA)
[sür/tə fīd/ nür/sĭng ə sĭs/tənt] / [sē/ĕn/ā/]
120–12
chain [chān] **51**–33, **95**–33, **180**–41
chair [chër] **7**–11
armchair [ärm/chër] **56**–22
beach chair [bēch/ chër/] **225**–22
dining room chair [dī/nĭng rōōm/chër/] **55**–8

easy chair [ē/zē/ chër/] **56**–22
folding chair [fōld/ĭng chër/] **102**–5
high chair [hī/ chër/] **37**–6, **82**–3
rocking chair [räk/ĭng chër/] **37**–21
wheelchair [wēl/chër/] **113**–9
chalk [chök] **7**–18
chalkboard [chök/börd/] **6**–1
challenged [chăl/əngd] **32**–10
change [chānj] **36**–G, **60**–P, **148**–C
change purse [chānj/ pürs/] **94**–14
changing [chān/jĭng]
changing pad [chān/jĭng păd/] **59**–2
changing table [chān/jĭng tā/bəl] **59**–1
charger [chär/jər] **14**–10, **234**–17, **235**–27
chart [chärt] **121**–24
cheap [chēp] **23**–20
check [chĕk] **132**–13
check book [chĕk/ bŏŏk/] **132**–12
check-in kiosk [chĕk/ĭn/ kē/ösk] **160**–2
checkstand [chĕk/stănd/] **73**–12
paycheck [pā/chĕk/] **165**–14
check [chĕk]
check blood pressure [chĕk/ blŭd/ prĕsh/ər] **118**–A
check email [chĕk/ ē/ māl/] **39**–W
check in [chĕk/ ĭn/] **160**–A
check Internet job sites
[chĕk/ ĭn/tər nĕt/ jäb/ sīts/] **173**–D
check messages [chĕk/ mĕs/ə jĭz] **171**–R
check out [chĕk/ owt/] **133**–C
check the correct boxes
[chĕk/ dhə kə rĕkt/ bäk/səz] **9**–U
check the oil [chĕk/ dhə oyl/] **157**–H
check the pronunciation
[chĕk/ dhe prə nən sē ā/ shən] **8**–D
check your bags [chĕk/ yər băgz/] **160**–B
check pulse [chĕk/ pŭls/] **122**–A
check your spelling [chĕk/ yər spĕl/ĭng] **197**–F
check your understanding
[chĕk/ yər ŭn/dər stănd/ĭng] **12**–N
check your work [chĕk/ yər würk/] **10**–L
checked [chĕkt] **96**–24
checkers [chĕk/ərz] **232**–7
checking account number
[chĕk/ĭng ə kownt/ nŭm/bər] **132**–14
checkout [chĕk/owt/] **133**–10
Checkpoint [chĕk/poynt/] **160**
cheddar cheese [chĕd/ər chēz/] **71**–28
cheek [chēk] **106**–3
cheese [chēz] **66**–4
American cheese [ə mĕr/ə kən chēz/] **71**–26
cheddar cheese [chĕd/ər chēz/] **71**–28
cheeseburger [chēz/bür/gər] **79**–3
cheesecake [chēz/kāk/] **81**–34
grilled cheese sandwich
[grĭld/ chēz/ săn/wĭch, –sănd/–] **80**–10
Swiss cheese [swĭs/ chēz/] **71**–27
Cheesy Tofu Vegetable Casserole
[chē/zē tō/fōō vĕj/tə bəl kăs/ə rōl] **77**
chef [shĕf] **83**–16
chef's hat [shĕfs/ hăt/] **93**–28
chef's jacket [shĕfs/ jăk/ət] **93**–29
chef's salad [shĕfs/ săl/ əd] **80**–14

executive chef [ĭg zĕk/yə tĭv shĕf/] **185**–7
head chef [hĕd/ shĕf/] **185**–7
sous chef [sōō/ shĕf/] **185**–6
Chef [shĕf] **93**
chemist [kĕm/ĭst] **195**–25
Chemistry [kĕm/ə strē] **195**
cherries [chĕr/ēz] **68**–11
cherry picker [chĕr/ē pĭk/ər] **178**–5
chess [chĕs] **232**–8
chest [chĕst] **59**–16, **104**–4, **107**–25
chest of drawers [chĕst/ əv drörz/] **59**–6
chicken [chĭk/ən] **66**–3, **70**–16
chicken pox [chĭk/ən päks/] **111**–6
chicken sandwich [chĭk/ən săn/wĭch, –sănd–] **79**–5
fried chicken [frīd/ chĭk/ən] **76**–1
roast chicken [rōst/ chĭk/ən] **81**–22
Chicken [chĭk/ən] **77**
chief justice [chēf/ jŭs/təs] **138**–13
CHILDCARE AND PARENTING
[chīld/kër ən për/ən tĭng] **36**–37
child / children [chīld] / [chĭl/ drən]
childcare center [chīld/kër sĕn/tər] **129**–30
childcare worker [chīld/kër wür/kər] **166**–16
children's program [chĭl/drənz prō/grăm] **236**–9
child safety seat [chīld/ sāf/tē sēt/] **159**–53
grandchild [grăn/chīld/, grănd/–] **34** ✦
lost child [löst/ chīld/] **144**–1
Childhood Diseases [chīld/hŏŏd dĭ zē/zəz] **111**
chili peppers [chĭl/ē pĕp/ərz] **69**–29
chill [chĭl] **76**–D
chills [chĭlz] **110**–9
chimney [chĭm/nē] **53**–5
chimpanzee [chĭm/păn zē/] **217**–27
chin [chĭn] **106**–1
chipmunk [chĭp/mŭngk] **215**–20
chips [chĭps] **73**–35
chiropractors [kī/rō prăk/tərz] **120**
chisel [chĭz/əl] **181**–55
choke [chōk] **116**–L
choose [chōōz] **9**–P
chop [chäp] **77**–L
chops [chäps] **70**–10, **70**–15
Christmas [krĭs/məs] **22**–18
Christmas tree [krĭs/məs trē/] **239**–16
chromosome [krō/mə zōm/] **194**–8
chrysanthemum [krĭ săn/thə məm] **211**–21
church [chürch] **127**–14
chute [shōōt] **51**–26
circle [sür/ kəl] **193**–34
circle [sür/ kəl] **9**–Q
circular saw [sür/kyə lər sö/] **180**–9
circulation desk [sür/kyə lā/shən dĕsk/] **133**–2
circumference [sər kŭm/frəns] **193**–36
citizen [sĭt/ə zən] **30**–5
Citizenship Requirements
[sĭt/ə zən shĭp/ rĭ kwïr/mənts] **140**
city [sĭt/ē] **4**–7, **52**–1
city code [sĭt/ē kōd/] **15**–34
city council [sĭt/ē kown/səl] **139**–27
city hall [sĭt/ē häl/] **124**–8
City Government [sĭt/ē gŭ/vərn mənt] **139**
CITY STREETS [sĭt/ē strēts/] **126**–127

CIVIC RIGHTS AND RESPONSIBILITIES
[sĭ/vĭk rīts n rĭ spän/sə bĭl/ə tēz] **140**
Civilizations [sĭ/və lə zā/shenz] **199**
claim [klām] **160**–L
clamp [klămp] **180**–6
clams [klămz] **71**–15
clarinet [klăr/ə nĕt/] **238**–2
classical [kla/sĭ kəl] **237**–21
classical concert [kla/sĭ kəl kän/sərt] **223**–14
classified ad [klăs/e fīd] **48**–2
Classmates [klăs/māts/] **8**
classroom [klăs/rōōm/] **5**–7
CLASSROOM [klăs/rōōm/] **6**–7
claw [klö] **214**–2
clean [klēn] **101**–16
clean [klēn] **76**–A
clean teeth [klēn/ tēth/] **119**–A
clean the house [klēn/ dhə hows/] **39**–O
clean the lint trap [klēn/ dhə lĭnt/ trăp/] **101**–D
clean the oven [klēn/ dhə ŭv/ən] **60**–C
clean up [klēn/ ŭp/] **147**–M
cleaner [klēn/ər]
dry cleaners [drī/ klēn/ərz] **128**–2
glass cleaner [glăs/ klēn/ər] **61**–14
oven cleaner [ŭv/ən klēn/ər] **61**–3
vacuum cleaner [văk/yōōm klēn/ər] **61**–10
vacuum cleaner attachments
[văk/yōōm klēn/ər ə tăch/mənts] **61**–11
vacuum cleaner bag [văk/yəm klēn/ər băg/] **61**–12
CLEANING SUPPLIES [klē/nĭng sə plīz/] **61**
cleanser [klēn/zər] **61**–18
CLEANUP [klēn/ŭp/] **148**–149
clear [klĭr] **13**–9
clear tape [klĭr/tāp/] **183**–30
clear [klĭr] **82**–G
clear off [klĭr/ äf/] **10**–I
clerk [klürk] **5**–13, **182**–2
admissions clerk [əd mĭsh/ənz klürk/] **120**–14
desk clerk [dĕsk/ klürk/] **184**–11
DMV clerk [dē/ĕm/vē/ klürk/] **136**–3
file clerk [fīl/ klürk/] **182**–10
grocery clerk [grōs/rē klürk/, grōsh/–, grō/sə–] **72**–4
library clerk [lī/brĕr ē klürk/] **133**–1
payroll clerk [pā/rōl/ klürk/] **165**–10
postal clerk [pō/stəl klürk/] **135**–7
retail clerk [rē/tāl/ klürk/] **169**–53
salesclerk [sālz/klürk/] **94**–3
shipping clerk [shĭp/ĭng klürk/] **175**–16
stock clerk [stäk/ klürk/] **169**–59
click [klĭk] **197**–B
climb [klīm] **224**–C
climbing apparatus [klīm/ĭng ă/pə ră/təs] **224**–14
clinic [klĭn/ĭk] **186**–2
clip-on earrings [klĭp/än ĭr/ĭngz, –ön–] **95**–37
clipper [klĭp/ər] **109**–31, **176**–11
clips [klĭps] **108**–19, **183**–31, **194**–24
clock [kläk] **7**–9, **58**–24, **165**–7
clock radio [kläk/ rā/dē ō] **102**–6
close [klōz] **6**–H
closet [kläz/ət] **57** ✦, **58**–5
Closures [klō/zhərz] **99**

cloth [klöth] **181**–54
cloth diaper [klöth/ dī/pərz] **37**–8
tablecloth [tā/bəl klöth/] **55**–12
washcloth [wäsh/klöth/] **57**–4
clothes [klōz] **146**–6
clothesline [klōz/lĭn/] **101**–9
clothespin [klōz/pĭn/] **101**–10
CLOTHES [klōz] **86**–87, **88**–89, **96**–97, **98**–99
clothing [klō/dhĭng] **102**–2
CLOTHING [klō/dhĭng] **90**, **92**–93
Clothing Problems [klō/dhĭng präb/ləmz] **97**
cloudy [klow/dē] **13**–10
club [klŭb] **162**–4, **223**–12, **231**–1
club sandwich [klŭb săn/wĭch/, –sănd–] **80**–12
clubs [klŭbz] **233**–32
clutch [klŭch] **159**–49
clutch bag [klŭch/ băg/] **89**–19
CNA (certified nursing assistant) [sē/ĕn/ā/] /
[sür/tə tə fīd/ nür/sĭng ə sĭs/tənt] **120**–12
coach [kōch] **5**–20, **229**–2
coal [kōl] **218**–4
coarse adjustment knob
[körs/ ə jüst/mənt näb/] **194**–22
Coast Guard [kōst/ gärd/] **138**–18
coat [kōt] **90**–2, **216**–19
lab coat [lăb/ kōt/] **93**–33
raincoat [rān/ kōt/] **90**–18
sports coat [spörts/ kōt/] **89**–14
trench coat [trĕnch/ kōt/] **90**–21
cobra [kō/brə] **213**–41
cockpit [käk/pĭt/] **161**–10
cockroaches [käk/rō/chəz] **63**–26
cocktail dress [käk/tāl/ drĕs/] **89**–20
coconuts [kō/kə nŭts/] **68**–24
cod [käd] **71**–8, **212**–5
code [kōd]
area code [ĕr/ē ə kōd/] **15**–29
bar code [bär/ kōd/] **27**–4
city code [sĭt/ē kōd/] **15**–34
country code [kŭn/trē kōd/] **15**–33
coffee [kö/fē] **73**–33, **81**–37, **81**–38
coffeemaker [kö/fē mā/kər] **54**–11
coffee mug [kö/fē mŭg/] **55**–7
coffee shop [kö/fē shäp/] **126**–11
coffee table [kö/fē tā/bəl] **56**–19
COFFEE SHOP MENU [kö/fē shäp/ mĕn/yōō] **80**–81
coins [koynz] **146**–17
coin purse [koyn/ pürs/] **94**–14
Coins [koynz] **26**
colander [käl/ən dər] **78**–17
cold [kōld] **13**–6, **42**–4, **111**–1
cold tablets [kōld tăb/ləts] **113**–27
cold water [kōld wö/tər] **57**–7
coleslaw [kōl/slö/] **80**–18
collar [käl/ər] **100**–
collate [kō/lāt/, kə lāt/] **171**–E
collect [kə lĕkt/] **232**–A
college [käl/ĭj] **127**–17, **188**–6, **188**–7
college degree [käl/ĭj də grē/] **41**–7
college dormitory [käl/ĭj dör/mə tör/ē] **52**–8
cologne [kə lōn/] **108**–6
colon [kō/lən] **190**–17

Colonial Period [kə lō/nē əl pĭr/ē əd] **198**
colonies [kä/lə nēz] **198**–1
colonists [kä/lə nĭsts] **198**–2
color [kŭl/ər]
watercolor [wö/tər kŭl/ər] **233**–21
color [kŭl/ər] **33**–D
coloring book [kŭl/ə rĭng bŏok/] **59**–13
Colors [kŭl/ərs] **24**
COLORS [kŭl/ərs] **24**
Columbus Day [kə lŭm/bəs dā/] **22**–15
column [käl/ŭm] **107**–49
comb [kōm] **33**–21, **108**–13
comb [kōm] **108**–G
come [kŭm] **39**–R
comedy [käm/ə dē] **236**–2, **237**–13
comet [käm/ət] **205**–24
comfort [kŭm/fərt] **36**–I
comma [käm/ə] **190**–14
commercial fisher [kə mür/shəl fĭsh/ər] **167**–17
commit a crime [kə mĭt/ ə krīm/] **142** ✦
Common Illnesses and Childhood Diseases
[käm/ən ĭl/nə səz ən chĭld/hŏod-dĭ zē/zəz] **111**
COMMUNITY CLEANUP
[kə myōō/nə tē klēn/ŭp] **148**–149
community college
[kə myōō/nə tə käl/ĭj] **127**–17, **188**–6
Comparing Clothing [kəm pĕr/ĭng klō/dhĭng] **97**
compartment [kəm pärt/mənt] **159**–44, **161**–13
complaint [kəm plānt/] **97** ✦
Complex [käm/plĕks/] **51**
compliment [käm/plə mĕnt/] **12** ✦
compliment [käm/plə mĕnt/] **12**–C
composer [kəm pō/zər] **199**–15
composition [käm/pə zĭsh/ən] **199**–14
compost [käm/pōst/] **219**–M
compost pile [käm/pōst pil/] **53**–25
computer [kəm pyōō/tər] **7**–15, **183**–17
computer lab [kəm pyōō/tər lăb/] **5**–15
computer software engineer
[kəm pyōō/tər söft/wĕr/ ĕn/jə nîr/] **167**–18
computer technician [kəm pyōō/tər tĕk nĭsh/ən]
167–19, **182**–12
Computer [kəm pyōō/tər] **196**
COMPUTERS [kəm pyōō/tərz] **196**
conceal [kən sēl/] **143**–C
concert [kän/sərt] **222**–5, **223**–14
concierge [kän/sē ĕrzh/, kön/–] **184**–4
conclusion [kən klōō/zhən] **190**–8
concrete [käng/krēt, kän krēt/] **178**–10
conditioner [kən dĭsh/ə nər] **108**–11, **159**–39
Conditions [kən dĭsh/ənz] **13**, **111**
CONDITIONS [kən dĭsh/ənz] **111**
condominium [kän/də mĭn/ē əm] **52**–5
conduct [kən dŭkt/] **238**–C
conductor [kən dŭk/tər] **152**–13
cone [kōn] **79**–13, **193**–40
pinecone [pīn/kōn] **210**–11
conference room [kän/frəns rōōm/] **182**–4
confetti [kən fĕt/ē] **239**–3
confused [kən fyōōzd/] **43**–26
congestion [kən jĕs/chən] **110**–7
Congress [käng/grəs] **138**–2, **198**–6

congressperson [kän/grəs pür/sən] **138**–4
CONSERVATION [kän/sər vā/shən] **218**–**219**
Conserve Energy and Resources
[kən sürv/ ēn/ər jē ən rē/sörs/əz] **219**
console [kän/sōl] **232**–3
constellation [kän/stə lā/shən] **205**–14
Constitution [kän/stə tōō/shən] **198**–19
construction [kən strŭk/shən]
construction paper [kən strŭk/shən pā/pər] **232**–12
construction site [kən strŭk/shən sīt/] **126**–2
construction worker
[kən strŭk/shən wür/kər] **178**–1
CONSTRUCTION [kən strŭk/shən] **178**
Construction Worker [kən strŭk/shən wür/kər] **92**
contact [kän/tăkt] **146**–2
contact lenses [kän/tăkt lĕn/zəz] **115**–8
container [kən tā/nər] **74**–5, **74**–17, **78**–4
CONTAINERS AND PACKAGING
[kən tā/nərz ən păk/ĭ jĭng] **74**
continental [kän/tə nĕnt/əl] **198**–6
contractor [kän/trăk tər] **186**–5
control [kən trōl/] **121**–27, **232**–4
convenience store [kən vēn/yəns stör/] **128**–3
convention center [kən vĕn/shən sĕn/tər] **127**–24
convert [kən vürt/] **17**–D, **75**–C
convertible [kən vür/tə bəl] **156**–5
conveyer belt [kən vā/ər bĕlt/] **175**–16
convict [kän/vĭkt] **141**–15
convict [kən vĭkt/] **141**–E
cook [kŏŏk] **185**–1, **185** ✦
cook [kŏŏk] **39**–Q, **76**–C, **170**–C
cooked [kŏŏkt] **70**–25
cookies [kŏŏk/ēz] **73**–38
cookie sheet [kŏŏk/ē shēt/] **78**–27
cool [kōōl] **13**–5
cooler [kōō/lər] **225**–19
co-op [kō/äp/] **52** ✦
copier [kä/pē ər]
photocopier [fō/tō kä/pē ər]**183**–23
copies / copy [kä/pēz] / [kä/pē]
copies of ID and credit cards
[käp/ēz əv ī/dē ən krĕd/ət kärdz/] **146**–19
copies of important papers
[käp/ēz əv ĭm pört/ənt pā/pərz] **146**–20
copy center [käp/ē sĕn/tər] **129**–18
copy [käp/ē] **8**–E
coral [kör/əl] **220**–5
cord [körd] **14**–2
bungee cord [bŭn/jē körd/] **181**–15
cordless phone [körd/ləs fōn/] **15**–24
extension cord [ĭk stĕn/shən körd/] **181**–14
frayed cord [frād/ körd/] **179**–5
power cord [pow/ər körd/] **196**–2
corduroy [kör/də roy/] **99**–11
core course [kör/ körs/] **189** ✦
corn [körn] **69**–12, **177**–4
corn rows [körn/ rōz/] **33**–14
corned beef [körnd/ bēf/] **71**–22
corner [kör/nər] **128**–7
coronary disease [kör/ə nĕ/rē dĭ zēz/] **111** ✦
corral [kə răl/] **177**–17
correct [kə rĕkt/] **10**–N

correction [kə rĕk/shən]
correction fluid [kə rĕk/shən flōō/əd] **183**–36
correction tape [kə rĕk/shən tāp/] **183**–37
cost [köst] **27**–7, **122**–1
costume [käs/tōōm] **239**–11
cotton [kät/n] **98**–1, **177**–6
couch [kowch] **56**–18
cough [köf] **110**–A
cough syrup [köf/ sĭr/əp, –sür/–] **113**–29
council [kown/səl] **139**–27
councilperson [kown/səl pür/sən] **139**–28
counselor [kown/slər] **5**–6, **172**–10
count [kownt] **84**–A
counter [kown/tər] **54**–22, **113**–18
counterperson [kown/tər pür/sən] **79**–17
Counterperson [kown/tər pür/sən] **93**
country [kŭn/trē] **52**–4, **227**–3, **237**–27
country code [kŭn/trē kōd/] **15**–33
county fair [kown/tē fër/] **223**–13
coupe [kōōp] **156**–2
couple [kŭ/pəl] **35**–20, **35**–21, **239**–4
coupons [kōō/pönz/] **67**–15
courier [kür/ē ər, kŏŏr/–] **168**–40
course [körs] **172**–8, **189** ✦
court [kört]
basketball court [băs/kət böl/ kört/] **229**–7
courthouse [kört/hows/] **125**–13
courtroom [kört/rōōm/] **141**–7
court reporter [kört/ rĭ pör/tər] **141**–12
courtyard [kört/yärd/] **51**–21
food court [fōōd/ kört/] **131**–15
Supreme Court [sə prēm/ kört/] **138**–11
tennis court [tĕ/nəs kört/] **224**–6
cousin [kŭz/ən] **34**–9
cover [kŭv/ər] **158**–9, **181**–46
coveralls [kŭv/ər ölz/] **92**–8
cover-up [kŭv/ər ŭp/] **90**–25
cow [kow] **215**–1
cowboy hat [kow/boy/ hăt/] **92**–18
coyote [kī ō/tē, kī/ōt/] **216**–3
CPR (cardiopulmonary resuscitation) [sē/pē/är/] /
[kär/dē ō pŏŏl/mə nër/ē-rē sŭs/ə tā/shən] **117**–17
CPU [sē/pē/yōō/] **196**–4
crab [krăb] **71**–9, **212**–20
cracked [krăkt] **62**–4
cradle [krād/l] **59**–20
crane [krān] **178**–7
crash [krăsh] **144**–3
crayons [krā/änz] **59**–14
cream [krēm] **24**–16, **81**–41, **113**–25
antihistamine cream
[ăn/tī hĭs/tə mēn krēm/] **117**–11
ice-cream [īs/ krēm/] **72**–26
ice-cream cone [īs/ krēm kōn/] **79**–13
ice cream shop [īs/ krēm shäp/] **131**–16
shaving cream [shā/vĭng krēm/] **109**–29
sour cream [sow/ər krēm/] **72**–21
creamer [krē/mər] **55**–15
credit [krĕd/ət] **146**–19
creek [krēk, krĭk] **204** ✦
crescent moon [krĕs/ənt mōōn/] **205**–10

crew [krōō] **176**–1, **176**–4
crewneck [krōō/nĕk] **96**–7
crew socks [krōō/säks/] **91**–8
crib [krĭb] **59**–3
cricket [krĭk/ət] **214**–23
crime [krīm] **142** ✦
CRIME [krīm] **142**
criminal [krĭm/ə nəl] **142** ✦
crocheting [krō shā/ĭng] **233**–25
crocodile [kräk/ə dīl/] **213**–37
crocus [krō/kəs] **211**–17
Crops [kräps] **177**
cross [krös]
cross-country skiing [krös/kŭn/trē skē/ĭng] **227**–3
crosswalk [krös/wök/] **128**–15
cross [krös] **128**–A
cross out [krös/ owt/] **9**–R
crossing [krö/sĭng] **154**–13, **154**–14, **154**–15
crown [krown] **119**–9
crucible tongs [krōō/sə bəl tängz/, –töngz/] **195**–44
crutches [krŭch/əz] **113**–10
cry [krī] **206**–B
cube [kyōōb] **193**–38
cubicle [kyōōb/ə kəl] **182**–7
cucumbers [kyōō/kŭm bərz] **69**–10
cuff [kŭf] **100**–9
cup [kŭp] **75**–2, **75**–10, **83**–24
1/2 cup [hăf/ kŭp/] **75**–9
1/4 cup [kwör/tər kŭp/] **75**–8
teacup [tē/kŭp/] **55**–6
curb [kürb] **129**–21
curling iron [kür/lĭng ī/ərn] **108**–17
curly hair [kür/lē hër/] **33**–11
cursor [kür/sər] **197**–14
curtains [kür/tnz] **57**–12, **58**–7
curved line [kürvd/ līn/] **193**–23
cushion [kŏŏ/shən] **56** ✦, **100**–13
customer [kŭs/tə mər] **72**–1, **94**–4, **132**–2, **164**–2
customer service [kŭs/tə mər sür/vəs] **97** ✦
customer service representative
[kŭs/tə mər-sür/vəs rĕ/prə zĕn/tə tĭv] **167**–20
Customs [kŭs/təmz] **161**
customs officer [kŭs/təmz ö/fə sər] **161**–17
cut [kŭt] **91**–10, **110**–13
cut [kŭt] **33**–A, **109**–N
cut up [kŭt/ ŭp/] **77**–I
cute [kyōōt] **32**–14
cutlets [kŭt/ləts] **70**–6
cutter [kut/ər] **183**–22, **232**–16
cutting board [kŭt/ĭng börd/] **54**–27
cycling [sī/klĭng] **228**–5
cyclist [sī/klĭst] **224**–2
cylinder [sĭl/ən dər] **193**–41, **195**–38
cytoplasm [sī/tə plăzm] **194**–9
daffodil [dăf/ə dĭl/] **211**–25
daily [dā/lē] **20**–21
DAILY ROUTINES [dā/lē rōō tēnz/] **38**–**39**
Dairy [dër/ē] **72**
daisy [dā/zē] **211**–14
dance [dăns] **64**–A
dangerous [dān/jər əs] **186**–1
dark blue [därk/ blōō/] **24**–10

Dashboard and Instrument Panel
  [dăsh/börd/ ən ĭn/strə mənt păn/əl] **159**
dates [dāts] **20**–1, **68**–28
  date of birth [dāt əv bürth/] **4**–13
  expiration date
    [ĕk/spə rā/shən dāt/] **112**–7, **136**–10
daughter [dö/tər] **34**–14
  daughter-in-law [dö/tər ĭn lö/] **34** ✦
  granddaughters [grăn/dö/tərz] **34** ✦
  stepdaughter [stĕp/dö/tər] **35** ✦
day [dā] **20**–2
  birthday [bürth/dā/] **22**–1
  Columbus Day [kə lŭm/bəs dā/] **22**–15
  daylight saving time [dā/līt/ sā/vĭng tīm/] **19**–25
  every day [ĕv/rē dā/] **20**–21
  Independence Day [ĭn/də pĕn/dəns dā/] **22**–13
  Labor Day [lā/bər dā/] **22**–14
  Martin Luther King Jr. Day
    [mär/tən loo/thər kĭng/ joon/yər-dā/] **22**–10
  Memorial Day [mə mör/ē əl dā/] **22**–12
  New Year's Day [noo/ yĭrz/ dā/] **22**–9
  Presidents' Day [prĕz/ə dənts dā/] **22**–11
  Veterans Day [vĕt/ər ənz dā/] **22**–16
Day [dā] **18**
DAY AT SCHOOL [dā/ ăt skool/] **11**
DAY AT WORK [dā/ ăt würk/] **186**–187
Days of the Week [dāz/ əv dhə wēk/] **20**
dead [dĕd]
  dead-bolt lock [dĕd/bōlt/ läk/] **51**–34
  dead end [dĕd/ĕnd/] **154**–6
deaf [dĕf] **32**–12
Dealer [dē/lər] **158**
dealership [dē/lər shĭp/] **126**–4
death certificate [dĕth/ sər tĭf/ə kət] **41**–11
debate [də bāt/] **139**–B
decaf coffee [dē/kăf/ kö/fē] **81**–38
decay [də kā/] **119**–7
December [dĭ sĕm/bər] **21**–36
decimal point [dĕ/sə məl poynt/] **17**–7
Decimals [dĕ/sə məlz] **17**
deck [dĕk] **240**–2
declaration [dĕk/lə rā/shən]
  declaration form [dĕk/lə rā/shən förm/] **161**–16
  Declaration of Independence
    [dĕk/lə rā/shən əv ĭn/də pĕn/dəns] **198**–5
decline [də klīn/] **12**–J
decorations [dĕk/ə rā/shənz] **240**–1
deductions [də dŭk/shənz] **165**–13
deed [dēd] **41**–9
deer [dĭr] **216**–14
defendant [dĭ fĕn/dənt] **141**–5
defense attorney [dĭ fĕns/ ə tür/nē] **141**–4
defroster [də frös/tər] **159**–41
degrees [də grēz/] **13**–8, **193**–26
delayed flight [də lād/ flīt/] **161**–30
delete [də lēt/] **196**–C
DELI [dĕl/ē] **71**
deliver [də lĭv/ər] **11**–G, **135**–E
delivery person [də lĭv/ə rē pür/sən] **167**–21
dementia [də mĕn/shə] **111**–18
demonstration [dĕ/mən strā/shən] **122**–6
denim [dĕ/nəm] **99**–7

denominator [də nömə nā/tər] **192**–6
dental [dĕn/təl]
  dental assistant [dĕn/təl ə sĭs/tənt] **119**–2, **167**–22
  dental floss [dĕn/təl flös/, –fläs/] **109**–24
  dental hygienist [dĕn/təl hī jē/nĭst, –jē/nĭst] **119**–3
  dental instruments [dĕn/təl ĭn/strə mənts] **119**–4
DENTAL CARE [dĕn/təl kër/] **119**
Dental Problems [dĕn/təl präb/ləmz] **119**
dentist [dĕn/tĭst] **119**–1
Dentistry [dĕn/təs trē/] **119**
dentures [dĕn/chərz] **119**–10
deodorant [dē ō/dər ənt] **108**–5
department [dĭ pärt/mənt] **95**–7, **95**–8
  Department of Motor Vehicles
    [dĭ pärt/mənt əv mō/tər vē/ĭ kəlz] **124**–4
  department store [dĭ pärt/mənt stör/] **131**–13
DEPARTMENT OF MOTOR VEHICLES (DMV)
    [dĭ pärt/mənt əv mō/tər vē/ĭ kəlz] / [dē/ĕm/vē/]
    136–137
departure [dĭ pär/chər] **161**–5, **161**–7
deposit [dĭ päz/ət] **132**–3, **132**–7
  deposit slip [dĭ päz/ət slĭp/] **132**–4
depression [də prĕ/shən] **115**–5
depth [dĕpth] **17**–18
DESCRIBING CLOTHES [dĭ skrī/bĭng klōz/] **96**–97
DESCRIBING HAIR [dĭ skrī/bĭng hër/] **33**
DESCRIBING PEOPLE [dĭ skrī/bĭng pē/pəl] **32**
DESCRIBING THINGS [dĭ skrī/bĭng thĭngz/] **23**
desert [dĕz/ərt] **204**–4
design [dĭ zīn/] **175**–A
designated drivers [dĕz/ĭg nā/təd drī/vərz] **143** ✦
designer [dĭ zī/nər] **98** ✦, **167**–30, **175**–2, **176**–5
desk [dĕsk] **6**–7, **182**–9
  circulation desk [sür/kyə lā/shən dĕsk/] **133**–2
  desk clerk [dĕsk klürk/] **184**–11
  front desk [frŭnt/ dĕsk/] **184**–12
Desktop Computer [dĕsk/täp/ kəm pyoo/tər] **196**
Desserts [dĭ zürts] **81**
  dessert tray [dĭ zürt/ trā/] **83**–10
destination [dĕs/tə nā/shən] **161** ✦
detector [dĭ tĕk/tər] **51**–29
detergent [dĭ tür/jənt] **101**–8
device [də vīs/] **225**–20
diabetes [dī/ə bē/tēz, –təs] **111**–12
diagonal [dī ăg/ə nəl, –ăg/nəl] **193**–31
diameter [dī ăm/ə tər] **193**–37
diamonds [dī/məndz] **233**–29
diaper [dī/pər] **37**–8, **37**–10
  diaper pail [dī/pər pāl/] **37**–7
diaphragm [dī/ə frăm] **194**–19
dice [dīs] **232**–6
dice [dīs] **77**–J
dictate [dĭk/tāt] **8**–N
dictator [dĭk/tā/tər] **199**–6
dictionary [dĭk/shə nër/ē] **7**–30, **7**–31
die [dī] **41**–R
dietician [dī/ə tĭsh/ən] **120**–15
difference [dĭf/rəns] **192**–8
different [dĭ/frənt, dĭ/fə rənt] **23**–16
DIFFERENT [dĭ/frənt, dĭ/fə rənt] **28**–29

DIFFERENT PLACES TO LIVE
    [dĭ/frənt plā/səz tə lĭv, dĭ/fə rənt] **52**
difficult [dĭf/ĭ kŭlt/] **23**–24
digital [dĭ/jə təl]
  digital camera [dĭ/jə təl kăm/rə] **235**–19
  digital photo album [dĭ/jə təl fō/tō ăl/bəm] **235**–32
dime [dīm] **26**–3
Dimensions [də mĕn/shənz] **17**
diner [dī/nər] **82**–6, **185**–9
dining [dī/nĭng]
  dining area [dī/nĭng ër/ē ə] **46**–7
  dining room [dī/nĭng room/] **82**–1
  dining room chair [dī/nĭng room/ chër/] **55**–8
  dining room table [dī/nĭng room/tā/bəl] **55**–9
Dining [dī/nĭng] **185**
DINING AREA [dī/nĭng ër/ē ə] **55**
dinner [dĭn/ər] **72**–28
  dinner fork [dĭn/ər förk/] **83**–28
  dinner plate [dĭn/ər plāt/] **83**–18
  dinner salad [dĭn/ər săl/əd] **80**–15
Dinner [dĭn/ər] **81**
diploma [də plō/mə] **40**–3
direct flight [də rĕkt/ flīt/, dī–] **161** ✦
Directions [də rĕk/shənz] **9**, **155**
DIRECTIONS AND MAPS
    [də rĕk/shənz ən măps/, dī–] **155**
directory [də rĕk/tə rē, dī–] **131**–24
  directory assistance
    [də rĕk/tə rē ə sĭs/təns, dī–] **14**–22
dirty [dür/tē] **101**–15
Disabilities [dĭ/sə bĭ/lə tēz] **32**
disagree [dĭ/sə grē/] **12**–L
disappointed [dĭ/sə poyn/təd] **28**–4
DISASTERS [dĭ/zăs tərz] **144**–145
disc [dĭsk] **231**–27
discipline [dĭs/ə plən] **36**–K
discuss [dĭ skŭs/] **8**–G
disease [dĭ zēz/] **111**–11, **111** ✦, **119**–11
Diseases [dĭ zē/zəz] **111**
disgusted [dĭ skŭs/təd] **42**–7
dish [dĭsh] **55**–1
  casserole dish [kăs/ə rōl dĭsh/] **78**–10
  dish rack [dĭsh/ răk/] **54**–5
  dish room [dĭsh/ room/] **83**–13
  dish towel [dĭsh/ tow/əl] **61**–22
  dishwasher [dĭsh/wä/shər, –wö/–]
    54–8, **83**–14, **185**–2
  dishwashing liquid [dĭsh/wä/shĭng lĭk/wəd] **61**–21
  satellite dish [să/tə lĭt dĭsh/] **53**–6
  soap dish [sōp/ dĭsh/] **57**–25
disinfectant wipes [dĭs/ən fĕk/tənt wīps/] **61**–23
display case [dĭ splā/ kās/] **94**–5
disposable [dĭ spō/zə bəl]
  disposable diaper [dĭ spō/zə bəl dī/pər] **37**–10
  disposable gloves [dĭ spō/zə bəl glŭvz/] **93**–27
disposal [dĭ spō/zəl] **54**–7, **121**–31
dive [dīv] **230**–K
divide [də vīd/] **17**–A, **192**–D
diving [dī/vĭng] **227**–12
  diving mask [dī/vĭng măsk/] **225**–6
divorced couple [də vörst/ kŭ/pəl] **35**–21
DJ [dē/jā/] **64**–4

DMV [dē/ĕm/vē/]
  DMV clerk [dē/ĕm/vē/ klürk/] **136**–3
  DMV handbook [dē/ĕm/vē/ hănd/bŏŏk/] **136**–1
do [dōō] **39**–T
  do an experiment [dōō ən ĭk spĕr/ə mənt] **195**–B
  do crafts [dōō krăfts/] **232**–D
  do errands [dōō ĕr/əndz] **128** ✦
  do manual labor [dōō măn/yōō əl lā/bər] **170**–D
  do not drink [dōō nät drĭnk/] **112**–F
  do not enter [dōō nät/ ĕn/tər] **154**–2
  do not operate [dōō nät/ äp/ə rāt/] **112**–E
  do not take [dōō nät/ tāk/] **112**–F
  don't be late [dōnt/ bē/ lāt/] **174**–E
  don't litter [dōnt/ lĭ/tər] **219**–L
  don't smoke [dōnt/ smōk/] **114**–G
dock [däk] **175**–15, **234**–3
  dockworker [däk/wür/kər] **167**–23
doctor [däk/tər] **118**–5
DOCUMENTS [dä/kyə mənts] **40**–**41**
dog [dög] **79**–6, **215**–11, **215**–22
dogwood [dög/wŏŏd/] **210**–15
DOING THE LAUNDRY [dō/ĭng dhə lön/drē] **101**
doll [däl] **59**–21, **233**–28
  dollhouse [däl/hows/] **59**–16
  doll making kit [däl/ mā/kĭng kĭt/] **232**–13
dollar [däl/ər] **26**–7
  dollar coin [däl/ər koyn/] **26**–6
  fifty dollars [fĭf/tē däl/ərz] **26**–11
  five dollars [fĭv/ däl/ərz] **26**–8
  half dollar [hăf/ däl/ər] **26**–5
  one hundred dollars
    [wŭn/ hŭn/drəd däl/ərz] **26**–12
  ten dollars [tĕn/ däl/ərz] **26**–9
  twenty dollars [twĕn/tē däl/ərz] **26**–10
dolphin [däl/fən, döl/–] **213**–31
domesticated [də mĕs/tə kā/təd] **215** ✦
DOMESTIC ANIMALS AND RODENTS
  [də mĕs/tĭk ăn/ə məlz ən rōd/nts] **215**
donkey [däng/kē, dŭng/–, döng/–] **215**–3
donut [dō/nŭt] **79**–15
  donut shop [dō/nŭt shäp/] **129**–17
door [dör] **46**–3
  doorbell [dör/bĕl/] **53**–14
  door chain [dör/ chān/] **51**–33
  doorknob [dör/näb/] **53**–12
  door lock [dör/ läk/] **159**–25
  doorman [dör/măn/] **184**–1
  4-door car [för/ dör kär/] **156**–1
  front door [frŭnt/ dör/] **53**–11
  garage door [gə räj/ dör/] **53**–7
  revolving door [rĭ väl/vĭng dör/] **184**–2
  screen door [skrēn/ dör/] **53**–15
  sliding glass door [slī/dĭng glăs/dör/] **53**–18
  storm door [störm/ dör/] **53**–10
  2-door car [tōō/dör kär/] **156**–2
dorm / dormitory [dörm] / [dör/mə tör/ē] **52**–8
dosage [dō/sĭj] **112**–6
double [dŭb/əl]
  double bed [dŭb/əl bĕd/] **184**–14
  double boiler [dŭb/əl boy/lər] **78**–8

down [down]
  break down [brāk/ down/] **162**–D
  downhill skiing [down/hĭl/ skē/ĭng] **227**–1
  down jacket [down jăk/ət] **90**–16
  down vest [down vĕst/] **90**–14
  drop-down menu [dräp/ down/ mĕn/yōō/] **197**–8
  put down [pŏŏt/ down/] **6**–J
  sit down [sĭt down/] **6**–F
  walk down [wäk down/] **153**–D
downstairs [down/stĕrz/] **51** ✦
DOWNTOWN [down/town/] **124**–**125**
drain [drān] **57**–5
drama [drä/mə] **236**–12
drapes [drāps] **56**–16
draw [drö] **8**–F, **118**–F, **195**–E
drawer [drör] **54**–23, **58**–2, **59**–6
dress [drĕs] **86**–3, **88**–5, **89**–20
  dressmaker [drĕs/mā/kər] **100**–1
  dressmaker's dummy [drĕs/mā/kərz dŭ/mē] **100**–2
  dress socks [drĕs/ säks/] **91**–9
dress [drĕs] **36**–H, **174**–B
dressed [drĕst] **38**–D
dresser [drĕs/ər] **58**–1
Dressings [drĕs/ĭngz] **80**
dribble [drĭb/əl] **230**–J
drill [drĭl] **178**–9, **180**–8
  drill bit [drĭl bĭt/] **180**–28
drill [drĭl] **119**–D
drink [drĭnk] **11**–J
  do not drink alcohol
    [dōō/ nät/ drĭnk/ ăl/kə höl/] **112**–F
  don't drink and **drive** [dōnt/ drĭnk ən drĭv/] **143**–G
  drink fluids [drĭnk flōō/ədz] **114**–C
drip [drĭp] **121**–25
dripping [drĭp/ĭng] **63**–17
drive [drĭv] **196**–6, **196**–8, **196**–9
  drive-thru window [drĭv/thrōō/ wĭn/dō] **128**–11
  driveway [drĭv/wā/] **53**–8
drive [drĭv]
  don't drink and **drive** [dōnt/drĭnk ən drĭv/] **143**–G
  drive a truck [drĭv ə trŭk] **170**–E
  drive through [drĭv/ thrōō] **153**–K
  drive to work [drĭv/ tə würk/] **38**–I
driver [drī/vər] **152**–21, **169**–61
  designated drivers [dĕz/ĭg nā/təd drī/vərz] **143** ✦
  driver's license [drī/vərz lī/səns] **40**–4, **136**–9
  driver's license number
    [drī/vərz lī/səns nŭm/bər] **136**–11
  Phillips screwdriver [fĭl/ĭps skrōō/drī/vər] **180**–31
  screwdriver [skrōō/drī/vər] **180**–30
driving [drī/vĭng] **142**–5
drop [dräp]
  drop cloth [dräp/ klöth/] **181**–54
  drop-down menu [dräp/ down/ mĕn/yōō/] **197**–8
drop off [dräp/ öf/] **38**–G
dropper [dräp/ər] **195**–45
drops [dräps] **113**–31
drought [drowt] **145**–11
drown [drown] **116**–I
drugs [drŭgz] **116**–K, **142**–6
drums [drŭmz] **238**–16
drumsticks [drŭm/stĭks/] **70**–23
drunk driving [drŭngk/ drī/vĭng] **142**–5

dry [drī] **101**–18
  dry cleaners [drī/ klē/nərz] **128**–2
  dry erase marker [drī/ ĭ rās/ mär/kər] **7**–17
  drywall [drī/wöl/] **178**–19
dry [drī] **60**–N, **108**–H
dryer [drī/ər] **50**–13, **101**–4
  blow dryer [blō/ drī/ər] **33**–23, **108**–18
  dryer sheets [drī/ər shēts/] **101**–5
Dry Measures [drī/ mĕzh/ərz] **75**
duck [dŭk] **70**–18, **214**–12
duct tape [dŭkt/ tāp/] **181**–49
dummy [dŭ/mē] **100**–2
dump truck [dŭmp/ trŭk/] **156**–19
dune [dōōn] **204**–5
duplex [dōō/plĕks/] **52** ✦
During an Emergency [dōō/rĭng ən ĭ mür/jən sē] **147**
dust [dŭst]
  dustpan [dŭst/ păn/] **61**–17
  dust ruffle [dŭst/ rŭf/əl] **58**–17
  dust storm [dŭst/ störm/] **13**–19
dust [dŭst] **60**–A
duster [dŭs/tər] **61**–1
DVD [dē/vē/dē/] **133**–19, **234**–11
  DVD and CD-ROM drive
    [dē/vē/dē/ ən sē/dē/räm/ drĭv/] **196**–9
  DVD player [dē/vē/dē/ plā/ ər] **56**–7, **234**–10
dye [dī] **33**–D
eagle [ē/gəl] **214**–9
ear [ĭr] **32**–17, **105**–11
  earache [ĭr/āk/] **110**–3
  ear infection [ĭr/ ĭn fĕk/shən] **111**–3
  earmuffs [ĭr/mŭfs/] **90**–13, **179**–16
  ear plugs [ĭr/ plŭgz/] **179**–15
  pierced earrings [pïrst/ ĭr/ĭngz] **95**–36
early [ür/lē] **19**–22
Earth [ürth] **205**–3
earthquake [ürth/kwāk/] **144**–5
easel [ē/zəl] **233**–18
east [ēst] **155**–4
Eastern time [ē/stərn tīm/] **19**–32
easy [ē/zē] **23**–23, **76**–11
  easy chair [ē/zē chĕr/] **56**–22
Easy Chicken Soup [ē/zē chĭk/ən sōōp/] **77**
eat [ēt] **11**–1
  eat a healthy diet [ēt ə hĕl/thē dī/ət] **114**–F
  eat breakfast [ēt brĕk/fəst] **38**–E
  eat dinner [ēt dĭn/ər] **39**–S
  eat out [ēt/ owt/] **82** ✦
eater [ē/tər] **176**–12
eclipse [ĭ klĭps/] **205**–16, **205** ✦
edit [ĕd/ət] **191**–I
education [ĕ jyōō/ kā/shən] **189**–17
eel [ēl] **212**–12
eggplants [ĕg/plănts/] **69**–23
eggs [ĕgz] **66**–7
  eggbeater [ĕg/bē/tər] **78**–20
  eggs over easy [ĕgz ō/vər ē/zē] **76**–11
  eggs sunny-side up [ĕgz sŭn/ē sïd/ ŭp/] **76**–10
  hardboiled eggs [härd/ boyld/ ĕgz/] **76**–8
  poached eggs [pōcht/ ĕgz/] **76**–9
  scrambled eggs [skrăm/bəld ĕgz/] **76**–7
Eggs [ĕgz] **76**

Index

eight [āt] **16**
eighteen [ā/tēn/] **16**
eighteenth [ā/tēnth/] **16**
eighth [ātth, āth] **16**
eightieth [ā/tē/əth] **16**
eighty [ā/tē] **16**
elastic bandage [ĭ lăs/tĭk băn/dĭj] **117**–12
elbow [ĕl/bō] **106**–12
elderly [ĕl/dər lē] **32**–3
elected [ĭ lĕk/təd] **139**–C
 elected official [ĭ lĕk/təd ə fĭ/shəl] **139**–32
Election [ĭ lĕk/shən] **139**
election results [ĭ lĕk/shən rĭ zŭltz/] **139**–31
elective [ĭ lĕk/tĭv] **189** ✦
electric [ĭ lĕk/trĭk] **116**–F
 electric can opener [ĭ lĕk/trĭk kăn/ ō/pə nər] **54**–14
 electric drill [ĭ lĕk/trĭk drĭl/] **180**–8
 electric keyboard [ĭ lĕk/trĭk kē/bördʼ] **238**–18
 electric mixer [ĭ lĕk/trĭk mĭk/sər] **54**–25
 electric pencil sharpener
  [ĭ lĕk/trĭk pĕn/səl shär/pə nər] **183**–26
 electric shaver [ĭ lĕk/trĭk shā/vər] **109**–26
electrical [ĭ lĕk/trĭ kəl]
 electrical hazard [ĭ lĕk/trĭ kəl hăz/ərd] **186**–6
 electrical tape [ĭ lĕk/trĭ kəl tāp/] **181**–43
electrician [ĭ lĕk trĭsh/ən] **62**–9
electron [ĭ lĕk/trän] **195**–30
electronics [ĭ lĕk trän/ĭks]
 electronics repair person
  [ĭ lĕk trän/ĭks rĭ pĕr/ pür/sən] **167**–24
 electronics store [ĭ lĕk trän/ĭks stör/] **131**–20
ELECTRONICS AND PHOTOGRAPHY
 [ĭ lĕk trän/ĭks ən fə tä g/rə fē] **234**–235
elementary school [ĕl/ə mĕn/trē skool/] **188**–2
elephant [ĕl/ə fənt] **217**–42
elevator [ĕl/ə vā/tər] **50**–9, **131**–21, **184**–9
eleven [ĭ lĕv/ən] **16**
eleventh [ĭ lĕv/ənth] **16**
elm [ĕlm] **210**–16
Email [ē/māl/] **197**
embarrassed [ĭm băr/əst] **43**–24
embroidery [ĭm broy/də rē] **233**–24
EMERGENCIES [ĭ mür/jən sēz] **116**
EMERGENCIES AND NATURAL DISASTERS
 [ĭ mür/jən sēz ən năch/rəl dĭ zăs/tərz,–năch/ə rəl–]
 144–145
emergency [ĭ mür/jən sē] **117**–3
 emergency card [ĭ mür/jən sē kärd/] **161**–26
 emergency exit
  [ĭ mür/jən sē ĕg/zət,–ĕk/sət] **51**–25, **161**–14
 emergency medical technician (EMT) [ĭ mür/jən sē
  mĕd/ĭ kəl tĕk nĭsh/ən] / [ē/ĕm/tē/] **121**–32
Emergency [ĭ mür/jən sē] **146**–147
Emergency Call [ĭ mür/jən sē köl/] **15**
EMERGENCY PROCEDURES
 [ĭ mür/jən sē prə sē/jərz] **146**–147
Emergency Room Entrance
 [ĭ mür/jən sē room/ ĕn/trəns] **121**
Emergency Worker [ĭ mür/jən sē wür/kər] **93**
emery board [ĕm/ə rē börd/, ĕm/rē-] **109**–32
emperor [ĕm/pər ər] **199**–3
employee [ĕm ploy/ē] **165**–9

employer [ĕm ploy/ər] **164**–4
empty [ĕmp/tē] **23**–10
empty [ĕmp/tē] **60**–L
EMT (emergency medical technician) [ē/ĕm/tē/] /
 [ĭ mür/jən sē mĕd/ĭ kəl tĕk nish/ən] **121**–32
end [ĕnd] **154**–6
 endpoint [ĕnd/poynt] **193**–21
 end table [ĕnd/ tā/bəl] **56**–14
energy [ĕn/ər jē] **218**–1, **218**–7, **218**–8
 bioenergy [bī/ō ĕn/ər jē] **218**–9
ENERGY AND CONSERVATION
 [ĕn/ər jē ən kän/sər vā/shən] **218**–219
Energy and Resources [ĕn/ər jē ən rē/sör/səz] **219**
Energy Sources [ĕn/ər jē sör/səz] **218**
engine [ĕn/jən] **158**–18, **197**–6
engineer [ĕn/jə nïr/] **167**–18, **167**–25
ENGLISH COMPOSITION
 [ĭng/glĭsh käm/pə zĭsh/ən] **190**–191
English muffin [ĭng/glĭsh mŭf/ən] **80**–5
enter [ĕn/tər]
 do not **enter** [doo/ nät/ ĕn/tər] **154**–2
 enter data [ĕn/tər dā/tə] **171**–B
 enter the room [ĕn/tər dhe room/] **11**–A
 enter your PIN [ĕn/tər yər pĭn/] **132**–E
ENTERTAINMENT [ĕn/tər tān/mənt] **236**–237
entertainment center [ĕn/tər tān/mənt sĕn/tər] **56**–5
entrance [ĕn/trəns] **164**–1
Entrance [ĕn/trəns] **50**, **121**
entry-level job [ĕn/trē lĕv/əl jäb/] **172**–1
Entryway [ĕn/trē wā/] **51**
envelope [ĕn/və lōp/] **134**–14, **183**–43
equation [ĭ kwā/zhən] **192**–13
equipment [ĭ kwĭp/mənt] **177**–12, **179**–4
Equipment [ĭ kwĭp/mənt] **179**, **183**
EQUIPMENT [ĭ kwĭp/mənt] **231**
Equivalencies [ĭ kwĭ/və lən sēz/] **17**, **75**
erase [ĭ rās/] **10**–M
eraser [ĭ rā/sər] **7**–19, **7**–21
errands [ĕr/əndz] **128** ✦
eruption [ĭ rŭp/shən] **145**–16
escalator [ĕs/kə lā/tər] **131**–23
escape [ĭs kāp/] **50**–2
 escape route [ĭs kāp/ root/, rowt/] **146**–3
ESL [ē/ĕs/ĕl/] **189**–14
ESOL [ē/ĕs/ō/ĕl/] **189**–14
essay [ĕs/ā] **190**–4
Essay [ĕs/ā] **190**
e-ticket [ē/tĭ kət] **161**–19
evacuate [ĭ văk/yoo/ āt/] **147**–K
evacuation route [ĭ văk/yoo/ā shən root/, rowt/] **146**–5
evening [ēv/nĭng] **18**–19
 evening gown [ēv/nĭng gown/] **89**–18
even numbers [ē/vən nŭm/bərz] **192**–4
EVENTS [ĭ vĕnts/] **22**, **40**–41
every day [ĕv/rē dā/] **20**–21
EVERYDAY CLOTHES [ĕv/rē dā/ klōz/] **86**–87
EVERDAY CONVERSATION
 [ĕv/rē dā/ kän/vər sā/shən] **12**
evidence [ĕv/ī dəns/] **141**–9
exam [ĭg zăm/] **122**–1, **136**–6
examination table [ĭg zăm/ə nā/shən tā/bəl] **118**–7
examine [ĭg zăm/ən] **118**–D, **118**–E

Examining Room [ĭg zăm/ə nĭng room/] **118**
exchange [ĭks chänj/] **27**–I
excited [ĭk sī/təd] **43**–22
exclamation mark [ĕk/sklə mā/shən märk/] **190**–13
executive [ĭg zĕk/yə tĭv] **182**–5
 executive chef [ĭg zĕk/yə tĭv shĕf/] **185**–7
Executive Branch [ĭg zĕk/yə tĭv brănch/] **138**
exercise [ĕk/sər sĭz/] **122**–4
exercise [ĕk/sər sĭz/] **39**–P, **230**–N
Exercise Wear [ĕk/sər sĭz/wĕr] **89**
exhausted [ĭg zö/stəd] **43** ✦
ex-husband [ĕks/ hŭz/bənd] **35** ✦
exit [ĕg/zət, ĕk/sət] **51**–25, **51** ✦, **161**–14
expensive [ĭk spĕn/sĭv] **23**–19, **97**–44
Experiment [ĭk spĕr/ə mənt] **195**
expiration date [ĕk/spə rā/shən dāt/] **112**–7, **136**–10
expire [ĕk/spīr/] **136** ✦
explain [ĭk splān/] **12**–M
exploration [ĕk/splə rā/shən] **199**–8
explorer [ĭk splör/ər] **199**–9
explosion [ĭk splō/zhən] **144**–4
exposed [ĭk spōzd/]
 overexposed [ō/vər ĭk spōzd/] **235**–34
 underexposed [ŭn/dər ĭk spōzd/] **235**–35
Express Mail® [ĭk sprĕs/ māl/] **134**–2
Extended Family [ĭk stĕn/dəd făm/lē, făm/ə lē] **34**
extension cord [ĭk stĕn/shən körd/] **181**–14
exterminate [ĭk stür/mə nāt/] **62** ✦
exterminator [ĭk stür/mə nā/tər] **63**–21
extinguisher [ĭk stĭn/gwə shər] **179**–21
extra [ĕk/strə]
 extra large [ĕk/strə lärj/] **96**–5
 extra small [ĕk/strə smöl/] **96**–1
ex-wife [ĕks/ wīf/] **35** ✦
eye [ī] **99**–27, **105**–11
 eyebrow [ī/brow/] **106**–9
 eyebrow pencil [ī/brow/ pĕn/səl] **109**–34
 eye drops [ī/dräps/] **113**–31
 eye hook [ī/hook/] **180**–40
 eyelashes [ī/lăsh/əz] **106**–11
 eyelid [ī/lĭd/] **106**–10
 eyeliner [ī/lī/nər] **109**–36
 eyepiece [ī/pēs/] **194**–14
 eye shadow [ī/shă/dō] **109**–35
Eye [ī] **106**
fabric [făb/rĭk] **98**–15
 fabric softener [făb/rĭk sö/fə nər] **101**–6
Fabric Store [făb/rĭk stör/] **99**
face [fās] **193**–44
 face mask [fās măsk/] **93**–32
 face powder [fās/ pow/dər] **109**–41
Face [fās] **106**
factory [făk/tə rē, –trē] **126**–3
 factory owner [făk/tə rē ō/nər] **175**–1
 factory worker [făk/tə rē wür/kər] **175**–3
Factory [făk/tə rē] **98**
FACTORY [făk/tə rē] **175**
Fahrenheit [făr/ən hīt/] **13**–1
fair [fĕr] **172**–13, **223**–13
 fair trial [fĕr/ trī/əl] **140**–5
FAIR [fĕr] **122**–123
fall [föl] **21**–39

fall [föl] **40**–H, **116**–O
FAMILIES [făm/lēz, făm/ə lēz] **34**–**35**
Family [făm/lē, făm/ə lē] **34**
FAMILY REUNION
[făm/lē rē yōōn/yən, făm/ə lē] **44**–**45**
famine [fă/mĭn] **145**–12
fan [făn] **55**–19, **229**–4
fancy [făn/sē] **97**–34
far from [fär/ frŭm/, –frəm/] **25** ✦
fare [fër] **152**–2
fare card [fër kärd/] **152**–11
farm [färm] **52**–9
farm equipment [färm ĭ kwĭp/mənt] **177**–12
farmworker [färm/ wür/kər] **177**–8
Farm Animals [färm/ ăn/ə məlz] **215**
farmer [fär/mər] **177**–13
FARMERS' MARKET [fär/mərz mär/kət] **84**–**85**
FARMING AND RANCHING
[fär/mĭng ən răn/chĭng] **177**
Farmworker [färm/ wür/kər] **92**
fashion [făsh/ən] **88** ✦
fashion designer [făsh/ən dĭ zī/nər] **98** ✦
fast [făst] **23**–3
fast food restaurant [făst/ fōōd/ rĕs/tə rənt, –ränt]
128–10
fasten [făs/ən] **160**–H
fastener [făs/nər] **99**–29
FAST FOOD RESTAURANT
[făst/ fōōd/ rĕs/tə rənt, –ränt] **79**
fast forward [făst/ för/wərd] **235**–D
fat [făt] **32**–7
father [fä/dhər] **34**–4, **35**–23
father-in-law [fä/dhər ĭn lö/] **34**–11
grandfather [grăn/fä/dhər, grănd/–] **34**–2
stepfather [stĕp/fädhər] **35**–25
faucet [fö/sət] **57**–6
fax [făks] **171**–G
fax machine [făks/ mə shēn/] **183**–21
feast [fēst] **239**–13
feather [fĕdh/ər] **214**–4
feather duster [fĕdh/ər dŭs/tər] **61**–1
February [fĕb/yōō ër/ē, fĕb/rōō–] **21**–26
Federal Government
[fĕ/də rəl gŭ/vərn mənt, fĕ/drəl] **138**
feed [fēd] **36**–C, **176**–D, **177**–D
feed dog / feed bar [fēd/dög/ / fēd/ bär/] **98**–20
feel [fēl] **110**–C, **110**–D
FEELINGS [fē/lĭngz] **42**–**43**
female [fē/māl/] **4**–18
fence [fĕns] **177**–19
fencing [fĕn/sĭng] **228**–7
ferry [fĕr/ē] **220**–4
fertilize [fürt/ əl īz/] **176**–D
fever [fē/vər] **110**–8
fiction [fĭk/shən] **237**–18
field [fēld] **5**–2, **177**–7
ball field [böl/ fēld/] **224**–1
track and field [trăk/ ən fēld/] **228**–18
fifteen [fĭf/tēn/] **16**
fifteenth [fĭf/tēnth/] **16**
fifth [fĭfth] **16**
fiftieth [fĭf/tē əth] **16**

fifty [fĭf/tē] **16**
fifty dollars [fĭf/tē däl/ərz] **26**–11
50 percent [fĭf/tē pər sĕnt/] **17**–10
fighter [fī/tər]
firefighter [fīr/fī/tər] **144**–9, **167**–26
figs [fĭgz] **68**–27
figure [fĭg/yər] **233**–26
figure skating [fĭg/yər skā/tĭng] **227**–5
figurine [fĭg/yə rēn/] **232**–1
file [fīl] **183**–44
file cabinet [fīl kăb/ə nət] **182**–11
file clerk [fīl klürk/] **182**–10
file folder [fīl fōl/dər] **183**–50
fill [fĭl]
fill a cavity [fĭl/ ə kăv/ə tē] **119**–E
fill prescriptions [fĭl/ prĭ skrĭp/shənz] **112** ✦
fill in [fĭl/ ĭn] **9**–O
fill out [fĭl/ owt/] **173**–J
fill the tank [fĭl/ dhe tăngk/] **157**–G
fill the tires [fĭl/ dhe tīrz/] **157**–L
filling [fĭl/ĭng] **119**–8
Filling Out a Form [fĭl/ĭng owt ə förm/] **4**
film [fĭlm] **235**–22
film camera [fĭlm kăm/rə] **235**–21
find [fīnd] **160**–F
FINDING A HOME [fīn/dĭng ə hōm/] **48**–**49**
fine adjustment knob [fīn/ ə jŭst/mənt näb/] **194**–23
fingers [fĭng/gərz] **105**–16, **110**–16
fingernail [fĭng/gər nāl/] **106**–18
fingerprint [fĭng/gər prĭnt/] **136**–5
Fingers [fĭng/gərz] **106**
finish [fĭn/ĭsh] **112**–C, **230**–T
fins [fĭnz] **212**–1, **225**–7
fire [fīr] **144**–7, **144**–8
campfire [kămp/fīr/] **226**–11
fire escape [fīr ĭ skāp/] **50**–2
fire exit [fīr/ ĕg/zət, –ĕk/sət] **51** ✦
fire extinguisher [fīr ĭk stĭng/gwĭ shər] **179**–21
firefighter [fīr/fī/tər] **144**–9, **167**–26
fire hydrant [fīr hī/drənt] **129**–27
fireplace [fīr/plās/] **56**–13
fire screen [fīr skrēn/] **56**–12
fire station [fīr stā/shən] **125**–12
fire truck [fīr trŭk/] **144**–10
fireworks [fīr/würks/] **239**–7
first [fürst] **16**
first aid kit [fürst/ ād/ kĭt/] **117**–1, **146**–18
first aid manual [fürst/ ād/ măn/yōō əl] **117**–2
First Continental Congress
[fürst/ kän/tə nĕnt/ əl käng/grəs] **198**–6
first name [fürst/ nām/] **4**–2
first president [fürst/ prĕz/ə dənt] **198**–11
First Aid [fürst/ ād/] **117**
FIRST AID [fürst/ ād/] **117**
First Aid Procedures [fürst/ ād/ prə sē/ jərz] **117**
First Floor [fürst/ flör/] **50**
First License [fürst/ lī/səns] **137**
fish [fĭsh] **66**–1, **81**–29, **209**–14
catfish [kăt/fĭsh/] **71**–2
goldfish [gōld/fĭsh/] **215**–16
jellyfish [jĕ/lē fĭsh/] **212**–14
starfish [stär/fĭsh/] **212**–16
swordfish [sörd/fĭsh/] **71**–5

Fish [fĭsh] **71, 212**
fisher [fĭsh/ər] **167**–17
fishing [fĭsh/ĭng] **226**–4
fishing net [fĭsh/ĭng nĕt/] **226**–17
fishing pole [fĭsh/ĭng pōl/] **226**–18
fitted sheet [fĭt/əd shēt/] **58**–12
fittings [fĭt/ĭngz] **181**–18
five [fĭv] **16**
five after one [fĭv ăf/tər wŭn/] **18**–7
five dollars [fĭv däl/ərz] **26**–8
fix [fĭks] **62** ✦, **219**–F
fixture [fĭks/chər] **55**–18
flag [flăg] **239**–8
flammable liquids [flăm/ə bəl lĭk/wədz] **179**–8
flashlight [flăsh/līt/] **146**–14
flat [flăt]
flat panel TV [flăt/ păn/əl tē/vē/] **234**–7
flat screen TV [flăt/ skrēn/ tē/vē/] **234**–7
flat sheet [flăt/ shēt/] **58**–13
have a flat tire [hăv/ ə flăt/ tīr/] **162**–F
flats [flăts] **95**–27
fleas [flēz] **63**–25
flea market [flē/ mär/kət] **222**–6
flight [flīt] **161**–30, **161** ✦
flight attendant [flīt/ ə tĕn/dənt] **161**–12
Flight [flīt] **160**
float [flōt/] **239**–2
flood [flŭd] **145**–19
floor [flör] **46**–6, **58**–21, **179**–6
floor lamp [flör lămp/] **56**–15
floor plan [flör plăn/] **186**–4
Floor [flör] **50**
floral [flör/əl] **96**–25
florist [flör/ĭst] **130**–8, **167**–27
floss [flös, fläs] **109**–24
floss [flös, fläs] **109**–K
flounder [flown/dər] **212**–15
flour [flow/ər] **73**–29
Flower [flow/ər] **211**
flowers [flow/ərz] **208**–7
flower bed [flow/ər bĕd/] **53**–20
FLOWERS [flow/ərz] **211**
flu [flōō] **111**–2
fluid [flōō/əd] **183**–36
fluid ounce [flōō/əd owns/] **75**–1
flute [flōōt] **238**–1
fly [flī] **214**–28
fly [flī] **170**–F
flyer [flī/ər] **102**–1
flying disc [flī/ĭng dĭsk/] **231**–27
foam pad [fōm/ păd/] **226**–13
focus [fō/kəs] **235**–33
foggy [fö/gē, fäg/ē] **13**–20
foil [foyl] **72**–23
fold [fōld] **101**–F
folder [fōl/dər] **183**–50
folding [fōl/dĭng]
folding card table [fōl/dĭng kärd/ tā/bəl] **102**–4
folding chair [fōl/dĭng chër/] **102**–5
folk [fōk] **237**–29
follow [fäl/ō] **114**–J, **147**–F
Following Directions [fäl/ō də rĕk/shənz, –dī–] **9**

Index

food [fo͞od]
   baby food [bā/bē fo͞od/] **37**–4
   canned food [kănd/ fo͞od/] **146**–9
   fast food restaurant [făst/ fo͞od/ rĕs/tə rănt] **128**–10
   food court [fo͞od/ kört] **131**–15
   food preparation worker
      [fo͞od/ prĕ/pə rā/shən wür/kər] **185**–4
   food processor [fo͞od/ prä/sĕ sər] **54**–26
   packaged food [păk/ĭjd fo͞od/] **146**–10
   pet food [pĕt/ fo͞od/] **72**–5
FOOD [fo͞od] **79**
FOOD PREPARATION AND SAFETY
   [fo͞od/ prĕ/pə rā/shən ən săf/tē] **76**–**77**
Food Processor [fo͞od/ prä/sĕ sər] **92**
Foods [fo͞odz] **72, 73**
Food Safety [fo͞od/ săf/tē] **76**
FOOD SERVICE [fo͞od/ sür/vəs] **185**
foot [fo͝ot] **104**–8
   football [fo͝ot/böl/] **229**–11, **231**–21
   football helmet [fo͝ot/böl/ hĕl/mət] **231**–19
   footnote [fo͝ot/nōt/] **190**–10
Foot [fo͝ot] **106**
for [för] **128**–B, **173**–C
forceps [för/səps, –sĕps] **195**–43
forearm [för/ärm/] **106**–13
forehead [för/əd/, –hĕd/, fär/–] **106**–2
forest [för/əst, fär/–] **204**–1, **204**–11
   forest fire [för/əst fir/] **144**–7
fork [förk] **55**–3, **83**–27, **83**–28
   forklift [förk/lĭft/] **175**–12
Form [förm] **4**
Formal Clothes [förm/əl klōz/] **89**
former husband [för/mər hŭz/bənd] **35** ✦
former wife [för/mər wif/] **35** ✦
forms [förmz] **118**–4, **134**–19, **161**–16
formula [för/myə lə] **37**–3, **195**–34
fortieth [för/tē əth] **16**
forty [för/tē] **16**
forward [för/wərd] **235**–D
   forward button [för/wərd bŭt/n] **197**–3
foundation [fown dā/shən] **109**–40
founders [fown/dərz] **198**–7
fountain [fown/tn] **224**–5, **224**–9
four [för] **16**
   4-door car [för/dör kär/] **156**–1
   2 x 4 (two by four) [to͞o/ bi för/] **181**–19
fourteen [för/tēn/] **16**
fourteenth [för/tēnth/] **16**
fourth [förth] **16**
Fourth Floor [förth flör/] **50**
Fourth of July [förth əv jo͞o li/] **22**–13
fox [fäks] **216**–15
Fractions [frăk/shənz] **192**
Fractions and Decimals [frăk/shənz ən dĕ/sə məlz] **17**
frame [frām] **58**–4, **58**–18
frayed cord [frād/ körd/] **179**–5
free [frē] **122**–7
   free speech [frē/ spēch/] **140**–2
freedom [frē/dəm]
   freedom of religion [frē/dəm əv rĭ li/jən] **140**–3
   freedom of the press [frē/dəm əv dhə prĕs/] **140**–4
freezer [frē/zər] **54**–10, **185**–3

freezing [frē/zĭng] **13**–7
French [frĕnch]
   french fries [frĕnch/ friz/] **79**–2
   French horn [frĕnch/ hörn/] **238**–13
Frequency [frē/kwən sē/] **20**
fresh [frĕsh] **71**–16
Friday [fri/dā, –dē] **20**–13
fried [frid] **76**–6
   fried chicken [frid/ chĭk/ən] **76**–1
fringe [frĭnj] **99**–34
frog [frög, fräg] **212**–25
front [frŭnt] **25**–7
   front desk [frŭnt/ dĕsk/] **184**–12
   front door [frŭnt/ dör/] **53**–11
   front seat [frŭnt/ sēt/] **159**–51
   front walk [frŭnt/ wök/] **53**–2
Front Porch [frŭnt/ pörch/] **53**
Font Yard and House [frŭnt/ yärd/ en hows/] **53**
frostbite [fräst/bit/] **116**–G
frozen [frō/zən] **63**–16, **71**–17
   frozen dinner [frō/zən dĭn/ər] **72**–28
   frozen vegetables [frō/zən vĕj/tə bəlz] **72**–27
Frozen Foods [frō/zən fo͞odz/] **72**
fruit [fro͞ot] **67**–9
   fruit salad [fro͞ot săl/əd] **80**–21
FRUIT [fro͞ot] **68**
frustrated [frŭs/trā/təd] **43**–27
frying pan [fri/ĭng păn/] **78**–5
fuel injection system
   [fyo͞o/əl ĭn jĕk/shən sĭs/təm] **158**–17
full [fo͝ol] **23**–9, **42**–6
   full-length mirror [fo͝ol/lĕnth/ mĭr/ər] **58**–6
   full moon [fo͝ol/ mo͞on/] **205**–12
   full slip [fo͝ol/ slĭp/] **91**–22
fumes [fyo͞omz] **179**–3
funnel [fŭn/əl] **195**–40
funny photo [fŭn/ē fō/tō] **206**–2
fur [für] **216**–19
furious [fyo͝or/ē əs] **43** ✦
furnished apartment [für/nĭsht ə pärt/mənt] **48**–3
furniture [für/nĭ chər] **53**–19
   furniture polish [für/nĭ chər päl/ĭsh] **61**–8
   furniture store [für/nĭ chər stör/] **126**–8
Furniture and Accessories
   [für/nĭ chər ən ĭk sĕs/ə rēz] **59**
fuse box [fyo͞oz/ bäks/] **62**–13
fusion [fyo͞o/zhən] **218**–10
galaxy [găl/ək sē] **205**–15
gallbladder [göl/blăd/ər] **107**–44
gallon [găl/ən] **75**–5
game [gām]
   baseball game [bās/böl găm/] **44**–2
   board game [börd/ găm/] **232**–5
   game show [gām/ shō/] **236**–8
   video game console [vĭd/ē ō găm/ kän/sōl] **232**–3
   video game control [vĭd/ē ō găm kən trōl/] **232**–4
Games [gāmz] **59**
GAMES [gāmz] **232**–**233**
gang violence [găng/ vi/ə ləns] **142**–4
garage [gə räzh/, –räj/] **47**–14, **124**–1
   garage door [gə räzh/ dör/] **53**–7
Garage [gə räzh/, –räj/] **50**

GARAGE SALE [gə räzh/ säl/] **102**–**103**
garbage [gär/bĭj]
   garbage can [gär/bĭj kăn/] **53**–24
   garbage disposal [gär/bĭj dĭ spō/zəl] **54**–7
   garbage truck [gär/bĭj trŭk/] **127**–22
garden [gär/dn]
   botanical garden [bə tăn/ə kəl gär/dn] **222**–3
   roof garden [ro͞of/gär/dn] **50**–4
   vegetable garden [vĕj/tə bəl gär/dn] **53**–27, **177**–14
garden [gär/dn] **53**–B
gardener [gär/dn er, gärd/nər] **167**–28
gardenia [gär dēn/yə] **211**–18
gardening [gärd/nĭng]
   gardening crew [gärd/nĭng kro͞o/] **176**–1
   gardening crew leader
      [gärd/nĭng kro͞o lēd/ər] **176**–4
GARDENING [gärd/nĭng] **176**
gargle [gär/gəl] **109**–L
garlic [gär/lĭk] **69**–30
   garlic bread [gär/lĭk brĕd/] **81**–28
   garlic press [gär/lĭk prĕs/] **78**–11
Garment Factory [gär/mənt făk/tə rē, făk/trē] **98**
garment worker [gär/mənt wür/kər] **167**–29
garter [gär/tər]
   garter belt [gär/tər bĕlt/] **91**–16
   garter snake [gär/tər snāk/] **213**–39
gas [găs] **218**–3
   gas gauge [găs/gāj/] **159**–31
   gas meter [găs mē/tər] **62**–14
   gas pedal [găs pĕd/l] **159**–46
   gas shut-off valve [găs/ shŭt/öf vălv/] **146**–4
   gas station [găs stā/shən] **125**–10
   gas station attendant
      [găs stā/shən ə tĕn/dənt] **162**–3
   gas tank [găs tăngk/] **158**–10
gate [gāt] **50**–16, **53**–9, **161**–8
Gate [gāt] **161**
gauge [gāj]
   blood pressure gauge [blŭd/ prĕsh/ər gāj/] **118**–9
   gas gauge [găs/gāj/] **159**–31
   oil gauge [oyl/gāj/] **159**–29
   temperature gauge [tĕm/prə chər gāj/] **159**–30
gauze [göz] **117**–8
gear shift [gĭr/ shĭft/] **159**–47
gel [jĕl] **108**–2, **108**–16
GEOGRAPHY AND HABITATS
   [jē äg/rə fē ən hă/bə tăts/] **204**
Geometric Solids [jē ə mĕ/trik săl/ədz] **193**
geometry [jē äm/ə trē] **192**–17
geothermal energy [jē/ō thür/məl ĕn/ər jē] **218**–7
get [gĕt]
   get a job [gĕt/ ə jäb/] **40**–F
   get a learner's permit
      [gĕt/ ə lürn/ərz pür/mĭt] **137**–F
   get a library card [gĕt/ ə li/brĕr ē kärd/] **133**–A
   get a loan [gĕt/ ə lōn/] **49**–J
   get an electric shock [gĕt/ ən ĭ lĕk/trik shäk/] **116**–F
   get a speeding ticket [gĕt/ ə spē/dĭng tĭk/ət] **162**–C
   get bed rest [gĕt/ bĕd/ rĕst/] **114**–B
   get change [gĕt/ chānj/] **26**–A
   get dressed [gĕt/ drĕst/] **38**–D
   get elected [gĕt/ ĭ lĕk/təd] **139**–C

get engaged [gĕt/ ĭn gājd/] **41**–J

get feedback [gĕt/ fēd/băk/] **191**–K

get frostbite [gĕt/ fröst/bit/] **116**–G

get good grades [gĕt/ good/ grādz/] **10**–H

get hired [gĕt/ hīrd/] **173**–L

get home [gĕt/ hōm/] **39**–R

get immunized [gĕt/ ĭm/yə nizd/] **114**–I

get into [gĕt/ ĭn/tōō] **153**–E

get lost [gĕt/ löst/] **162**–B

get married [gĕt/ măr/ēd] **41**–K

get off [gĕt/ öf/] **153**–J

get on [gĕt/ än/, ön/] **153**–I

get out of [gĕt/ owt/ əv] **153**–F

get the title [gĕt/ dhə tit/l] **157**–E

get up [gĕt/ ŭp/] **38**–B

get your license [gĕt/ yər li/səns] **137**–I

Getting Your First License
[gĕt/ĭng yər fürst/ li/səns] **137**

Get Well [gĕt/ wĕl/] **114**

gift [gĭft] **94** ✦, **240**–3

gift shop [gĭft/ shäp/] **130** ✦, **184**–5

gills [gĭlz] **212**–2

giraffe [jə räf/] **217**–32

girder [gür/dər] **178**–3

girdle [gür/dl] **91**–15

girl [gürl] **31**–10

give [gĭv] **15**–F, **122**–B, **148**–A,

glad [glăd] **44**–5

glass [glăs] **53**–18, **83**–22, **83**–23

glass cleaner [glăs klē/nər] **61**–14

glasses [glăs/əz] **92**–10, **115**–7, **179**–10

sunglasses [sŭn/glăs/əz] **90**–27

global positioning system (GPS) [glō/bəl
pə zi/shə nĭng sĭs/təm] / [jē/pē/ĕs/] **155**–11

gloves [glŭvz] **90**–6, **231**–17

disposable gloves [dĭ spō/ zə bəl glŭvz/] **93**–27

glove compartment [glŭv/ kəm pärt/mənt] **159**–44

latex gloves [lā/tĕks glŭvz/] **93**–34

rubber gloves [rŭb/ər glŭvz/] **61**–4

surgical gloves [sür/jĭ kəl glŭvz/] **121**–39

work gloves [würk/ glŭvz/] **92**–17, **179**–17

glue [glōō] **183**–33

glue stick [glōō/ stĭk] **232**–11

go [gō]

go back [gō/ băk/] **11**–M

go for [gō/ fər] **157**–J

go on [gō/ än/] **173**–K

go over [gō/ ō/vər] **153**–B

go past [gō/ păst/] **155**–E

go straight [gō/ strāt/] **155**–A

go through [gō/ thrōō/] **160**–D

go to an employment agency
[gō/ tə ən ĭm ploy/mənt ā/jən sē] **173**–E

go to bed [gō/ tə bĕd/] **39**–Y

go to college [gō/ tə käl/ĭj] **41**–I

go to jail [gō/ tə jāl/] **141**–G

go to prison [gō/ tə prĭz/ən] **141**–G

go to school [gō/ tə skōōl/] **38**–J

go to sleep [gō/ tə slēp/] **39**–Z

go to the grocery store
[gō/ tə dhə grōs/rē stör/, grösh/rē] **38**–L

go to the next line [gō/ tə dhə nĕkst/ lĭn] **196**–D

go to work [gō/ tə würk/] **38**–I

go under [gō/ ŭn/dər] **153**–A

to-go box [tə gō/ bäks/] **82**–5

GO [gō] **222**–223

goat [gōt] **215**–5

goggles [gäg/əlz] **179**–11

goldfish [gōld/fĭsh] **215**–16

golf [gälf, gölf] **228**–8

golf club [gälf/ klŭb/] **231**–1

good [good] **23**–17

Goods [goodz] **73**

goose [gōōs] **214**–13

gopher [gō/fər] **215**–19

gorilla [gə rĭl/ə] **217**–29

gospel [gäs/pəl] **237**–30

Government [gŭ/ vərn mənt] **138**–139

GOVERNMENT AND MILITARY SERVICE
[gŭ/ vərn mənt ən mĭl/ lə tër ē sür/vəs]**138**–139

governor [gŭ/ vər nər] **139**–20, **139**–21

gown [gown] **206**–8

evening gown [ēv/nĭng gown/] **89**–18

hospital gown [häs/pĭ tl gown/] **121**–19

nightgown [nĭt/gown/] **91**–25

surgical gown [sür/jə kəl gown/] **93**–37, **121**–38

GPS (global positioning system) [jē/pē/ĕs/] /
[glō/bəl pə zi/shə nĭng sĭs/təm] **155**–11

grab bar [grăb/ bär/] **57**–9

grades [grādz] **10**–4

graduate [grăj/ōō ăt/] **40**–D

graduated cylinder [grăj/ōō ā/təd sĭl/ən dər] **195**–38

GRADUATION [grăj/ōō ā/shən] **206**–207

graffiti [grə fēt/tē] **148**–1

grandchild [grăn/chĭld/, grănd/–] **34** ✦

granddaughters [grăn/dö/tərz] **34** ✦

grandfather [grăn/fä/dhər, grănd/–] **34**–2

grandmother [grăn/mŭdh/ər, grănd/–] **34**–1

Grandparents [grăn/për/ənts, grănd/–] **34**

grandson [grăn/sŭn/, grănd/–] **34** ✦

grapefruit [grāp/frōōt/] **68**–6

grapes [grāps] **68**–3

graph [grăf] **192**–15

graphic designer [grăf/ĭk dĭ zi/nər] **167**–30

grasshopper [grăs/häp/ər] **214**–24

grate [grāt] **77**–G

grater [grā/tər] **78**–2

gray [grā] **24**–15

gray hair [grā hër/] **33**–13

grease [grēs] **77**–B

green [grēn] **24**–5

green card [grēn/ kärd/] **40**–2

green onions [grēn/ ŭn/yənz] **69**–20

greet [grēt] **3**–G, **171**–M, **174**–H

GREETING [grē/tĭng] **2**–3

greeting card [grē/tĭng kärd/] **134**–15

grill [grĭl] **53**–17

grilled [grĭld/]

grilled cheese sandwich
[grĭld/ chēz/ săn/wĭch, –sănd/–] **80**–10

grilled fish [grĭld/ fĭsh/] **81**–29

grilled ribs [grĭld/ rĭbz/] **76**–2

grocery [grōs/rē, grösh/rē]

grocery bag [grōs/rē băg/] **67**–13

grocery clerk [grōs/rē klürk/] **72**–4

Grocery Products [grōs/rē präd/ŭkts] **72**

GROCERY STORE [grōs/ rē stör/] **72**–73

ground [grownd]

ground beef [grownd/ bēf/] **70**–4

ground post [grownd/ pōst/] **134**–6

playground [plā/grownd/] **50**–3

group [grōōp] **115**–15

grower [grō/ər] **177**–13

guard [gärd] **141**–3

Coast Guard [kōst/ gärd/] **138**–18

lifeguard [lif/gärd/] **225**–19

lifeguard station [lif/gärd/ stā/shən] **225**–21

National Guard [nă/shə nəl gärd/] **138**–19

security guard [sĭ kyōōr/ə tē gärd/] **132**–5, **169**–55

shin guards [shĭn/ gärdz/] **231**–13

guest [gĕst] **184**–10

guest room [gĕst/ rōōm] **184**–13

guest services [gĕst/ sür/vəs əs] **130**–12

guest speaker [gĕst/ spē/kər] **206**–4

guinea pig [gĭn/ē pĭg/] **215**–14

guitar [gĭ tär/] **238**–9

gums [gŭmz] **106**–6

gum disease [gŭm/ dĭ zēz/] **119**–11

gun [gŭn] **142**–13, **181**–21

gurney [gür/nē] **121**–33

gutter [gŭt/ər] **53**–4

gym [jĭm] **5**–19, **126**–10, **184**–24

gymnastics [jĭm năs/tĭks] **228**–9

gynecologists [gi/nə käl/ə jĭsts] **120** ✦

habitat [hă/bə tăt/] **194**–12

HABITATS [hă/bə tăts/] **204**

hacksaw [hăk/sö/] **180**–5

hail a taxi [hāl/ ə tăx/ē/]] **152** ✦

hailstorm [hāl/störm/] **13**–21

hair [hër] **104**–2

black hair [blăk/ hër/] **33**–16

blond hair [bländ/ hër/] **33**–17

brown hair [brown/ hër/] **33**–18

curly hair [kür/lē hër/] **33**–11

gray hair [grā/ hër/] **33**–13

hair clip [hër klĭp/] **108**–19

hairdresser [hër/drĕs/ər] **167**–31

hair gel [hër jĕl/] **108**–16

hairnet [hër nĕt/] **93**–25

hair salon [hër sə län/] **131**–18

hair spray [hër sprā/] **108**–12

hair stylist [hër stī/lĭst] **167**–31

long hair [löng/ hër/] **33**–3

red hair [rĕd/ hër/] **33**–15

short hair [shört/hër/] **33**–1

shoulder-length hair [shōl/dər lĕnth/ hër/] **33**–2

straight hair [strāt/ hër/] **33**–9

wavy hair [wā/vē hër/] **33**–10

HAIR [hër] **33**

Index

half [hăf]
  half bath [hăf/ băth/] **57** ✦
  half brother [hăf/ brŭdh/ər] **35**–28
  1/2 cup [hăf/ kŭp/] **75**–9
  half dollar [hăf/ däl/ər] **26**–5
  half past one [hăf/ păst/ wŭn/] **18**–11
  half sister [hăf/ sĭs/tər] **35**–27
  half slip [hăf/ slĭp/] **91**–23
halibut steak [hăl/ə bət stāk/] **71**–6
hall [höl] **124**–8
  hallway [höl/wā/] **5**–10, **184**–18
Hallway [höl/wā/] **51**
ham [hăm] **70**–9, **76**–5
hamburger [hăm/bür/gər] **79**–1
hammer [hăm/ər] **180**–1
  jackhammer [jăk/hăm/ər] **178**–9
  sledgehammer [slĕj/ hăm/ər] **178**–23
hammer [hăm/ər] **178**–D
hammock [hăm/ək] **53**–23
hamper [hăm/pər] **57**–1
hand [hănd] **105**–15, **177**–20
  DMV handbook [dē/ĕm/vē/ hănd/bŏŏk] **136**–1
  handbag [hănd/băg/] **87**–9, **94**–2
  handbrake [hănd/ brāk/] **59**–48
  handcuffs [hănd/kŭfs/] **141**–2
  handsaw [hănd/sö/] **180**–4
  handset [hănd/sĕt/] **14**–1
  hand towel [hănd tow/əl] **57**–15
  hand truck [hănd trŭk/] **175**–11
Hand [hănd] **106**
handicapped parking [hăn/dē kăpt pär/kĭng]
  128–6, **154**–12
hand in [hănd/ ĭn/] **10**–O
hanger [hăng/gər] **101**–11
hang up [hăng/ ŭp/] **15**–D, **101**–H
happy [hăp/ē] **28**–6, **43**–31
hard [härd] **23**–5, **23**–24
  hardboiled eggs [härd/boyld/ ĕgz/] **76**–8
  hard drive [härd/ drĭv/] **196**–6
  hard hat [härd/ hăt/] **92**–1, **179**–9
hardware store [härd/wër/stör/] **148**–4
harmonica [här mä/ nĭ kə] **238**–21
harvest [här/vəst] **177**–B
hash browns [hăsh/ brownz/] **80**–3
hats [hăts] **90**–1, **95**–11
  chef's hat [shĕfs/ hăt/] **93**–28
  cowboy hat [kow/boy/ hăt/] **92**–18
  hard hat [härd/ hăt/] **92**–1, **179**–9
  ski hat [skē/ hăt/] **90**–11
  straw hat [strö/ hăt/] **90**–23
have [hăv]
  have a baby [hăv/ ə bā/bē/] **41**–L
  have a conversation [hăv/ ə kän/vər sā/shən] **11**–L
  have a heart attack [hăv/ ə härt/ ə tăk/] **116**–D
  have an allergic reaction
    [hăv/ ən ə lür/jĭk rē ăk/shən] **116**–E
  have a picnic [hăv/ ə pĭk/nĭk] **224**–D
  have dinner [hăv/ dĭn/ər] **39**–S
  have regular checkups
    [hăv/ rĕg/yə lər chĕk/ups] **114**–H
Hawaii-Aleutian time [hə wī/ē ə lōō/shən tīm/] **19**–27

hay [hā] **177**–18
hazard [hăz/ərd] **186**–6
  hazard lights [hăz/ərd lĭts/] **159**–36
Hazardous Materials [hăz/ər dəs mə tĭr/ē əlz] **179**
hazardous waste [hăz/ər dəs wāst/] **218**–12
Hazards [hăz/ərdz] **179**
head [hĕd] **69**–32, **104**–1
  headache [hĕd/āk/] **110**–1
  headband [hĕd/bănd/] **90**–3
  headboard [hĕd/börd/] **58**–10
  head chef [hĕd/ shĕf/] **185**–7
  headlight [hĕd/līt/] **158**–7
  headline [hĕd/līn/] **133**–7
  headphones [hĕd/fōnz/] **6**–8, **234**–4
  headset [hĕd/sĕt/] **14**–13
  headwaiter [hĕd/wā/tər] **185**–12
  headwrap [hĕd/răp/] **90**–7
  letterhead [lĕt/ər hĕd/] **183**–42
  overhead compartment
    [ō/vər hĕd/ kəm pärt/mənt] **161**–13
  overhead projector [ō/vər hĕd/prə jĕk/tər] **7**–16
  wireless headset [wīr/ləs hĕd/sĕt/] **14**–14
health [hĕlth] **167**–32
  health history form [hĕlth/ hĭs/tə rē förm/] **118**–4
  health insurance card
    [hĕlth/ ĭn shŏŏr/əns kärd/] **118**–3
HEALTH [hĕlth] **114**–115
HEALTH FAIR [hĕlth/ fër/] **122**–123
Health Problems [hĕlth/ präb/ləmz] **115**
hear [hĭr] **106**–B
hearing [hĭr/ĭng]
  hearing aid [hĭr/ĭng ād/] **115**–10
  hearing impaired [hĭr/ĭng ĭm përd/] **32**–12
  hearing loss [hĭr/ĭng lös/] **115**–2
heart [härt] **107**–38, **116**–D, **239**–6
  heart disease [härt/ dĭ zēz/] **111**–11
hearts [härts] **233**–31
heater [hē/tər] **159**–40
heating pad [hē/tĭng păd/] **113**–13
heat wave [hēt/ wāv/] **13**–13
heavy [hĕv/ē] **23**–13, **32**–7, **97**–27
hedge clippers [hĕj/ klĭp/ərz] **176**–11
heel [hēl] **94**–22, **106**–24
  high heels [hī/ hēlz/] **89**–21, **95**–25
height [hīt] **17**–16, **32**–5
Height [hīt] **32**
Heimlich maneuver [hīm/lĭk mə nōō/vər] **117**–18
helicopter [hĕl/ə kăp/tər] **151**–9
helmet [hĕl/mət] **93**–23, **231**–19
help [hĕlp] **8**–J, **147**–G
Help with Health Problems
  [hĕlp/ wĭth/ hĕlth/ präb/ləmz] **115**
hem [hĕm] **100**–8
hen [hĕn] **215**–8
herbal tea [ür/bəl tē/, hür/bəl–] **81**–40
herbs [ürbz, hürbz] **84**–9
hibiscus [hī bĭs/kəs, hĭ–] **211**–12
hide [hīd] **240**–D
high [hī] **91**–12, **97**–32, **188**–3
  high blood pressure [hī/ blŭd/ prĕsh/ər] **111**–14
  high chair [hī/ chër/] **37**–6, **82**–3
  high heels [hī/ hēlz/] **89**–21, **95**–25

high-rise [hī/ rīz/] **127**–13
high school [hī/ skōōl] **188**–4
highway [hī/wā] **155**–9
  highway marker [hī/wā mär/kər] **154**–17
hiking [hī/kĭng] **226**–7
  hiking boots [hī/kĭng bōōts/] **95**–31
hills [hĭlz] **204**–16
  downhill skiing [down/hĭl/ skē/ĭng] **227**–1
hip hop [hĭp/häp/] **237**–26
hippopotamus [hĭp/ə pät/ə məs] **217**–43
hire [hīr] **141**–B
  hired hand [hīrd/ hănd/] **177**–20
Historical Terms [hĭs/tör/ə kəl türmz/] **199**
history [hĭs/tə rē] **118**–4, **189**–12
HISTORY [hĭs/tə rē] **198**–199
hit [hĭt] **230**–B
HIV (human immunodeficiency virus)
  [āch/ī/vē/] / [hyōō/mən ĭm/yə nō
  dĭ fĭsh/ən sē vī/rəs] **111**–17
Hi-Visibility safety vest [hī/vĭ/zə bĭl/ə tē vĕst/] **92**–4
HOBBIES AND GAMES [häb/ēz ən gāmz/] **232**–233
hockey [häk/ē] **229**–13
  hockey stick [häk/ē stĭk/] **231**–11
hold [hōld] **36**–A
holder [hōl/dər]
  candle holder [kăn/dl hōl/dər] **56**–21
  cell phone holder [sĕl/ fōn/ hōld/ər] **94**–15
  magazine holder [măg/ə zēn/ hōld/ər] **56**–23
  pot holders [pät/ hōl/dərz] **78**–29
  toothbrush holder [tōōth/brŭsh/ hōld/ər] **57**–22
holiday [häl/ə dā/] **22**–7, **22**–8
Holidays [häl/ə dāz/] **22**
HOLIDAYS [häl/ə dāz/] **239**
holly [häl/ē] **210**–19
home [hōm] **52**–7, **52**–12
  home health care aide [hōm/ hĕlth/ kër ād] **167**–32
  home improvement store
    [hōm/ ĭm prōōv/mənt stör/] **127**–20
  homemaker [hōm/mā/kər] **168**–33
  homesick [hōm/sĭk/] **43**–20
HOME [hōm] **46**–47, **48**–49
honeybee [hŭn/ē bē/] **214**–25
hood [hŏŏd] **158**–4
Hood [hŏŏd] **158**
hoof / hooves [hŏŏf/] / [hŏŏvz] **216**–17
hook [hŏŏk] **180**–39, **180**–40
  hook and eye [hŏŏk/ ən ī/] **99**–27
  hook and loop fastener
    [hŏŏk/ ən lōōp/ făs/sən ər] **99**–29
horn [hörn] **159**–32, **216**–21, **238**–11
  French horn [frĕnch/ hörn] **238**–13
horror story [hör/ər stör/ē, här/–] **237**–17
horse [hörs] **215**–4
  horseback riding [hörs/băk rī/dĭng] **226**–9
  horse racing [hörs/ rā/sĭng] **228**–19
  seahorse [sē/hörs/] **212**–13
hose [hōz] **53**–21, **91**–18
hospital [häs/pĭ tl] **125**–9, **154**–18
  hospital bed [häs/pĭ tl bĕd/] **121**–22
  hospital gown [häs/pĭ tl gown/] **121**–19
HOSPITAL [häs/pĭ tl] **120**–121
Hospital Room [häs/pĭ tl rōōm/] **121**

Hospital Staff [häs′pĭ tl stăf′] **120**
hostess [hō′stəs] **82**–2
hot [hät] **13**–3, **42**–1
  hot cereal [hät sïr′ē əl] **80**–9
  hot dog [hät′ dög′] **79**–6
  hot water [hät′ wö′tər] **57**–8
  hot water bottle [hät′ wö′tər bät′l] **113**–15
hotel [hō tĕl′] **124**–3
A HOTEL [hō tĕl′] **184**
hour [ow′ər] **18**–1
house [hows]
  courthouse [kört′hows′] **125**–13
  dollhouse [däl′hows′] **59**–18
  housekeeper [hows′kē′pər] **168**–34, **184**–20
  housekeeping cart [hows′kē′pĭng kärt′] **184**–19
  House of Representatives
    [hows′ əv rĕp′rĭ zĕn′tə tĭvz] **138**–3
  house painter [hows′ pān′tər] **168**–46
  houseplant [hows′plănt′] **56**–4, **211**–27
  townhouse [town′hows′] **52**–6
  two-story house [tōō′stör′ē hows′] **52** ✦
  warehouse [wër′hows′] **175**–7
  White House [wīt′ hows′] **138**–7
House [hows] **49, 53**
A HOUSE AND YARD [hows′ən yärd′] **53**
HOUSEHOLD PROBLEMS AND REPAIRS
  [hows′hōld′ präb′ləmz ən rĭ përz′] **62**–63
HOUSEWORK [hows′würk′] **60**
housing [how′zĭng] **52**–11
hubcap [hŭb′kăp′] **158**–9
hug [hŭg] **2**–E
human immunodeficiency virus (HIV)
  [hyōō′mən ĭm′yə nō dĭ fĭsh′ən sē vī′rəs] /
  [āch′ī/vē′] **111**–17
humid [hyōō′məd] **13**–15
humidifier [hyōō mĭd′ə fī/ər] **113**–11
humiliated [hyōō mĭl′ē ā′təd] **43** ✦
hummingbird [hŭm′ĭng bürd′] **214**–10
hump [hŭmp] **217**–51
hungry [hŭng′grē] **42**–5
hurricane [hür′ə kān′] **145**–14
hurt [hürt] **42**–16, **116**–C
husband [hŭz′bənd] **34**–13
  ex-husband [ĕks′ hŭz′bənd] **35** ✦
  former husband [för′mər hŭz′bənd] **35** ✦
hutch [hŭch] **55**–22
hybrid [hy′brĭd] **156**–3
hydrant [hī′drənt] **129**–27
hydroelectric power [hī′drō ĭ lĕk′trĭk pow′ər] **218**–5
hydrogen peroxide [hī′drə jən pə räk′sīd] **117**–9
hyena [hī ē′nə] **217**–30
HYGIENE [hy′jēn] **108**–109
hygienist [hī jē′nĭst, –jĕn′ĭst] **119**–3
hypertension [hī′pər tĕn′shən] **111**–14
hyphen [hy′fən] **190**–20
hypoallergenic [hī′pō ăl′ər jĕn′ĭk] **108** ✦
I beam [ī′ bēm′] **178**–3
ice [īs]
  ice cream [īs′ krēm′] **72**–26
  ice-cream cone [īs′ krēm′ kōn′] **79**–13
  ice cream shop [īs′ krēm′ shäp′] **131**–16
  ice hockey [īs′ häk′ē] **229**–13

ice pack [īs′ păk′] **117**–13
ice skates [īs′ skāts′] **231**–9
ice skating [īs′ skā′tĭng] **227**–4
iced tea [īst′ tē′] **79**–12
icy [ī′sē] **13**–22
ID [ī′dē′] **146**–19
identity theft [ī dĕn′tə tē thĕft′] **142**–9
ignition [ĭg nĭsh′ən] **159**–33
illegal drugs [ĭ lē′gəl drŭgz′] **142**–6
Illnesses and Childhood Diseases
  [ĭl′nə səz ən chīld′hōōd dĭ zēz′ əz] **111**
ILLNESSES AND MEDICAL CONDITIONS
  [ĭl′nə səz ən mĕd′ĭ kəl kən dĭsh′ənz] **111**
Immediate Family
  [ĭ mē′ dē ət făm′lē, –fă′məlē] **34**
immigrant [ĭm′ə grənt] **199**–19
immigrate [ĭm′ə grāt′] **40**–C
immigration [ĭm′ə grā′shən] **199**–18
immunization [ĭm′yə nə zā′shən] **114** ✦
immunodeficiency [ĭm′yə nō dĭ fĭsh′ən sē] **111**–17
impaired [ĭm përd′] **32**–11, **32**–12
important [ĭm pört′ənt] **146**–19
improvement [ĭm prōōv′mənt] **127**–20
in [ĭn] **25**–6
  be in shock [bē′ ĭn shäk′] **116**–B
  bubble in [bŭb′l ĭn′] **10**–K
  call in [käl′ ĭn′] **186**–A
  check in [chĕk′ ĭn′] **160**–A
  check-in kiosk [chĕk′ĭn kē′äsk′] **160**–2
  fall in love [fäl′ ĭn lŭv′] **40**–H
  fill in [fĭl′ ĭn′] **9**–O
  hand in [hănd′ĭn′] **10**–O
  in fashion [ĭn făsh′ən] **88** ✦
  in front of [ĭn frŭnt′ əv] **24**–7
  in love [ĭn lŭv′] **42**–18
  in pain [ĭn pān′] **42**–11
  in style [ĭn stīl′] **88** ✦
  in the middle [ĭn dhə mĭd′l] **24**–2
  look in [lōōk′ ĭn] **173**–B
  move in [mōōv′ ĭn′] **48**–F
  send in [sĕnd′ ĭn′] **173**–H
  take in [tāk′ ĭn′] **100**–D
  turn in [türn′ ĭn′] **191**–M
  walk-in freezer [wäk′ĭn frē′zər] **185**–3
inch [ĭnch] **17**–15
indent [ĭn dĕnt′] **190**–D
independence [ĭn′də pĕn′dəns]
  Declaration of Independence
    [dĕk′lə rā′shən əv ĭn′də pĕn′dəns] **198**–5
  Independence Day [ĭn′də pĕn′dəns dā′] **22**–13
INDIVIDUAL SPORTS [ĭn′də vĭj′ōō əl spörts′] **228**
infant [ĭn′fənt] **31**–6
infection [ĭn fĕk′shən] **111**–3
infectious disease [ĭn fĕk′shəs dĭ zēz′] **111** ✦
influenza [ĭn′flōō ĕn′zə] **111** ✦
INFORMATION [ĭn′fər mā′shən] **4**
inhaler [ĭn hā′lər] **113**–33
injection [ĭn jĕk′shən] **114** ✦, **158**–17
injured [ĭn′jərd] **116**–C
INJURIES [ĭn′jə rēz] **110**

ink [ĭnk]
  ink cartridge [ĭnk′ kär′trĭj] **183**–45
  inkjet printer [ĭnk′jĕt prĭn′tər] **183**–18
  ink pad [ĭnk′ păd′] **183**–46
inline [ĭn′līn′]
  inline skates [ĭn′līn′ skāts′] **231**–10
  inline skating [ĭn′līn′ skā′tĭng] **228**–10
inquire about benefits
  [ĭn kwīr′ ə bowt′bĕn′ə fĭts] **174** ✦
insects [ĭn′sĕkts] **209**–11
  insect bite [ĭn′sĕkt bīt′] **110**–11
  insect repellent [ĭn′sĕkt rĭ pĕl′ənt] **226**–23
Insects [ĭn′sĕkts] **214**
INSECTS [ĭn′sĕkts] **214**
insert [ĭn sürt′] **132**–D
INSIDE AND OUTSIDE THE BODY
  [ĭn′sīd′ ən owt′sīd′ dhə băd′ē] **106**–107
Inside the Car [ĭn′sīd′ dhə kär′] **159**
Inside the Kit [ĭn′sīd′ dhə kĭt′] **117**
Inside the Trunk [ĭn′sīd′ dhə trŭnk′] **158**
inspect [ĭn spĕkt′] **147**–N
install [ĭn stäl′] **176**–H, **178**–C
instructor [ĭn strŭk′tər] **6**–4
Instrument Panel [ĭn′strə mənt păn′əl] **159**
instruments [ĭn′strə mənts] **119**–4, **238**
insulation [ĭn′sə lā′shən] **178**–14
insurance [ĭn shōōr′əns] **118**–3, **136**–8
integers [ĭn′tə jərz] **192**–1, **192**–2
Integers [ĭn′tə jərz] **192**
intercom [ĭn′tər käm′] **50**–5
interest inventory [ĭn′trəst ĭn′vən tör′ ē] **172**–11
international call [ĭn′tər näsh′ə nəl köl′] **15**–35
Internet [ĭn′tər nĕt′]
  Internet listing [ĭn′tər nĕt′ lĭst′ĭng] **48**–1
  Internet map [ĭn′tər nĕt′ măp′] **155**–12
  Internet phone call [ĭn′tər nĕt′ fōn′ käl′] **14**–20
INTERNET [ĭn′tər nĕt′] **197**
internist [ĭn′tür′nĭst] **120**–1
internship [ĭn′türn shĭp′] **172**–6
interpreter [ĭn tür′prə tər] **168**–35
INTERSECTION [ĭn′tər sĕk′shən] **128**–129
INTERVIEW SKILLS [ĭn′tər vyōō′ skĭlz′] **174**
intestinal parasites [ĭn tĕs′tə nəl păr′ə sīts′] **111**–13
intestines [ĭn tĕs′tənz] **107**–42
In the Airline Terminal [ĭn dhə ër′līn tür′mə nəl] **160**
In the Examining Room
  [ĭn dhə ĭg zăm′ə nĭng rōōm′] **118**
In the Waiting Room [ĭn dhə wā′tĭng rōōm′] **118**
into [ĭn′tōō, –tə] **153**–E
intravenous drip (IV)
  [ĭn′trə vē′nəs drĭp′] / [ī′vē′] **121**–25
introduce [ĭn′trə dōōs′] **2**–C, **3**–I
introduction [ĭn′trə dŭk′shən] **190**–6
invention [ĭn vĕn′shən] **199**–12
inventor [ĭn vĕn′tər] **199**–13
inventory [ĭn′vən tör′ ē] **172**–11, **172**–12
invertebrates [ĭn vür′ tə brəts′] **194**–13
invitation [ĭn və tā′shən] **12**–I, **12**–J, **64**–9
invite [ĭn vīt′] **12**–H
iris [ī′rəs] **211**–16
iron [ī′ərn] **101**–13, **108**–17
iron [ī′ərn] **101**–G

ironed [i/ərnd] **101**–20

ironing board [i/ər nĭng börd/] **101**–14

irritated [ĭr/ə tā/təd] **64**–6

island [i/lənd] **204**–8

IV (intravenous drip)
[i/vē/] / [ĭn/trə vē/nəs drĭp/] **121**–25

ivory [i/vər ē] **24**–16

ivy [i/vē] **210**–25

jack [jăk] **158**–24

jacket [jăk/ət] **90**–8
chef's jacket [shĕfs/ jăk/ət] **93**–29
down jacket [down/ jăk/ət] **90**–16
leather jacket [lĕdh/ər jăk/ət] **90**–4
sports jacket [spörts/ jăk/ət] **89**–14

jackhammer [jăk/ hăm/ər] **178**–9

jack-o'-lantern [jăk/ə lăn/tərn] **239**–10

janitor [jăn/ĭ tər] **182**–3

January [jăn/yōō ër/ē] **21**–25

jar [jär] **74**–2, **74**–14

jasmine [jăz/mən] **211**–22

jaw [jö] **106**–4

jay [jā] **214**–6

jaywalk [jā/wäk] **128**–C

jazz [jăz] **237**–24

jeans [jēnz] **86**–2, **92**–19

jellyfish [jĕl/ē fĭsh/] **212**–14

jewelry [jōō/əl rē]
jewelry department [jōō/əl rē dĭ pärt/mənt] **95**–8
jewelry store [jōō/əl rē stör/] **130**–2

jigsaw [jĭg/sö/] **180**–10

job [jäb] **172**–1, **172**–3, **172**–7
job fair [jäb/ fër] **172**–13

JOB SAFETY [jäb/ sāf/tē] **179**

JOBS AND OCCUPATIONS
[jäbz/ ən äk/yə pā/shənz] **166–169**

JOB SEARCH [jäb/ sürch/] **173**

JOB SKILLS [jäb/ skĭlz/] **170**

Job Training [jäb/ trān/ĭng] **172**

jockstrap [jäk/străp/] **91**–6

join [joyn] **143**–L

judge [jŭj] **141**–6

Judicial Branch [jōō dĭ/shəl brănch/] **138**

juice [jōōs] **73**–32

July [jōō li/] **21**–31

jump [jŭmp] **230**–I

jumper cables [jŭm/pər kā/bəlz] **158**–21

jump rope [jŭmp/ rōp] **224**–4

jumpsuit [jŭmp/sōōt/] **93**–24

June [jōōn] **21**–30

junior high school [jōōn/yər hi/ skōōl] **188**–3

junk mail [jŭnk/ māl/] **135** ✦

Jupiter [jōō/pə tər] **205**–5

jury [jür/ē] **141**–8

justices [jŭs/tə səz] **138**–12, **138**–13

kangaroo [kăng/gə rōō/] **217**–44

keep [kēp] **28**–B

ketchup [kĕch/əp, kăch/–] **79**–21

kettle [kĕt/l] **54**–21

key [kē] **51**–30, **155**–9
key pad [kē/ păd/] **14**–5
pound key [pownd/ kē/] **14**–7
star key [stär/ kē/] **14**–6

keyboard [kē/börd/] **196**–14, **238**–18

Keyboarding [kē/börd/ĭng] **196**

kick [kĭk] **230**–E

kidney [kĭd/nē] **107**–43

kids' bedroom [kĭdz/ bĕd/rōōm/] **47**–9

KIDS' BEDROOM [kĭdz/ bĕd/rōōm/] **59**

king-size bed [kĭng/siz/ bĕd/] **184**–15

kiosk [kē/äsk/] **131**–22, **160**–2

kiss [kĭs] **3**–K, **36**–P

kit [kĭt]
doll making kit [däl/ mā/kĭng kĭt/] **232**–13
first aid kit [fürst/ ād/ kĭt/] **117**–1, **146**–18
model kit [mäd/l kĭt/] **232**–9
woodworking kit [wŏŏd/wür/kĭng kĭt/] **232**–14

Kit [kĭt] **117**

kitchen [kĭch/ən] **46**–5, **83**–15
kitchen timer [kĭch/ən ti/mər] **78**–18

A KITCHEN [ə kĭch/ən] **54**

Kitchen [kĭch/ən] **185**

KITCHEN UTENSILS [kĭch/ən yōō tĕn/səlz] **78**

kite [kit] **225**–2

kitten [kĭt/n] **215**–10

kiwi [kē/wē] **68**–22

knee [nē] **106**–20
knee highs [nē/hiz/] **91**–12
knee pads [nē/pădz/] **179**–19

knife [nif] **55**–4, **83**–30
carving knife [kär/vĭng nif/] **78**–12
multi-use knife [mŭl/tē yōōs/nif/, mŭl/ti–] **226**–20
paring knife [për/ĭng nif/] **78**–16
steak knife [stāk/ nif/] **83**–29

knit [nĭt] **233**–F

knitting needles [nĭt/ĭng nēd/lz] **233**–23

knit top [nĭt/ täp/] **88**–7

knob [näb] **194**–22, **194**–23
doorknob [dör/näb/] **53**–12

knuckle [nŭk/l] **106**–17

koala [kō ä/lə] **217**–45

lab [lăb] **5**–15
lab coat [lăb/ kōt/] **93**–33

Lab [lăb] **195**

label [lā/bəl]
mailing label [mā/lĭng lā/bəl] **183**–41
nutrition label [nōō trĭ/shən lā/bəl] **122**–8
prescription label [prĭ skrĭp/shən lā/bəl] **112**–4
warning label [wär/nĭng lā/bəl] **112**–8

label [lā/bəl] **9**–V

Labor Day [lā/bər dā/] **22**–14

lace [lās] **99**–9
shoelaces [shōō/lā səz] **94**–24

ladder [lăd/ər] **178**–2

ladle [lā/dl] **78**–7

ladybug [lā/dē bŭg/] **214**–26

lake [lāk] **204**–13

lamb [lăm] **70**–14
lamb chops [lăm/ chäps/] **70**–15
lamb shanks [lăm/ shăngks/] **70**–13

Lamb [lăm] **70**

lamp [lămp] **56**–15, **58**–25
lampshade [lămp/shād/] **56** ✦, **58**–26

land [lănd] **160**–K

landlord [lănd/lörd/] **51**–27

landmarks [lănd/märks/] **220**–1

landscape designer [lănd/skāp/ dĭ zi/nər] **176**–5

LANDSCAPING AND GARDENING
[lănd/skā/pĭng ən gärd/nĭng] **176**

languages [lăng/gwĭ jəz] **189**–13
language arts [lăng/gwĭj ärts/] **189**–9

lantern [lăn/tərn] **226**–22, **239**–10

laptop [lăp/täp/] **196**–16

large [lärj] **96**–4, **96**–5

laser printer [lā/zər prĭn/tər] **183**–19

lashes [lăsh/əz]
eyelashes [i/lăsh/əz] **106**–11

last [lăst]
last name [lăst/ nām/] **4**–4
last week [lăst/wēk/] **20**–18

late [lāt] **19**–24

latex gloves [lā/tĕks glŭvz/] **93**–34

laugh [lăf] **44**–A

laundromat [lön/drə măt/] **128**–1

laundry [lön/drē] **101**–1
laundry basket [lön/drē băs/kət] **101**–2
laundry detergent [lön/drē dĭ tür/jənt] **101**–8

LAUNDRY [lön/drē] **101**

Laundry Room [lön/drē rōōm/] **50**

lawn [lön] **53**–26
lawn mower [lön/ mō/ər] **176**–6

lawyer [lö/yər] **168**–36

lay [lā] **178**–B

layer cake [lā/ər kāk/] **81**–33

LCD projector [ĕl/sē/dē/ prə jĕk/tər] **6**–6, **235**–29

leader [lē/dər] **176**–4

leaf / leaves [lēf] / [lēvz] **210**–6, **211**–6
leaf blower [lēf/ blō/ər] **176**–2

leaking [lē/kĭng] **62**–3

learn [lürn] **40**–E

Learning New Words [lür/nĭng nōō/ würdz/] **8**

lease [lēs] **48** ✦, **51**–28

leather [lĕdh/ər] **98**–6
leather jacket [lĕdh/ər jăk/ət] **90**–4

leave [lēv] **11**–O, **38**–N, **82**–J, **160**–J, **171**–P

leaves / leaf [lēvz] / [lēf] **210**–6, **211**–6
leaf blower [lēf/ blō/ər] **176**–2

lecture [lĕk/chər] **122**–9

left [lĕft] **25**–1, **154**–8, **155**–C

legal [lē/gəl]
legal holiday [lē/gəl hăl/ə dā/] **22**–8
legal pad [lē/gəl păd/] **183**–38

Legal Holidays [lē/gəl hăl/ə dāz/] **22**

LEGAL SYSTEM [lē/gəl sĭs/təm] **141**

Leg and Foot [lĕg/ ən fŏŏt/] **106**

leggings [lĕg/ĭngz] **90**–12

Legislature [lĕ/jəs lā/chər] **139**–23

legs [lĕgz] **70**–21, **105**–9
leg of lamb [lĕg/ əv lăm/] **70**–14

lemonade [lĕm/ə nād/] **84**–2

lemons [lĕm/ənz] **68**–7

lend [lĕnd] **26**–C

length [lĕngkth] **17**–17, **96**–17

lengthen [lĕngk/thən] **100**–A

lens / lenses [lĕnz] / [lĕnz/əz] **115**–8, **235**–23

leopard [lĕp/ərd] **217**–34

let out [lĕt/ owt/] **100**–C

letter [lĕt′ər] **134**–13
letter carrier [lĕt′ər kăr′ē ər] **134**–20
letterhead [lĕt′ər hĕd′] **183**–42
lettuce [lĕt′əs] **69**–1
level [lĕv′əl] **172**–1, **180**–29
librarian [lī brër′ē ən] **133**–9
library [lī′brër ē] **5**–17, **125**–15
library clerk [lī′brër ē klŭrk′] **133**–1
library patron [lī′brër ē pā′trən] **133**–3
LIBRARY [lī′brër ē] **133**
license [lī′səns]
driver's license [drī′vərz lī′səns] **40**–4, **136**–9
driver's license number
[drī′vərz lī′səns nŭm′bər] **136**–11
license plate [lī′səns plāt′] **136**–12, **158**–12
marriage license [măr′ĭj lī′səns] **41**–8
renew a license [rĭ nōō′ ə lī′səns, –nyōō′–] **136** ✦
taxi license [tăk′sē lī′səns] **152**–22
License [lī′səns] **137**
licensed practical nurse (LPN)
[lī′sənst prăk′tə kəl nürs′] / [ĕl′pē′ĕn′] **120**–11
lid [lĭd] **78**–24
lieutenant governor [lōō tĕ′nənt gŭ′ vər nər] **139**–21
life [līf]
lifeguard [līf′gärd′] **225**–19
lifeguard station [līf′gärd stā′shən] **225**–21
lifesaving device [līf′sā′vĭng dĭ vīs′] **225**–20
life vest [līf′ vĕst′] **161**–25, **226**–14
wildlife [wīld′ līf′] **220**–3
LIFE [līf] **212**–**213**
LIFE EVENTS AND DOCUMENTS
[līf′ ĭ vĕnts′ ən dä′kyə mənts] **40**–**41**
lift [lĭft] **11**–E
light [līt] **23**–14, **97**–28
brake light [brāk′ līt′] **158**–14
daylight saving time [dā′līt′ sā′vĭng tīm′] **19**–25
flashlight [flăsh′līt′] **146**–14
hazard lights [hăz′ərd līts′] **159**–36
headlight [hĕd′ līt′] **158**–7
light blue [līt′ blōō′] **24**–11
light bulb [līt′ bŭlb′] **56** ✦
light fixture [līt′ fĭks′chər] **55**–18
light source [līt′ sörs′] **194**–21
light switch [līt′ swĭch′] **58**–27
night light [nīt′ līt′] **37**–27
porch light [pörch′ līt′] **53**–13
streetlight [strēt′līt′] **148**–3
string lights [strĭng′ līts′] **239**–18
tail light [tāl′ līt′] **158**–13
traffic light [trăf′ĭk līt′] **128**–8
work light [würk′ līt′] **181**–44
lightning [līt′nĭng] **13**–17
lily [lĭl′ē] **211**–26
limbs [lĭmz] **106** ✦, **210**–3
limes [līmz] **68**–8
limit [lĭ′mət] **154**–4
limo / limousine [lĭ′mō] / [lĭ′mə zēn] **156**–11
line [līn] **73**–11
assembly line [ə sĕm′blē līn] **175**–6
clothesline [klōz′līn′] **101**–9
curved line [kürvd′ līn′] **193**–23
headline [hĕd′līn′] **133**–7

line cook [līn′ kŏŏk′] **93, 185** ✦
line segment [līn′ sĕg′mənt] **193**–20
line supervisor [līn′ sōō′pər vī zər] **175**–4
parallel lines [pă′rə lĕl līnz′] **193**–25
perpendicular lines
[pür′pən dĭk′yə lər līnz′] **193**–24
straight line [strāt′ līn′] **193**–22
linen [lĭn′ən] **98**–2
linen closet [lĭn′ən kläz′ət] **57** ✦
liner [lī′nər]
eyeliner [ī′lī′nər] **109**–36
Lines [līnz] **193**
lingerie [län′zhə rā′, –jə–] **91** ✦
links [lĭnkz] **197**–10
lion [lī′ən] **213**–33, **216**–2, **217**–36
lip [lĭp] **106**–5
lipstick [lĭp′stĭk′] **109**–38
Liquid Measures [lĭk′wəd mĕzh′ərz] **75**
liquids [lĭk′wədz] **61**–21, **179**–8
list [lĭst] **67**–14
listen [lĭs′ən] **6**–C, **118**–C, **174**–K
listing [lĭst′ĭng] **48**–1
litter [lĭ′tər] **148**–2
litter [lĭ′tər] **219**–L
little [lĭt′l] **23**–1
Little League [lĭt′l lēg′] **229** ✦
live [līv] **140**–H
LIVE [līv] **52**
live music [līv′ myōō′zĭk] **84**–1
liver [lĭv′ər] **70**–7, **107**–40
livestock [līv′stäk′] **177**–15
living room [lĭv′ĭng rōōm′] **47**–12
LIVING ROOM [lĭv′ĭng rōōm′] **56**
lizard [lĭz′ərd] **213**–40
llama [lä′mə] **217**–25
load [lōd] **101**–C
loading dock [lō′dĭng däk′] **175**–15
loaf [lōf] **74**–10, **74**–22
meatloaf [mēt′lōf′] **81**–31
loafers [lō′fərz] **95**–30
Lobby [läb′ē] **50**
lobster [läb′stər] **71**–10
local call [lō′kəl köl′] **15**–31
lock [läk] **51**–34, **159**–25
locksmith [läk′smĭth′] **62**–11
lock [läk] **143**–E
locker [lä′kər] **5**–11, **50**–17
locket [läk′ət] **95**–35
Logging on and Sending Email
[lög′ĭng än′ ən sĕnd′ĭng ē′māl, –ön–] **197**
lonely [lōn′lē] **42**–17
long [löng] **96**–18
long distance call [löng′dĭs′təns köl′] **15**–32
long hair [löng′ hër′] **33**–3
long-sleeved [löng′slēvd′] **96**–14
long underwear [löng′ ŭn′dər wër′] **91**–3
look [lŏŏk]
look at [lŏŏk′ ăt′, –ət] **49**–H, **157**–A
look for [lŏŏk′ för′] / [lŏŏk′ fər] **133**–B, **173**–C
look in [lŏŏk′ ĭn′] **173**–B
look up [lŏŏk′ ŭp′] **8**–A
loop [lōōp] **99**–29

loose [lōōs] **97**–30
lose [lōōz] **229** ✦
loss [lös] **115**–2
lost child [löst′ chīld′] **144**–1
lotion [lō′shən] **37**–13, **108**–9
loud [lowd] **23**–11
loungewear [lownj′wër′] **91** ✦
love [lŭv] **40**–H, **42**–18
love seat [lŭv′ sēt′] **56**–1
low [lō] **97**–31
low-cost exam [lō′köst ĭg zăm′] **122**–1
low-cut socks [lō′kŭt′ säks′] **91**–10
low-fat milk [lō′făt′ mĭlk′] **81**–42
lower back [lō′ər băk′] **107**–29
lozenges [läz′ən jəz] **113**–30
LPN (licensed practical nurse) [ĕl′pē′ĕn′] /
[lī′sənst präk′tə kəl nürs′] **120**–11
luggage [lŭg′ĭj] **161**–18
luggage cart [lŭg′ĭj kärt′] **184**–8
lug wrench [lŭg′ rĕnch′] **158**–22
lumber [lŭm′bər] **178**–17
Lunch [lŭnch] **80**
lung [lŭng] **107**–39
machine [mə shēn′]
answering machine [ăn′sər ĭng mə shēn′] **14**–17
ATM (Automated Teller Machine) [ā′tē′ĕm′] /
[ö′tə māt ĭd tĕ′lər mə shēn′] **132**
fax machine [făks′ mə shēn′] **183**–21
machine operator [mə shēn′ äp′ə rā tər] **168**–37
machine screw [mə shēn′ skrōō′] **180**–32
sewing machine [sō′ĭng mə shēn′] **98**–13
sewing machine operator
[sō′ĭng mə shēn′ äp′ə rā′tər] **98**–14
stamp machine [stămp′ mə shēn′] **135**–11
vending machine [vĕnd′ĭng mə shēn′] **152**–9
Machine [mə shēn′] **98, 132**
magazine [măg′ə zēn′, măg′ə zēn′] **133**–5
magazine holder [măg′ə zēn′ hōl′dər] **56**–23
magnet [măg′nət] **195**–36
magnolia [măg nōl′yə] **210**–8
mail
airmail [ër′māl′] **134**–5
Certified Mail® [sür′tə fīd māl′] **134**–4
Express Mail® [ĭk sprĕs′ māl′] **134**–2
junk mail [jŭnk′ māl′] **135** ✦
mailboxes [māl′bäk′səz] **50**–11, **53**–1, **128**–13,
135–12
media mail [mē′dē ə māl′] **134**–3
overnight / next day mail
[ō′vər nīt′ / nĕkst′ dā′ māl′] **135** ✦
Priority Mail® [prī′ör ə tē māl′] **134**–1
mail [māl′] **135**–D
mailer [mā′lər] **183**–40
mailing [mā′lĭng]
mailing address [mā′lĭng ə drĕs′, ă′drĕs] **134**–22
mailing label [mā′lĭng lā′bəl] **183**–41
main office [mān′ ö′fəs] **5**–12
MAINTAINING A CAR [mān′tā nĭng ə kär′] **157**
maintenance [mān′tn əns] **184**–23
maitre d' [mā′trə dē′] **185**–11
make [māk] **156** ✦

make [māk]
  make a deposit [māk/ ə dǐ pǎz/ət] **132**–B
  make a disaster kit [māk/ ə dǐz/ās tər kǐt/] **146**–B
  make a mortgage payment
    [māk/ ə mör/gəj pā/mənt] **49**–L
  make an offer [māk/ ən ö/fər] **49**–I
  make a wish [māk/ ə wǐsh/] **240**–B
  make copies [māk/ käp/ēz] **171**–D
  make dinner [māk/ dǐn/ər] **39**–Q
  make eye contact [māk/ ī/ kän/tăkt] **174**–J
  make furniture [māk/ für/nǐ chər] **170**–G
  make lunch [māk/ lŭnch/] **38**–F
  make progress [māk/ prä/grəs] **10**–G
  make small talk [māk/ smöl/tök] **12**–B
  make the bed [māk/dhə bĕd/] **60**–F
maker [mā/kər]
  dressmaker [drĕs/mā/kər] **100**–1
  dressmaker's dummy [drĕs/mā/kərz dŭ/mē] **100**–2
  homemaker [hōm/mā/kər] **168**–33
Makeup [māk/ŭp] **109**
makeup remover [māk/ŭp rǐ mōōv/ər] **109**–42
making [mā/kǐng] **232**–13
MAKING ALTERATIONS [māk/ǐng öl/tə rā/shənz] **100**
MAKING CLOTHES [māk/ǐng klōz/] **98**–**99**
Making an Emergency Call
  [mā/kǐng ən ǐ mür/jən sē köl/] **15**
Making a Phone Call [mā/kǐng ə fōn/ köl/] **15**
male [māl] **4**–17
mall [möl] **126**–7
MALL [möl] **130**–**131**
mallet [māl/ət] **180**–2
mammals [măm/əlz] **209**–10
Mammals [măm/əlz] **213**
MAMMALS [măm/əlz] **216**–**217**
manager [măn/ǐ jər] **50**–8, **72**–8
  account manager [ə kownt/ măn/ǐ jər] **132**–9
  office manager [ö/fəs măn/ǐ jər] **182**–8
Manager [măn/ǐ jər] **92**
mane [mān] **217**–49
maneuver [mə nōō/vər] **117**–18
mangoes [măng/gōz] **68**–21
manicurist [măn/ə kyōō/rǐst] **168**–38
man / men [măn] / [mĕn] **30**–1, **30**–4
  doorman [dör/măn/] **184**–1
mantle [măn/təl] **56**–11
manual [măn/yōō əl] **117**–2
Manual Transmission [măn/yōō əl trănz mǐsh/ən] **159**
manufacture [măn/yə făk/chər] **175**–B
map [măp] **7**–12, **155**–12
Map [măp] **13**
maple [mā/pəl] **210**–12
Maps [măps] **155**
MAPS [măps] **155**
March [märch] **21**–27
margarine [mär/jər ən] **72**–20
marigold [măr/ə gōld/] **211**–13
MARINE LIFE, AMPHIBIANS, AND REPTILES
  [mə rēn/ līf/ ăm fǐb/ē ənz ən rĕp/tīlz] **212**–**213**
Marines [mə rēnz/] **138**–17
mark [märk] **190**–12, **190**–13, **190**–15
  postmark [pōst/märk/] **134**–24

markers [mär/kərz] **7**–17, **7**–24, **154**–17
market [mär/kət] **222**–6
  supermarket [sōō/pər mar/kət] **127**–18
MARKET [mär/kət] **66**–**67**
marriage license [măr/ǐj lī/səns] **41**–8
married couple [măr/ēd kŭ/pəl] **35**–20
Mars [märz] **205**–4
martial arts [mär/shəl ärts/] **228**–11
Martin Luther King Jr. Day
  [mär/tən lōō/thər-kǐng/ jōōn/yər dā/] **22**–10
mascara [mă skär/ə] **109**–39
mashed potatoes [măsht/ pə tā/tōz] **81**–23
mask [măsk] **239**–9
  catcher's mask [kăch/ərz măsk/] **231**–15
  diving mask [dī/vǐng măsk/] **225**–6
  face mask [fās/ măsk/] **93**–32
  oxygen mask [äk/sǐ jən măsk/] **161**–24
  particle mask [pär/tǐ kəl măsk/] **179**–14
  ski mask [skē/ măsk/] **90**–15
  surgical mask [sür/jǐ kəl măsk/] **93**–36
  ventilation mask [vĕnt/əl ā/shən măsk/] **92**–7
masking tape [măs/kǐng tāp/] **181**–53
mat [măt] **57**–3, **57**–28
  placemat [plās/măt/] **55**–11
match [măch] **9**–T
matches [măch/əz] **146**–16, **226**–21
matching [mă/chǐng] **28**–3
Material [mə tǐr/ē əl] **98**
materials [mə tǐr/ē əlz] **98** ✦, **179**–7
Materials [mə tǐr/ē əlz] **179**
maternity [mə tür/nə tē]
  maternity dress [mə tür/nə tē drĕs/] **88**–5
  maternity store [mə tür/nə tē stör/] **131**–19
math [măth] **189**–10
MATHEMATICS [măth/ə măt/ǐks] **192**–**193**
Math Operations [măth/ äp/ə rā/shənz] **192**
Math Problem [măth/ präb/ləmz] **192**
mattress [mă/trəs] **58**–20
May [mā] **21**–29
mayonnaise [mā/ə nāz/, mā/ə nāz/] **79**–23
mayor [mā/ər] **139**–26
meadow [mĕd/ō] **204**–20
measles [mē/zəlz] **111**–5
measure [mĕzh/ər] **100**–17, **181**–45
measure [mĕzh/ər] **17**–C
Measurement [mĕzh/ər mənt] **17**
MEASUREMENTS [mĕzh/ər mənts] **17, 75**
Measures [mĕzh/ərz] **75**
Measuring Area and Volume
  [mē/zhər ǐng ĕr/ē ə ən văl/yəm, –yōōm] **193**
meat [mēt] **66**–2
  meatballs [mēt/bölz] **81**–27
  meatloaf [mēt/lōf/] **81**–31
Meat [mēt] **70, 76**
MEAT AND POULTRY [mēt/ n pōl/trē] **70**
mechanic [mə kăn/ĭk] **166**–8
Mechanic [mə kăn/ĭk] **158**
media mail [mē/dē ə māl/] **134**–3
medical [mĕd/ĭ kəl] **121**–32
  medical chart [mĕd/ĭ kəl chärt/] **121**–24
  medical emergency bracelet
    [mĕd/ĭ kəl ĭ mür/jən sē brās/lət] **117**–3

medical records technician
  [mĕd/ĭ kəl rĕkərdz tĕk nĭsh/ən] **168**–39
medical waste disposal
  [mĕd/ĭ kəl wāst/ dĭ spō/zəl] **121**–31
MEDICAL CARE [mĕd/ĭ kəl kër/] **118**
MEDICAL CONDITIONS [mĕd/ĭ kəl kən dĭsh/ənz] **111**
MEDICAL EMERGENCIES [mĕd/ĭ kəl ĭ mür/jən sēz] **116**
Medical Procedures [mĕd/ĭ kəl prə se/jərz] **118**
Medical Specialists [mĕd/ĭ kəl spĕ/shə lĭsts] **120**
Medical Technician [mĕd/ĭ kəl tĕk nĭsh/ən] **93**
Medical Warnings [mĕd/ĭ kəl wör/nĭngz] **112**
medication [mĕd/ə kā/shən] **112**–3, **112** ✦,
  113–18, **121**–20
Medication [mĕd/ə kā/shən] **113**
medicine cabinet [mĕd/ə sən kăb/ə nət] **57**–20
medium [mē/dē əm] **96**–3
meet [mēt] **222**–6
meet [mēt] **49**–G, **49**–R
meeting [mē/tĭng]
  meeting place [mē/tĭng plās/] **146**–1
  meeting room [mē/tĭng rōōm/] **184**–25
MEETING AND GREETING [mē/tĭng ən grē/tĭng] **2**–**3**
melons [mĕl/ənz] **68**–19
  watermelons [wö/tər mĕl/ənz] **68**–18
membrane [mĕm/brān] **194**–6
Memorial Day [mə mör/ē əl dā/] **22**–12
memory card [mĕm/ə rē kärd/] **235**–20
men / man [mĕn] / [măn] **30**–1, **30**–4
  doorman [dör/măn/] **184**–1
  men's store [mĕnz/ stör/] **130** ✦
Men's Underwear [mĕnz/ un/dər wër/] **91**
menu [mĕn/yōō] **82**–7, **197**–8
  menu bar [mĕn/yōō bär/] **197**–1
MENU [mĕn/yōō] **80**–**81**
Mercury [mür/kyə rē] **205**–1
merge [mürj] **154**–10
mess [mĕs] **64**–8
message [mĕs/ĭj] **14**–18, **14**–19
messenger [mĕs/ən jər] **168**–40
meter [mē/tər] **62**–14, **129**–25, **152**–23
mice / mouse [mīs] / [mows] **63**–28, **196**–15, **215**–18
microphone [mī/krə fōn/] **234**–18
microprocessor [mī/krō prä/sĕ sər] **196**–4
Microscope [mī/krə skōp/] **194**
microwave [mī/krə wāv/] **77**–T
microwave oven [mī/krə wāv/ ŭv/ən] **54**–13
middle [mĭd/l] **25**–2
  middle-aged [mĭd/l ājd/] **32**–2
  middle initial [mĭd/l ĭ nĭsh/əl] **4**–3
  middle school [mĭd/l skōōl/] **188**–3
mid-length [mĭd/lĕnth] **96**–17
midnight [mĭd/nīt/] **18**–21
Military [mĭl/ə tër ē] **138**
MILITARY SERVICE [mĭ/lə tër ē sür/vəs] **138**–**139**
milk [mĭlk] **66**–5, **81**–42
  milkshake [mĭlk shāk/] **79**–14
milk [mĭlk] **177**–C
mini [mĭn/ē] **96**–15
  mini-blinds [mĭn/ē blĭndz/] **58**–8
  minivan [mĭn/ē văn/] **156**–8
minister [mĭ/nə stər] **199**–7

minutes [mĭn′əts] **18**–2
mirror [mĭr′ər] **57**–16
   full-length mirror [fŏŏl′lĕnth mĭr′ər] **58**–6
   rearview mirror [rĭr′vyōō′ mĭr′ər] **159**–35
   sideview mirror [sīd′vyōō′ mĭr′ər] **158**–3
misbehave [mĭs′bĭ hāv′] **44**–B
miss the bus [mĭs dhə bŭs′] **152** ✦
missing [mĭs′ĭng] **97**–40
mittens [mĭt′nz] **90**–10
mix [mĭks] **77**–R
mixed berries [mĭkst′ bĕr′ēz] **81**–36
mixer [mĭk′sər] **54**–25
mixing bowl [mĭk′sĭng bōl′] **54**–28, **78**–31
mobile [mō′bēl] **59**–5
   mobile home [mō′bəl hōm′] **52**–7
model [mäd′l] **156** ✦, **168**–41
   model kit [mäd′l kĭt′] **232**–9
   model trains [mäd′l trānz′] **233**–27
modern [mä′dərn] **199**–2
moist towelettes [moyst′ tow′əl ĕts] **146**–12
moisturizer [moys′chə ri′zər] **108**–9
mole [mōl] **32**–16
molecule [mäl′ĭ kyōōl′] **195**–27
monarch [mä′nərk, mä′närk] **199**–4
Monday [mŭn′dā, –dē] **20**–9
MONEY [mŭn′ē] **26**
monitor [män′ə tər] **196**–11
   arrival and departure monitors
     [ə rī′vəl ən dĭ pär′chər män′ə tərz] **161**–7
   baby monitor [bā′bē män′ə tər] **59**–7
   vital signs monitor [vī′təl sīnz män′ə tər] **121**–26
monkey [mŭng′kē] **217**–26
month [mŭnth] **20**–3
Months of the Year [mŭnths′ əv dhə yĭr′] **21**
moon [mōōn]
   crescent moon [krĕs′ənt mōōn′] **205**–10
   full moon [fŏŏl′ mōōn′] **205**–12
   new moon [nōō′ mōōn′] **205**–9
   quarter moon [kwör′tər mōōn′] **205**–11
Moon [mōōn] **205**
moose [mōōs] **216**–1
mop [mäp] **61**–6
mop [mäp] **60**–D
morning [mör′nĭng] **18**–15
mosque [mäsk] **126**–5
mosquito [mə skē′tō] **214**–22
motel [mō tĕl′] **126**–12
moth [möth] **214**–21
mother [mŭdh′ər] **34**–3, **35**–22
   grandmother [grăn′mŭdh′ər, grănd′–] **34**–1
   motherboard [mŭdh′ər börd′] **196**–5
   mother-in-law [mŭdh′ər ĭn lö′] **34**–10
   stepmother [stĕp′mŭdh′ər] **35**–26
MOTION [mō′shən] **153**
motor [mō′tər] **124**–4
motorcycle [mō′tər sī′kəl] **150**–4
mountain [mown′tn]
   mountain biking [mown′tn bī′kĭng] **226**–8
   mountain lion [mown′tn lī′ən] **216**–2
   mountain peak [mown′tn pēk′] **204**–14
   mountain range [mown′tn rānj′] **204**–15
   Mountain time [mown′tn tīm′] **19**–30

mouse / mice [mows] / [mīs] **63**–28, **196**–15, **215**–18
mouth [mowth] **104**–7
   mouthwash [mowth′wäsh′, –wösh′] **109**–25
Mouth [mowth] **106**
move in [mōōv′ ĭn′] **48**–F
move out [mōōv′ owt′] **48** ✦
movement [mōōv′mənt] **199**–16
mover [mōō′vər] **168**–42
movies [mōō′vēz] **222**–2
   movie theater [mōō′vē thē′ə tər] **126**–6
Movies [mōō′vēz] **237**
Moving In [mōō′vĭng ĭn] **49**
moving van [mōō′vĭng văn′] **156**–18
mow [mō] **176**–A
mower [mō′ər] **176**–6
mozzarella cheese [möts′ə rĕ lə chēz′] **71**–29
MP3 player [ĕm′pē′thrē′ plā′ər] **234**–2
mudslide [mŭd′slīd′] **144**–6
muffin [mŭf′ən] **79**–16, **80**–5
muffler [mŭf′lər] **158**–16
muffs [mŭfs] **179**–16
mug [mŭg] **55**–7
mugging [mŭg′ĭng] **142**–11
multiply [mŭl′tə plī] **192**–C
multi-use knife [mŭl′tē yōōs′ nīf′, mŭl′tī–] **226**–20
mumps [mŭmps] **111**–7
murder [mŭr′dər] **142**–12
muscle [mŭs′əl] **107**–32
mushrooms [mŭsh′rōōmz′] **69**–27
music [myōō′zĭk] **64**–3, **189**–15
   live music [lĭv′ myōō′zĭk] **84**–1
   music store [myōō′zĭk stör′] **130**–1
   world music [würld′ myōō′zĭk] **237**–32
Music [myōō′zĭk] **237**
MUSIC [myōō′zĭk] **238**
musician [myōō zĭsh′ən] **168**–43
mussels [mŭs′əlz] **71**–13, **212**–17
mustache [mŭs′tăsh] **33**–5
mustard [mŭs′tərd] **79**–22
mystery [mĭs′tə rē] **237**–20
nachos [nä′chōz] **79**–7
nail [nāl] **180**–34
   fingernail [fĭng′gər nāl′] **106**–18
   nail clipper [nāl klĭp′ər] **109**–31
   nail polish [nāl päl′ĭsh] **109**–33
   nail salon [nāl sə län′] **130**–3
   toenail [tō′nāl′] **106** ✦
name [nām] **4**–1, **4**–2, **4**–4
   name tag [nām′ tăg′] **92**–15
napkin [năp′kĭn] **55**–10, **83**–26
narrow [năr′ō] **97**–35
nasal [nā′zəl]
   nasal congestion [nā′zəl kən jĕs′chən] **110**–7
   nasal spray [nā′zəl sprā′] **113**–32
National Guard [nă′shə nəl gärd′] **138**–19
NATIONAL PARKS [nă′shə nəl pärks′] **220**–221
Native Americans [nā′tĭv ə mĕr′ə kənz] **198**–3
natural [năch′rəl, năch′ər əl]
   natural gas [năch′rəl găs′] **218**–3
   natural materials [năch′rəl mə tïr′ē əlz] **98** ✦
NATURE CENTER [nā′chər sĕn′tər] **208**–209
nature program [nā′chər prō′grăm] **236**–7

Navigating a Webpage [nă′və gā′tĭng ə wĕb′pāj] **197**
Navy [nā′vē] **138**–15
navy blue [nā′vē blōō′] **28**–5
near [nïr] **25** ✦
neck [nĕk] **96**–8, **96**–10, **104**–3
   crewneck [krōō′nĕk] **96**–7
   necklaces [nĕk′lə sĕz] **95**–10
   turtleneck [tür′tl nĕk′] **96**–9
needle [nēd′l] **98**–17, **100**–10, **210**–10, **233**–23
   needle plate [nēd′l plāt′] **98**–18
negative integers [nĕ′gə tĭv ĭn′tə jərz] **192**–1
negotiate [nĭ gō′shē āt′] **157**–D
neighborhood [nā′bər hŏŏd′] **128** ✦
nephew [nĕf′yōō] **34**–19
Neptune [nĕp′tōōn] **205**–8
nervous [nür′vəs] **42**–10
nest [nĕst] **209**–12
net [nĕt] **226**–17
   hairnet [hĕr′nĕt′] **93**–25
network [nĕt′würk′] **173**–A
Neutral Colors [nōō′trəl kŭl′ərz] **24**
neutron [nōō′trän] **195**–32
new [nōō]
   new job [nōō′ jäb′] **172**–3
   new moon [nōō′ mōōn′] **205**–9
   New Year's Day [nōō′ yïrz′ dā′] **22**–9
Newfoundland time [nōō′fən lənd tīm′, –fənd–] **19**–34
news [nōōz]
   newspaper [nōōz′pā′pər] **133**–6
   news program [nōōz prō′grăm] **236**–1
   newsstand [nōōz′stănd′] **128**–12
newt [nōōt] **212**–26
New Words [nōō′ würdz′] **8**
next [nĕkst]
   next day mail [nĕkst′ dā′ māl′] **135** ✦
   next to [nĕkst′ tōō, –tə] **24**–9
   next week [nĕkst′ wēk′] **20**–20
nickel [nĭk′əl] **26**–2
niece [nēs] **34**–18
night [nīt] **18**–20
   nightclub [nīt′klŭb′] **223**–12
   nightgown [nīt′gown′] **91**–25
   night light [nīt′līt′] **37**–27
   nightshirt [nīt′shürt′] **91**–28
   nightstand [nīt′stănd′] **58**–23
   night table [nīt′ tā′bəl] **58**–23
nine [nīn] **16**
nineteen [nīn′tēn′] **16**
nineteenth [nīn′tēnth′] **16**
ninetieth [nīn′tē əth] **16**
ninety [nīn′tē] **16**
   90° angle [nīn′tē də grē′ ăng′gəl] **193**–26
ninth [nīnth] **16**
nipple [nĭp′əl] **37**–2
no [nō]
   no left turn [nō′ lĕft′ türn] **154**–8
   no outlet [nō′ owt′lĕt, –lət] **154**–6
   no parking [nō′ pär′kĭng] **154**–11
noise [noyz] **64**–5
noisy [noy′zē] **23**–11
noon [nōōn] **18**–16
   afternoon [ăf′tər nōōn′] **18**–17

north [nörth] **155**–1
NORTH AMERICA AND CENTRAL AMERICA
[nörth/ ə mĕr/ə kə ən sĕn/trəl ə mĕr/ə kə] **200**–**201**
nose [nōz] **104**–6, **110**–17
revolving nosepiece [rə văl/vĭng nōz/pēs] **194**–17
not [nät]
can't breathe [kănt/ brēdh/] **116**–N
do not drink [dōō/ nät/ drĭnk/] **112**–F
do not enter [dōō/ nät/ ĕn/tər] **154**–2
do not operate [dōō/ nät/ äp/ər ät/] **112**–E
do not take [dōō nät/ tāk/] **112**–D
don't be late [dōnt/ bē/ lāt/] **174**–E
don't litter [dōnt/ lĭt/ər] **219**–L
don't smoke [dōnt/ smōk/] **114**–G
not working [nät/ wür/kĭng] **62**–1
note [nōt] **183**–39
footnote [fōōt/nōt/] **190**–10
notebook [nōt/bōōk/] **7**–27
notebook paper [nōt/bōōk/ pāp/ər] **7**–28
spiral notebook [spī/rəl nōt/bōōk/] **7**–29
novel [nä/vəl] **133**–16
November [nō vĕm/bər] **21**–35
nuclear energy [nōō/klē ər ĕn/ər jē] **218**–8
nucleus [nōō/klē əs] **194**–7, **195**–29
numb [nŭm] **119**–C
number [nŭm/bər]
access number [ăk/sĕs/ nŭm/bər] **14**–16
apartment number [ə pärt/mənt nŭm/bər] **4**–6
cell phone number [sĕl/ fōn/ nŭm/bər] **4**–12
checking account number
[chĕk/ĭng ə kownt/ nŭm/bər] **132**–14
driver's license number
[drī/vərz lī/səns nŭm/bər] **136**–11
even numbers [ēv/ən nŭm/bərz] **192**–4
odd numbers [öd/ nŭm/bərz] **192**–3
phone number [fōn/ nŭm/bər] **4**–11, **15**–30
prescription number
[prĭ skrĭp/shən nŭm/bər] **112**–5
savings account number
[sā/vĭngz ə kownt/ nŭm/bər] **132**–11
SKU number [ĕs/kā/yōō/ nŭm/bər] **27**–5
Social Security number
[sō/shəl sĭ kyōōr/ə tē nŭm/bər] **4**–15
Numbers [nŭm/bərz] **16**
NUMBERS [nŭm/bərz] **16**
Numerals [nōō/mər əlz] **16**
numerator [nōō/mər ā/ tər] **192**–5
nurse [nürs] **118**–8, **168**–44
licensed practical nurse (LPN) [lī/sənst
präk/tə kəl nürs/] / [ĕl/pē/ĕn/] **120**–11
nurse midwives [nürs/ mĭd/wīvz] **120** ✦
nurse practitioners [nürs/ präk tĭ/shən ərz] **120** ✦
registered nurse (RN) [rĕj/ə stərd nürs/] / [är/ĕn/]
120–10
surgical nurse [sür/jĭ kəl nürs/] **120**–9
nurse [nürs] **36**–B
Nurse [nürs] **93**
nursery [nür/sə rē]
nursery rhymes [nür/sə rē rīmz/] **37**–22
nursery school [nür/sə rē skōōl/] **188**–1
nursing [nür/sĭng] **120**–12
nursing home [nür/sĭng hōm/] **52**–12

Nursing Staff [nür/sĭng stăf/] **120**
nutrition label [nōō trĭ/shən lā/bəl] **122**–8
nuts [nŭts] **73**–36, **180**–36
nylon [nī/län] **99**–12
oak [ōk] **210**–17, **210**–24
obey [ō bā/] **140**–C
objective [əb jĕk/tĭv] **194**–18
oboe [ō/bō] **238**–3
observatory [əb zür/və tör/ē] **205**–21
observe [əb zürv/] **195**–C
obstetrician [äb/stə trĭsh/ən] **120**–2
obtuse angle [äb/tōōs ăng/gəl] **193**–27
occupational therapist
[äk/yə pā/shən əl thĕr/ə pĭst] **168**–45
OCCUPATIONS [äk/yə pā/shənz] **166**–**169**
ocean [ō/shən] **204**–6, **225**–1
o'clock [ə kläk/] **18**–6
October [äk tō/bər] **21**–34
octopus [äk/tə pəs] **212**–9
odd numbers [öd/ nŭm/bərz] **192**–3
odometer [ō däm/ə tər] **159**–28
off [öf]
clear off [klĭr/ öf/] **10**–I
drop off [dräp/ öf/] **38**–G
gas shut-off valve [găs/ shŭt/öf vălv/] **146**–4
get off [gĕt/ öf/] **153**–J
take off [tăk/ öf/] **109**–Q
turn off [türn/ öf/] **11**–P, **160**–I, **174**–G, **219**–G
offer [ö/fər] **12**–D
office [ö/fəs] **164**–3
main office [mān/ ö/fəs] **5**–12
office building [ö/fəs bĭld/ĭng] **124**–2
office manager [ö/fəs măn/ĭ jər] **182**–8
office supply store [ö/fəs sə plī/ stör/] **127**–21
post office [pōst/ ö/fəs] **125**–11
post office box (PO box) [pōst/ ö/fəs bäks/] /
[pē/ō bäks/] **135**–9
run for office [rŭn/ fər ö/fəs] **139**–A
Office [ö/fəs] **51**
OFFICE [ö/fəs] **134**–**135**, **182**–**183**
Office Equipment [ö/fəs ĭ kwĭp/mənt] **183**
officer [ö/fə sər] **161**–17, **168**–48
Office Skills [ö/fəs skĭlz/] **171**
OFFICE SKILLS [ö/fəs skĭlz/] **171**
Office Supplies [ö/fəs sə plīz/] **183**
Office Visit [ö/fəs vĭ/zət] **119**
official [ə fĭsh/əl] **139**–32, **229**–6
oil [oyl] **73**–31, **218**–6
oil gauge [oyl/ gāj/] **159**–29
oil paint [oyl/ pānt/] **233**–19
oil spill [oyl/ spĭl/] **218**–17
ointment [oynt/mənt] **113**–24, **117**–10
OK [ō kā/] **154**–5
old [ōld] **31**–9, **31**–10
omelet [äm/lət, ä/mə lət] **76**–12
on [än, ön] **25**–11
get on [gĕt/ än, –ön] **153**–I
go on [gō/ än, –ön] **173**–K
on-the-job training [än dhə jäb/ trā/nĭng, –ön]
172–7
on the left [än dhə lĕft/, –ön] **25**–1
on the right [än dhə rīt/, –ön] **25**–3

on time [än tīm/, –ön] **19**–23, **16**–29
overdose on drugs [ō/vər dōs/ än drŭgz/] **116**–K
put on [pōōt/ än/, –ön/] **87**–B, **108**–D, **109**–P
try on [trī/ än/, –ön/] **95**–C
turn on [türn/ än/, –ön/] **11**–B
once a week [wŭns/ə wēk/] **20**–22
oncologist [ön/kö lə jĭst/] **120**–5
one [wŭn] **16**
five after one [fīv/ ăf/ tər wŭn/] **18**–7
one billion [wŭn/ bĭl/yən] **16**
one eighth [wŭn/ ātth/, –āth/] **17**–5
one-fifteen [wŭn/fĭf/tēn/] **18**–9
one-forty [wŭn/för/tē] **18**–12
one-forty-five [wŭn/för/tē fīv/] **18**–13
one fourth [wŭn/ förth/] **17**–4
one half [wŭn/ hăf/] **17**–2
one hundred [wŭn/ hŭn/drəd] **16**
one hundred dollars
[wŭn/ hŭn/drəd däl/ərz] **26**–12
one hundred one [wŭn/ hŭn/drəd wŭn/] **16**
100 percent [wŭn/ hŭn/drəd pər sĕnt/] **17**–8
one hundredth [wŭn/ hŭn/drəth] **16**
one hundred thousand
[wŭn/ hŭn/drəd thow/zənd] **16**
one million [wŭn/ mĭl/yən] **16**
one o'clock [wŭn/ ə kläk/] **18**–6
one-oh-five [wŭn/ō fīv/] **18**–7
one-size-fits-all [wŭn/sīz fĭts/äl] **96**–6
one-ten [wŭn/tĕn/] **18**–8
one third [wŭn/ thürd/] **17**–3
one-thirty [wŭn/thür/tē] **18**–11
one thousand [wŭn/ thow/zənd] **16**
one thousandth [wŭn/ thow/zənth] **16**
one-twenty [wŭn/twĕn/tē] **18**–10
one way [wŭn/ wā/] **154**–3
one-way trip [wŭn/wā/ trĭp/] **152**–16
one whole [wŭn/hōl/] **17**–1
quarter after one [kwör/tər ăf/tər wŭn/] **18**–9
ten after one [tĕn/ ăf/tər wŭn/] **18**–8
twenty after one [twĕn/tē ăf/tər wŭn/] **18**–10
onions [ŭn/yənz] **69**–19, **69**–20
onion rings [ŭn/yən rĭngz/] **79**–4
online [än/lĭn/, ön–]
online catalog [än/lĭn/ kă/tə lög, ön–] **133**–11
online course [än/lĭn/ körs/, ön–] **172**–8
only [ön/lē] **154**–7
On the Airplane [än/ dhe ĕr/plān/] **161**
open [ō/pən] **6**–G, **143**–F
opener [ō/pən ər] **54**–8, **78**–1, **146**–8
Opening an Account [ö/pə nĭng ən ə kownt/] **132**
opera [äp/rə] **223**–11, **236**–5
operate [äp/ə rāt/] **112**–E, **170**–H
Operating Room [äp/ə rā/tĭng rōōm/] **121**
operating table [äp/ə rā/tĭng tā/bəl] **121**–40
Operations [äp/ə rā/shənz] **192**
operator [äp/ə rā/tər] **14**–21, **98**–14, **168**–37
ophthalmologist
[äf/thəl mäl/ə jĭst, –thə mäl/–, äp/–] **120**–7
opinion [ə pĭn/yən] **44**–3
opossum [ə päs/əm, päs/əm] **216**–4
opponent [ə pō/nənt] **139**–30
optician [äp tĭsh/ən] **130**–9

optometrist [äp täm/ə trïst] **115**–6
orange [ör/ənj, är/–] **24**–4
oranges [ör/ən jəz, är/–] **68**–5
orangutan [ə răng/ə tăng/, –tăn/] **217**–39
orchard [ör/chərd] **177**–10
orchid [ör/kïd] **211**–19
order [ör/dər] **185**–1
   order puller [ör/dər pŏŏl/ər] **175**–10
order [ör/dər] **82**–D
orderly [ör/dər lē] **120**–16
Ordinal Numbers [ör/dn əl nŭm/bərz] **16**
organ [ör/gən] **238**–20
organic [ör gă/nïk] **84**–2
organisms [ör/gə nïzmz] **194**–1
organize [ör/gə nïz/] **171**–L, **191**–G
organizer [ör/gə nï/zər] **183**–49
ornament [ör/nə mənt] **239**–15
Orthodontics [ör/thə dän/tïks] **119**
orthodontist [ör/thə dän/tïst] **119**–5
orthopedists [ör/thə pē/dïsts] **120** ✦
otter [ät/ər] **213**–35
ounce [owns] **75**–1, **75**–11
out [owt] **62**–2
   blow out [blō/ owt/] **240**–C
   check out [chĕk/ owt/] **133**–C
   cross out [krös/ owt/] **9**–R
   eat out [ēt/ owt/] **82** ✦
   fill out [fïl/ owt/] **173**–J
   get out of [gĕt/ owt/ əv] **153**–F
   let out [lĕt/ owt/] **100**–C
   move out [mōōv/ owt/] **48** ✦
   outfit [owt/fït] **88** ✦
   out of focus [owt/ əv fō/kəs] **235**–33
   out-of-state contact [owt/əv stāt/ kän/täkt] **146**–2
   run out of gas [rŭn/ owt/ əv găs/] **162**–E
   take out [tāk/ owt/] **9**–Y, **60**–Q, **82** ✦
   work out [würk/ owt/] **230**–N
OUTDOOR RECREATION [owt/dör rĕk/rē ā/shən] **226**
outlet [owt/lĕt, –lət] **58**–28, **154**–6, **159**–42
   outlet cover [owt/lĕt kŭv/ər] **181**–46
OUTSIDE THE BODY [owt/sïd/ dhe bä/dē] **106**–**107**
oven [ŭv/ən] **54**–15, **54**–20
   oven cleaner [ŭv/ən klē/nər] **61**–3
over [ō/vər] **76**–11, **153**–B
   overalls [ō/vər ölz/] **88**–6
   overcoat [ō/vər kōt/] **90**–2
   overexposed [ō/vər ïk spōzd/] **235**–34
   overflowing [ō/vər flō/ïng] **63**–17
   overhead compartment
      [ō/vər hĕd/ kəm pärt/mənt] **161**–13
   overhead projector [ō/vər hĕd/ prə jĕk/tər] **7**–16
   overjoyed [ō/vər joyd/] **43** ✦
   overnight mail [ō/vər nït/ māl/] **135** ✦
   over-the-counter medication
      [ō/vər dhə -kown/tər mĕd/ə kā/shən] **113**–18
overdose [ō/vər dōs/, ō/vər dōs/] **116**–K
Over-the-Counter Medication
   [ō/vər dhə kown/tər mĕd/ə kā/shən] **113**
owl [owl] **214**–5
owner [ō/nər] **166**–11, **175**–1
oxfords [äks/fərdz] **95**–29

oxygen mask [äk/sï jən mäsk/] **161**–24
oysters [oy/stərz] **71**–14
Pacific time [pə sïf/ïk tïm/] **19**–29
pacifier [päs/ə fï/ər] **37**–24
pack [päk] **74**–9, **117**–13, **235**–26
   backpack [băk/păk/] **94**–18, **226**–15
pack [päk] **49**–M, **162**–A
package [päk/ïj] **74**–8, **74**–20, **134**–17
packaged food [päk/ïjd fōōd/] **146**–10
PACKAGING [päk/ə jïng] **74**
packer [päk/ər] **175**–18
packing tape [päk/ïng tāp/] **183**–32
pad [päd]
   bumper pad [bŭm/pər päd/] **59**–4
   changing pad [chănj/ïng päd/] **59**–2
   foam pad [fōm/ päd/] **226**–13
   heating pad [hē/tïng päd/] **113**–13
   ink pad [ïnk/ päd/] **183**–46
   knee pads [nē/ pădz/] **179**–19
   legal pad [lē/gəl päd/] **183**–38
   shoulder pads [shōl/dər pădz/] **231**–20
   steel-wool soap pads [stēl/wŏŏl/sōp/ pădz/] **61**–5
   sterile pad [stĕr/əl päd/] **117**–6
pail [pāl] **37**–7, **61**–7, **225**–8
pain [pān] **42**–11, **115**–3
   pain reliever [pān rï lē/vər] **113**–26
paint [pānt] **181**–25, **232**–10, **233**–19
   paintbrush [pānt/brŭsh/] **181**–22, **233**–20
   paint pan [pānt/ pän/] **181**–51
   paint roller [pānt/ rō/lər] **181**–23
paint [pānt] **49**–P, **178**–A, **233**–E
painter [pān/tər] **168**–46
Painter [pān/tər] **92**
painting [pān/tïng] **56**–9
pair of scissors [pĕr/ əv sïz/ərz] **100**–16
paisley [pāz/lē] **96**–26
pajamas [pə jä/məz, –jä/–] **91**–24
pallet [pä/lət] **175**–13
palm [päm] **106**–15, **210**–14
pan [pän] **54**–24
   bed pan [bĕd/ pän/] **121**–28
   cake pan [kāk/ pän/] **78**–26
   dustpan [dŭst/ pän/] **61**–17
   frying pan [frï/ïng pän/] **78**–5
   paint pan [pānt/ pän/] **181**–51
   pancakes [pän/kāks/] **80**–7
   pie pan [pï/ pän/] **78**–28
   roasting pan [rō/stïng pän/] **78**–13
   saucepan [sös/pän/] **78**–25
pancreas [pän/krē əs] **107**–45
panda [pän/də] **217**–41
pane [pān] **178**–16
panel [pän/əl] **234**–7
Panel [pän/əl] **159**
panther [pän/thər] **217**–40
panties [pän/tēz] **91**–13
pants [pänts] **87**–12
   security pants [sï kyōōr/ə tē pänts/] **93**–22
   training pants [trā/nïng pänts/] **37**–11
   work pants [würk/ pänts/] **92**–5
panty hose [pän/tē hōz/] **91**–18
papayas [pə pï/əz] **68**–20

paper [pā/pər]
   construction paper [kən strŭk/shən pā/pər] **232**–12
   copies of important papers
      [kä/pēz əv ïm pört/ənt pā/pərz] **146**–20
   newspaper [nōōz/pā/pər] **133**–6
   notebook paper [nōt/bŏŏk/ pā/pər] **7**–28
   paper clip [pā/pər klïp/] **183**–31
   paper cutter [pā/pər kŭt/ər] **183**–22
   paper dolls [pā/pər dälz/] **233**–28
   paper shredder [pā/pər shrĕd/ər] **183**–24
   paper towels [pā/pər tow/əlz] **54**–3
   sandpaper [sänd/ pā/pər] **181**–56
   toilet paper [toy/lət pā/pər] **57**–17, **146**–13
   wallpaper [wäl/ pā/pər] **59**–8
parade [pə räd/] **239**–1
paragraph [pär/ə grăf/] **190**–3
parakeet [pär/ə kēt/] **215**–15
parallel lines [pär/ə lĕl/ lïnz/] **193**–25
parallelogram [pär/ə lĕl/ə grăm/] **193**–33
paramedic [pär/ə mĕ/dïk] **116**–2
parasites [pär/ə sïts/] **111**–13
parcel post [pär/səl pōst/] **134**–6
parentheses [pə rĕn/thə sēz/] **190**–19
PARENTING [pär/ən tïng, pĕr/–] **36**–**37**
Parents [pär/ənts, pĕr/–] **34**
parent-teacher conference
   [pär/ənt tē/chər kän/frəns, pĕr/–] **22**–5
paring knife [pĕr/ïng nïf/] **78**–16
park [pärk] **223**–10
   park ranger [pärk/ rāng/jər] **220**–2
park [pärk] **129**–E
parka [pär/kə] **90**–9
PARK AND PLAYGROUND [pärk/ ən plā/grownd/] **224**
parking [pär/kïng] **128**–6, **154**–11, **154**–12
   parking attendant [pär/kïng ə tĕn/dənt] **184**–3
   parking garage [pär/kïng gə räzh/, –räj/] **124**–1
   parking meter [pär/kïng mē/tər] **129**–25
   parking space [pär/kïng spās/] **50**–18, **128**–5
PARKS [pärks] **220**–**221**
parochial school [pə rō/kē əl skōōl/] **5** ✦
parsley [pär/slē] **69**–28
part [pärt] **33**–4
participate [pär tï/sə pāt/] **10**–B
particle [pär/tï kəl]
   particle board [pär/tï kəl börd/] **181**–20
   particle mask [pär/tï kəl mäsk/] **179**–14
Partner [pärt/nər] **8**
parts [pärts] **175**–5
Parts of a Bird [pärts/ əv ə bürd/] **214**
PARTS OF A CAR [pärts/ əv ə kär/] **158**–**159**
Parts of a Fish [pärts/ əv ə fïsh/] **212**
Parts of a Flower [pärts/ əv ə flow/ər] **211**
Parts of an Essay [pärts/ əv ən ĕs/ā] **190**
Parts of a Phone [pärts/ əv ə fōn/] **14**
Parts of a Sewing Machine
   [pärts/ əv ə sō/ïng mə shēn] **98**
Parts of a Tree [pärts/ əv ə trē/] **210**
party [pär/tē] **64**–2
pass [päs] **161**–20
   passbook [päs/bŏŏk/] **132**–10
   passport [päs/pört/] **41**–10
pass [päs] **10**–E, **137**–H, **230**–G

Index

passenger [păs/ən jər] **150**–2, **161**–15
past [păst] **155**–E
pasta [päs/tə] **67**–12
　pasta salad [päs/tə săl/əd] **80**–20
paste [pāst]
　toothpaste [tōōth/pāst/] **109**–23
pastrami [pə strä/mē] **71**–23
path [păth] **208**–3, **224**–3
Path [păth] **172**
patient [pā/shənt] **118**–6, **121**–18
patio [păt/ē ō] **53**–16
　patio furniture [păt/ē ō für/nĭ chər] **53**–19
patron [pā/trən] **82**–6, **133**–3
pattern [păt/ərn] **99**–22
PATTERNS [păt/ərnz] **96**
pause [pöz] **235**–E
paw [pö] **216**–20
pay [pā]
　paycheck [pā/chĕk/] **165**–14
　payroll clerk [pā/rōl klürk/] **165**–10
　pay stub [pā/ stŭb/] **165**–11
pay [pā]
　pay a late fine [pā/ ə lāt/ fīn/] **133**–E
　pay attention [pā/ ə tĕn/shən] **147**–D
　pay back [pā/ băk/] **26**–D
　pay cash [pā/ kăsh/] **27**–A
　pay for [pā/ för/, –fər] **27**–G
　pay phone [pā/ fōn/] **15**–25, **129**–23
　pay taxes [pā/ tăks/əz] **140**–B
　pay the application fee
　　[pā/ dhe ăp/lə kā/shən fē/] **137**–D
　pay the check [pā/ dhe chĕk/] **82**–I
　pay the rent [pā/ dhe rĕnt/] **48**–E
Pay [pā] **27**
PBX [pē/ bē/ ĕks/] **182**–13
peaceful assembly [pēs/fəl ə sĕm/blē] **140**–1
peaches [pē/chəz] **68**–10
peacock [pē/käk/] **214**–14
peak [pēk] **204**–14
pearls [pürlz] **95**–39
pears [përz] **68**–4
peas [pēz] **69**–21
pedal [pĕd/əl] **159**–45, **159**–46
pedestrian [pə dĕs/trē ən] **128**–14
　pedestrian crossing [pə dĕs/trē ən krö/sĭng] **154**–13
pediatrician [pē/dē ə trĭsh/ən] **120**–4
peel [pēl] **77**–K
peeler [pē/lər] **78**–15
peephole [pēp/hōl/] **51**–32
pelvis [pĕl/vəs] **107**–50
pen [pĕn] **7**–22
pencil [pĕn/səl] **7**–20, **109**–34
　pencil eraser [pĕn/səl ĭ rā/sər] **7**–21
　pencil sharpener [pĕn/səl shär/pə nər] **7**–23, **183**–26
penguin [pĕng/win] **214**–11
peninsula [pĕ nĭn/sə lə] **204**–7
penny [pĕn/ē] **26**–1
PEOPLE [pē/pəl] **32**
pepper [pĕp/ər] **55**–13, **69**–7, **69**–29
percent [pər sĕnt/]
　50 percent [fif/tē pər sĕnt/] **17**–10
　100 percent [wŭn/ hŭn/drəd pər sĕnt/] **17**–8

75 percent [sĕv/ən tē fĭv/ pər sĕnt/] **17**–9
10 percent [tĕn/ pər sĕnt/] **17**–12
25 percent [twĕn/tē fĭv/ pər sĕnt/] **17**–11
Percents [pər sĕnts/] **17**
Percussion [pər kŭsh/ən] **238**
perfume [pür/fyōōm/, pər fyōōm/] **108**–6
perimeter [pə rĭ/mə tər] **193**–43
period [pïr/ē əd] **190**–11
Period [pïr/ē əd] **198**
periodicals [pïr/ē äd/ĭ kəlz] **133**–4
periodic table [pïr/ē äd/ĭk tā/bəl] **195**–26
perm [pürm] **33**–B
peroxide [pə räk/ sĭd] **117**–9
perpendicular lines [pür/pən dĭk/yə lər lĭnz/] **193**–24
person [pür/sən]
　appliance repair person
　　[ə plī/əns rĭ për/ pür/sən] **166**–4
　assemblyperson [ə sĕm/blē pür/sən] **139**–24
　businessperson [bĭz/nəs pür/sən] **166**–12
　bus person [bŭs/ pür/sən] **185**–13
　congressperson [kän/grəs pür/sən] **138**–4
　councilperson [kown/səl pür/sən] **139**–28
　counterperson [kown/tər pür/sən] **79**–17
　delivery person [də lĭv/ə rē pür/sən] **167**–21
　electronics repair person
　　[ĭ lĕk trän/ĭks rĭ për/ pür/sən] **167**–24
　repair person [rĭ për/ pür/sən] **62**–10
personal CD player [pür/sə nəl sē/dē/ plā/ər] **234**–5
PERSONAL HYGIENE [pür/sə nəl hī/jēn/] **108**–109
PERSONAL INFORMATION
　[pür/sə nəl ĭn/fər mā/shən] **4**
pesticide poisoning [pĕs/tə sīd/ poy/zə nĭng] **218**–16
pests [pĕsts] **62** ✦
pet [pĕt]
　pet food [pĕt fōōd/] **72**–5
　pet store [pĕt stör/] **130**–6
petals [pĕt/lz] **211**–8
petition [pə tĭ/shən] **148**–5
petroleum [pə trō/lē əm] **218**–6
Pets [pĕts] **215**
pharmacist [fär/mə sĭst] **112**–1
pharmacy [fär/mə sē] **128**–4
PHARMACY [fär/mə sē] **112**–113
Phase of the Moon [fāz/ əf dhə mōōn/] **205**
Phillips screwdriver [fĭl/ĭps skrōō/drī/vər] **180**–31
phlebotomist [flĭ bä/tə mĭst] **121**–29
phone [fōn]
　automated phone system
　　[ö/tə māt ĭd fōn/ sĭs/təm] **14**–23
　cell phone holder [sĕl/ fōn/ hōl/dər] **94**–15
　cell phone kiosk [sĕl/ fōn/ kē/ösk] **131**–22
　cell phone number [sĕl/ fōn/ nŭm/bər] **4**–12
　cellular phone [sĕl/yə lər fōn/] **14**–8
　cordless phone [körd/ləs fōn/] **15**–24
　headphones [hĕd/fōnz/] **6**–8, **234**–4
　Internet phone call [ĭn/tər nĕt/ fōn/ käl/] **14**–20
　microphone [mī/krə fōn/] **234**–18
　pay phone [pā/ fōn/] **15**–25, **129**–23
　phone bill [fōn/ bĭl/] **15**–28
　phone jack [fōn/ jăk/] **14**–3
　phone line [fōn/ lĭn/] **14**–4
　phone number [fōn/ nŭm/bər] **4**–11, **15**–30
　smart phone [smärt/ fōn/] **15**–27

Phone [fōn] **14**
Phone Bill [fōn/ bĭl/] **15**
Phone Call [fōn/ köl/] **15**
photo [fō/tō] **58**–3, **136**–4
　digital photo album [dĭ/jə təl fō/tō ăl/bəm] **235**–32
　funny photo [fŭn/ē fō/tō] **206**–2
　photo album [fō/tō ăl/bəm] **235**–31
　photocopier [fō/tə käp/ē ər] **183**–23
　serious photo [sïr/ē əs fō/tō] **206**–3
photographer [fə täg/rə fər] **206**–1
PHOTOGRAPHY [fə täg/rə fē] **234**–235
photosynthesis [fō/tō sĭn/thə səs] **194**–10
physical [fĭz/ĭ kəl]
　physical education [fĭz/ĭ kəl ĕ jə kā/shən] **189**–17
　physical therapist [fĭz/ĭ kəl thĕr/ə pĭst] **115**–12
　physical therapy [fĭz/ĭ kəl thĕr/ə pē] **115**–11
physically challenged [fĭz/ĭ klē chăl/ənjd] **32**–10
physician assistant [fĭz/ĭ shən ə sĭs/tənt] **168**–47
physicist [fĭz/ĭ sĭst/] **195**–33
Physics [fĭz/ĭks] **195**
pi (π) [pī] **193**–46
piano [pē ăn/ō] **238**–14
pick [pĭk] **108**–15
pickax [pĭk/ăks/] **178**–21
picker [pĭ/kər] **178**–5
pickle [pĭk/l] **80**–11
pick up [pĭk/ ŭp/] **6**–I, **11**–E, **38**–M, **112** ✦
pickup truck [pĭk/ŭp trŭk/] **156**–12
picnic [pĭk/nĭk] **224**–D
picnic table [pĭk/nĭk tā/bəl] **224**–8
picture [pĭk/chər]
　picture book [pĭk/chər bōōk/] **133**–12
　picture dictionary [pĭk/chər dĭk/shə nër ē] **7**–31
　picture frame [pĭk/chər frām/] **58**–4
pie [pī] **81**–35
　pie pan [pī/ păn/] **78**–28
pier [pïr] **225**–18
pierced [pïrst]
　pierced ear [pïrst/ ïr/] **32**–17
　pierced earrings [pïrst/ ïr/ĭngz] **95**–36
pig [pĭg] **215**–2, **215**–14
pigeon [pĭj/ən] **214**–15
pile [pīl] **53**–25
pill [pĭl] **113**–21
pillow [pĭl/ō] **56**–2, **58**–11
　pillowcase [pĭl/ō kās/] **58**–14
pilot [pī/lət] **161**–11
pin [pĭn] **95**–38
　bobby pins [bäb/ē pĭnz/] **108**–21
　clothespin [klōz/ pĭn/] **101**–10
　pin cushion [pĭn/ kōōsh/ən] **100**–13
　pushpin [pōōsh/pĭn/] **183**–35
　rolling pin [rō/lĭng pĭn/] **78**–30
　safety pin [sāf/tē pĭn/] **37**–9, **100**–14
　straight pin [strāt pĭn/] **100**–12
pine [pīn] **210**–9
　pinecone [pīn/kōn/] **210**–11
pineapples [pī/năp/əlz] **68**–23
pink [pĭnk] **24**–7
pint [pīnt] **75**–3
pipe [pīp] **158**–15, **181**–17
　pipe wrench [pīp rĕnch/] **181**–47

pitch [pĭch] **230**–A
pizza [pēt/sə] **79**–10
place [plās] **146**–1
fireplace [fīr/plās/] **56**–13
placemat [plās/măt/] **55**–11
place of birth [plās/ əv bürth/] **4**–14
place setting [plās/ sĕt/ĭng] **83**–17
PLACES TO GO [plā/səz tə gō/] **222**–**223**
PLACES TO LIVE [plā/səz tə lĭv/] **52**
plaid [plăd] **96**–22
plain [plān] **97**–33
plains [plānz] **204**–19
plan [plăn] **186**–4
plan [plăn] **146**–A
plane [plān] **144**–3, **150**–8, **181**–57
Planets [plăn/əts] **205**
Planning a Career [plă/nĭng ə kə rēr/] **172**
plant [plănt] **176**–E, **177**–A, **219**–N
plants [plănts] **208**–5
houseplant [hows/plănt/] **56**–4, **211**–27
Plants [plănts] **210**
PLANTS [plănts] **210**
plaque [plăk] **119**–12
plastic [plăs/tĭk]
plastic storage bags [plăs/tĭk stör/ĭj băgz] **72**–25
plastic storage container
[plăs/tĭk stör/ĭj kən tā/nər] **78**–4
plastic utensils [plăs/tĭk yōō tĕn/ səlz] **79**–19
plastic wrap [plăs/tĭk răp/] **72**–24
plate [plāt] **55**–1
bread-and-butter plate [brĕd/n bŭt/ər plāt/] **83**–19
dinner plate [dĭn/ər plāt/] **83**–18
license plate [lī/səns plāt/] **136**–12, **158**–12
salad plate [săl/əd plāt/] **83**–20
vanity plate [vă/nə tē plāt/] **136** ✦
platform [plăt/förm/] **152**–7
platter [plăt/ər] **55**–20
platypus [plăt/ĭ pəs, –pōōs/] **217**–46
play [plā] **223**–8
play area [plā/ ër/ē ə] **130**–11
playground [plā/grownd/] **50**–3
play [plā] **235**–B
play an instrument [plā/ ən ĭn/strə mənt] **238**–A
play cards [plā/ kärdz/] **233**–H
play games [plā/ gāmz/] **232**–B
play with [plā/ wĭth/] **36**–M
player [plā/ər] **229**–5
CD player [sē/dē plā/ər] **159**–38
DVD player [dē/vē/dē/ plā/ər] **56**–7, **234**–10
MP3 player [ĕm/pē/thrē/ plā/ər] **234**–2
personal CD player [pür/sə nəl sē/dē plā/ər] **234**–5
portable cassette player
[pör/tə bəl kə sĕt/ plā/ər] **234**–6
portable DVD player
[pör/tə bəl dē/vē/dē/ plā/ər] **234**–11
video player [vĭd/ē ō plā/ər] **197**–11
PLAYGROUND [plā/grownd/] **224**
pliers [plī/ərz] **180**–7
plugs [plŭgz] **179**–15, **234**–16
plumber [plŭm/ər] **63**–20
plums [plŭmz] **68**–13
plunger [plŭn/jər] **181**–50

plywood [plī/wŏŏd/] **178**–18
p.m. [pē/ĕm/] **18**–5
pneumatic drill [nŏŏ măt/ĭk dril/] **178**–9
poached eggs [pōcht/ ĕgz/] **76**–9
PO box (post office box) [pē/ō bäks/] /
[pōst/ ö/fəs bäks/] **135**–9
pocket [päk/ət] **100**–7
podium [pō/dē əm] **206**–5
poinsettia [poyn sĕt/ē ə, –sĕt/ə] **211**–24
point [poynt] **17**–7,
endpoint [ĕnd/poynt/] **193**–21
pointer [poyn/tər] **197**–12
poison [poy/zən] **116**–J
poison ivy [poy/zən ī/vē] **210**–25
poison oak [poy/zən ōk/] **210**–24
poison sumac [poy/zən sōō/măk, –shōō/–] **210**–23
poisoning [poy/zən ĭng] **218**–16
poisonous fumes [poy/zən əs fyōōmz/] **179**–3
poles [pōlz] **226**–18, **231**–25
police [pə lēs/]
police officer [pə lēs/ ö/fə sər] **141**–1, **168**–48
police station [pə lēs/ stā/shən] **124**–6
polish [päl/ĭsh] **61**–8, **109**–33
polish [päl/ĭsh] **60**–E, **109**–O
political [pə lĭ/tĭ kəl]
political campaign [pə lĭ/tĭ kəl kăm pān/] **139**–29
political movement [pə lĭ/tĭ kəl mōōv/mənt] **199**–16
political party [pə lĭ/tĭ kəl pär/tē] **139** ✦
polka-dotted [pō/kə dät/əd] **96**–21
pollution [pə lōō/shən] **218**–11, **218**–14
Pollution [pə lōō/shən] **218**
polo [pō/lō] **229**–15
polo shirt [pō/lō shïrt/] **92**–14
poncho [pän/chō] **90**–19
pond [pänd] **204**–21
pool [pōōl] **51**–22, **184**–22, **228**–2
pool service [pōōl/ sür/vəs] **184**–21
pool table [pōōl/ tā/bəl] **50**–14
pop [päp] **73**–34, **237**–25
pop-up ad [päp/ŭp/] **197**–9
porch light [pörch/ līt/] **53**–13
porcupine [pör/kyə pīn/] **216**–10
Pork [pörk] **70**
pork chops [pörk/ chäps/] **70**–10
porpoise [pör/pəs] **213**–30
port [pört] **196**–7
airport [ër/pört/] **151**–10
portable [pör/tə bəl]
portable cassette player
[pör/tə bəl kə sĕt/ plā/ər] **234**–6
portable DVD player
[pör/tə bəl dē/vē/dē/ plā/ər] **234**–11
portable TV [pör/tə bəl tē/ vē/] **234**–8
positive integers [pö/zə tĭv ĭn/tə jərz] **192**–2
post [pōst] **134**–6
post card [pōst/kärd] **134**–16
postmark [pōst/märk/] **134**–24
post office [pōst/ ö/fəs] **125**–11
post office box (PO box) [pōst/ ö/fəs bäks/] /
[pē/ō bäks/] **135**–9
postage [pō/stĭj] **135** ✦

postal [pō/stəl] **135**–10
postal clerk [pō/stəl klürk/] **135**–7
postal forms [pō/stəl förmz/] **134**–19
postal scale [pō/stəl skāl/] **183**–27
postal worker [pō/stəl wür/kər] **169**–49
POST OFFICE [pōst/ ö/fəs] **134**–**135**
pot [pät] **54**–16, **78**–6
pot holders [pät hōl/dərz] **78**–29
teapot [tē/pät/] **55**–16
potatoes [pə tā/tōz] **69**–17
baked potato [bākt/ pə tā/tō] **81**–25
mashed potatoes [măsht/ pə tā/tōz] **81**–23
potato chips [pə tā/tō chĭps/] **73**–35
potato salad [pə tā/tō săl/əd] **80**–19
sweet potatoes [swēt/ pə tā/tōz] **69**–18
potty seat [pät/ē sēt/] **37**–12
pouch [powch] **217**–50
Poultry [pōl/trē] **70**, **76**
POULTRY [pōl/trē] **70**
pound [pownd] **75**–12
pound key [pownd/ kē/] **14**–7
pour [pör] **82**–C
powder [pow/dər] **37**–14, **108**–4, **109**–41
power [pow/ər] **218**–2, **218**–5
power cord [pow/ər körd/] **196**–2
power outlet [pow/ər owt/lĕt] **159**–42
power sander [pow/ər săn/dər] **180**–11
pox [pöks] **111**–6
practical [prăk/tə kəl] **120**–11
prairie dog [prër/ē dög/] **215**–22
praise [prāz] **36**–J
pregnant [prĕg/nənt] **32**–15
preheat [prē/hēt/] **77**–A
preparation [prĕ/pə rā/shən] **185**–4
PREPARATION [prĕ/pə rā/shən] **76**–**77**
prepare [prī/për/] **174**–A
PREPOSITIONS [prĕp/ə zish/ənz] **25**
PREPOSITIONS OF MOTION
[prĕp/ə zish/ənz əv mō/shən] **153**
preschool [prē/skōōl/] **188**–1
prescribe medication [prī skrīb/mĕd/ə kā/shən] **112** ✦
prescription [prī skrĭp/shən] **112**–2
pick up a prescription
[pĭk/ ŭp/ə prī skrĭp/shən] **112** ✦
prescription label [prī skrĭp/shən lā/bəl] **112**–4
prescription medication
[prī skrĭp/shən mĕd/ə kā/shən] **112**–3
prescription number [prī skrĭp/shən nüm/bər]
112–5
present [prĕz/ənt] **94** ✦, **240**–3
presentation [prĕ/zən tā/shən] **182**–6
president [prĕz/ə dənt] **138**–8, **199**–5
first president [fürst/ prĕz/ə dənt] **198**–11
Presidents' Day [prĕz/ə dənts dā/] **22**–11
vice president [vīs/ prĕz/ə dənt] **138**–9
press [prĕs] **78**–11, **140**–4
press [prĕs] **15**–B, **15**–D
presser foot [prĕs/ər fŏŏt/] **98**–19
pressure [prĕsh/ər] **111**–14, **118**–9
pretend [prī tĕnd/] **233**–G
Prewriting [prē/rī/tĭng] **191**

price [prīs] **27**–2, **27**–3, **27**–7
   price tag [prīs tăg/] **27**–1
prime minister [prīm/ mĭn/ə stər] **199**–7
principal [prĭn/sə pəl] **5**–4
print [prĭnt] **96**–23
   fingerprint [fĭng/gər prĭnt/] **136**–5
print [prĭnt] **4**–C, **171**–I
printer [prĭn/tər] **169**–50, **196**–17
   inkjet printer [ĭnk/jĕt prĭn/tər] **183**–18
   laser printer [lā/zər prĭn/tər] **183**–19
Priority Mail® [prī ör/ə tē māl/, –âr/–] **134**–1
prism [prĭz/əm] **195**–35
prisoner [prĭz/nər] **141**–15
private school [prī/vət skool/] **5** ✦
Problem [präb/ləm] **192**
problems [präb/ləmz] **115**–1, **192**–11
Problems [präb/ləmz] **115**, **119**
PROBLEMS [präb/ləmz] **62**–63
Procedures [prə sē/jərz] **117**, **118**
PROCEDURES [prə sē/jərz] **146**–147
Process [prä/sĕs] **191**
processor [prä/sĕ sər] **54**–26
Processor [prä/sĕ sər] **92**
produce section [prō/doos sĕk/shən] **72**–2
product [präd/ŭkt] **192**–9
Products [präd/ŭkts] **72**, **73**
program [prō/grăm]
   children's program [chĭl/drənz prō/grăm] **236**–9
   nature program [nā/chər prō/grăm] **236**–7
   news program [nooz/ prō/grăm] **236**–1
   shopping program [shäp/ĭng prō/grăm] **236**–10
   sports program [spörtz/ prō/grăm] **236**–11
program [prō/grăm] **170**–I
Programs [prō/grămz] **236**
projector [prə jĕk/tər] **6**–6, **7**–16, **235**–29
promotion [prə mō/shən] **172**–4
proof of insurance [proof/ əv/ĭn shoor/əns] **136**–8
proofread [proof/rēd/] **191**–I
prosecuting attorney
   [präs/ĭ kyoo/tĭng ə tür/nē] **141**–10
protect [prə tĕkt/] **143**–D
protector [prə tĕk/tər] **196**–1
proton [prō/tön] **195**–31
proud [prowd] **43**–21
prunes [proonz] **68**–26
pruning shears [proo/nĭng shĭrz/] **176**–11
psychiatrist [sī kī/ə trĭst, sə–] **120**–8
PUBLIC SAFETY [pŭb/lĭk sāf/tē] **143**
public school [pŭb/lĭk skool/] **5** ✦
PUBLIC TRANSPORTATION
   [pŭb/lĭk trăns/pər tā/shən] **152**
pull [pool] **119**–F, **224**–A
puller [pool/ər] **175**–10
pullover sweater [pool/ō/vər swĕt/ər] **88**–3
pulse [pŭls] **122**–A
pumps [pŭmps] **95**–26
Punctuation [pŭngk/choo ā/shən] **190**
puppy [pŭp/ē] **215**–12
purchase [pür/chəs] **94**–A
purifier [pyoo/rə fī/ ər] **113**–13
purple [pür/pəl] **24**–6
purses [pür/səz] **94**–2, **94**–14

push [poosh] **224**–B
pushpin [poosh/pĭn/] **183**–35
put [poot] **9**–X
put away
   [poot/ə wā/] **9**–Z, **60**–G
   put down [poot/ down/] **6**–J
   put in coolant [poot/ ĭn koo/lənt] **157**–I
   put on [poot/ än/, –ön/] **87**–B, **108**–D, **109**–P, **135**–C
   put on hold [poot/ än höld/, –ön] **171**–N
   put the utilities in your name
     [poot/ dhe yoo tĭl/ə tēz ĭn yər nām/] **49**–O
puzzle [pŭz/əl] **59**–17
pyramid [pĭr/ə mĭd] **193**–39
quad [kwäd] **5**–1
quart [kwört] **75**–4
quarter [kwör/tər] **26**–4
   quarter after one [kwör/tər ăf/tər wŭn/] **18**–9
   1/4 cup [kwör/tər kŭp/] **75**–8
   quarter moon [kwör/tər moon/] **205**–11
   quarter to two [kwör/tər tə too/] **18**–13
   3/4 sleeved [thrē/ kwör/tər slēvd/] **96**–13
question mark [kwĕs/chən märk/] **190**–12
Quick and Easy Cake [kwĭk/ ən ē/zē kāk/] **77**
quiet [kwī/ət] **23**–12
quill [kwĭl] **216**–23
quilt [kwĭlt] **58**–16
   quilt block [kwĭlt/ bläk/] **232**–15
quilt [kwĭlt] **232**–C
quotation [kwōt tā/shən] **190**–9
   quotation marks [kwō tā/shən märks/] **190**–15
quotient [kwō /shənt] **192**–10
rabbit [răb/ət] **215**–13
raccoon [ră koon/] **216**–13
race [rās] **230**–S
racing [rā/sĭng] **228**–19
rack [răk] **98**–16
   dish rack [dĭsh/ răk/] **54**–5
   roasting rack [rō/stĭng răk/] **78**–14
   towel rack [tow/əl răk/] **57**–13
racket [răk/ət] **231**–2
racquetball [răk/ət böl/] **228**–12
radiation [rā/dē ā/shən] **218**–15
radiator [rā/dē ā/tər] **158**–19
radio [rā/dē ō] **102**–6, **159**–37, **179**–22
radioactive materials
   [rā/dē ō ăk/tĭv mə tĭr/ē əlz] **179**–7
radiologist [rā/dē äl/ə jĭst] **120**–6
radishes [răd/ĭ shəz] **69**–4
radius [rā/dē əs] **193**–35
rafting [răf/tĭng] **226**–2
rags [răgz] **61**–9
rail [rāl] **59**–10
railroad crossing [rāl/rōd krö/sĭng] **154**–14
rain [rān] **218**–13
   rain boots [rān/ boots/] **90**–20
   raincoat [rān/kōt/] **90**–18
   rain forest [rān/ för/əst, fär/–] **204**–1
raining [rā/nĭng] **13**–11
raise [rāz] **6**–A
raisins [rā/zənz] **68**–25
rake [rāk] **176**–8
rake [rāk] **176**–C

ranch [rănch] **52**–10
rancher [răn/chər] **177**–22
Ranch Hand [rănch hănd/] **92**
RANCHING [răn/chĭng] **177**
R&B [är/n bē/] **237**–28
range [rānj] **204**–15
ranger [rān/jər] **220**–2
rash [răsh] **110**–10
raspberries [răz/bĕr/ēz] **68**–15
rats [răts] **63**–27, **215**–17
rattle [răt/l] **37**–26
   rattlesnake [răt/l snāk/] **213**–38
raw [rö] **70**–24
ray [rā] **212**–11
razor [rā/zər] **109**–27
   razorblade [rā/zər blād/] **109**–28
reaction [rē/ăk shən] **116**–E
read [rēd]
   proofread [proof/rēd/] **191**–I
   read the card [rēd/ dhe kärd/] **135**–G
   read the definition [rēd/ dhe dĕ/fə nĭ/shən] **8**–B
   read the paper [rēd/ dhe pā/pər] **39**–V
   read to [rēd/ too] **36**–N
Reading a Phone Bill [rē/dĭng ə fōn/ bĭl/] **15**
reality show [rē ă lə tē shō/] **236**–6
rearview mirror [rĭr/vyoo/ mĭr/ər] **159**–35
receipt [rĭ sēt/] **27**–6
receive [rĭ sēv/] **135**–F
receiver [rĭ sē/vər] **14**–1
reception area [rĭ sĕp/shən ĕr/ē ə] **182**–15
receptionist [rĭ sĕp/shə nĭst] **118**–2, **164**–5,
   169–51, **182**–14
reclined seat [rĭ klīnd/ sēt/] **161**–27
record [rĭ körd/] **195**–D, **235**–A
records [rĕk/ərdz] **168**–39
RECREATION [rĕk/rē ā/shən] **226**
recreational vehicle (RV)
   [rĕk/rē ā/shən əl vē/ə kəl] / [är/vē/] **156**–10
Recreation Room [rĕk/rē ā/shən room/] **50**
recruiter [rə kroo/tər] **172**–14
rectangle [rĕk/tăng/gəl] **193**–29
recycle [rē sī/kəl] **60**–B, **219**–C
recycling bin [rē sī/klĭng bĭn/] **61**–2
red [rĕd] **24**–1
   red hair [rĕd/ hĕr/] **33**–15
   redwood [rĕd/wood/] **210**–18
redecorate [rē dĕk/ə rāt/] **48** ✦
reduce [rĭ doos/] **219**–A
referee [rĕf/ə rē/] **229**–6
reference librarian [rĕf/rəns lī brĕr/ē ən] **133**–9
refrigerator [rĭ frĭj/ə rā/tər] **54**–9
refund [rē/fŭnd] **97** ✦
reggae [rĕ gā/] **237**–31
register [rĕj/ə stər] **73**–15
register [rĕj/ə stər] **140**–D, **157**–F
registered nurse (RN)
   [rĕj/ə stərd nürs/] / [är/ĕn/] **120**–10
registration [rĕj/ə strā/shən]
   registration sticker
     [rĕj/ə strā/shən stĭk/ər] **136**–13
   registration tag [rĕj/ə strā/shən tăg/] **136**–13
regular price [rĕg/yə lər prīs/] **27**–2

regulations [rĕ gyə lā′shənz] **164**–6
relatives [rĕ lə tĭvz] **44**–6
relax [rĭ lăks] **39**–U
relieved [rĭ lēvd] **42**–15
reliever [rĭ lēv′ər] **113**–26
religious holiday [rĭ lĭj′əs hăl′ə dā′] **22**–7
remain [rĕ′ mān] **147**–E
remarried [rē măr′ ēd] **35**–24
remote [rĭ mōt′] **234**–9
remove [rĭ mōōv′] **109**–Q, **132**–G
remover [rĭ mōō′vər] **109**–42
renew a license [rĭ nōō′ ə lī′səns, –nyōō′–] **136** ✦
rental agreement [rĕn′təl ə grē′mənt] **51**–28
Rental Office [rĕn′təl ö′fəs] **51**
Renting an Apartment [rĕn′tĭng ən ə pärt′mənt] **48**
repair [rĭ pĕr′] **166**–4, **167**–24
    repair person [rĭ pĕr′ pür′sən] **62**–10
repair [rĭ pĕr′] **170**–J
REPAIRS [rĭ pĕrz′] **62–63**
repellent [rĭ pĕl′ənt] **226**–23
replace [rĭ plās′] **157**–K
report [rĭ pört′] **143**–J, **143**–K
reporter [rĭ pör′tər] **169**–52
representative [rĕ′prĭ zĕn′tə tĭv] **138**–3, **167**–20
Reptiles [rĕp′tĭlz] **213**
REPTILES [rĕp′tĭlz] **212–213**
request [rĭ kwĕst′] **12** ✦
Requirements [rĭ kwīr′mənts] **140**
rescue [rĕs′kyōō] **145**–20
    rescue breathing [rĕs′kyōō brē′dhĭng] **117**–16
Resident Alien card [rĕz′ə dənt ā′lē ən kärd′] **40**–2
resource center [rē′sörs sĕn′tər] **172**–9
Resources [rē′sörs′səz, rĭ sör′səz] **219**
respirator [rĕs′pə rā′tər] **179**–13
Responding [rĭ spän′dĭng] **191**
Responsibilities [rĭ spän′sə bĭl′ə tēz] **140**
RESPONSIBILITIES [rĭ spän′sə bĭl′ə tēz] **140**
restaurant [rĕs′tə rənt, –ränt′] **125**–14, **128**–10
RESTAURANT [rĕs′tə rənt, –ränt′] **79, 82–83**
Restaurant Dining [rĕs′tə rənt dī′nĭng, –ränt′] **185**
Restaurant Kitchen [rĕs′tə rənt kĭ′chən, –ränt′] **185**
restrooms [rĕst′ rōōmz′] **5**–10
results [rĭ zŭltz′] **139**–31
resuscitation [rĭ sə sə tā′shən] **117**–17
retail clerk [rē′tāl′ klürk′] **169**–53
retire [rĭ tīr′] **41**–O
return [rĭtürn′] **73**–16
    return address [rĭ türn′ ə drĕs′, –ă′drĕs] **134**–21
return [rĭ türn′] **27**–H, **133**–D
REUNION [rē yōōn′yən] **44–45**
reuse [rē yōōz′] **219**–B
revise [rĭ viz′] **191**–J
Revising [rĭ vī′zĭng] **191**
Revolutionary War [rĕ′və lōō′shə nĕr ē wör′] **198**–8
revolving [rĭ väl′vĭng]
    revolving door [rĭ väl′vĭng dör′] **184**–2
    revolving nosepiece [rĭ väl′vĭng nōz′pēs] **194**–17
rewind [rē wind′] **235**–C
rewrite [rē rit′] **191**–J
rhinoceros [rĭ näs′ər əs] **217**–28
ribbon [rĭ′bən] **99**–30

ribs [rĭbz] **70**–5, **76**–2
    rib cage [rĭb′ kāj′] **107**–48
rice [ris] **67**–10, **81**–30, **177**–1
ride [rid] **129**–D
rider [ri′dər] **152**–3
riding [rī′dĭng] **226**–9
right [rit] **25**–3, **155**–B, **198**–10
    right angle [rit′ ăng′gəl] **193**–26
    right turn only [rit′ türn′ ōn′lē] **154**–7
Rights [rĭts] **140**
RIGHTS AND RESPONSIBILITIES
    [rĭts′ ən rĭ spän′sə bĭl′ə tēz] **140**
ring [rĭng] **37**–25, **79**–4, **95**–40
    clip-on earrings [klĭp′än ĭr′ĭngz, –ön–] **95**–37
    pierced earrings [pĭrst′ ĭr′ĭngz] **95**–36
rinse [rĭns] **108**–F
ripe [rĭp] **68**–30
ripped [rĭpt] **97**–41
ripper [rĭ′pər] **100**–18
rise [riz] **127**–13
    sunrise [sŭn′riz′] **18**–14
river [rĭv′ər] **155**–10, **204**–3
RN (registered nurse) [är′ĕn′] / [rĕj′ə stərd nürs′]
    120–10
road work [rōd′ würk′] **154**–16
Road Worker [rōd′ wür′kər] **92**
roast [rōst] **70**–1
    roast beef [rōst bēf′] **71**–21
    roast chicken [rōst chĭk′ən] **81**–22
    roasted turkey [rō′stəd tür′kē] **76**–4
    roasting pan [rō′stĭng păn′] **78**–13
    roasting rack [rō′stĭng răk′] **78**–14
robe [rōb] **91**–29
robin [räb′ən] **214**–16
rock [räk] **36**–D
rock concert [räk′ kän′sərt] **222**–5
rocking chair [räk′ĭng chĕr′] **37**–21
rocks [räks] **208**–6, **237**–23
Rodents [rōd′nts] **215**
RODENTS [rōd′nts] **215**
rollers [rō′lərz] **33**–19, **181**–23
rolling pin [rō′lĭng pĭn′] **78**–30
rolls [rōlz] **74**–11, **74**–23, **80**–17
romance [rō măns′, rō′măns] **237**–16
Roman Numerals [rō′mən nōō′mər əlz] **16**
roof [rōōf] **46**–1
roof garden [rōōf′ gär′dn] **50**–4
roofer [rōō′fər] **62**–8
room [rōōm]
    baby's room [bā′bēz rōōm′] **47**–10
    ballroom [böl′ rōōm′] **184**–26
    banquet room [băn′kwət rōōm′] **185**–14
    bathroom [băth′rōōm′] **46**–4
    bedroom [bĕd′rōōm′] **46**–2
    conference room [kän′frəns rōōm′] **182**–4
    dining room [dī′nĭng rōōm′] **82**–1
    dining room chair [dī′nĭng rōōm′ chĕr′] **55**–8
    dining room table [dī′nĭng rōōm′ tā′bəl] **55**–9
    dish room [dĭsh′ rōōm′] **83**–13
    guest room [gĕst′ rōōm′] **184**–13
    kids' bedroom [kĭdz′ bĕd′rōōm′] **47**–9

living room [lĭv′ĭng rōōm′] **47**–12
meeting room [mē′tĭng rōōm′] **184**–25
roommates [rōōm′māts′] **64**–1
room service [rōōm′ sür′vəs] **184**–17
storeroom [stör′rōōm′] **185**–5
Room [rōōm] **50, 118, 121**
ROOM [rōōm] **56**
rooster [rōō′stər] **215**–7
roots [rōōts] **210**–5, **211**–3
rope [rōp] **224**–4, **226**–19
rose [rōz] **211**–15
rotary [rō′tə rē]
    rotary card file [rō′tə rē kärd′ fil′] **183**–44
    rotary cutter [rō′tə rē kŭt′ər] **232**–16
rotten [rät′n] **68**–32
round trip [rownd′ trĭp′] **152**–17
route [rōōt] / [rowt]
    bus route [bŭs′ rōōt, –rowt] **152**–1
    escape route [ĕs′kāp rōōt, –rowt] **146**–3
    evacuation route
        [ĭ văk′yōō′ā shən rōōt, –rowt] **146**–5
    U.S. route [yōō′ĕs′ rōōt, –rowt] **154**–17
router [row′tər] **180**–12
ROUTINES [rōō tēnz′] **38–39**
rubber [rŭb′ər]
    rubber band [rŭb′ər bănd′] **183**–34
    rubber gloves [rŭb′ər glŭvz′] **61**–4
    rubber mat [rŭb′ər măt′] **57**–3
ruffle [rŭ′fəl] **58**–17
rug [rŭg] **58**–22
ruler [rōō′lər] **17**–13
rules [rōōlz] **64**–8
Rules [rōōlz] **190**
run [rŭn] **11**–D
    run across [rŭn′ə krös′] **153**–G
    run around [rŭn′ə rownd′] **153**–H
    run for office [rŭn′ fər ö′fəs] **139**–A
    run out [rŭn′owt′] **162**–E
runner [rŭ′nər] **185**–15
rural area [rŏŏr′əl ĕr′ē ə] **52**–4
RV (recreational vehicle)
    [är′vē′] / [rĕk′rē ā′shən əl vē′ə kəl] **156**–10
rye bread [ri′ brĕd′] **71**–20
sad [săd] **43**–19
safety [săf′tē] **37**–19, **92**–4, **159**–53
    safety boots [săf′tē bōōts′] **179**–20
    safety deposit box [săf′tē dĭ păz′ət bäks′] **132**–7
    safety glasses [săf′tē glăs′əz] **92**–10, **179**–10
    safety goggles [săf′tē gäg′əlz] **179**–11
    safety pin [săf′tē pĭn′] **37**–9, **100**–14
    safety rail [săf′tē rāl′] **59**–10
    safety regulations [săf′tē rĕ′gyə lā′shənz] **164**–6
    safety visor [săf′tē vī′zər] **179**–12
Safety [săf′tē] **76**
SAFETY [săf′tē] **76–77, 143, 179**
Safety Equipment [săf′tē ĭ kwĭp′mənt] **179**
Safety Hazards and Hazardous Materials
    [săf′tē hăz′ərdz ən hăz′ər dəs-mə tĭr′ē əlz] **179**
sailboat [sāl′bōt′] **225**–3
sailing [sā′lĭng] **227**–8

Index

salad [săl/əd]
  chef's salad [shĕfs/ săl/əd] **80**–14
  dinner salad [dĭn/ər săl/əd] **80**–15
  fruit salad [frōōt/ săl/əd] **80**–21
  pasta salad [päs/tə săl/əd] **80**–20
  potato salad [pə tā/tō săl/əd] **80**–19
  salad bar [săl/əd bär/] **79**–24
  salad fork [săl/əd förk/] **83**–27
  salad plate [săl/əd plāt/] **83**–20
  spinach salad [spĭ/nĭch săl/əd] **80**–13
Salad Dressings [săl/əd drĕ/sĭngz] **80**
Salads [săl/ədz] **80**
salamander [săl/ə măn/dər] **212**–27
salami [sə lä/mē] **71**–24
SALE [sāl] **102**–**103**
sales [sālz]
  sale price [sāl/ prīs/] **27**–3
  salesclerk [sālz/klürk/] **94**–3
  sales tax [sālz/ tăks/] **27**–8
Salesperson [sālz/pür/sən] **92**
salmon [săm/ən] **71**–3
  salmon steak [săm/ən stāk/] **71**–4
salon [sə lön/] **130**–3, **131**–18
salt and pepper shakers
  [sölt/ n pĕp/ər shā/kərz] **55**–13
same [sām] **23**–15
SAME AND DIFFERENT
  [sām/ ən dĭ/frənt, –dĭ fə rənt] **28**–**29**
samples [săm/pəlz] **84**–5
sand [sănd] **225**–23
  sandbox [sănd/bäks/] **224**–15
  sand castle [sănd kăs/əl] **225**–12
  sand dune [sănd dōōn/] **204**–5
  sandpaper [sănd/pā/pər] **181**–56
sandals [săn/dlz] **88**–9
sander [săn/dər] **180**–11
sandwich [săn/wĭch, –sănd/–] **79**–5, **80**–10, **80**–12
sanitation worker [săn/ə tā/shən wür/kər] **169**–54
satellite [săt/əl īt/] **205**–20
  satellite dish [săt/əl īt/ dĭsh/] **53**–6
satisfied [săt/ĭs fīd/] **42**–6
Saturday [săt/ər dā/, –dē] **20**–14
Saturn [săt/ərn] **205**–6
saucepan [sös/păn/] **78**–25
saucer [sö/sər] **83**–25
sausage [sö/sĭj] **70**–12, **80**–2
sauté [sö tā/, sö –] **77**–E
save [sāv] **219**–E
saving [sā/vĭng] **19**–25, **225**–20
savings account number
  [sā/vĭngz ə kownt/ nŭm/bər] **132**–11
saw [sö] **180**–9
  hacksaw [hăk/sö/] **180**–5
  jigsaw [jĭg/sö/] **180**–10
saxophone [săk/sə fōn/] **238**–5
say [sā] **2**–A, **3**–L, **4**–A
scaffolding [skăf/əl dĭng] **178**–4
scales [skālz] **57**–27, **72**–3, **135**–8, **155**–7, **195**–41, **212**–3
  postal scale [pō/stəl skāl/] **183**–27
scallions [skăl/yənz] **69**–20
scallops [skăl/əps, skäl/–] **71**–12, **212**–19

scan [skăn] **171**–H
scanner [skăn/ər] **183**–20
scared [skĕrd] **43**–23
scarf / scarves [skärf] / [skärvz] **95**–12
  winter scarf [wĭn/tər skärf/] **90**–5
scenery [sē/ nə rē] / [sēn/rē] **162**–3
schedule [skĕj/ōōl, –ōō əl] **152**–4
schedule [skĕj/ōōl, –ōō əl] **171**–J
school [skōōl] **126**–9
  adult school [[ə dŭlt/–, ăd/ŭlt skōōl/] **188**–8
  elementary school [ĕl/ə mĕn/trē skōōl/] **188**–2
  high school [hī/ skōōl/] **188**–4
  junior high school [jōōn/yər hī/ skōōl/] **188**–3
  middle school [mĭd/l skōōl/] **188**–3
  nursery school [nür/sə rē skōōl/] **188**–1
  parochial school [pə rō/kē əl skōōl/] **5** ✦
  preschool [prē/skōōl] **188**–1
  private school [prī/vət skōōl/] **5** ✦
  public school [pŭb/lĭk skōōl/] **5** ✦
  school bus [skōōl/ bŭs/] **156**–21
  school crossing [skōōl/ krö/sĭng] **154**–15
  technical school [tĕk/nĭ kəl skōōl/] **188**–5
  vocational school [vō kā/shə nəl skōōl/] **188**–5
SCHOOL [skōōl] **5, 10, 11**
School Registration Form
  [skōōl/ rĕj/ə strā/shən förm/] **4**
SCHOOLS AND SUBJECTS
  [sklōōz ən sŭb/jĭkts] **188**–**189**
science [sī/əns] **189**–11
SCIENCE [sī/əns] **194**–**195**
Science Lab [sī/əns lăb/] **195**
scissors [sĭz/ərz] **33**–20, **100**–16
scoop neck [skōōp/ nĕk/] **96**–10
score [skör] **10**–3, **229**–1
scorpion [skör/pē ən] **214**–30
scrambled eggs [skrăm/bəld ĕgz/] **76**–7
scraper [skrā/pər] **181**–52
screen [skrēn] **6**–2, **196**–11, **235**–30
  big-screen TV [bĭg/skrēn/ tē/ vē/] **50**–15
  fire screen [fīr/ skrēn/] **56**–12
  flat screen TV [flăt/ skrēn/ tē/vē/] **234**–7
  screen door [skrēn/ dör/] **53**–15
  sunscreen [sŭn/skrēn/] **108**–7, **225**–10
screener [skrēn/ər] **160**–5
screening area [skrē/nĭng ĕr/ē ə] **160**–4
screw [skrōō] **180**–32, **180**–33
  Phillips screwdriver [fĭl/ĭps skrōō/drī/vər] **180**–31
  screwdriver [skrōō/drī/vər] **180**–30
scroll bar [skrōl/bär/] **197**–15
scrub [skrŭb] **60**–K
scrubs [skrŭbz] **93**–31
  scrub brush [skrŭb/ brŭsh/] **61**–20
  surgical scrub cap [sür/jĭ kəl skrŭb/ kăp/] **93**–35
  surgical scrubs [sür/jĭ kəl skrŭbz/] **93**–38
scuba [skōō/bə]
  scuba diving [skōō/bə dī/vĭng] **227**–12
  scuba tank [skōō/bə tăngk/] **225**–5
sea [sē]
  sea anemone [sē/ ə nĕm/ə nē] **212**–24
  seahorse [sē/ hörs/] **212**–13
  sea lion [sē/ lī/ən] **213**–33
  sea otter [sē/ ät/ər] **213**–35

seashell [sē/shĕl/] **225**–24
sea urchin [sē/ ür/chən] **212**–21
seaweed [sē/ wēd/] **225** ✦
Sea Animals [sē/ ăn/ə məlz] **212**
SEAFOOD AND DELI [sē/fōōd/ ən dĕ/lī] **71**
seal [sēl] **213**–34
Sea Mammals [sē/ măm/əlz] **213**
seam ripper [sēm/ rĭp/ər] **100**–18
search [sürch]
  search and rescue team
    [sürch/ ən rĕs/kyōō tēm/] **145**–20
  search box [sürch/ bäks/] **197**–5
  search engine [sürch/ ĕn/jən] **197**–6
SEARCH [sürch] **173**
SEASONAL CLOTHING [sē/zə nəl klō/dhĭng] **90**
Seasons [sē/zənz] **21**
seat [sēt]
  backseat [băk/ sēt/] **159**–54
  car safety seat [kär/ sāf/tē sēt/] **37**–19
  child safety seat [chīld/ sāf/tē sēt/] **159**–53
  front seat [frŭnt/ sēt/] **159**–51
  love seat [lŭv/ sēt/] **56**–1
  potty seat [pät/ē sēt/] **37**–12
  reclined seat [rĭ klīnd/ sēt/] **161**–27
  seat belt [sēt/ bĕlt/] **159**–52
  upright seat [ŭp/rīt/ sēt/] **161**–28
seat [sēt] **82**–B
second [sĕk/ənd] **16**
Second Floor [sĕk/ənd flör/] **50**
seconds [sĕk/əndz] **18**–3
section [sĕk/shən] **72**–2
security [sĭ kyŏŏr/ə tē]
  security camera [sĭ kyŏŏr/ə tē kăm/rə] **50**–19
  security gate [sĭ kyŏŏr/ə tē gāt/] **50**–16
  security guard [sĭ kyŏŏr/ə tē gärd/] **132**–5, **169**–55
  security pants [sĭ kyŏŏr/ə tē pănts/] **93**–22
  security screener [sĭ kyŏŏr/ə tē skrē/nər] **160**–5
  security shirt [sĭ kyŏŏr/ə tē shürt/] **93**–20
Security Checkpoint [sĭ kyŏŏr/ə tē chĕk/poynt/] **160**
Security Guard [sĭ kyŏŏr/ə tē gärd/] **93**
sedan [sə dăn/] **156**–1
see [sē] **106**–A
seed [sēd] **211**–1
  seedling [sēd/lĭng] **211**–4
seek [sēk] **114**–A, **147**–H
seesaw [sē/sö/] **224**–16
select [sə lĕkt/] **196**–B
self-checkout [sĕlf/ chĕk/owt/] **73**–10, **133**–10
sell [sĕl] **170**–K
semi [sĕm/ī] **156**–15
semicolon [sĕm/ē kō/lən] **190**–18
Senate [sĕn/ət] **138**–5
senator [sĕn/ə tər] **138**–6
  state senator [stāt/ sĕn/ə tər] **139**–25
send [sĕnd] **197**–I
  send in [sĕnd/ ĭn] **173**–H
Sending a Card [sĕn/dĭng ə kärd/] **135**
Sending Email [sĕn/dĭng ē/māl/] **197**
senior [sēn/yər]
  senior citizen [sēn/yər sĭt/ə zən] **30**–5
  senior housing [sēn/yər howz/ĭng] **52**–11
Senses [sĕn/səz] **106**

sentence [sĕn/tns] **190**–2
sentence [sĕn/tns] **141**–E
separate [sĕ/pə rāt/] **76**–B
September [sĕp tĕm/bər] **21**–33
sequins [sē/kwĭnz/] **99**–33
Serious Medical Conditions
[sïr/ē əs mĕd/ĭ kəl kən dĭsh/ənz] **111**
serious photo [sïr/ē əs fō/tō] **206**–3
serve [sürv] **139**–D, **230**–P
serve on a jury [sürv/ ăn ə jŏŏr/ē, –ŏn–] **140**–E
serve the meal [sürv/ dhə mēl/] **82**–F
Serve [sürv] **76**
server [sür/vər] **82**–8, **83**–9, **169**–56, **185**–8
service [sür/vəs]
customer service [kŭs/tə mər sür/vəs] **97** ✦
customer service representative
[kŭs/tə mər-sür/vəs rĕ/prə zĕn/tə tĭv] **167**–20
guest services [gĕst/ sür/vəs əz] **130**–12
pool service [pŏŏl/ sür/vəs] **184**–21
room service [rŏŏm/ sür/vəs] **184**–17
SERVICE [sür/vəs] **138**–**139**, **185**
serving bowl [sür/vĭng bōl/] **55**–21
set [sĕt] **10**–A, **33**–C, **82**–A
set up [sĕt/ ŭp/] **173**–I
sunset [sŭn/sĕt/] **18**–18
setting [sĕ/tĭng] **83**–17
seven [sĕv/ən] **16**
seventeen [sĕv/ən tēn/] **16**
seventeenth [sĕv/ən tēnth/] **16**
seventh [sĕv/ənth] **16**
seventieth [sĕv/ən tē əth] **16**
seventy [sĕv/ən tē] **16**
75 percent [sĕv/ən tē fīv/ pər sĕnt/] **17**–9
sew [sō] **98**–A, **98**–B, **170**–L
sewing [sō/ĭng]
sewing machine [sō/ĭng mə shēn/] **98**–13
sewing machine operator
[sō/ĭng mə shēn/ äp/ə rā/ tər] **98**–14
Sewing Machine [sō/ĭng mə shēn/] **98**
Sewing Supplies [sō/ĭng sə plīz/] **100**
sex [sĕks] **4**–16
shade [shād] **225**–13
lampshade [lămp/shād/] **56** ✦, **58**–26
shadow [shă/dō/] **109**–35
shake [shāk]
milkshake [mĭlk/shāk/] **79**–14
shake [shāk] **3**–J, **174**–I
shakers [shā/kərz] **55**–13
shampoo [shăm pŏŏ/] **108**–10
shanks [shănks] **70**–13
shaper [shā/pər] **91**–15
Shapes [shāps] **193**
share [shër] **8**–M
Sharing and Responding
[shër/ĭng ən rĭ spän/dĭng] **191**
shark [shärk] **212**–4
sharpener [shär/pən ər] **183**–26
shave [shāv]
aftershave [ăf/tər shāv/] **109**–30
shave [shāv] **109**–M
shaver [shā/vər] **109**–26
shaving cream [shā/vĭng krēm/] **109**–29

shears [shïrz] **176**–9
sheep [shēp] **215**–6
sheet [shēt]
cookie sheet [kŏŏk/ē shēt/] **78**–27
dryer sheets [drī/ər shēts/] **101**–5
fitted sheet [fĭt/əd shēt/] **58**–12
flat sheet [flăt/ shēt/] **58**–13
shelf [shĕlf] **54**–2
shell [shĕl]
seashell [sē/shĕl/] **225**–24
Shellfish [shĕl/fĭsh/] **71**
shelter [shĕl/tər] **52**–13
shield [shēld]
windshield [wĭnd/shēld/] **158**–1
windshield wipers [wĭnd/shēld wī/pərz] **158**–2
shift [shĭft] **159**–49, **159**–50
shin [shĭn] **106**–21
shin guards [shĭn/ gärdz/] **231**–13
shingles [shĭng/gəlz] **178**–20
ship [shĭp] **175**–D
shipping clerk [shĭp/ĭng klürk/] **175**–14
shirt [shürt] **86**–1
nightshirt [nīt/shürt/] **91**–28
polo shirt [pō/lō shürt/] **92**–14
security shirt [sĭ kyŏŏr/ə tē shürt/] **93**–20
sports shirt [spörts/ shürt/] **88**–4
T-shirt [tē/shürt/] **86**–4
work shirt [würk/ shürt/] **92**–2
shock [shäk] **116**–B, **116**–F
shoes [shŏŏz] **86**–7, **87**–13, **95**–32
shoe department [shŏŏ/ dĭ pärt/mənt] **95**–7
shoelaces [shŏŏ/lās əz] **94**–24
shoe store [shŏŏ/ stör/] **130**–10
SHOES AND ACCESSORIES
[shŏŏz/ ən ĭk sĕs/ə rēz] **94**–**95**
shoot [shŏŏt] **211**–5
shoot [shŏŏt] **230**–H
shop [shäp]
barbershop [bär/bər shäp/] **129**–19
beauty shop [byŏŏ/tē shäp/] **130** ✦
coffee shop [kö/fē shäp/] **126**–11
donut shop [dō/nŭt shäp/] **129**–17
gift shop [gĭft/ shäp/] **130** ✦, **184**–5
ice cream shop [īs/ krēm shäp/] **131**–16
shop [shäp] **28**–A, **143**–H
Shop [shäp] **100**
SHOP [shäp] **80**–81
shoplifting [shäp/lĭf/tĭng] **142**–8
shopping [shäp/ĭng]
shopping basket [shäp/ĭng bäs/kət] **73**–9
shopping list [shäp/ĭng lĭst/] **67**–14
shopping mall [shäp/ĭng mäl/] **126**–7
shopping program [shäp/ĭng mäl/] **236**–10
SHOPPING [shäp/ĭng] **27**
shore [shör] **204**–12
short [shört] **32**–6, **96**–16
short hair [shört/ hër/] **33**–1
short-order cook [shört/ör/dər kŏŏk/] **185**–1
short-sleeved [shört/slēvd/] **96**–12
shorten [shört/ən] **100**–B
shorts [shörts] **89**–25, **91**–4

shoulder [shōl/dər] **105**–13
shoulder bag [shōl/dər băg/] **94**–17
shoulder blade [shōl/dər blād/] **107**–28
shoulder-length hair [shōl/dər lĕngkth/ hër/] **33**–2
shoulder pads [shōl/dər pädz/] **231**–20
shovel [shŭv/əl] **176**–7, **178**–22
show [shō] **236**–4, **236**–6, **236**–8
show [shō] **137**–C, **160**–C
shower [show/ər]
shower cap [show/ər kăp/] **108**–1
shower curtain [show/ər kür/tn] **57**–12
shower gel [show/ər jĕl/] **108**–2
showerhead [show/ər hĕd/] **57**–11
stall shower [stöl/ show/ər] **57** ✦
shredder [shrĕ/dər] **183**–24
shrimp [shrĭmp] **71**–11, **212**–18
shut [shŭt] **146**–4
shuttle [shŭt/l] **152**–19, **205**–19
sick [sĭk] **42**–12
homesick [hōm/sĭk/] **43**–20
side [sīd] **76**–10
sideburns [sīd/bürnz/] **33**–7
sideview mirror [sīd/vyŏŏ/ mĭr/ər] **158**–3
Side Salads [sīd/ săl/ədz] **80**
sidewalk [sīd/wök/] **129**–24
sight impaired [sīt/ ĭm përd/] **32**–11
sign [sīn] **4**–D
street sign [strēt/ sīn/] **129**–26
vacancy sign [vā/kən sē sīn/] **50**–7
vital signs monitor [vīt/l sīnz/ män/ə tər] **121**–26
sign [sīn] **48**–D
signal [sĭg/nəl]
strong signal [sträng/ sĭg/nəl] **14**–11
turn signal [türn/ sĭg/nəl] **158**–6, **159**–34
weak signal [wēk/ sĭg/nəl] **14**–12
signature [sĭg/nə chər] **4**–19
SIGNS [sīnz] **154**
silk [sĭlk] **98**–5
simmer [sĭm/ər] **77**–P
sing [sĭng] **36**–O, **238**–B
single [sĭng/gəl]
single father [sĭng/gəl fä/dhər] **35**–23
single mother [sĭng/gəl mŭdh/ər] **35**–22
sink [sĭnk] **54**–4, **57**–23
Sirius [sïr/ē əs] **205** ✦
sister [sĭs/tər] **34**–5, **35**–27
sister-in-law [sĭs/tər ĭn lö/] **34**–16
stepsister [stĕp/sĭs/tər] **35**–29
sitcom (situation comedy)
[sĭt/käm/] / [sĭch/ŏŏ ā/shən käm/ə dē] **236**–2
sit down [sĭt/ down/] **6**–F
site [sīt] **126**–2
sitter [sĭt/ər] **166**–9
situation comedy (sitcom)
[sĭch/ŏŏ ā/shən-käm/ə dē] / [sĭt/käm/] **236**–2
six [sĭks] **16**
six-pack [sĭks/păk/] **74**–9, **74**–21
6-year-old boy [sĭks/yïr ōld/boy/] **31**–9
sixteen [sĭks/tēn/] **16**
sixteenth [sĭks/tēnth/] **16**
sixth [sĭksth] **16**
sixtieth [sĭks/tē əth] **16**

Index

sixty [sĭks/tē] **16**

Sizes [sī/zəz] **96**

skate [skāt] **230**–U

skates [skāts] **231**–9, **231**–10

    skateboard [skāt/bôrd/] **224**–7

    skateboarding [skāt/bôr/dĭng] **228**–13

skating [skā/tĭng] **227**–4, **227**–5, **227** ✦, **228**–10

ski [skē] **230**–V

skiing [skē/ĭng] **227**–1, **227**–3

    waterskiing [wö/tər skē/ĭng] **227**–7

skill inventory [skĭl/ ĭn/vən tör/ē] **172**–12

Skills [skĭlz] **171**

SKILLS [skĭlz] **170, 171, 174**

skin [skĭn] **107**–31

    skinless [skĭn/ləs] **70** ✦

skirt [skürt] **87**–10

skis [skēz] **231**–24

    ski boots [skē/ boots] **231**–26

    ski hat [skē/ hăt/] **90**–11

    ski mask [skē/ măsk/] **90**–15

    ski poles [skē/ pölz/] **231**–25

skull [skŭl] **107**–47

skunk [skŭngk] **216**–12

SKU number [ĕs/kā/yōō/ nŭm/bər, skyōō/] **27**–5

sky [skī] **209**–9

    skycap [skē/kăp/] **160**–1

    skyscraper [skī/skrā/pər] **127**–13

slacks [slăks] **87**–12

slaves [slāvz] **198**–4

sledding [slĕd/ĭng] **227**–6

sledgehammer [slĕj/hăm/ər] **178**–23

sleeper [slē/pər] **91**–27

sleeping bag [slē/pĭng băg/] **226**–12

Sleepwear [slēp/wër] **91**

SLEEPWEAR [slēp/wër] **91**

sleepy [slē/pē] **42**–3

sleeve [slēv] **100**–6

    long-sleeved [löng/slēvd/] **96**–14

    short-sleeved [shört/slēvd/] **96**–12

    sleeveless [slēv/ləs] **96**–11

    3/4 sleeved [thrē/kwör/tər slēvd/] **96**–13

slender [slĕn/dər] **32**–9

slice [slīs] **77**–C

slide [slīd] **194**–3, **224**–13

    mudslide [mŭd/slīd/] **144**–6

sliding glass door [slī/dĭng glăs/ dör/] **53**–18

sling [slĭng] **113**–19

slip [slĭp] **91**–22, **91**–23, **132**–4

slippers [slĭp/ərz] **91**–26

slippery floor [slĭ/pər ē flör/] **179**–6

slow [slō] **23**–4

small [smöl] **96**–1, **96**–2, **97**–37

    small town [smöl/ town/] **52**–3

smart phone [smärt/ fōn/] **15**–27

smell [smĕl] **106**–C

smile [smil] **2**–D

smock [smök] **93**–26

smog [smäg, smög] **218**–11

smoggy [smä/gē, smö/–] **13**–14

smoke [smök] **114**–G

smoke detector [smök/ dĭ tĕk/tər] **51**–29

smoked turkey [smökt/ tür/kē] **71**–25

Snack Foods [snăk/ foodz/] **73**

snail [snāl] **212**–22

snake [snāk] **213**–39

    rattlesnake [ră/təl snāk/] **213**–38

snap [snăp] **99**–26

sneeze [snēz] **110**–B

snorkeling [snör/kə lĭng] **227**–11

snow [snō]

    snowboard [snō/börd/] **231**–23

    snowboarding [snō/bör/dĭng] **227**–2

    snowstorm [snō/störm/] **13**–23

snowing [snō/ĭng] **13**–12

soap [sōp] **57**–24, **61**–5, **108**–3

    soap dish [sōp/ dĭsh/] **57**–25

    soap opera [sōp/ äp/rə] **236**–5

sober [sō/ bər] **143** ✦

soccer [säk/ər] **229**–12

    soccer ball [säk/ər böl/] **231**–12

social [sō/shəl]

    Social Security card

        [sō/shəl sĭ kyoor/ə tē kärd/] **40**–5

    Social Security number

        [sō/shəl sĭ kyoor/ə tē nŭm/bər] **4**–15

    social worker [sō/shəl wür/kər] **169**–57

socks [säks] **86**–6

    ankle socks [ang/kəl säks/] **91**–7

    crew socks [kroo/ säks/] **91**–8

    dress socks [drĕs/ säks/] **91**–9

    low-cut socks [lō/kŭt säks/] **91**–10

Socks [säks] **91**

soda [sō/də] **73**–34, **79**–11

sofa [sō/fə] **56**–18

    sofa cushions [sō/fə koo/shənz] **56** ✦

soft [söft] **23**–6

    softball [söft/böl/] **229**–10

softener [sö/fən ər] **101**–6

software [söft/wër/] **167**–18, **196**–10

soil [soyl] **208**–2

solar [sō/lər]

    solar eclipse [sō/lər ĭ klĭps/] **205**–16, **205** ✦

    solar energy [sō/lər ĕn/ər jē] **218**–1

Solar System and the Planets

    [sō/lər sĭs/təm ən dhə plăn/əts] **205**

soldier [sōl/jər] **169**–58

sole [sōl] **94**–21

solid [säl/əd] **96**–19

Solids [säl/ədz] **193**

solution [sə loo/ shən] **192**–14

solve [sölv] **170**–M

son [sŭn] **34**–15

    grandson [grăn/sŭn/, grănd/–] **34** ✦

    son-in-law [sŭn/ĭn lö/] **34** ✦

sore throat [sör/ thrōt/] **110**–6

sort [sört] **101**–A

soul [sōl] **237**–28

soup [soop] **72**–18, **80**–16

    soup bowl [soop/ böl/] **83**–21

    soupspoon [soop/spoon/] **83**–32

Soup [soop] **77**

sour [sow/ər] **84**–4

    sour cream [sow/ər krēm/] **72**–21

Sources [sör/səz] **218**

sous chef [soo/ shĕf/] **185**–6

south [sowth] **155**–3

soybeans [soy/bēnz/] **177**–3

space [spās] **50**–18, **128**–5

    space shuttle [spās/ shŭt/əl] **205**–19

    space station [spās/ stā/shən] **205**–18

Space [spās] **205**

Space Exploration [spās/ ĕk/splə rā/shən] **205**

spades [spādz] **233**–30

spaghetti [spə gĕt/ē] **81**–26

spare tire [spër/ tir/] **158**–23

sparrow [spăr/ō] **214**–7

spatula [spăch/ə lə] **78**–19

speak [spēk] **170**–N

speakers [spē/kərz] **50**–5, **206**–4, **234**–14

Special [spĕ/shəl] **80**

Specialists [spĕsh/ə lĭsts/] **120**

speech [spēch] **140**–2

speed limit [spēd/ lĭm/ət] **154**–4

speedometer [spĭ däm/ə tər] **159**–27

speed skating [spēd/skā/tĭng] **227** ✦

spell [spĕl] **4**–B

sphere [sfir] **193**–42

spider [spi/dər] **214**–29

spill [spĭl] **218**–17

spinach [spĭn/ĭch] **69**–11

    spinach salad [spĭn/ĭch săl/əd] **80**–13

spinal column [spi/nəl käl/əm] **107**–49

spiral notebook [spi/rəl nōt/book/] **7**–29

splint [splĭnt] **117**–14

sponge [spŭnj] **61**–19

    sponge mop [spŭnj/ mäp/] **61**–6

spoon [spoon] **55**–5, **78**–9

    soupspoon [soop/spoon/] **83**–32

    tablespoon [tā/bəl spoon/] **75**–7

    teaspoon [tē/spoon/] **75**–6, **83**–31

spoon [spoon] **77**–F

sports [spörts]

    sports car [spörts/ kär/] **156**–4

    sports coat [spörts/ kōt/] **89**–14

    sports jacket [spörts/ jăk/ət] **89**–14

    sports program [spörts/ prō/grăm] **236**–11

    sports shirt [spörts/ shürt/] **88**–4

    sport-utility vehicle (SUV) [spört/

        yoo tĭl/ə tē vē/ĭ kəl] / [ĕs/yoo/vē/] **156**–7

SPORTS [spörts] **228, 229, 230, 231**

SPORTS EQUIPMENT [spörts/ ĭ kwĭp/mənt] **231**

SPORTS VERBS [spörts/ vürbz/] **230**

sprained ankle [sprānd/ ăng/kəl] **110**–18

spray [sprā] **108**–12, **113**–32

    spray gun [sprā/ gŭn/] **181**–21

    spray starch [sprā/ stärch/] **101**–12

spread [sprĕd]

    bedspread [bĕd/sprĕd] **59**–11

spring [sprĭng] **21**–37, **58**–19

sprinkler [sprĭng/klər] **53**–22

square [skwër] **193**–30

squash [skwäsh, skwösh] **69**–24

squeegee [skwē/jē] **61**–15

squid [skwĭd] **212**–7

squirrel [skwür/əl] **215**–21

stadium [stā/dē əm] **126**–1

staff [stăf] **185** ✦
Staff [stăf] **120**
stage [stāj] **194**–16
   stage clips [stāj/ klĭps/] **194**–24
stain [stān] **181**–24
stained [stānd] **97**–42
stairs [stĕrz] **50**–10
stairway [stĕr/ wā/] **50**–10
stall shower [stöl/ show/ər] **57** ✦
stamps [stămps] **134**–18, **134**–23, **183**–47
   stamp machine [stămp/ mə shēn/] **135**–11
stand [stănd] **152**–18
   checkstand [chĕk/ stănd/] **73**–12
   newsstand [nooz/ stănd/] **128**–12
   nightstand [nīt/ stănd/] **58**–23
stand [stănd] **141**–D
   stand up [stănd/ ŭp/] **6**–D
standard time [stăn/ dərd tīm/] **19**–26
staple [stā/ pəl] **171**–F
stapler [stā/ plər] **183**–28
staples [stā/ pəlz] **183**–29
star [stär] **205**–13
   starfish [stär/ fĭsh/] **212**–16
   star key [stär/ kē/] **14**–6
starch [stärch] **101**–12
start [stärt] **12**–A, **40**–B, **230**–R
starting point [stär/ tĭng poynt/] **162**–1
starving [stär/ vĭng] **43** ✦
state [stāt] **4**–8, **146**–2
   state capital [stāt kă/ pət əl] **139**–22
   state senator [stāt sĕn/ ə tər] **139**–25
state [stāt] **15**–G, **195**–A
State Government [stāt gŭ/ vərn mənt] **139**
statement [stāt/ mənt] **132**–16
station [stā/ shən]
   bus station [bŭs/ stā/ shən] **124**–7
   fire station [fīr/ stā/ shən] **125**–12
   gas station [găs/ stā/ shən] **125**–10
   gas station attendant
     [găs/ stā/ shən ə tĕn/ dənt] **162**–3
   lifeguard station [lïf/ gärd stā/ shən] **225**–21
   police station [pə lēs/ stā/ shən] **124**–6
   space station [spās/ stā/ shən] **205**–18
   station wagon [stā/ shən wăg/ ən] **156**–6
   subway station [sŭb/ wā/ stā/ shən] **151**–11
Station [stā/ shən] **152**
stationery [stā/ shə nĕr/ ē] **183**–42
stay [stā]
   stay away [stā ə wā/] **147**–I
   stay fit [stā fĭt/] **114**–E
   stay on the line [stā ön dhə lïn/] **15**–H
   stay on well-lit streets [stā ön wĕl lĭt/ strēts/] **143**–B
Stay Well [stā wĕl/] **114**
steak [stāk] **70**–2, **81**–24
   broiled steak [broyld/ stāk/] **76**–3
   halibut steak [hăl/ ə bŭt stāk/] **71**–6
   salmon steak [săm/ ən stāk/] **71**–4
   steak knife [stāk/ nīf/] **83**–29
steal [stēl] **142** ✦
steam [stēm] **77**–D
steamed vegetables [stēmd/ vĕj/ tə bəlz] **81**–32
steamer [stē/ mər] **78**–3

steel [stēl]
   steel toe boots [stēl/ tō/ boots/] **92**–6
   steel-wool soap pads [stēl/ wool/ sōp/ pădz/] **61**–5
steering wheel [stïr/ ĭng wēl/] **159**–26
stems [stĕmz] **211**–9
step [stĕp]
   stepbrother [stĕp/ brŭdh/ ər] **35**–30
   stepdaughter [stĕp/ dö/ tər] **35** ✦
   stepfather [stĕp/ fä/ dhər] **35**–25
   stepladder [stĕp/ lăd/ ər] **61**–13
   stepmother [stĕp/ mŭdh/ ər] **35**–26
   steps [stĕps] **53**–3
   stepsister [stĕp/ sĭs/ tər] **35**–29
stereo system [stĕr/ ē ö sĭs/ təm] **56**–8
sterile [stĕr/ əl]
   sterile pad [stĕr/ əl păd/] **117**–6
   sterile tape [stĕr/ əl tāp/] **117**–7
stethoscope [stĕth/ ə skōp/] **118**–10
stewing beef [stoo/ ĭng bēf/] **70**–3
stick [stĭk] **231**–11, **232**–11
   drumsticks [drŭm/ stĭks/] **70**–23
   lipstick [lĭp/ stĭk/] **109**–38
   stick shift [stĭk/ shĭft/] **159**–50
   yardstick [yärd/ stĭk/] **181**–16
sticker [stĭk/ ər] **102**–3, **136**–13
sticky notes [stĭk/ ē nōts/] **183**–39
stir [stür] **77**–O
   stir-fried beef [stür/ frīd/ bēf/] **76**–6
stitches [stĭch/ əz] **117**–15
stock clerk [stäk/ klürk/] **169**–59
stockings [stäk/ ĭngz] **91**–17
stomach [stŭm/ ək] **107**–41
   stomachache [stŭm/ ək āk/] **110**–4
stop [stäp] **129**–16, **151**–13, **154**–1
   stopover [stäp/ ō/ vər] **161** ✦
stop [stäp] **155**–D
Stop [stäp] **152**
stopped up [stäpt/ ŭp/] **63**–19
storage [stör/ ĭj] **72**–25, **78**–4
   storage locker [stör/ ĭj läk/ ər] **50**–17
store [stör]
   bookstore [book/ stör/] **130**–4
   candy store [kăn/ dē stör/] **131**–17
   card store [kärd/ stör/] **130**–7
   convenience store [kən vēn/ yəns stör/] **128**–3
   department store [dĭ pärt/ mənt stör/] **131**–13
   electronics store [ē lĕk trän/ ĭks stör/] **131**–20
   furniture store [für/ nĭ chər stör/] **126**–8
   hardware store [härd/ wĕr/ stör/] **148**–4
   home improvement store
     [hōm/ ĭm proov/ mənt stör/] **127**–20
   jewelry store [joo/ əl rē stör/] **130**–2
   maternity store [mə tür/ nə tē stör/] **131**–19
   men's store [mĕnz/ stör/] **130** ✦
   music store [myoo/ zĭk stör/] **130**–1
   office supply store [ö/ fəs sə plī/ stör/] **127**–21
   pet store [pĕt/ stör/] **130**–6
   shoe store [shoo/ stör/] **130**–10
   toy store [toy/ stör/] **130**–5
   video store [vĭd/ ē ō stör/] **129**–20
Store [stör] **99**
STORE [stör] **72**–**73**

storeroom [stör/ room/] **185**–3
storm [störm] **13**–19
   hailstorm [hāl/ störm/] **13**–21
   snowstorm [snō/ störm/] **13**–23
   storm door [störm/ dör/] **53**–10
   thunderstorm [thŭn/ dər störm/] **13**–16
story [stör/ ē]
   action story [ăk/ shən stör/ ē] **237**–19
   adventure story [ăd vĕn/ chər stör/ ē] **237**–19
   horror story [hör/ ər stör/ ē, här/–] **237**–17
   science fiction story [sī/ əns fĭk/ shən stör/ ē] **237**–18
   two-story house [too/ stör/ ē hows/] **52** ✦
stove [stōv] **54**–18, **226**–16
stow [stō] **160**–G
straight [strāt] **155**–A
   straight hair [strāt/ hĕr/] **33**–9
   straight line [strāt/ lïn/] **193**–22
   straight pin [strāt/ pĭn/] **100**–12
strainer [strā/ nər] **78**–22
straw [strö] **79**–18
   strawberries [strö/ bĕr/ ēz] **68**–14
   straw hat [strö/ hăt/] **90**–23
stream [strēm] **204** ✦
street [strēt] **150**–5, **155**–8
   streetlight [strēt/ līt/] **148**–3
   street sign [strēt/ sīn/] **129**–26
   street vender [strēt/ vĕn/ dər] **129**–29
STREETS [strēts] **126**–**127**
strep throat [strĕp/ thrōt/] **111**–4
stress [strĕs] **115**–4
stretch [strĕch] **230**–M
stretcher [strĕch/ ər] **121**–33
string [strĭng]
   string beans [strĭng/ bēnz/] **69**–8
   string lights [strĭng/ līts/] **239**–18
   string of pearls [strĭng/ əv pürlz/] **95**–39
Strings [strĭngz] **238**
striped [strīpt] **96**–20
stripper [strĭ/ pər] **181**–42
stroller [strō/ lər] **37**–18
strong signal [ströng/ sĭg/ nəl] **14**–11
stub [stŭb] **165**–11
stucco [stŭk/ ō] **178**–15
student [stood/ nt] **6**–5
study [stŭ/ dē] **10**–D, **137**–A
STUDYING [stŭ/ dē ĭng] **8**–**9**
stuffed animals [stŭft/ ăn/ ə məlz] **59**–15
style [stīl/] **88** ✦
Styles [stīlz] **96**
STYLES [stīlz] **96**
stylist [stī/ lĭst] **167**–31
SUBJECTS [sŭb/ jĭkts/] **188**–**189**
submit [səb mĭt/] **48**–C
substitute [sŭb/ stə toot/] **79**–20
subtract [səb trăkt/] **192**–B
suburbs [sŭb/ ürbz] **52**–2
subway [sŭb/ wā/] **151**–12
   subway car [sŭb/ wā/ kär/] **152**–6
   subway station [sŭb/ wā/ stā/ shən] **151**–11
Subway Station [sŭb/ wā/ stā/ shən] **152**
Succeed [sək sēd/] **10**
SUCCEEDING IN SCHOOL [sək sē/ dĭng ən skool/] **10**

suede [swād] **99**–8

sugar [shŏŏg/ər] **73**–30

    sugar bowl [shŏŏg/ər bōl/] **55**–14

    sugar-free [shŏŏg/ər frē/] **122**–7

    sugar substitute [shŏŏg/ər sŭb/stə tōōt/] **79**–20

suit [sōōt] **87**–11

    bathing suit [bā/dhǐng sōōt/] **90**–26

    business suit [bǐz/nəs sōōt/] **88**–11

    jumpsuit [jŭmp/sōōt/] **93**–24

    three piece suit [thrē/pēs/ sōōt/] **88** ✦

    wet suit [wĕt/ sōōt/] **225**–4

suite [swēt] **184**–16

sum [sŭm] **192**–7

sumac [sōō/măk] **210**–23

summer [sŭm/ər] **21**–38

sun [sŭn] **209**–8

    sunblock [sŭn/blăk/] **108**–8, **225**–0

    sunburn [sŭn/bürn/] **110**–14

    sunflower [sŭn/flow/ər] **211**–10

    sunglasses [sŭn/glăs/əz] **90**–27

    sunrise [sŭn/ rīz] **18**–14

    sunscreen [sŭn/skrēn/] **108**–7, **225**–10

    sunset [sŭn/ sĕt] **18**–19

Sunday [sŭn/dā, –dē] **20**–8

sunny [sŭn/ē] **13**–9, **76**–10

superintendent [sōō/prǐn tĕn/dənt, sōō/pər ǐn–] **50**–8

supermarket [sōō/pər/ mär/kət] **127**–18

supervise [sōō/pər vīz/] **170**–O

supervisor [sōō/pər vī/zər] **165**–8, **175**–4

Supplies [sə plīz/] **100, 183**

SUPPLIES [sə plīz/] **61, 180**–**181**

supply [sə plī/] **127**–21

    supply cabinet [sə plī/ kăb/ə nət] **182**–1

support [sə pört/] **179**–18

    support group [sə pört/ grōōp/] **115**–15

supporter [sə pör/tər] **91**–6

Supreme Court [sə prēm/ kört/] **138**–11

surfboard [sürf/börd/] **225**–16

surfer [sür/fər] **225**–15

surfing [sür/fǐng] **227**–9, **227**–10, **227** ✦

surgeon [sür/jən] **121**–36

Surgeon [sür/jən] **93**

surge protector [sürj/ prə tĕk/tər] **196**–1

surgical [sür/jǐ kəl]

    surgical cap [sür/jǐ kəl kăp/] **121**–37

    surgical gloves [sür/jǐ kəl glŭvz/] **121**–39

    surgical gown [sür/jǐ kəl gown/] **93**–37, **121**–38

    surgical mask [sür/jǐ kəl măsk/] **93**–36

    surgical nurse [sür/jǐ kəl nürs/] **120**–9

    surgical scrub cap [sür/jǐ kəl skrŭb/ kăp/] **93**–35

    surgical scrubs [sür/jǐ kəl skrŭbz/] **93**–38

Surgical Assistant [sür/jǐ kəl ə sǐs/tənt] **93**

surprised [sər prīzd/, sə–] **43**–30

suspenders [sə spĕn/dərz] **94**–1

suspense [sŭs/pĕns] **237**–20

SUV (sport-utility vehicle) [ĕs/yōō/vē/] / [spört/ yōō tǐl/ə tē vē/ǐ kəl] **156**–7

swallow [swäl/ō] **116**–J

swap meet [swäp/ mēt/] **222**–6

sweat [swĕt]

    sweatpants [swĕt/ pănts/] **89**–23

    sweatshirt [swĕt/ shürt/] **89**–22

sweater [swĕt/ər] **28**–2, **87**–14

    cardigan sweater [kär/də gən swĕt/ər] **88**–2

    pullover sweater [pōōl/ō/vər swĕt/ər] **88**–3

sweep [swēp] **60**–J

sweet potatoes [swĕt pə tā/tōz] **69**–18

sweets [swēts] **84**–9

swim [swǐm] **230**–L

    swimsuit [swǐm/sōōt/] **90**–26

swimming [swǐm/ǐng]

    swimming pool [swǐm/ǐng pōōl/] **51**–22

    swimming trunks [swǐm/ǐng trŭngks/] **90**–22

swing [swǐng] **230**–Q

swings [swǐngz] **224**–11

Swiss cheese [swǐs/ chēz/] **71**–27

switch [swǐch] **58**–27

swollen finger [swō/lən fǐng/gər] **110**–16

swordfish [sörd/fǐsh/] **71**–5, **212**–10

symbol [sǐm/bəl] **155**–8

SYMPTOMS AND INJURIES

    [sǐmp/təmz ən ǐn/jə rēz] **110**

synagogue [sǐn/ə gäg/] **127**–16

synthetic materials [sǐn thĕ/tǐk mə tïr/ē əlz] **98** ✦

syringe [sə rǐnj/] **118**–12

syrup [sǐr/əp, sür/–] **113**–29

system [sǐs/təm]

    fuel injection system [fyōō/əl ǐn jĕk/shən sǐs/təm] **158**–17

    stereo system [stĕr/ē ō sǐs/təm] **56**–8

SYSTEM [sǐs/təm] **141**

tab [tăb] **197**–7

table [tā/bəl]

    bed table [bĕd/ tā/bəl] **121**–21

    changing table [chān/jǐng tā/bəl] **59**–1

    coffee table [kö/fē tā/bəl] **56**–19

    dining room table [dī/nǐng rōōm/ tā/bəl] **55**–9

    end table [ĕnd/ tā/bəl] **56**–14

    examination table [ǐg zăm/ə nā/shən tā/bəl] **118**–7

    folding card table [fōl/dǐng kärd/ tā/bəl] **102**–4

    night table [nīt/ tā/bəl] **58**–23

    operating table [äp/ə rā/tǐng tā/bəl] **121**–40

    periodic table [pǐr/ē äd/ǐk tā/bəl] **195**–26

    picnic table [pǐk/nǐk tā/bəl] **224**–8

    pool table [pōōl/ tā/bəl] **50**–15

    tablecloth [tā/bəl klöth/] **55**–12

    tablespoon [tā/bəl spōōn/] **75**–7

    table tennis [tā/bəl tĕn/əs] **228**–14

    tray table [trā/ tā/bəl] **161**–21

    turntable [türn/tā/bəl] **234**–12

tablet [tăb/lət] **113**–22, **113**–27

tackle [tăk/əl] **230**–F

taco [tä/kō] **79**–8

tags [tăgz] **92**–15, **136**–13

tail [tāl] **216**–22

tail light [tāl/ līt/] **158**–13

tail pipe [tāl/ pīp/] **158**–15

tailor [tā/lər] **100**–3

take [tāk]

    do not take with dairy products [dōō nät/ tāk/ wǐth dër/ē präd/ŭkts] **112**–A

    take a bath [tāk/ ə băth/] **108**–B

    take a break [tāk/ ə brāk/] **11**–H

    take a citizenship test [tāk/ ə sǐt/ə zən shǐp tĕst/] **140**–I

take a driver education course [tāk/ ə drī/vərz ĕj/ə kā/shən körs/] **137**–B

take a driver's training course [tāk/ ə drī/vərz trā/nǐng körs/] **137**–G

take a message [tāk/ ə mĕs/ǐj] **171**–Q

take a nap [tāk/ ə năp/] **53**–A

take a picture [tāk/ ə pǐk/chər] **206**–B

take a seat [tāk/ ə sēt/] **6**–F

take a shower [tāk/ ə show/ər] **38**–C, **108**–A

take a tour [tāk/ ə tōōr/] **220**–A

take a written test [tāk/ ə rǐt/ən tĕst] **137**–E

take care of children [tāk/ kër/ əv chǐl/drən] **170**–P

take cover [tāk/ kŭv/ər] **147**–J

take dictation [tāk/ dǐk/tā shən] **171**–K

take in [tāk/ ǐn] **100**–D

take medicine [tāk/ mĕd/ə sən] **114**–D

take notes [tāk/ nōts/] **10**–C

take off [tāk/ öf/] **109**–Q, **160**–J

take one hour before eating [tāk/ wŭn/ ow/ər bǐ för/ ē/tǐng] **112**–B

take out [tāk/ owt/] **9**–Y, **60**–Q, **82** ✦

take ownership [tāk/ ō/nər shǐp/] **49**–K

take temperature [tāk/ tĕm/prə chər] **118**–B

take the bus to school [tāk/ dhə bŭs/ tə skōōl/] **38**–H

take the car to a mechanic [tāk/ dhə kär/ tə dhə mə kăn/ǐk] **157**–C

take the children to school [tāk/ dhə chǐl/drən tə skōōl/] **38**–G

take the order [tāk/ dhē ör/dər] **82**–E

take with food [tāk/ wǐth fōōd/] **112**–A

take x-rays [tāk/ ĕks/rāz/] **119**–B

Taking a Flight [tā/kǐng ə flīt/] **160**

Taking a Test [tā/kǐng ə tĕst/] **10**

TAKING A TRIP [tā/kǐng ə trǐp/] **162**–**163**

Taking Care of Your Car [tā/kǐng kër/ əv yər kär/] **157**

TAKING CARE OF YOUR HEALTH [tā/kǐng kër əv yər hĕlth/] **114**–**115**

talk [tök]

    talk show [tök/ shō/] **236**–4

    talk therapy [tök/ thër/ ə pē] **115**–13

talk [tök]

    talk about [tök ə bowt/] **174**–L

    talk on the phone [tök/ ön dhə fōn/] **15**–C

    talk to friends [tök/ tə frĕndz/] **173**–A

    talk to the teacher [tök/ tə dhə tē/chər] **6**–B

tall [töl] **32**–4

tambourine [tăm/bə rēn/] **238**–17

tan [tăn] **24**–18

tangerines [tăn/jə rēnz/] **68**–9

tank [tăngk] **158**–10, **225**–5

    tank top [tăngk/ täp/] **89**–24

    tank truck [tăngk/ trŭk/] **156**–20

tape [tāp]

    clear tape [klër/ tāp/] **183**–30

    correction tape [kə rĕk/shən tāp/] **183**–37

    duct tape [dŭkt/ tāp/] **181**–49

    electrical tape [ǐ lek/trǐ kəl tāp/] **181**–43

    masking tape [măs/kǐng tāp/] **181**–53

    packing tape [păk/ǐng tāp/] **183**–32

    sterile tape [stĕr/ əl tāp/] **117**–7

    tape measure [tāp mĕzh/ər] **100**–17, **181**–45

target [tär/gət] **231**–7
taste [tāst] **106**–D
tattoo [tă tōō/] **32**–18
tax / taxes [tăks] / [tăks/əz] **27**–8
taxi [tăk/sē] **150**–3
    hail a taxi [hāl/ ə tăk/sē] **152** ✦
    taxi driver [tăk/sē drī/vər] **152**–21
    taxi license [tăk/sē lī/səns] **152**–22
    taxi stand [tăk/sē stănd/] **152**–18
TB (tuberculosis) [tē/bē/] / [tōō bûr/kyə lō/səs] **111**–15
TDD [tē/dē/dē/] **15**–26
tea [tē] **79**–12, **81**–39, **81**–40
    teacup [tē/kŭp] **55**–6
    tea kettle [tē/ kĕt/l] **54**–21
    teapot [tē/pät/] **55**–16
    teaspoon [tē/spōōn/] **75**–6, **83**–31
teach [tēch] **170**–Q
teacher [tē/chər] **5**–8, **6**–4, **22**–5
    teacher's aide [tē/chərz ād/] **5**–16
team [tēm] **145**–20, **229**–3
TEAM SPORTS [tēm/ spörts/] **229**
technical school [tĕk/nĭ kəl skōōl/] **188**–5
technician [tĕk nĭsh/ən]
    computer technician
        [kəm pyōō/tər tĕk nĭsh/ən] **167**–19, **182**–12
    emergency medical technician (EMT)
        [ĭ mûr/jən sē mĕd/ĭ kəl tĕk nĭsh/ən] / [ē/ĕm/tē/]
            121–32
    medical records technician
        [mĕd/ĭ kəl rĕk/ərdz tĕk nĭsh/ən] **168**–39
Technician [tĕk nĭsh/ən] **93**
teddy bear [tĕd/ē bër/] **37**–23
teen / teenager [tēn] / [tē/nā/jər] **31**–11
teething ring [tē/dhĭng rĭng/] **37**–25
teeth / tooth [tēth] / [tōōth] **106**–7
    toothache [tōōth/āk/] **110**–2
    toothbrush [tōōth/brŭsh/] **57**–21, **109**–22
    toothbrush holder [tōōth/brŭsh/ hōl/dər] **57**–22
    toothpaste [tōōth/pāst/] **109**–23
telemarketer [tĕl/ə mär/kə tər] **169**–60
TELEPHONE [tĕl/ə fōn/] **14**–15
Telephone Skills [tĕl/ə fōn/ skĭlz/] **171**
telescope [tĕl/ə skōp/] **205**–23
television / TV [tĕl/ə vĭzh/ən] / [tē/vē/] **56**–6
    big-screen TV [bĭg/skrēn/ tē/vē/] **50**–14
    flat panel TV [flăt/ păn/əl tē/vē/] **234**–7
    flat screen TV [flăt/ skrēn/ tē/vē/] **234**–7
    portable TV [pör/tə bəl tē/vē/] **234**–8
teller [tĕl/ər] **132**–1
Teller [tĕl/ər] **132**
Telling Time [tĕ/lĭng tīm/] **18**
temperature [tĕm/prə chər] **110**–8
    temperature gauge [tĕm/prə chər gāj/] **159**–30
Temperature [tĕm/prə chər] **13**
ten [tĕn] **16**
    ten after one [tĕn/ ăf/tər wŭn/] **18**–8
    ten dollars [tĕn/ däl/ərz] **26**–9
    10 percent [tĕn/ pər sĕnt/] **17**–12
    ten thousand [tĕn/ thow/zənd] **16**
    10-year-old girl [tĕn/yïr ōld/ gûrl/] **31**–10
tenant [tĕn/ənt] **50**–6
TENANT MEETING [tĕn/ənt mē/tĭng] **64**–65

tennis [tĕn/əs] **228**–15
    table tennis [tā/bəl tĕn/əs] **228**–14
    tennis court [tĕn/əs kört/] **224**–6
    tennis racket [tĕn/əs răk/ət] **231**–2
    tennis shoes [tĕn/əs shōōz/] **95**–32
tent [tĕnt] **226**–10
tenth [tĕnth] **16**
Terminal [tûr/mə nəl] **160**
termites [tûr/mīts] **63**–22
term [tûrm] **139** ✦
Terms [tûrmz] **199**
terrified [tĕr/ə fīd/] **43** ✦
test [tĕst] **121**–30
    test booklet [tĕst/ bŏŏk/lət] **10**–1
    testing area [tĕs/tĭng ër/ē ə] **136**–2
    test tube [tĕst/ tōōb/] **195**–42
Test [tĕst] **10**
text [tĕkst]
    textbook [tĕkst/bŏŏk/, tĕks/-] **7**–25
    text box [tĕkst/ bäks/, tĕks/-] **197**–13
    text message [tĕkst/ mĕs/ĭj, tĕks/-] **14**–19
thank [thăngk] **12**–E, **174**–N
Thanksgiving [thăngks gĭv/ĭng] **22**–17
theater [thē/ə tər] **126**–6, **127**–23
theft [thĕft] **142**–9
therapist [thĕr/ ə pĭst] **115**–12, **115**–14, **168**–45
therapy [thĕr/ ə pē] **115**–11, **115**–13
thermal undershirt [thûr/məl ŭn/dər shûrt/] **91**–2
thermometer [thər mäm/ə tər] **118**–11
thick [thĭk] **23**–7
thighs [thīz] **70**–22, **106**–19
thimble [thĭm/bəl] **100**–15
thin [thĭn] **23**–8, **32**–9
THINGS [thĭngz] **23**
think [thĭnk] **191**–E
third [thûrd] **16**
Third Floor [thûrd/ flör/] **50**
thirsty [thûr/stē] **42**–2
thirteen [thûr/tēn/] **16**
    thirteen colonies [thûr/tēn/ kä/lə nēz] **198**–1
thirteenth [thûr/tēnth/] **16**
thirtieth [thûr/tē əth] **16**
thirty [thûr/tē] **16**
    35 mm camera
        [thûr/tē fīv/ mĭl/ə mē/tər kăm/rə] **235**–21
this week [dhĭs/ wēk/] **20**–19
thorn [thörn] **211**–29
thread [thrĕd] **99**–23, **100**–11
three [thrē] **16**
    three piece suit [thrē/pēs/ sōōt/] **88** ✦
    3-ring binder [thrē/ rĭng/ bīn/dər] **7**–27
    3/4 sleeved [thrē/kwör/tər slēv/] **96**–13
    three times a week [thrē/ tīmz/ ə wēk/] **20**–24
throat [thrōt] **107**–35, **110**–6, **111**–4
    throat lozenges [thrōt/ läz/ən jəz] **113**–30
through [thrōō] **153**–K
throw [thrō] **230**–C
    throw away [thrō/ ə wā/] **11**–N
    throw up [thrō/ ŭp/] **110**–E
throw pillow [thrō/ pĭl/ō] **56**–2
thumb [thŭm] **106**–16
thunderstorm [thŭn/dər störm/] **13**–16

Thursday [thûrz/dā, –dē] **20**–12
tick [tĭk] **214**–27
ticket [tĭk/ət] **152**–15, **161**–19
    ticket agent [tĭk/ət ā/jənt] **160**–3
    ticket window [tĭk/ət wĭn/dō/] **152**–12
tidal wave [tīd/l wāv/] **145**–17
tide [tīd] **225** ✦
tie [tī] **88**–12, **89**–16, **92**–13, **229** ✦
tie [tī] **86**–A
tiger [tī/gər] **217**–37
tight [tīt] **97**–29
tights [tīts] **91**–19
tile [tīl] **57**–10, **178**–11, **178**–D
time [tīm]
    Alaska time [ə lăs/kə tīm/] **19**–28
    arrival time [ə rī/vəl tīm/] **161** ✦
    Atlantic time [ət lăn/tĭk tīm/] **19**–33
    Central time [sĕn/trəl tīm/] **19**–31
    daylight saving time [dā/līt/ sā/vĭng tīm/] **19**–25
    departure time [dĭ pär/chər tīm/] **161** ✦
    Eastern time [ē/stərn tīm/] **19**–32
    Hawaii-Aleutian time
        [hə wī/ē ə lōō/shən tīm/] **19**–27
    Mountain time [mown/tn tīm/] **19**–30
    Newfoundland time
        [nōō/fən lənd tīm/, –fənd–] **19**–34
    on time [än/ tīm/, ön/ tīm/] **19**–23, **161**–29
    Pacific time [pə sĭf/ĭk tīm/] **19**–29
    standard time [stăn/dərd tīm/] **19**–26
    three times a week [thrē tīmz/ ə wēk/] **20**–24
    time clock [tīm/ kläk/] **165**–7
Time [tīm] **18**
TIME [tīm] **18**–19
timer [tī/mər] **78**–18
Times of Day [tīmz/ əv dā/] **18**
Time Zones [tīm/ zōnz/] **19**
tire [tīr] **158**–5, **158**–23, **162**–F
tired [tīrd] **43**–32
title [tīt/l] **133**–14, **190**–5
toad [tōd] **212**–28
toast [tōst] **80**–4
toaster [tō/stər] **54**–6
    toaster oven [tō/stər ŭv/ən] **54**–15
today [tə dā/] **20**–5
toddler [täd/lər] **31**–8
toe [tō] **92**–6, **94**–23, **105**–10
    toenail [tō/nāl/] **106** ✦
Tofu [tō/fōō/] **77**
toggle bolt [täg/əl bōlt/] **180**–38
to-go box [tə gō/ bäks/] **82**–5
toilet [toy/lət] **57**–19
    toilet brush [toy/lət brŭsh/] **57**–18
    toilet paper [toy/lət pā/pər] **57**–17, **146**–13
token [tō/kən] **152**–10
tomatoes [tə mā/tōz] **69**–6
tomorrow [tə mär/ō, –mör/ō] **20**–6
tongs [tängz, töngz] **78**–23, **195**–44
tongue [tŭng] **106**–8
too [tōō]
    too big [tōō/ bĭg/] **97**–38
    too expensive [tōō/ ĭk spĕn/sĭv] **97**–44
    too small [tōō/ smöl/] **97**–37

Index

tool belt [tool/ bĕlt/] **92**–3
TOOLS AND BUILDING SUPPLIES
    [toolz/ ən bĭl/dĭng sə plīz/] **180**–**181**
tooth / teeth [tooth] / [tĕth] **106**-7
    toothache [tooth/āk/] **110**–2
    toothbrush [tooth/brŭsh/] **57**–21, **109**–22
    toothbrush holder [tooth/brŭsh/ hōl/dər] **57**–22
    toothpaste [tooth/pāst/] **109**–23
top [täp] **88**–7, **89**–24
torn [törn] **97**–41
tornado [tör nā/dō] **145**–15
torso [tör/sō/] **106** ✦
tortoise [tör/təs] **213**–42
total [tōt/l] **27**–9
totebag [tōt/ băg/] **94**–19
touch [tŭch] **106**-E
towel [tow/əl]
    bath towel [băth/ tow/əl] **57**–14
    dish towel [dĭsh/ tow/əl] **61**–22
    hand towel [hănd/ tow/əl] **57**–15
    paper towels [pā/pər tow/əlz] **54**–3
    towel rack [tow/əl răk/] **57**–13
towelettes [tow/əl ĕts] **146**–12
tower [tow/ər] **196**–3
town [town] **52**–3
    town car [town/ kär/] **152**–20
    townhouse [town/hows/] **52**–6
tow truck [tō/ trŭk/] **156**–14
toy [toy]
    toy chest [toy/ chĕst/] **59**–16
    toy store [toy/ stör/] **130**–5
Toys and Games [toyz/ ən gāmz/] **59**
track [trăk] **5**–21, **152**–14
    track and field [trăk/ ən fēld/] **228**–18
tractor [trăk/tər] **177**–9
    tractor trailer [trăk/tər trā/lər] **156**–15
traffic light [trăf/ĭk līt/] **128**–8
TRAFFIC SIGNS [trăf/ĭk sīnz/] **154**
tragedy [trăj/ə dē] **237**–14
trailer [trā/lər] **156**–15, **156**–17
training [trā/nĭng] **172**–2, **172**–5, **172**–7
    training pants [trā/nĭng pănts/] **37**–11
Training [trā/nĭng] **172**
Train Station [trān/ stā/shən] **152**
transcribe [trăn skrīb/] **171**-C
transfer [trăns für/, trăns/fər] **152**–5
transfer [trăns für/, trăns/fər] **171**-O
translate [trănz/lāt] **8**-C
translator [trănz/lā/tər, trăns/–] **168**–35
Transmission [trănz mĭsh/ən, trăns–] **159**
Transportation [trăns/pər tā/shən] **152**
TRANSPORTATION [trăns/pər tā/shən] **150**–**151**, **152**
trash [trăsh]
    trash bags [trăsh/ băgz/] **61**–24
    trash bin [trăsh/ bĭn/] **51**–23
    trash chute [trăsh/ shoot/] **51**–26
travel [trăv/əl] **41**-P
travel agency [trăv/əl ā/jən sē] **131**–14
tray [trā] **55**–17, **83**–10
    tray table [trā tā/bəl] **161**–21
Tree [trē] **210**

trees [trēz] **208**–1, **239**–16
TREES AND PLANTS [trēz/ ən plănts/] **210**
trench coat [trĕnch/ kōt/] **90**–21
trial [trī/əl] **140**–5
triangle [trī/ăng/gəl] **193**–32
tricycle [trī/sĭ kəl] **224**–12
trigonometry [trĭg/ə năm/ə trē] **192**–18
trim [trĭm] **176**-B
trip [trĭp] **152**–16, **152**–17
tripe [trīp] **70**–8
tripod [trī/päd] **235**–25
trombone [trăm bōn/] **238**–10
trout [trowt] **71**–1
trowel [trow/əl] **176**–10, **178**–13
truck [trŭk] **150**–5
    dump truck [dŭmp/trŭk/] **156**–19
    fire truck [fīr/ trŭk/] **144**–10
    garbage truck [gär/bĭj trŭk/] **127**–22
    hand truck [hănd/ trŭk/] **175**–11
    pickup truck [pĭk/ŭp trŭk/] **156**–12
    tank truck [tăngk/ trŭk/] **156**–20
    tow truck [tō/ trŭk/] **156**–14
    truck driver [trŭk/ drī/vər] **169**–61
TRUCKS [trŭks] **156**
trumpet [trŭm/pət] **238**–11
Trunk [trŭngk] **158**
trunks [trŭngks] **158**–11, **210**–4, **217**–47
    swimming trunks [swĭm/ĭng trŭngks/] **90**–22
try on [trī/ön] **95**-C
TSA agent [tē/ĕs/ā/ ā/jənt] **160**–5
T-shirt [tē/shürt/] **86**–4
tsunami [soo nä/ mē/, tsoo–] **145**–17
tub [tŭb]
    bathtub [băth/tŭb/] **57**–2
tuba [too/bə] **238**–12
tube [toob] **74**–12, **74**–24, **195**–42
tuberculosis (TB)
    [too bür/kyə lō/səs] / [tē/bē/] **111**–15
Tuesday [tooz/dā, –dē] **20**–10
tulip [too/ləp] **211**–11
tuna [too/nə] **71**–7, **72**–19, **212**–8
tuner [too/nər] **234**–13
turbulence [tür/byə ləns] **161**–22
turkey [tür/kē] **70**–17, **239**–14
    roasted turkey [rōs/təd tür/kē] **76**–4
    smoked turkey [smōkt/ tür/kē] **71**–25
turn [türn] **154**–5, **154**–7, **154**–8
    turn signal [türn/ sĭg/nəl] **158**–6, **159**–34
    turnstile [türn/stīl/] **152**–8
    turntable [türn/tā/bəl] **234**–12
turn [türn]
    turn in [türn/ ĭn/] **191**-M
    turn left [türn/ lĕft/] **155**-C
    turn off [türn/ öf/] **11**-P, **160**-I, **174**-G, **219**-G
    turn on [türn/ ön/, –än/] **11**-B
    turn right [türn/ rīt/] **155**-B
turnips [tür/nəps] **69**–16
turquoise [tür/koyz, –kwoyz] **24**–9
turtle [tür/tl] **213**–43
    turtleneck [tür/tl nĕk/] **96**–9
tusk [tŭsk] **217**–48
tuxedo [tŭk sē/dō] **89**–17

TV Programs [tē/vē/ prō/grămz] **236**
TV / television [tē/vē/] / [tĕl/ə vĭzh/ən] **56**–6
    big-screen TV [bĭg/skrēn/ tē/vē/] **50**–14
    flat panel TV [flăt/ păn/əl tē/vē/] **234**–7
    flat screen TV [flăt/ skrēn/ tē/ vē/] **234**–7
    portable TV [por/tə bəl tē/vē/] **234**–8
tweezers [twē/zərz] **117**–4
twelfth [twĕlfth] **16**
twelve [twĕlv] **16**
twentieth [twĕn/tē əth] **16**
twenty [twĕn/tē] **16**
    twenty after one [twĕn/tē ăf/tər wŭn/] **18**–10
    twenty dollars [twĕn/tē däl/ərz] **26**–10
    twenty-first [twĕn/tē fürst/] **16**
    twenty-five [twĕn/tē fīv/] **16**
    25 percent [twĕn/fīv/ pər sĕnt/] **17**–11
    twenty-four [twĕn/tē för/] **16**
    twenty-one [twĕn/tē wŭn/] **16**
    twenty-three [twĕn/tē thrē/] **16**
    twenty to two [twĕn/tē tə too/] **18**–12
    twenty-two [twĕn/tē too/] **16**
twice a week [twis/ ə wēk/] **20**–23
twig [twĭg] **210**–1
twins [twĭnz] **28**–1
two [too] **16**
    2-door car [too/dör kär/] **156**–2
    two-story house [too/stör/ē hows/] **52** ✦
    two-way radio [too/wā rā/dē ō] **179**–22
    2 x 4 (two by four) [too/ bī/ för/] **181**–19
type [tīp] **170**-R, **196**-A
    type a letter [tīp/ə lĕt/ər] **171**-A
    type the message [tīp/ dhə mĕs/ĭj] **197**-E
    type the subject [tīp/ dhə sŭb/jĭkt] **197**-D
    type your password [tīp/ yər păs/würd/] **197**-A
Types of Health Problems
    [tīps/ əv hĕlth/ präb/ləmz] **115**
Types of Job Training [tīps/ əv jäb/ trā/nĭng] **172**
Types of Material [tīps/ əv mə tïr/ē əl] **99**
Types of Math [tīps/ əv măth/] **192**
Types of Medication [tīps/ əv mĕd/ə kā/shən] **113**
Types of Movies [tīps/ əv moo/vēz] **237**
Types of Music [tīps/ əv myoo/zĭk] **237**
Types of TV Programs [tīps/ əv tē/vē/ prō/grămz] **236**
ugly [ŭg/lē] **23**–22
umbrella [ŭm brĕl/ə] **90**–17, **225**–14
umpire [ŭm/pīr] **229** ✦
uncle [ŭng/kəl] **34**–8
uncomfortable [ŭn kŭmf/tə bəl, –tər–] **42**–9
unconscious [ŭn/kän/shəs] **116**-A
under [ŭn/dər] **25**–10, **153**-A
    long underwear [löng/ ŭn/dər wër] **91**–3
    thermal undershirt [thür/məl ŭn/dər shürt] **91**–2
    underexposed [ŭn/dər ĭk spōzd/] **235**–35
    underpants [ŭn/dər pănts/] **91**–14
    undershirt [ŭn/dər shürt/] **91**–1
underline [ŭn/dər līn/] **9**-S
Under the Hood [ŭn/dər dhə hood/] **158**
Underwear [ŭn/dər wër/] **91**
UNDERWEAR AND SLEEPWEAR
    [ŭn/dər wër/ ən slēp/wër/] **91**
undress [ən drĕs/] **36**-E

unfurnished apartment
[ŭn/fŭr nĭsht ə pärt/ mənt] **48**–4
uniform [yōō/nə förm/] **88**–10, **231**–16
Unisex Socks [yōō/nə sĕks/ säks/] **91**
Unisex Underwear [yōō/nə sĕks/ ŭn/dər wër] **91**
universal remote [yōō/nə vür/səl rĭ mōt/] **234**–9
UNIVERSE [yōō/nə vürs/] **205**
university [yōō/nə vür/sə tē] **188**–7
unload [ŭn lōd/] **101**–E
unpack [ŭn păk/] **49**–N
unraveling [ŭn răv/əl ĭng] **97**–43
unripe [ŭn rip/] **68**–31
unscented [ŭn sĕn/təd] **108** ✦
unscramble [ŭn skrăm/bəl] **9**–W
up [ŭp]
    buckle up [bŭk/əl ŭp/] **36**–L
    clean up [klēn/ ŭp/] **147**–M
    cut up [kŭt/ ŭp/] **77**–I
    eggs sunny-side up [ĕgz/ sŭn/ē sid/ ŭp/] **76**–10
    get up [gĕt/ ŭp/] **38**–B
    hang up [hăng/ ŭp/] **15**–D, **101**–H
    look up [lōōk/ ŭp/] **8**–A
    pick up [pĭk/ ŭp/] **6**–I, **11**–E, **38**–M
    pop-up ad [päp/ ŭp ăd/] **197**–9
    set up [sĕt/ ŭp/] **173**–I
    stand up [stănd/ ŭp/] **6**–D
    stopped up [stäpt/ ŭp/] **63**–19
    throw up [thrō/ ŭp/] **110**–E
    wake up [wāk/ ŭp/] **38**–A
    walk up [wôk/ ŭp/] **153**–C
upright seat [ŭp/rit/ sēt/] **161**–28
upset [ŭp sĕt/] **43**–28
upstairs [ŭp/stërz/] **51** ✦
Uranus [yōōr/ə nəs, yōō rā/nəs] **205**–7
urban area [ür/bən ër/ē ə] **52**–1
urchin [ür/chən] **212**–21
URL [yōō/är/ĕl/] **197**–4
U.S. [yōō/ĕs/]
    U.S. Capitol [yōō/ĕs/ kă/pət əl] **138**–1
    U.S. route [yōō/ĕs/ rōōt/, –rowt/] **154**–17
USB port [yōō/ĕs/ bē/ pört/] **196**–7
use [yōōz]
    use a cash register [yōōz/ə kăsh/ rĕj/ə stər] **170**–S
    use a credit card [yōōz/ə krĕ/dət kärd/] **27**–B
    use a debit card [yōōz/ə dĕ/bət kärd/] **27**–C
    use a gift card [yōōz/ ə gĭft/ kärd/] **27**–E
    use deodorant [yōōz/ə dē ō/dər ənt] **108**–C
    use energy-efficient bulbs
        [yōōz/ ĕn/ər jē ĭ fĭ/shənt bŭlbz] **219**–H
    use punctuation [yōōz/ pŭngk/chōō ā/shən] **190**–C
Used Car [yōōzd/ kär/] **157**
used clothing [yōōzd/ klō/dhĭng] **102**–2
U.S. HISTORY [yōō/ĕs/ hĭs/tə rē] **198**
U.S. NATIONAL PARKS
    [yōō/ĕs nä/shə nəl pärks/] **220**–**221**
utensils [yōō tĕn/səlz] **79**–19
utility / utilities [yōō tĭl/ə tē] / [yōō tĭl/ə tēz]
    48–5, **156**–7
U-turn [yōō/türn/] **154**–5
vacancy sign [vā/kən sē sin/] **50**–7
vacation [vā kā/shən] **22**–6
vaccination [văk/sə nä/shən] **114** ✦

vacuum [văk/yōōm]
    vacuum cleaner [văk/yōōm klē/nər] **61**–10
    vacuum cleaner attachments
        [văk/yōōm klē/nər ə tăch/mənts] **61**–11
    vacuum cleaner bag
        [văk/yōōm klē/nər băg/] **61**–12
vacuum [văk/yōōm] **60**–H
valley [văl/ē] **204**–17
valuables [văl/yə bəlz, –yə wə–] **132**–8
valve [vălv] **146**–4
van [văn] **156**–13, **156**–18
vandalism [văn/də lĭz/əm] **142**–1
vanity plate [vă/nə tē plāt/] **136** ✦
variable [vër/ē ə bəl] **192**–12
vase [vās, vāz, väz] **55**–23
vault [völt] **132**–6
VCR [vē/sē/är/] **102**–7
veal cutlets [vēl/ kŭt/ləts] **70**–6
Vegetable [vĕj/tə bəl] **77**
vegetables [vĕj/tə bəlz] **66**–8, **72**–27, **81**–32
    vegetable garden [vĕj/tə bəl gär/dn] **53**–27, **177**–14
    vegetable peeler [vĕj/tə bəl pē/lər] **78**–15
VEGETABLES [vĕj/tə bəlz] **69**
vegetarian [vĕj/ə tër/ē ən] **70** ✦
vehicles [vē/ĭ kəlz] **124**–4, **156**–7, **156**–10
vein [văn] **107**–37
velvet [vĕl/vət] **99**–10
vending machine [vĕn/dĭng mə shēn/] **152**–9
vendors [vĕn/dərz] **84**–7, **129**–29
ventilation mask [vĕnt/əl ā/shən măsk/] **92**–7
Venus [vē/nəs] **205**–2
verdict [vür/dĭkt] **141**–14
vertebrates [vür/ tə brəts] **194**–13
vest [vĕst] **89**–15
    down vest [down/ vĕst/] **90**–14
    Hi-Visibility safety vest
        [hi/vĭz/ə bĭl/ə tē sāf/tē vĕst/] **92**–6
    life vest [lif/ vĕst/] **161**–25, **226**–14
Veterans Day [vĕt/ər ənz dā/] **22**–16
veterinarian [vĕt/ər ə nër/ē ən] **169**–62
vice president [vis/ prĕz/ə dənt] **138**–9
victim [vĭk/təm] **142**–10
video [vĭd/ē ō]
    videocassette [vĭd/ē ō kə sĕt/] **133**–18
    video game console [vĭd/ē ō gām/ kän/sōl/] **232**–3
    video game control [vĭd/ē ō gām/ kän trōl/] **232**–4
    video player [vĭd/ē ō plā ər] **197**–11
    video store [vĭd/ē ō stör/] **129**–20
videotape [vĭd/ē ō tāp/] **240**–A
view [vyōō]
    rearview mirror [rĭr/vyōō/ mĭr/ər] **159**–35
    sideview mirror [sid/vyōō/ mĭr/ər] **158**–3
village [vĭ/lĭj] **52**–3
vine [vin] **210**–22
vineyard [vĭn/yərd] **177**–16
violence [vi/ləns, vi/ə–] **142**–4
violet [vi/ə lət, vi/lət] **24**–8, **211**–23
violin [vi/ə lĭn/] **238**–6
virus [vi/rəs] **111**–17
vise [vis] **180**–26
vision [vi/zhən]
    vision exam [vĭ/zhən ĭg zăm/] **136**–6
    vision problems [vĭ/zhən präb/ləmz] **115**–1

Visit [vĭ/zət] **119**
visor [vi zər] **179**–12
vital signs monitor [vit/l sinz/ män/ə tər] **121**–26
vitamins [vi/tə mənz] **113**–17
v-neck [vē/nĕk/] **96**–8
vocational [vō kā/shə nəl]
    vocational school [vō kā/shə nəl skōōl/] **188**–5
    vocational training [vō kā/shə nəl trā/nĭng] **172**–5
voice message [voys mĕs/ĭj] **14**–18
volcanic eruption [väl kăn/ĭk ĭ rŭp/shən] **145**–16
volleyball [väl/ē böl/] **229**–14, **231**–3
Volume [väl/yəm, –yōōm] **75, 193**
volunteer [väl/ən tĭr/] **121**–17
volunteer [väl/ən tĭr/] **41**–Q
vomit [väm/ət] **110**–E
vote [vōt] **140**–A
waffles [wä/fəlz, wö/–] **80**–8
wages [wā/jĭz] **165**–12
wagon [wă/gən] **156**–6
waist [wāst]
    waist apron [wāst/ ā/prən] **93**–30
    waistband [wāst/bănd/] **100**–5
wait [wāt] **94**–B, **128**–B, **170**–T
waiter [wā/tər] **82**–8
    headwaiter [hĕd/wā/tər] **185**–12
waiting area [wā/tĭng ër/ē ə] **182**–16
Waiting Room [wā/tĭng rōōm/] **118**
waitress [wā/trəs] **83**–9
wait staff [wāt/ stăf/] **185** ✦
wake up [wāk/ ŭp/] **38**–A
walk [wôk] **53**–2
    crosswalk [krös/wôk/] **128**–15
    walk-in freezer [wôk/ĭn frē/zər] **185**–3
walk [wôk]
    walk a dog [wôk ə dög/] **129**–F
    walk down [wôk/ down/] **153**–D
    walk to class [wôk/ tə klăs/] **11**–C
    walk up [wôk/ ŭp/] **153**–C
    walk with a friend [wôk/ wĭth ə frĕnd/] **143**–A
walker [wö/kər] **113**–11
wall [wöl] **56**–10, **194**–5
    drywall [dri/wöl/] **178**–19
    wallpaper [wöl/pā/pər] **59**–8
wallet [wä/lət, wö/–] **94**–13
walrus [wöl/rəs] **213**–32
war [wör] **199**–10
    Revolutionary War [rē/və lōō/shə nër/ē wör/] **198**–8
warehouse [wër/hows/] **175**–7
warm [wörm] **13**–4
    warm clothes [wörm/ klōz/] **146**–6
warning label [wör/nĭng lā/bəl] **112**–8
Warnings [wör/nĭngz] **112**
wash [wäsh, wösh]
    mouthwash [mowth/wäsh/, –wösh/–] **109**–25
    washcloth [wäsh/klöth/, wösh/–] **57**–4
wash [wäsh, wösh]
    wash clothes [wäsh/ klöz/, wösh/–] **219**–K
    wash hair [wäsh/ här/, wösh/–] **108**–E
    wash the dishes [wäsh/ dhə dĭsh/əz, wösh/–] **60**–M
    wash the windows
        [wäsh/ dhə wĭn/dōz, wösh/–] **60**–I
washer [wä/shər, wö/–] **50**–12, **101**–3, **180**–37
    dishwasher [dĭsh/wäsh/ər, –wö/–] **54**–8, **185**–2

Index

washing [wä′shĭng, wö′–] **61**–21
wasp [wäsp, wösp] **214**–17
waste [wāst] **121**–31, **218**–12
    wastebasket [wāst′băs′kət] **57**–26
watch [wäch, wöch] **94**–16
watch [wäch, wöch] **39**–X, **147**–C
water [wö′tər] **209**–3, **225**–1
    body of water [bäd′ē əv wö′tər] **204** ✦
    bottled water [bät′ld wö′tər] **146**–11
    cold water [kōld′ wö′tər] **57**–7
    hot water [hät′ wö′tər] **57**–8
    hot water bottle [hät′ wö′tər böt′l] **113**–15
    watercolor [wö′tər kŭl′ər] **233**–21
    waterfall [wä′tər föl′] **204**–2
    water fountain [wö′tər fown′tn] **224**–9
    water glass [wö′tər glăs′] **83**–22
    watermelons [wö′tər mĕl′ənz] **68**–18
    water pollution [wö′tər pə lōō′shən] **218**–14
    water polo [wö′tər pō′lō] **229**–15
    waterskiing [wö′tər skē′ĭng] **227**–7
water [wö′tər] **176**–F
WATER SPORTS [wö′tər spörts′] **227**
wave [wāv] **145**–17, **225**–17
wave [wāv] **2**–F
wavy hair [wā′vē hër′] **33**–10
way [wā]
    hallway [häl′wā′] **184**–18
    one way [wŭn′ wā′] **154**–3
    one-way trip [wŭn′wā′ trĭp′] **152**–16
    two-way radio [tōō′wā′ rā′dē ō] **179**–22
    wrong way [röng′ wā′] **154**–2
Ways to Conserve Energy and Resources
    [wāz′ tə kən sürv′ ĕn′ər jē n rē′sör′səz,
    –rĭ sör′səz] **219**
Ways to Get Well [wāz′ tə gĕt′ wĕl′] **114**
Ways to Pay [wāz′ tə pā′] **27**
Ways to Serve Eggs [wāz′ tə sürv′ ĕgz′] **76**
Ways to Serve Meat and Poultry
    [wāz′ tə sürv′ mēt′ n pōl′trē′] **76**
Ways to Stay Well [wāz′ tə stā′ wĕl′] **114**
Ways to Succeed [wāz′tə sək sēd′] **10**
weak signal [wēk′ sĭg′nəl] **14**–12
WEATHER [wĕdh′ər] **13**
Weather Conditions [wĕdh′ər kən dĭsh′ənz] **13**
Weather Map [wĕdh′ər măp′] **13**
webcam [wĕb′kăm′] **196**–12
Webpage [wĕb′pāg′] **197**
website address [wĕb′sīt ə drĕs′] **197**–4
wedding [wĕ′dĭng] **22**–2
Wednesday [wĕnz′dā, –dē] **20**–11
weed [wēd]
    seaweed [sē′ wēd′] **225** ✦
    weed eater [wēd′ ē′tər] **176**–12
    weed whacker [wēd′ wăk′ər] **176**–12
weed [wēd] **176**–G
week [wēk] **20**–15
    last week [lăst′ wēk′] **20**–18
    next week [nĕkst′ wēk′] **20**–20
    once a week [wŭns′ ə wēk′] **20**–22
    this week [dhĭs′ wēk′] **20**–19
    three times a week [thrē′ tīmz′ ə wēk′] **20**–24
    twice a week [twīs′ ə wēk′] **20**–23

weekdays [wēk′dāz′] **20**–16
    weekend [wēk′ĕnd′] **20**–17
Week [wēk] **20**
weigh [wā] **75**–B
weight [wāt] **32**–8
Weight [wāt] **32, 75**
weightlifting [wāt′lĭf′tĭng] **228**–16
weights [wāts] **231**–22
WEIGHTS AND MEASUREMENTS
    [wāts′ ən mĕzh′ər mənts] **75**
welder [wĕl′dər] **169**–63
well [wĕl] **42**–14
Well [wĕl] **114**
west [wĕst] **155**–2
western [wĕs′tərn] **237**–15
wet [wĕt] **101**–17
    wet suit [wĕt′ sōōt′] **225**–4
whacker [wăk′ər] **176**–12
whale [wāl] **213**–29
wheat [wēt] **177**–2
wheat bread [wēt′ brĕd′] **71**–19
wheel [wēl] **159**–26
    wheelbarrow [wēl′băr′ō] **176**–3
    wheelchair [wēl′chër′] **113**–9
    wheel cover [wēl′ kŭv′ər] **158**–9
whisk [wĭsk] **78**–21
whiskers [wĭs′kərz] **216**–18
white [wīt] **24**–14
    whiteboard [wīt′börd′] **6**–3
    white bread [wīt′ brĕd′] **71**–18
    White House [wīt′ hows′] **138**–7
whole salmon [hōl′ săm′ən] **71**–3
wide [wīd] **97**–36
widow [wĭd′ō] **41** ✦
widower [wĭd′ō ər] **41** ✦
width [wĭdth, wĭtth] **17**–19
wife [wīf] **34**–12
    ex-wife [ĕks′ wīf′] **35** ✦
    former wife [för′mər wīf′] **35** ✦
wild [wīld] **215** ✦
wildlife [wīld′līf′] **220**–3
willow [wĭl′ō] **210**–13
win [wĭn] **229** ✦
wind [wĭnd]
    windbreaker [wĭnd′brā′kər] **90**–24
    wind power [wĭnd′ pow′ər] **218**–2
    windshield [wĭnd′ shēld′] **158**–1
    windshield wipers [wĭnd′shēld′wī′pərz] **158**–2
    windsurfing [wĭnd′sür′fĭng] **227**–10, **227** ✦
window [wĭn′dō] **47**–11, **56**–17, **136**–7
    drive-thru window [drīv′thrōō′ wĭn′dō] **128**–11
    ticket window [tĭk′ət wĭn′dō] **152**–12
    window pane [wĭn′dō păn′] **178**–16
windy [wĭn′dē] **13**–18
wine glass [wīn′ glăs′] **83**–23
wing [wĭng] **70**–20, **214**–1
winter [wĭn′tər] **21**–40
    winter scarf [wĭn′tər skärf′] **90**–5
WINTER AND WATER SPORTS
    [wĭn′tər ən wö′tər spörts′] **227**
wipe [wīp] **60**–O
wipers [wī′pərz] **158**–2

wipes [wīps] **37**–15, **61**–23
wire [wīr] **181**–13
    wire stripper [wīr′ strĭp′ər] **181**–42
wireless headset [wīr′ləs hĕd′sĕt] **14**–14
wiring [wīr′ĭng] **186**–7
withdraw [wĭdh drö′, wĭth–] **132**–F
witness [wĭt′nəs] **141**–11
wolf [wŏōlf] **216**–5
woman [wŏŏm′ən] **30**–2
women [wĭ′mən] **30**–3
Women's Socks [wĭ′mənz säks′] **91**
Women's Underwear [wĭ′mənz ŭn′dər wër′] **91**
wood [wŏōd] **178**–18
    plywood [plī′wŏōd] **178**–17
    redwood [rĕd′wŏōd] **210**–18
    wood floor [wŏōd′ flör′] **58**–21
    woodpecker [wŏōd′pĕk′ər] **214**–8
    wood screw [wŏōd′ skrōō′] **180**–33
    wood stain [wŏōd′ stān′] **181**–24
    woodworking kit [wŏōd′wür′kĭng kĭt′] **232**–14
wooden spoon [wŏōd′n spōōn′] **78**–9
Woodwinds [wŏōd′wĭndz′] **238**
wool [wŏōl] **61**–5, **98**–3
word [würd] **190**–1
word problem [würd′ prä′bləm] **192**–11
Words [wördz] **8**
work [würk] **121**–30, **154**–16
    workbook [würk′bŏōk′] **7**–26
    work gloves [würk′ glŭvz′] **92**–17, **179**–17
    work light [würk′ līt′] **181**–44
    work pants [würk′ pănts′] **92**–5
    work shirt [würk′ shürt′] **92**–2
work [würk] **8**–I, **10**–J, **38**–K
WORK [würk] **186**–187
Work Clothes [würk′ klōz′] **88**
worker [wür′kər]
    careful worker [kër′fəl wür′kər] **179**–2
    careless worker [kër′ləs wür′kər] **179**–1
    childcare worker [chīld′kër wür′kər] **166**–16
    construction worker
        [kən strŭk′shən wür′kər] **178**–1
    dockworker [däk′wür′kər] **167**–23
    factory worker [făk′tə rē wür′kər, –trē] **175**–3
    farmworker [färm′wür′kər] **177**–8
    food preparation worker
        [fōōd′ prĕp ə rā′shən wür′kər] **185**–4
    garment worker [gär′mənt wür′kər] **167**–29
    postal worker [pō′stəl wür′kər] **169**–49
    sanitation worker [săn′ə tā′shən wür′kər] **169**–54
    social worker [sō′shəl wür′kər] **169**–57
Worker [wür′kər] **92, 93**
working [wür′kĭng]
    not working [nät′ wür′kĭng] **62**–1
    woodworking kit [wŏōd′wür′kĭng kĭt′] **232**–14
Working with a Partner [wür′kĭng wĭth ə pärt′nər] **8**
Working with Your Classmates
    [wür′kĭng wĭth yər klăs′māts′] **8**
work out [würk′ owt′] **230**–N
WORKPLACE [würk′ plās′] **164**–165
WORKPLACE CLOTHING
    [würk′ plās′ klō′dhĭng] **92**–93

world [würld]
    world languages [würld/ lăng/gwĭ jəz] **189**–13
    world music [würld/ myo͞o/zĭk] **237**–32
WORLD MAP [würld/măp/] **202**–**203**
WORLD HISTORY [würld hĭs/tə rē] **199**
worm [würm] **212**–23
worried [wür/ēd] **42**–13
wrap [răp] **72**–24
wrap [răp] **240**–F
wrench [rĕnch] **158**–22, **181**–47, **181**–48
wrestling [rĕs/lĭng] **228**–17
wrinkled [rĭng/kəld] **101**–19
wrist [rĭst] **106**–14
    wristwatch [rĭst/wäch/, –wŏch/] **94**–16
write [rīt]
    write a check [rīt/ ə chĕk/] **27**–D
    write a cover letter [rīt/ ə kŭv/ər lĕt/ər] **173**–G
    write a final draft [rīt/ ə fī/nəl drăft/] **191**–L
    write a first draft [rīt/ ə fürst/ drăft/] **191**–H
    write a note [rīt/ ə nōt/] **135**–A
    write a resume [rīt/ ə rĕ/zə mā/] **173**–F
    write a thank-you note
        [rīt/ ə thăngk/ yo͞o nōt/] **174**–O
    write back [rīt/ băk/] **135**–H
    write on the board [rīt/ ön dhə börd/] **6**–E
writer [rī/tər] **169**–64
Writing and Revising [rī/tĭng ən rĭ vī/ zĭng] **191**
Writing Process [rī/tĭng prä/sĕs] **191**
Writing Rules [rī/tĭng ro͞olz] **190**
wrong way [röng/ wā/] **154**–2
xylophone [zī/lə fōn/] **238**–15
yard [yärd]
    courtyard [kört/ yärd/] **51**–21
    yardstick [yärd/stĭk/] **181**–16
YARD [yärd] **53**
yarn [yärn] **233**–22
year [yïr] **20**–4, **31**–9, **31**–10
Year [yïr] **21**
yellow [yĕl/ō] **24**–2
yesterday [yĕs/tər dā/, –dē] **20**–7
yield [yēld] **154**–9
yoga [yō/gə] **122**–4
yogurt [yō/gərt] **72**–22
young [yŭng] **32**–1
Your First License [yər fürst/ lī/səns] **137**
YOUR HEALTH [yər hĕlth/] **114**–**115**
zebra [zē/brə] **217**–33
zero [zïr/ō] **16**
ZIP code [zĭp/ kōd/] **4**–9
zipper [zĭp/ər] **99**–25
Zones [zōnz] **19**
zoo [zo͞o] **222**–1
zoom lens [zo͞om/ lĕnz/] **235**–23
zucchini [zo͞o kē/nē] **69**–25

Geographical Index

Continents

Africa [ăf′rĭ kə] **202–5**
Antarctica [ănt ärk′tĭ kə, –är′tĭ–] **202–7**
Asia [ā′zhə] **202–4**
Australia [ö strāl′yə] **202–6**
Europe [yŏŏr′əp] **202–3**
North America [nörth′ ə mĕr′ə kə] **200–201, 202–1**
South America [sowth′ ə mĕr′ə kə] **202–2**

Countries and other locations

Afghanistan [ăf găn′ə stăn′] **203**
Albania [ăl bā′nē ə] **203**
Aleutian Islands [ə lōō′shən ĭ′ləndz] **200, 203**
Algeria [ăl jîr′ē ə] **203**
American Samoa [ə mĕr′ə kən sə mō′ə] **202**
Andaman Islands [ăn′də mən ĭ′ləndz] **203**
Angola [ăng gō′lə] **203**
Argentina [är′jən tē′nə] **202**
Armenia [är mē′nē ə] **203**
Austria [ö′strē ə] **203**
Azerbaijan [ăz′ər bī jän′] **203**
Azores [ā′zörz] **202**
Baffin Island [băf′ən ĭ′lənd] **200**
Bahamas [bə hä′məz] **200, 202**
Bahrain [bä rān′] **203**
Bangladesh [băng′glə dĕsh′, băng′–] **203**
Banks Island [bănks′ ĭ′lənd] **200**
Belarus [bē′lə rōōs′, byĕl′ə–] **203**
Belgium [bĕl′jəm] **203**
Belize [bə lēz′] **201, 202**
Benin [bə nĭn′, –nēn′] **203**
Bermuda Islands [bər myōō′də ĭ′ ləndz] **200, 202**
Bhutan [bōō tän′] **203**
Bolivia [bə lĭv′ē ə] **202**
Bosnia [bäz′nē ə] **203**
Botswana [bät swä′nə] **203**
Brazil [brə zĭl′] **202**
Brunei [brōō nī′] **203**
Bulgaria [bŭl gĕr′ē ə] **203**
Burkina Faso [bər kē′nə fä′sō] **203**
Burma [bûr′mə] **203**
Burundi [bōō rōōn′dē] **203**
Cambodia [kăm bō′dē ə] **203**
Cameroon [kăm′ə rōōn′] **203**
Canada [kăn′ə də] **200, 202**
Canary Islands [kə nĕr′ē ĭ′ ləndz] **203**
Cape Verde [kāp′ vûrd′] **202**
Central African Republic
   [sĕn′trəl ăf′rĭ kən rĭ pŭb′lĭk] **203**
Chad [chăd] **203**
Chile [chĭl′ē] **202**
China [chī′nə] **203**
Colombia [kə lŭm′bē ə] **202**
Comoros [kăm′ə rōz] **203**
Congo [käng′gō] **203**
Cook Islands [kŏŏk′ ĭ′ləndz] **202**
Corsica [kör′sĭ kə] **203**
Costa Rica [kös′tə rē′kə, käs′–] **201, 202**
Croatia [krō ā′shə] **203**
Cuba [kyōō′bə] **201, 202**
Cyprus [sī′prəs] **203**
Czech Republic [chĕk′ rĭ pŭb′lĭk] **203**

Democratic Republic of the Congo
   [dĕm′ə krăt′ĭk rĭ pŭb′lĭk əv dhə käng′gō] **203**
Denmark [dĕn′märk] **203**
Devon Island [dĕv′ən ĭ′lənd] **200**
Djibouti [jĭ bōō′tē] **203**
Dominican Republic [də mĭn′ĭ kən rĭ pŭb′lĭk] **201, 202**
Ecuador [ĕk′wə dör′] **202**
Egypt [ē′jĭpt] **203**
Ellesmere Island [ĕl′əs mïr′ ĭ′lənd] **200**
El Salvador [ĕl săl′və dör′] **201, 202**
Equatorial Guinea [ē′kwə tör′ē əl gĭn′ē, ĕk′wə–] **203**
Eritrea [ĕr′ə trē′ə] **203**
Estonia [ĕ stō′nē ə] **203**
Ethiopia [ē′thē ō′pē ə] **203**
Federated States of Micronesia
   [fĕ′də rā′təd stāts′ əv mī′krə nē′zhə] **203**
Fiji [fē′jē] **203**
Finland [fĭn′lənd] **203**
France [frăns] **203**
Franz Josef Land [fränz′ yō′səf länd′] **203**
French Guiana [frĕnch′ gē än′ə, –ä′nə] **202**
French Polynesia [frĕnch′ päl′ə nē′zhə] **202**
Gabon [gă bön′] **203**
Galápagos Islands [gə lä′pə gōs ĭ′ləndz] **202**
Gambia [găm′bē ə] **203**
Georgia [jör′jə] **203**
Germany [jûr′mə nē] **203**
Ghana [gä′nə] **203**
Greater Antilles [grā′tər ăn tĭl′ēz] **201**
Greece [grēs] **203**
Greenland [grēn′lənd, –lănd′] **200, 202**
Guam [gwäm] **203**
Guatemala [gwä′tə mä′lə] **201, 202**
Guinea [gĭn′ē] **203**
Guinea-Bissau [gĭn′ē bĭ sow′] **203**
Guyana [gī ăn′ə] **202**
Haiti [hā′tē] **201, 202**
Hawaiian Islands [hə wī′ən ĭ′ləndz] **200, 202**
Hispaniola [hĭs′pən yō′lə] **201**
Honduras [hän dŏŏr′əs] **201, 202**
Hong Kong [häng′ käng′] **203**
Hungary [hŭng′gə rē] **203**
Iceland [īs′lənd] **203**
India [ĭn′dē ə] **203**
Indonesia [ĭn′də nē′zhə] **203**
Iran [ĭ răn′, ī răn′] **203**
Iraq [ĭ räk′, ī räk′] **203**
Ireland [īr′lənd] **203**
Israel [ĭz′rē əl, –rā–] **203**
Italy [ĭt′l ē] **203**
Ivory Coast [īv′rē kōst′] **203**
Jamaica [jə mā′kə] **201, 202**
Japan [jə păn′] **203**
Jordan [jör′dn] **203**
Kazakhstan [kä′zäk stän′] **203**
Kenya [kĕn′yə, kēn′–] **203**
Kiribati [kĭr′ə bäs′] **203**
Kuwait [kōō wāt′] **203**
Kyrgyzstan [kîr′gī stän′, –stän′] **203**
Laos [lows, lä′ōs] **203**
Latvia [lăt′vē ə] **203**
Lebanon [lĕb′ə nən, –nän′] **203**

Lesotho [lə sō′tō, –sōō′tōō] **203**
Lesser Antilles [lĕ′sər ăn tĭl′ēz] **201, 202**
Liberia [lī bîr′ē ə] **203**
Libya [lĭb′ē ə] **203**
Lithuania [lĭth′ōō ā′nē ə] **203**
Luxembourg [lŭk′səm bûrg′] **203**
Macedonia [măs′ə dō′nē ə] **203**
Madagascar [măd′ə găs′kər] **203**
Madeira Islands [mə dîr′ə ĭ′ləndz] **203**
Malawi [mə lä′wē] **203**
Malaysia [mə lā′zhə] **203**
Maldives [möl′dēvz, mäl′–] **203**
Mali [mä′lē] **203**
Malta [möl′tə] **203**
Marshall Islands [mär′shəl ĭ′ləndz] **203**
Mauritania [mör′ə tā′nē ə] **203**
Mauritius [mö rĭsh′əs] **203**
Mexico [mĕk′sĭ kō′] **200, 201, 202**
Moldova [möl dō′və, mäl–] **203**
Monaco [män′ə kō′] **203**
Mongolia [mäng gō′lē ə] **203**
Montenegro [män′tə nē′grō, –nē′–] **203**
Morocco [mə räk′ō] **203**
Mozambique [mō′zəm bēk′] **203**
Namibia [nə mĭb′ē ə] **203**
Nepal [nə pöl′, –päl′] **203**
Netherlands [nĕdh′ər ləndz] **203**
New Caledonia [nōō′ kăl′ə dō′nē ə] **203**
New Zealand [nōō′ zē′lənd] **203**
Nicaragua [nĭk′ə rä′gwə] **201, 202**
Niger [nī′jər, nē zhĕr′] **203**
Nigeria [nī jîr′ē ə] **203**
Northern Mariana Islands
   [nördh′ərn mär′ē ä′nə ĭ′ləndz] **203**
North Korea [nörth′ kə rē′ə] **203**
Norway [nör′wā] **203**
Oman [ō män′] **203**
Pakistan [păk′ə stän′] **203**
Palau [pə low′] **203**
Panama [păn′ə mä′] **201, 202**
Papua New Guinea [păp′yōō ə nōō′ gĭn′ē] **203**
Paraguay [păr′ə gwī′, –gwä′] **202**
Peru [pə rōō′] **202**
Philippines [fĭl′ə pēnz′, fĭl′ə pēnz′] **203**
Poland [pō′lənd] **203**
Portugal [pör′chə gəl] **203**
Puerto Rico [pwĕr′tə rē′kō, pör′tə–] **201, 202**
Qatar [kä′tär, kə tär′] **203**
Romania [rō mā′nē ə, rōō–] **203**
Russia [rŭsh′ə] **203**
Rwanda [rōō än′də] **203**
Samoa [sə mō′ə] **202**
Saudi Arabia [sow′dē ə rā′bē ə, sö′dē–] **203**
Senegal [sĕn′ə göl′, –gäl′] **203**
Serbia [sûr′bē ə] **203**
Seychelles [sā shĕlz′, –shĕl′] **203**
Sierra Leone [sē ĕr′ə lē ōn′, –lē ō′nē] **203**
Singapore [sĭng′ə pör′] **203**
Slovakia [slō vä′kē ə] **203**
Slovenia [slō vē′nē ə] **203**
Society Islands [sə sī′ə tē ĭ′ləndz] **202**
Solomon Islands [säl′ə mən ĭ′ləndz] **203**

Somalia [sə mä/lē ə] **203**
South Africa [sowth/ ăf/rĭ kə] **203**
South Georgia [sowth/ jör/jə] **202**
South Korea [sowth/ kə rē/ə] **203**
Spain [spān] **203**
Sri Lanka [srē/ läng/kə, shrē/–] **203**
Sudan [so͞o dän/] **203**
Suriname [so͞or/ə nä/mə] **202**
Svalbard [sväl/bärd] **203**
Swaziland [swä/zē länd/] **203**
Sweden [swēd/n] **203**
Switzerland [swĭt/sər lənd] **203**
Syria [sĭr/ē ə] **203**
Tahiti [tə hē/tē] **202**
Taiwan [ti/wän/] **203**
Tajikistan [tä jĭk/ə stän/, –stän/] **203**
Tanzania [tăn/zə nē/ə] **203**
Tasmania [tăz mā/nē ə] **203**
Thailand [ti/lănd/, –lənd] **203**
Togo [tō/gō] **203**
Tonga [täng/gə] **202**
Tunisia [to͞o nē/zhə] **203**
Turkey [tür/kē] **203**
Turkmenistan [türk mĕn/ə stän/, –stän/] **203**
Uganda [yo͞o gän/də] **203**
Ukraine [yo͞o/krān, yo͞o krān/] **203**
United Arab Emirates [yo͞o nī/təd ăr/əb ĕm/ər əts] **203**
United Kingdom [yo͞o nī/təd kĭng/dəm] **203**
United States of America
    [yo͞o nī/təd stāts/ əv ə mĕr/ə kə] **200, 202**
Uruguay [yo͞or/ə gwī/, –gwä/] **202**
Uzbekistan [o͝oz bĕk/ə stän/, –stän/] **203**
Vanuatu [vä/no͞o ä/to͞o] **203**
Venezuela [vĕn/ə zwā/lə] **202**
Victoria Island [vĭk/tör ē ə ī/lənd] **200**
Vietnam [vē/ĕt näm/, –năm/] **203**
Wake Island [wāk/ ī/lənd] **203**
Western Sahara [wĕs/tərn sə här/ə] **203**
Yemen [yĕm/ən] **203**
Zambia [zăm/bē ə] **203**
Zanzibar [zăn/zə bär] **203**
Zimbabwe [zĭm bäb/wā] **203**

Bodies of water
Arctic Ocean [ärk/tĭk ō/shən] **200, 203**
Atlantic Ocean [ət lăn/ tĭk ō/shən] **200, 202–203**
Baffin Bay [băf/ən bā/] **200, 202**
Baltic Sea [böl/tĭk sē/] **203**
Beaufort Sea [bō/fərt sē/] **200**
Bering Sea [bĕr/ĭng sē/, bĭr/–] **200**
Black Sea [blăk/ sē/] **203**
Caribbean Sea [kăr/ə bē/ən sē/, kə rĭb/ē ən–] **201**
Caspian Sea [kăs/pē ən sē/] **203**
Coral Sea [kör/əl sē/] **203**
Gulf of Alaska [gŭlf/ əv ə lăs/kə] **200, 202**
Gulf of California [gŭlf/ əv kăl/ə förn/yə] **200**
Gulf of Mexico [gŭlf/ əv mĕk/sĭ kō/] **200, 202**
Hudson Bay [hŭd/sən bā/] **200, 202**
Indian Ocean [ĭn/dē ən ō/shən] **203**
Labrador Sea [lăb/rə dör/ sē/] **200**
Mediterranean Sea [mĕd/ə tə rā/nē ən sē/] **203**

North Atlantic Ocean [nörth/ ət lăn/tĭk ō/shən] **202**
North Pacific Ocean [nörth/ pə sĭf/ĭk ō/shən] **202, 203**
North Sea [nörth/ sē/] **203**
Pacific Ocean [pə sĭf/ĭk ō/shən] **200, 202, 203**
Philippine Sea [fĭl/ə pēn/ sē/] **203**
Red Sea [rĕd/ sē/] **203**
South Atlantic Ocean [sowth/ ət lăn/tĭk ō/shən] **203**
Southern Ocean [sŭdh/ərn ō/shən] **203**
South Pacific Ocean [sowth/ pə sĭf/ĭk ō/shən] **202, 203**

The United States of America
Capital: Washington, D.C. (District of Columbia)
    [wä/shĭng tən dē/sē/, wö/–] **200**

Regions of the United States
Mid–Atlantic States [mĭd/ət lăn/tĭk stāts/] **201–10**
Midwest [mĭd/wĕst/] **201–9**
New England [no͞o/ ĭng/glənd] **201–11**
Pacific States [pə sĭf/ĭk stāts/] **201–7**
Rocky Mountain States [räk/ē mown/tn stāts/] **201–8**
South [sowth] **201–13**
Southeast [sowth/ēst/] **201–13**
Southwest [sowth/wĕst/] **201–12**
West Coast [wĕst/ kōst/] **201–7**

States of the United States
Alabama [ăl/ə băm/ə] **200**
Alaska [ə lăs/kə] **200, 202**
Arizona [ăr/ə zō/nə] **200**
Arkansas [är/kən sö/] **200**
California [kăl/ə förn/yə] **200**
Colorado [kăl/ə răd/ō, –ra/dō] **200**
Connecticut [kə nĕt/ĭ kət] **200**
Delaware [dĕl/ə wër/] **200**
Florida [flör/ə də, flär/–] **200**
Georgia [jör/jə] **200**
Hawaii [hə wī/ē] **200**
Idaho [ī/də hō/] **200**
Illinois [ĭl/ə noy/] **200**
Indiana [ĭn/dē ăn/ə] **200**
Iowa [ī/ə wə] **200**
Kansas [kăn/zəs] **200**
Kentucky [kən tŭk/ē] **200**
Louisiana [lo͞o ē/zē ăn/ə] **200**
Maine [mān] **200**
Maryland [mĕr/ə lənd] **200**
Massachusetts [măs/ə cho͞o/səts] **200**
Michigan [mĭsh/ĭ gən] **200**
Minnesota [mĭn/ə sō/tə] **200**
Mississippi [mĭs/ə sĭp/ē] **200**
Missouri [mə zo͞or/ē, –zo͞or/ə] **200**
Montana [män tăn/ə] **200**
Nebraska [nə brăs/kə] **200**
Nevada [nə văd/ə, –vä/də] **200**
New Hampshire [no͞o/ hămp/shər] **200**
New Jersey [no͞o/ jür/zē] **200**
New Mexico [no͞o/ mĕk/sĭ kō/] **200**
New York [no͞o/ yörk/] **200**
North Carolina [nörth/ kăr/ə lī/nə] **200**
North Dakota [nörth/ də kō/tə] **200**
Ohio [ō hī/ō] **200**
Oklahoma [ō/klə hō/mə] **200**
Oregon [ör/ĭ gən, –găn/, är/–] **200**

Pennsylvania [pĕn/səl vān/yə] **200**
Rhode Island [rōd/ ī/lənd] **200**
South Carolina [sowth/ kăr/ə li/nə] **200**
South Dakota [sowth/ də kō/tə] **200**
Tennessee [tĕn/ə sē/] **200**
Texas [tĕk/səs] **200**
Utah [yo͞o/tö, –tä] **200**
Vermont [vər mänt/] **200**
Virginia [vər jĭn/yə] **200**
Washington [wä/shĭng tən, wö/–] **200**
West Virginia [wĕst/ vər jĭn/yə] **200**
Wisconsin [wĭs kän/sən] **200**
Wyoming [wī ō/mĭng] **200**

Canada
Capital: Ottawa [ät/ə wə] **201**

Regions of Canada
British Columbia [brĭt/ĭsh kə lŭm/bē ə] **201–2**
Maritime Provinces [mër/ə tim präv/ən səz] **201–6**
Northern Canada [nör/dhərn kăn/ə də] **201–1**
Ontario [än tër/ē ō/] **201–4**
Prairie Provinces [prër/ē präv/ən səz] **201–3**
Québec [kwĭ bĕk/] **201–5**

Provinces of Canada
Alberta [ăl bür/tə] **200**
British Columbia [brĭt/ĭsh kə lŭm/bē ə] **200**
Manitoba [măn/ə tō/bə] **200**
New Brunswick [no͞o/ brŭnz/wĭk] **200**
Newfoundland and Labrador
    [no͞o/fən lənd ən lä/brə dör/] **200**
Northwest Territories [nörth/wĕst/ tër/ə tör/ēz] **200**
Nova Scotia [nō/və skō/shə] **200**
Nunavut [no͞o/nə vo͞ot/] **200**
Ontario [än tër/ē ō/] **200**
Prince Edward Island [prĭns/ ĕd/wərd ī/lənd] **200**
Québec [kwĭ bĕk/] **200**
Saskatchewan [să skăch/ə wən, –wän/] **200**
Yukon [yo͞o/kän] **200**

Mexico
Capital: Mexico (City) [mĕk/sĭ kō/ (sĭt/ē)] **201**

Regions of Mexico
Chiapas Highlands [chē ä/pəs hī/ləndz] **201–18**
Gulf Coastal Plain [gŭlf/ kō/stəl plān/] **201–16**
Pacific Northwest [pə sĭf/ĭk nörth/wĕst] **201–14**
Plateau of Mexico [plă tō/ əv mĕk/sĭ kō/] **201–15**
Southern Uplands [sŭdh/ərn ŭp/ləndz] **201–17**
Yucatan Peninsula
    [yo͞o/kə tän/ pə nĭn/sə lə, yo͞o/kə tän/–] **201–19**

States of Mexico
Aguascalientes [ä/gwəs käl yĕn/tās] **201**
Baja California Norte [bä/hä käl/ə förn/yə nör/tā] **200**
Baja California Sur [bä/hä käl/ə förn/yə so͞or/] **200**
Campeche [käm pā/chā, käm pē/chē] **201**
Chiapas [chē ä/pəs] **201**
Chihuahua [chĭ wä/wä, –wə] **200**
Coahuila [kō/ə wē/lə] **200**
Colima Michoacán [kə lē/mə mē/chō ə kän/] **201**
Distrito Federal [dĭ strē/tō fĕd/ə räl/] **201**
Durango [do͞o răng/gō, –răng/–] **201**

Geographical Index

Guanajuato [gwä/nə hwä/tō] **201**
Guerrero [gə rër/ō] **201**
Hidalgo [hĭ däl/gō, ē dhäl/gō] **201**
Jalisco [hə lĭs/kō, –lēs/–] **201**
México [mĕk/sĭ kō/, mĕ/hē kō] **201**
Morelos [mö rēl/ōs] **201**
Nayarit [nä/yə rēt/] **201**
Nuevo León [nwā/vō lā ōn/] **200**
Oaxaca [wə hä/kə, wä–] **201**
Puebla [pwĕb/lä] **201**
Querétaro [kə rĕt/ə rō/] **201**
Quintana Roo [kēn tä/nə rō/] **201**
San Luis Potosí [sän/ lōō ēs/ pō/tə sē/] **201**
Sinaloa [sē/nə lō/ə] **200**
Sonora [sə nör/ə] **200**
Tabasco [tə bäs/kō] **201**
Tamaulipas [tä/mow lē/pəs] **201**
Tlaxcala [tlä skä/lə] **201**
Veracruz [vĕr/ə krōōz/, –krōōs/] **201**
Yucatán [yōō/kə tän/, –tän/] **201**
Zacatecas [zä/kə tä/kəs, sä/–] **201**

Research Bibliography

The authors and publisher wish to acknowledge the contribution of the following educators for their research on vocabulary development, which has helped inform the principals underlying OPD.

Burt, M., J. K. Peyton, and R. Adams. *Reading and Adult English Language Learners: A Review of the Research*. Washington, D.C.: Center for Applied Linguistics, 2003.

Coady, J. "Research on ESL/EFL Vocabulary Acquisition: Putting it in Context." In *Second Language Reading and Vocabulary Learning*, edited by T. Huckin, M. Haynes, and J. Coady. Norwood, NJ: Ablex, 1993.

de la Fuente, M. J. "Negotiation and Oral Acquisition of L2 Vocabulary: The Roles of Input and Output in the Receptive and Productive Acquisition of Words." *Studies in Second Language Acquisition* 24 (2002): 81–112.

DeCarrico, J. "Vocabulary learning and teaching." In *Teaching English as a Second or Foreign Language,* edited by M. Celcia-Murcia. 3rd ed. Boston: Heinle & Heinle, 2001.

Ellis, R. *The Study of Second Language Acquisition*. Oxford: Oxford University Press, 1994.

Folse, K. *Vocabulary Myths: Applying Second Language Research to Classroom Teaching*. Ann Arbor, MI: University of Michigan Press, 2004.

Gairns, R. and S. Redman. *Working with Words: A Guide to Teaching and Learning Vocabulary*. Cambridge: Cambridge University Press, 1986.

Gass, S. M. and M.J.A. Torres. "Attention When?: An Investigation Of The Ordering Effect Of Input And Interaction." *Studies in Second Language Acquisition* 27 (Mar 2005): 1–31.

Henriksen, Birgit. "Three Dimensions of Vocabulary Development." *Studies in Second Language Acquisition* 21 (1999): 303–317.

Koprowski, Mark. "Investigating the Usefulness of Lexical Phrases in Contemporary Coursebooks." *Oxford ELT Journal* 59(4) (2005): 322–32.

McCrostie, James. "Examining Learner Vocabulary Notebooks." *Oxford ELT Journal* 61 (July 2007): 246–55.

Nation, P. *Learning Vocabulary in Another Language*. Cambridge: Cambridge University Press, 2001.

National Center for ESL Literacy Education Staff. *Adult English Language Instruction in the 21st Century*. Washington, D.C.: Center for Applied Linguistics, 2003.

National Reading Panel. *Teaching Children to Read: An Evidenced-Based Assessment of the Scientific Research Literature on Reading and its Implications on Reading Instruction*. 2000. http://www.nationalreadingpanel.org/Publications/summary.htm/.

Newton, J. "Options for Vocabulary Learning Through Communication Tasks." *Oxford ELT Journal* 55(1) (2001): 30–37.

Prince, P. "Second Language Vocabulary Learning: The Role of Context Versus Translations as a Function of Proficiency." *Modern Language Journal* 80(4) (1996): 478-93.

Savage, K. L., ed. *Teacher Training Through Video - ESL Techniques: Early Production*. White Plains, NY: Longman Publishing Group, 1992.

Schmitt, N. *Vocabulary in Language Teaching*. Cambridge: Cambridge University Press, 2000.

Smith, C. B. *Vocabulary Instruction and Reading Comprehension*. Bloomington, IN: ERIC Clearinghouse on Reading English and Communication, 1997.

Wood, K. and J. Josefina Tinajero. "Using Pictures to Teach Content to Second Language Learners." *Middle School Journal* 33 (2002): 47–51.